PLAYING AWAY

The A–Z of Soccer Sex Scandals

Matthew Clark

EDINBURGH AND LONDON

First published in Great Britain in 2004 by
CUTTING EDGE PRESS LTD
7 Albany Street
Edinburgh EH1 3UG

ISBN 1 903813 06 9

A catalogue record for this book is available from the British Library

Typeset in Frutiger and Van Dijck
Printed in Great Britain by
Cox & Wyman Ltd

INTRODUCTION

Sexual intercourse began in 1963, said the poet Philip Larkin. The year George Best made his debut, he should have added. Before George, the boy genius who remains – touch wood – a living legend at boozing and birding, football and sex went together like, well, England and penalties.

The baggy-shorted players before him could barely afford Brylcreem with their maximum wages, let alone champagne, hotel suites and fun-loving blondes inside them. But George changed everything. Suddenly soccer was sexy. In the '60s, the pill and permissiveness fuelled the revolution; in the '70s, playboy stars boasted of their conquests; in the '80s, the tabloid kiss-and-tell became a boom industry; by the late '90s, players' lavish lifestyles inspired their own raunchy prime-time soap, *Footballers Wives*, which won more viewers than the Premiership highlights.

But if modern players have Best to thank for their sex-on-a-plate lifestyle, then they can curse him, too, for our fascination with their antics.

Until recently soccer sex was good clean fun – relatively speaking – with soccer studs and Page 3 stunners scoring three, four or five times a night. But the recent explosion in salaries for adolescents rich enough to indulge their every fantasy has bred a new style of bed-swapping superstar.

In Ayia Napa in 2000, three drunken young England stars were videoed having sex with women back at their hotel room. Just as this book was to have been published, in 2003, a series of sickening new scandals rocked the game. Police investigated alleged gang rapes by footballers on women in London and La Manga. For legal reasons, *Playing Away* had to be shelved for a year. All the stars were later cleared, but a new culture came to light.

Incredibly, the following year was even more torrid. England captain David Beckham's alleged philanderings with three different women were as surprising as they were shocking.

Beckham's carefully nurtured reputation as the perfect family man earned him millions in advertising deals. When his poor form contributed to his team's pitiful exit from Euro 2004, legitimate questions were asked about whether his private life was affecting his professional one . . . and our chances of victory.

Next, England's teenage sensation Wayne Rooney admitted having sex with prostitutes. Then, days before publication, the Football Association itself was exposed. England boss (and legendary ladies' man) Sven-Göran Eriksson and chief executive (and separated dad of five) Mark Palios had bedded the same FA secretary, Faria Alam. The FA had at first denied any improper relationship . . . then was forced into a catastrophic U-turn. Soon it was revealed that someone at the FA, the guardian of the game's moral code, had offered to leak every detail of the manager's affair to a newspaper if it kept the chief executive's name out. Palios resigned within hours. Eriksson was cleared of lying to his bosses.

But the men earning huge salaries to save our national game from financial ruin, rebuild Wembley and win the World Cup after 40 years of hurt had risked everything over sex with a secretary. This was a West End farce with Shakespearean themes of lust, power and betrayal. Anyone who says footballers' sex lives don't matter has a screw loose.

Sadly, not every soccer sex scandal could be included in *Playing Away*, due to legal reasons, deadlines and sheer lack of space. You have to draw a line somewhere. If only the stars could remember that!

Thanks: to the players of sexy football everywhere; to Fleet Street's finest for man-marking them; to Dennis Edensor and other friends for advice, encouragement and proofreading; to Mainstream Publishing; and, mostly, to Lydia, Ciara and Shauna for their patience as writing went into injury time, extra time, a silver goal, golden goal, penalties . . . and a replay.

Visit www.soccersexscandals.com

A

ABRAHAMS, Nadia

Twenty-one-year-old South African office worker who accused Manchester United boss Sir Alex FERGUSON of a sex assault. The case was dropped, but Abrahams and her businessman boyfriend Brian EBDEN sold their story to British newspapers for £75,000 and were spotted driving new cars weeks later.

ALAM, Faria

Lowly FOOTBALL ASSOCIATION secretary who had affairs with England boss Sven-Göran ERIKSSON and his boss Mark PALIOS, sparking a crisis that rocked the game. The FA at first denied the affair on the former model's behalf, before backtracking. Then a bid to leak details of Eriksson's affair if Palios's name was left out was exposed, leading to the chief executive's resignation and a high-level inquiry. Bangladesh-born Alam, 38 – married and divorced as a teenager – heaped more embarrassment on the FA by selling her story to newspapers and TV channels, reportedly for £500,000. She detailed her passionate sex with Sven, now dumped by long-term partner Nancy DELL'OLIO, including how she pleasured Eriksson with her speciality oral sex manouevre that left him gasping, and also revealed a macho culture at the game's headquarters.

See Ferrari.

ALLISON, Malcolm

Born: Bexleyheath 5.9.1927

Career: Player – Charlton Athletic, West Ham United. Manager – Bath City, Plymouth Argyle, Manchester City, Crystal Palace, Galatasaray, Memphis, Plymouth Argyle, Manchester City, Crystal Palace, Sporting Lisbon, Middlesbrough, Willington, Turkey, Kuwait, Setubal, Farense, Fisher Athletic, Bristol Rovers

The undisputed King of the Casanova soccer bosses. Allison was rarely seen without his famous fedora, a mighty Havana, a magnum of champagne . . . and a sexy blonde on his arm.

Big Mal, gambler, drinker, walking financial disaster and frequent illicit lover, was the antithesis of the soccer boss of old and the epitome of those who came afterwards. In 50 footballing years, Allison:

- BEDDED a PoW's wife while on National Service;
- MARRIED the girl he got pregnant;
- SEDUCED Christine KEELER, the beauty who nearly brought down a government;
- SLEPT with singing legend Dorothy Squires;
- BEDDED the wife of a football club director behind his back;
- DUMPED one Miss UK for another;
- PULLED a Brazilian beauty as she toasted her country's 1970 World Cup win;
- WED a Playboy Bunny Girl and . . .
- tried SUICIDE after another Bunny Girl dumped him;
- got FIRED for sharing the team bath with '70s porn queen Fiona Richmond;
- FATHERED six children by three partners – including one born when he was 63 – and was . . .
- CHASED for child maintenance when he lost all his money in a financial scandal.

Allison's amazing sex-and-soccer career began as a teenager when he joined his boyhood idols CHARLTON ATHLETIC, about to win their first major trophy – the 1947 FA Cup. Allison, a born rebel, found their training methods poor, inadequate and uninspiring. But his imagination was fired by a stint of National Service. The teenager was posted to Vienna, the Cold War hotspot immortalised by the spy movie *The Third Man*. It was a place ripe for black marketeering . . . and sexual intrigue.

It was in Vienna that Big Mal lost his virginity to (of course) a blonde, named Heidi. He recalled years later how they crept barefoot past the bedroom where her 17-stone butcher father was asleep and snoring. 'It was a day of many discoveries,' he revealed.

The next notch on his bedpost was the pretty, and persuasive, wife of an Austrian PoW, who led him from a dance hall to her home and bed. 'This is vhere ve vill sleep,' she announced. Her obliging grandmother woke him the next morning with a cup of coffee. For arriving back at base late he was confined to barracks for a week.

Fortunately for football, Allison got his first taste of coaching as he knocked the battalion team into shape. And he was inspired by the advanced Continental training methods he observed abroad. He returned to Charlton Athletic determined to succeed, despite their archaic training methods, and with his ambition to coach fired. Unable to break into the first team, he was sold to West Ham United, the club that would, in unexpected ways, help him achieve greatness.

At Upton Park, he explained later, 'My dedication was absolute. I didn't smoke, I didn't drink, and I never had sex within three days of a match. Incredible!'

Allison, an impressive specimen at 6 ft 1 in. and 12 st. 2 lb, and with rugged good looks, also claimed to be the first player in Britain to wear short shorts instead of the baggy Matthews style of old. He insisted it was to help his performance on the pitch.

He maintains he was for many years faithful to wife Beth, whom he met in a Bexleyheath dance hall and married in 1953. He wed not because he was in love, he recalled, but because she was pregnant. 'That's what one did in those days.'

But in November 1957, Allison's life was changed for ever. A persistent cough was diagnosed as tuberculosis and within days surgeons removed part of a lung. Told he would never play again, Allison, as usual, rebelled. For a year he worked relentlessly towards a comeback. But when injuries to others brought a chance to return, boss Benny Fenton instead chose a 17-year-old untried kid Allison had befriended and helped coach two evenings a week. Bobby Moore made an assured debut against Manchester United at Upton Park on Monday, 8 September 1958. That night Allison realised his career was over, after 255 appearances and 10 goals.

Beth sensed a change too. She said: 'The illness had a shattering effect on Malcolm. I think he came to the conclusion that he had only one life and he was going to live it to the full.'

Allison bought a club in London's West End. Its regulars included actors, singers and footballers. The late nights and early starts, as well as the easy accessibility of those tempting blondes, were to prove a lethal combination.

'I was never involved outside my marriage until after the illness,' he said. 'The girl was called Suzy. She was blonde. She came into my club with a girlfriend. It was a long time before I could forget her.'

But he did forget long enough to seduce the singer Dorothy Squires, recently divorced acrimoniously from actor Roger Moore and a frequent visitor to his club. 'I think she took a shine to me,' Big Mal recalled. 'I went back to her house several times to spend the night.'

Football, though, remained his true passion. After non-league jobs, he was made manager of Plymouth Argyle, and he arrived in the summer of 1964 to find rich pickings for casual sex. 'It was a hard job to keep from becoming entangled with some woman or another. My time in Plymouth was, in fact, a period of evasive tactics,' he said. 'Sometimes after a few drinks I might not be so evasive but there was never any question of getting involved in affairs. I was still suffering a hangover from Suzy.'

Sacked after a fall-out with the board, Allison moved on to Manchester City as assistant to new manager Joe Mercer. It was a magical partnership. Allison's revolutionary training methods and tactics, his inspired signings and supreme man-management helped City roar from Division Two to the League title itself in 1968, the FA Cup a year later and the League Cup and European Cup-Winners' Cup in 1970. Bitter rivals Manchester United, and their holy trinity of Best, Charlton and Law, were eclipsed, just as Allison had predicted. And not just at football.

At last City had a rival to take on George BEST in the sex stakes in swinging Manchester. In 1965, Allison met blonde model Jenny Lowe at a party where, despite the attentions of Best and City star Mike SUMMERBEE, Big Mal pulled. Jenny asked him to help her get fit for the 1966 Miss UK contest. Every Thursday she would train under him in the club gym at Maine Road, to the delight of City's jealous players. 'It was a small but pleasant affair,' he said later. Jenny later became another of Best's conquests.

Another conquest was a model named Jeanette, who at first turned down his advances. Allison phoned a city department store and ordered their biggest double bed to be delivered to her urgently. It was a masterstroke. 'We enjoyed a light-hearted, unforced affair, the sort most men hope for,' was his verdict.

In 1969, Allison, now living alone in a Manchester flat after splitting from Beth, fell for his second Miss UK, a strong-headed striking blonde named Jennifer Gurley. Amazingly, Jennifer would visit to do housework, cook and clean! 'It never went further than that,' he insisted. 'It was a great friendship but I knew she was fond of me.'

That summer, mighty Juventus courted the all-conquering coach. Allison spent weeks being wined and dined by the Italian giants and was offered a wage of £20,000 a year, a sum that would have cured his constant financial crises. He decided to reject the offer, but maintained: 'I would have taken her with me to Italy. I nearly fell in love with her.'

In the summer of 1970, Allison enjoyed his most exotic affair yet. After praising the brilliant Brazilian World Cup winners, he and fellow ITV panellists were invited to a party at their embassy in London. He explained: 'I was impressed by a very elegant girl in a white trouser suit managing, superbly, to cha-cha and play the bongo drums at the same time.' Allison wined and dined the girl, called Claudia, with bacon and eggs in the early hours. He dubbed her 'The Contessa' and romanced her secretly for two years until she announced she had met someone else and was to be married. 'Absurdly, I got angry. My ego had been dented,' said Allison. 'In the past it had always been me who said when something finished.'

If Claudia was exotic, Christine Keeler was electric. The former teenage call girl's affairs with the Secretary of State for War and the Russian naval attaché and spy suspect Yevgeny Ivanov sparked the PROFUMO AFFAIR in 1963 and scandalised the nation. Now she made it known at a pub they both used that she fancied the handsome soccer boss. They met for a steak at an upmarket West End restaurant. 'She had dyed her hair blonde but she remained instantly recognisable. There was still much of the tigress in her,' Allison recalled.

As transfixed waiters dropped plates and other male diners stared, Big Mal worked his magic. 'I found her a strong and interesting woman,' Allison said. 'We went out, in fact, a couple of times. I recall that we made love.' It was, he admitted, a relationship destined to be brief and fuelled by lust and curiosity.

In 1971, Mercer left Manchester City and Allison, always frustrated at being second fiddle, became manager in his own right. Their exciting attacking football, with the genius of Rodney Marsh now allied to Colin Bell, Summerbee and Tony Book's effective creativity, reflected his own life – thrilling, exhilarating yet ultimately flawed. With a wage of £100,000, Allison was in his element, spending his time in Tramp, London's hottest nightspot, and his money on women and horses.

In 1972, he began an affair with Playboy Bunny Girl Serena Williams and hammered the final nail into the coffin of his marriage to long-suffering Beth. He had first met Serena, then only 16, during his spell at Plymouth, at a dance in the hotel where he was staying.

Private happiness eased professional pain. At Maine Road, the trophies dried up and Allison left for Third Division Crystal Palace who, he felt, shared his ambition to win in style. It was a shock move but a defining moment.

Big Mal became engaged to Serena. He revealed: 'She wears a diamond ring I bought for her one day when the mood took me. It has become inevitable that we will marry.' He bought a medallion for himself inscribed 'No Longer Me, But We'. But within a year they were finished. On holiday in Spain, they rowed, as usual, about yet another financial disaster. A punch-up with a barman saw him splashed across the nation's newspapers and he returned home in disgrace, throwing himself into work. Alone in their now empty flat, he considered suicide. Beth, as ever, was the wayward boss's saviour. She returned with their children and they moved into a home near Palace's south London ground.

It wasn't long before Big Mal was back in hot water – literally. He agreed to let porn queen Fiona Richmond pose naked in the team bath at Crystal Palace for a photo shoot, then climbed in with her! Photos of the nude soccer boss and the porn model earned him a charge of bringing the game into disrepute. Three weeks later, on 19 May 1976, Allison was sacked as Third Division Palace's manager, despite their thrilling run to the FA Cup semi-final and narrow failure to win promotion. 'I got fired for it,' Allison remembered years later, 'but that appeared on the front page of newspapers in 19 countries.'

His increasingly shaky marriage to Beth had finally crumbled in 1975 after 22 years and 4 children. 'She has always been loyal,' he said. 'She has never nagged me; in fact, I cannot recall a single row between us. Not even when I disappeared one afternoon in Manchester to buy some FISH for tea and didn't get home until lunchtime the following day. She was a brilliant mother and a super girl. When I was gambling, I'd have £30,000, sometimes even £40,000, stuffed in drawers in notes and she never took a fiver.'

Wife number two was, inevitably, both blonde and a Bunny Girl, Sally-Ann Highley. It was a perfect mis-match. They met on Wimbledon Common at a wild open-air drinks party. They began skating on a frozen pond, the ice broke and she plunged in. She stripped off her wet clothes. He put his trench coat round her and carried her to his nearby flat, where he bedded her *and* her friend. He proposed, bizarrely, after her car somersaulted on the M1. 'As we climbed out of the wreckage, I asked her to marry me just because I thought, what a brave girl this is, I should marry her. It was the biggest mistake of my life.'

The couple had a daughter, Alexis, in 1979, but it was a stormy relationship. Sally-Ann appeared in the papers with a broken nose, two black eyes and missing teeth – he hit back with claims that she launched a teacup at him, leaving a gash so serious it needed 26 stitches.

His managerial career suffered amid the bedlam. He spent a year in Turkey at Galatasaray, a year in Memphis and one season back at Plymouth before finally returning to Manchester City.

But in January 1980, Allison suffered the ignominy of his second sacking by Manchester City as his expensively rebuilt team crashed out of the FA Cup to lowly Halifax Town. He headed instead, after a brief spell on the rebound back at Palace, for a series of jobs abroad, including a year with Sporting Lisbon, where he won the League and Cup double. His final parting from Sally-Ann came in 1983 when he returned to manage Middlesbrough. He had been 'dying to get rid of her', he said, especially as, he claimed, she had been having an affair with a rival soccer boss.

But Big Mal, now 55, had lost none of his legendary charm. He was already dating another blonde beauty he had spotted in an Italian restaurant. She was Lynn Salton, a 27-year-old Church of England primary schoolteacher. He had champagne sent to her table. Three months later, she moved into his two-bedroom flat. 'I should have married her when I was at Man City,' he joked. 'Trouble was, she was only 11 then.' Their daughter Gina – his sixth child – was born in 1990.

After a disappointing spell at Boro, soccer jobs became harder to find for the legendary boss, who also claimed he'd lost his savings with the £6 billion Bank of Credit and Commerce International collapse in July 1991. He spent his time caring for Gina, a child he finally had the time and inclination to dote on, and managing a local Sunday league team. In 1994, Allison was reportedly £30,000 behind in maintenance payments to Sally-Ann for Alexis, then 15.

Age, illness and mounting debts were catching up with him. In 1996, he had been diagnosed manic-depressive after losing his job as a radio pundit for swearing on air. In 2000, as his libido waned, Allison tried Viagra. 'Lynn kept saying, "You don't want to take them." You'd have thought she'd be pleased. I mean, we hadn't had sex for about six months,' he said.

They split for good in April 2000 when he tried to smash down the door of Lynn's home, from which he was barred by a court injunction. He spent 20 hours locked in a cell, was given a 12-month conditional discharge and ordered to pay £300 compensation. He claimed the house had been bought from the profits of the sale of his own home. Friends were not so sure where the blame lay.

In 2001, Allison's family announced he was an alcoholic. Living alone in a warden-controlled flat in Hale, Cheshire, he fell and broke his collarbone. After treatment, he entered the Priory Clinic, and the Professional Footballers' Association picked up the bill. Son Mark blamed Allison's troubles on his loneliness after the split from Lynn. 'He is very ill, but he's accepted for the first time that he's an alcoholic.'

Allison himself was in denial. 'You could say alcohol played a part in the break-up, but drink plays a part in everyone's relationship problems. I don't rule out a reconciliation with Lynn.'

By the end of the year, Alzheimer's disease was diagnosed. It was, at least, an explanation for his increasingly bizarre behaviour towards Lynn. Friends were heartbroken.

Allison's former skipper and assistant manager Tony Book said: 'He is living in a one-bed room, it has a lock on the door and he is obviously not allowed out, for his own good. Malcolm was as famous for his off-the-pitch activities as he was on it – and that makes it all the sadder now.'

Manchester City winger Mike Summerbee once dubbed him 'The Male Prostitute'. He quipped: 'He just sits there, waiting for offers.' And Buzzer wasn't far from the truth. In a life lived to the full – plus injury time – the flamboyant football man proved he was at least a tart with a heart.

ANDERSEN, Vetle

Born: Norway 20.4.1964
Career: IK Start, TB Berlin, Dunfermline, Viking Stavanger, Lyngby, West Bromwich Albion, Halmstad, Raith Rovers, Inverness Caledonian Thistle, Halmia

Maybe Raith Rovers should have checked out the veteran Norwegian's nickname *before* they signed him – for 'Hagar the Hunk' brought a longboat full of problems as he pillaged his way through Scottish football. Andersen, married with two children, joined the Kirkcaldy side after spells in Sweden and Germany. His class was always evident – in one cup tie he showboated so much that livid opponents tried to take the law into their own hands. No one could get near him until, on a nightclub dance floor, a love rival finally caught up with him.

Alan Wood, 23, approached the soccer star at Jackie O's bar in Kirkcaldy, Fife. Wood asked Andersen if he knew a woman called Shirley, then head-butted him. Andersen fell to the floor and police were called, Kirkcaldy Sheriff Court would later hear. He was taken to the town's Victoria Hospital with a broken nose. Police searched Wood's house and found bloodstained clothes. Wood confessed. In court, he claimed Andersen had been seeing his girlfriend behind his back and had taunted him over it. 'It was months of anger boiling over,' he told the court. Wood was fined £250 after admitting assault, and ordered to pay the soccer ace £350 compensation.

Andersen proclaimed his own innocence. 'I don't know anything about any girl called Shirley and I don't know anything about having an affair. He has just made it up as an excuse for what he did.'

ANDERSON, Viv

Born: Nottingham 29.7.1956
Career: Player – Nottingham Forest, Arsenal, Manchester United, Sheffield Wednesday. Manager – Barnsley. Asst. Manager – Middlesbrough

History-making England ace Viv Anderson was the perfect foil for rampant Middlesbrough boss Bryan ROBSON – on the training pitch and off it.

While Robson played away with Sky TV reporter Claire TOMLINSON, Anderson, his former Manchester United and England teammate turned right-hand man, romanced Nicole Burton, a striking red-headed restaurant manager.

With their wives and families hundreds of miles away in the Cheshire stockbroker belt, the pair played the old one–two on intimate dinner dates and trips to away matches and the 1998 World Cup. The Boro bad boys even booked the same hotel near their training ground and apparently spent the night bonking in rooms just yards apart.

Anderson, a long-legged yet elegant right-back and England's first black international, met Nicole at Middlesbrough's Purple Onion restaurant at a Christmas party for club officials in December 1996. Anderson, then 40, chatted up the 24-year-old beauty, left with her phone number and embarked on a torrid affair.

Nicole later told of:

● THREE-TIMES-A-WEEK meetings for sex for two and a half years;

● TRAINING SESSIONS where she taught him to be a brilliant lover;

● £20,000 of jewellery, gifts, champagne and cash he showered on her;

● A two-and-a-half week TRIP to the 1998 World Cup with Bryan Robson and his lover;

● Anderson's hollow PROMISE that he would leave his wife Debra for her.

She said: 'We had a fantastic time and Viv paid all the way. I will miss it, but I didn't go through all this just for the money. Of course I enjoy drinking champagne looking out over the sea in St Tropez. But I did it because I truly love Viv and wanted to be with him.'

Nicole admitted: 'I don't have a lot of money so Viv used to help me with my bills and rent. But then I helped him out in many ways. It took me six months to train him up to standard in the bedroom. Men don't know what they're doing in bed. Now it's going to take me a while to train somebody else. We had a healthy sex life, nothing kinky but a lot more than he got at home. He knew where to come for his oats and we lived like a couple.

'We had a passionate time. He would spend three nights a week with me either in my house, hotels or abroad. He said he loved me but to give him more time. He kept telling me he would leave his wife, but he just didn't have the bottle to tell her.'

Anderson and Robson would regularly wine and dine then bed their secret partners at Teesside hotels including the Posthouse Hotel in Thornaby, The Baltimore in Middlesbrough, and at Crathorne Hall in Yarm. Staff knew the women well.

As England battled in the 1998 World Cup, the mistresses joined Robson and Anderson in the PARIS Hilton and in Marseilles. Anderson even took Nicole to Ireland and Holland where, he told his wife, he was on a scouting mission for new talent.

Nicole kept a curious memento of her nights of passion – the keys to their rooms. 'I've got about 16 keys,' she explained. 'But I only kept the ones where the night meant something special to me.'

But when Robson's affair was exposed in 1998, it also spelt the end for Anderson's fling. With Debra already suspicious about his activities, and comforting Robson's wife Denise, the two women were sure to put two and two together to tumble their husbands' dangerous games.

When reporters from *The People* scented scandal and approached him, Anderson said: 'It is absolute nonsense. Of course I know Nicole. She is manager of the restaurant where people from the club eat.' Debra said simply: 'I don't know nothing about this. I'm going to speak to Viv now.'

Days later Anderson contacted Nicole. Their affair was over, he told her.

Nicole was shell-shocked: 'He told me he had looked into his wife's eyes and realised he still loved her. But I'm torn apart by all this. I really loved him. I've been faithful to Viv for two and a half years.

'I realise now he just wanted me as his bit on the side. I think his biggest fear was that Debra would ban him from seeing their son Charlie. He dotes on the seven-year-old lad and it would kill Viv not to be with him.'

She added: 'Viv and Bryan have gone running back to their wives with their tails between their legs. If the women are stupid enough to think their husbands will now stay faithful then they deserve them.'

But she admitted: 'I still love Viv and if he walked in now I would have him back.'

ASH, Leslie
Born: London 19.2.1960

The star of TV's *Men Behaving Badly* spent months crippled in a hospital bed after claiming an over-enthusiastic sex session with her soccer star husband Lee CHAPMAN went disastrously wrong.

Leslie, 43, was rushed to hospital after sustaining a punctured lung and broken rib in their luxury Chelsea Harbour apartment in April 2004. Chapman was arrested but both insisted it was an accident as they made love on a springy new mattress, and he was later released without charge.

But a timebomb was ticking. In hospital, Leslie, now famous for her 'Trout Pout' after plastic surgery went wrong, had contracted the deadly MSSA superbug. She was rushed back to hospital in agony and was said to have only a 50/50 chance of walking again.

It was another bizarre chapter in a tumultuous, and sometimes violent, relationship . . .

In October 1997, the actress won a temporary court order banning Chapman from going near her after a boozy argument ended in her receiving face and arm injuries. Two years before that, she forgave him when he confessed to spending a night with a model after storming off and blacking out during a holiday in Ibiza.

And in 1992, when French enfant terrible Eric CANTONA left Premier League Champions Leeds United for Manchester United, terrace rumours blamed his exit on an affair with TV star Leslie – who was pregnant with his teammate Chapman's baby. A decade later she described the rumour as 'a load of lies and garbage' and insisted her marriage to the 6 ft 4 in. tall striker turned restaurateur was unbreakable. 'When Lee was at Leeds,' she explained, 'a horrible rumour came out that I was having an affair with Eric Cantona. They put it about that I was the reason Cantona left Leeds. I didn't have an affair with him. The same thing happened to two other players' wives, but because I was on TV it stuck with me.'

ATKINSON, Ron

Born: Liverpool 18.3.1939

Career: Player – Aston Villa, Oxford United. Manager – Kettering Town, Cambridge United, West Bromwich Albion, Manchester United, West Bromwich Albion, Sheffield Wednesday, Aston Villa, Coventry City, Athletico Madrid, Sheffield Wednesday, Nottingham Forest

Big Ron plunged Manchester United into crisis after admitting he was cheating on his wife with a glamorous ex-model. Only six years earlier Tommy DOCHERTY had been fired for an affair – but Atkinson fared better. After winning the 1983 FA Cup, he confessed his love for 34-year-old Maggie Harrison, and, a year later, walked out on Margaret, his wife of 23 years.

Chairman Martin EDWARDS – gaining his own reputation for sex scandals – announced: 'I'm not interested in what happens outside this club', and Atkinson, 45, kept his job.

Maggie boasted: 'Ron's just my type – he's big and powerfully built.'

Champagne- and jewellery-loving Ron had a history, though: he had cheated once before while skippering Oxford United but been rumbled by his lover's husband and warned off by a private eye.

And Margaret warned: 'It was always soccer first, Ron second, me third. Maggie should remember that.' Margaret did make an audacious bid to keep hold of her teenage sweetheart, offering to *share him* with Maggie! He declined and 20 years on, Ron – a popular TV pundit until off-mic racist comments cost him his job – and Maggie remain together.

AYIA NAPA

The Cyprus beach resort is a popular haunt of footballers planning a post-season session.

See Kieron DYER, Rio FERDINAND, Don HUTCHISON, Frank LAMPARD, VIDEO.

B

BABAYARO, Celestine

Born: Kaduna, Nigeria, 29.8.1978
Career: Anderlecht, Chelsea

The GROUP-SEX-loving playboy suffered eight months of agony facing a jail sentence when his sex life went out of control. The Nigerian international was accused of a sex attack on one of two women allegedly plied with drink in a club and lured back to his luxury flat by his friends.

Colin Egebuige, 24, and Chibazo Obasi, 26, offered the women a lift in a taxi when they complained of feeling in a 'trance'. But instead of taking them home, the car took them to Babayaro's pad in Chiswick, west London, where a porn movie was playing on Baba's giant TV screen.

Inside, the soccer star tried to kiss one of the women, a hairdresser, Isleworth Crown Court heard.

'Babayaro tried to forcibly kiss the woman, pressing himself upon her, trying to put his tongue into her mouth,' said Brian O'Neill, prosecuting. 'She pushed him away and he left, going upstairs to bed, saying that he had training the next morning.'

Moments later, Egebuige pounced, prosecutors claimed, grappling with the girl's clothes and dragging her to the kitchen. Meanwhile, Obasi had climbed on her friend in the other room and put his hand up her skirt. Then, the court heard, Babayaro reappeared in the kitchen naked. Together with Egebuige, he pinned the first woman against the worktop. Babayaro, she said, pushed his groin against her. 'I was in shock,' she said. 'I thought I was going to be raped.'

Babayaro, Egebuige, of Seven Sisters, and Obasi, of Woolwich, all denied indecent assault. Babayaro told police he was in bed with his girlfriend when he heard his friends return to the house, said Mr O'Neill. He went to the kitchen to get a glass of water wearing just a pair of shorts.

And on 2 August 1999, as he stood in the dock, the Chelsea star looked to the heavens and sighed with relief as the judge directed the jury to find all three not guilty. He described the prosecution case as 'riddled with contradictions'.

Later Babayaro's spokesman said: 'Celestine now wishes to put this matter behind him and get back to playing.'

But Babayaro's penchant was exposed again three years later when soccer groupie Alicia DOUVALL revealed how she organised two three-in-a-bed sex sessions for the Chelsea ace after meeting at London's Chinawhite club.

'I had sex with Baba a number of times,' she said, 'mainly because it was all over very, very quickly. Then I had to wait ages for him to be ready again.'

To spice things up, Douvall claimed, she organised threesomes with a friend called Nina ('She was stunned by his physique, too, but once more Baba was a bit of a letdown') and Donna ('Baba loves big boobs and hers are huge but once more he got a little, er, "over excited"'). Alone with Alicia, Babayaro enjoyed kinky food sex, including a game with ice cream and Red Bull.

He eventually dumped Douvall over her secret fling with aptly named rapper Shaggy. But she did reveal Babayaro's admiration for her ex-boyfriend and fellow playboy – Dwight YORKE, with whom he once shared a foursome! 'He clearly looks up to Dwight and sees him as the King of the Playboys,' she said. 'Baba's a sort of junior playboy.'

BALDWIN, Tommy
Born: Gateshead 10.6.1945
Career: Arsenal, Chelsea, Millwall (loan), Manchester United, Seattle Sounders, Gravesend, Brentford
Some Managers Do 'Ave 'Em. If it wasn't the Geordie striker's

prodigious drinking that kept his Chelsea boss up at night it was his scandalous affair with the wife of TV's Frank Spencer.

Baldwin was the hardest drinker in Britain's hardest-drinking club. Chelsea idol and boozing pal Alan HUDSON said of him: 'Tommy was our greatest drinker. We called him the Sponge.'

Chelsea were the glamour side of their day, and the luvvies – from Raquel Welsh to Steve McQueen and dear, dear Dickie Attenborough – sashayed down the Kings Road to watch. But rising star Michael CRAWFORD would pay a heavy price for his devotion to the Blues.

Crawford had married Gabrielle, 19, the beautiful daughter of a surgeon, in a blaze of flashbulbs in December 1965. The star of *How I Won the War* (with John Lennon), *The Knack*, *The Games* and *Hello, Dolly!* had two children with Gabrielle – Lucy and Emma. But as Crawford found fame as the accident-prone beret-wearing fool Frank in the hit sitcom *Some Mothers Do 'Ave 'Em*, she was the one who fell head over heels – with the blond Chelsea star.

The Crawfords' marriage ended in 1974 – Baldwin's wife cited his adultery with Gabrielle in her divorce petition. Baldwin's career, too, was also on the rocks. He was convicted of assaulting a policeman and given a suspended sentence. Soon his high-flying days were over.

Gabrielle and Baldwin were together for seven years, and had two children of their own, Sam, born in 1976, and Harry, in 1983. Caring Crawford, today a megastar thanks to musicals *Barnum* and *Phantom of the Opera*, stayed close to his former wife and their children despite his pain.

BARNES, John

Born: Jamaica 7.11.1963
Career: Player – Watford, Liverpool, Newcastle United, Charlton Athletic. Manager – Celtic

Ever the showman, John Barnes, England's enigmatic winger and Liverpool's title-winning talisman, flaunted his beauty queen lover in a bar packed with hundreds of witnesses – and paid the ultimate price.

With his wife Suzy and four children hundreds of miles away in Liverpool, the Jamaican-born genius quaffed free champagne with stunning Miss Jamaica Nicole Haughton in the convivial atmosphere of 10 Room, in London's Piccadilly, at a showbiz bash.

He had met the 26-year-old beauty in late 2000 in Jamaica, then teamed up with her at various discreet night-time venues around London for the next nine months. But this time, as Nicole, in sexy skin-tight tan trousers and plunging black top, chatted to other celebrity guests, Barnes could pretend they were strangers no longer.

He signalled her over. They kissed at the bar. He ran his hands over her body. They retired to an inviting sofa and performed serious heavy petting, to the amazement of the other guests. Soon, Nicole, appropriately studying Public Relations at university, straddled him as the smooching got steamier and more obvious.

'It was almost as if they were having sex,' said an onlooker. While another eyewitness commented: 'It wasn't as if he was carrying on in a quiet corner of a restaurant where no one could see him. He didn't seem to care that people were watching and even taking pictures of him.'

It was one of those pictures, published by *The People* newspaper, which sealed the love rat's fate. Splashed over two pages of the red-top tabloid on 12 August 2001, the revelations were the final straw for his marriage.

Barnes, the son of a Jamaican police officer, starred for WATFORD in the 1980s, before a £900,000 move to Liverpool in 1987. There, he won two League titles and was voted Footballer of the Year by both the Professional Footballers' Association and the Football Writers' Association in 1988. Mysteriously inconsistent for his country – scoring just 11 goals in 79 games – his name will be forever linked with a stunning individual goal in the Maracana Stadium against Brazil in 1984. Just like those Brazilians, this time Barnes had no defence.

A friend told reporters: 'John is seeing Nicole and has been for a while. As far he is concerned, what his wife doesn't know can't hurt her. That's the way things work with John – his family's in Liverpool and whatever he gets up to in London is another thing. The two are kept separate. He loves beautiful women and finds it hard to resist them. That's just the way he is – he's a ladies' man.'

Four years earlier, Suzy had forgiven him for his fling with Zena Reid, a secretary on the *Financial Times*, whom he had met at a London party.

Pity Zena, then 24, didn't know Barnes was three-timing her and his wife with blonde timeshare saleswoman Pippa Hall.

John had met Pippa in Spain as he holidayed with friends. She told a newspaper how they had made love on the balcony of his hotel – a typically flamboyant performance from the crowd-pleasing number 10.

Now a TV soccer host after an unsuccessful spell as manager of CELTIC, Barnes retains his public popularity. But the last laugh, so far, in the love life and times of John Barnes has been his wife's.

After booting her errant husband out of the family's £600,000 mansion on Merseyside, Suzy, 40, met hunky, 23-year-old print worker David Foxhall in a Wirral disco and moved him in instead. As well as dropping him off at work in her expensive Mercedes and picking him up later, Suzy apparently gave him £200-a-week spending money and, according to one newspaper, let him wear Barnes's prized football shirts (and even his monogrammed purple silk pyjamas) between romps in the family jacuzzi!

'This is her revenge,' said a friend. 'She now has a young lover and is totally in control of her life.'

Let's call it a score draw.

● A woman-hating psychopath adopted John Barnes's name as a tribute to his Liverpool hero. Born Rodney Michael Smith, in Grays, Essex, Barnes raped, assaulted or robbed up to 25 women victims and targeted others including TV celebrities. At the Old Bailey in April 1997, the 31 year old was sent to Rampton psychiatric hospital indefinitely.

BARTHEZ, Fabien
Born: Lavelanet, France, 28.6.1971
Career: Toulouse, Olympique Marseille, Monaco, Manchester United, Marseille

A World Cup-winner's medal; a dream move to Manchester United on £40,000 a week; supermodel Linda Evangelista for your girlfriend. Was there a luckier man in the world than France's brilliant bald goalkeeper?

But for every silver lining there's a cloud. And for Barthez it was a giant Mancunian rain cloud. Girlfriend Linda, 35, told the goalie she could no longer cope with the bleak Manchester showers after the sunshine of Monaco, his previous club. Alone and apparently unloved, Barthez, a former boyfriend of Princess Stephanie of Monaco, found comfort in the arms of other women.

Caroline MARTIN, a call girl who had bedded United chairman Martin EDWARDS and Reds striker Dwight YORKE, told of her nights of passion with the athletic keeper after meeting him at Manchester's Living Room bar. They returned to his plush £1.2 million apartment in Deansgate, Manchester. 'He started caressing and kissing me,' said Caroline. 'We lay on the bed and had oral sex, but I decided I wanted to make him wait before we made love.'

A week later, Caroline, who insisted Barthez never knew she was a hooker, met Barthez again. This time they did the deed. She said: 'He was a better lover than Dwight, but he wasn't very considerate. He didn't even see me out and said he was staying in bed because he was tired.'

Alicia DOUVALL, a 32FF porn model, singer and another former Dwight Yorke conquest, met Barthez in London's hip Chinawhite club. They retired to his room at the St Martin's Lane Hotel, she told *The People*.

'You could tell he was a goalie because he was so good with his hands,' Alicia reported after the four-hour romp. 'He was very good at doing everything a woman enjoys. He certainly knew what he was doing.' But some of his saucy suggestions shocked the less than shy and retiring glamourpuss. 'In the morning I left him in bed while I got up, had a shower and left. I don't think that I will be seeing him again,' she told the paper.

When the summer came, Fabien *did* find love at last, with the sex-mad former girlfriend of diminutive pop star Prince. Beautiful French actress, model and singer Ophelie Winter had lived with the small one in his Paris pied-à-terre for a year. And an action-packed year it was. Ophelie claimed they had sex 500 times in 12 months! Bizarrely, she added, she had 'found God' during their sex sessions.

Ophelie had also starred in a no-holds-barred movie with, of all people, crooked Olympique Marseille owner Bernard Tapie. Their love scene was considered too hot for the final cut and was discarded from the movie, *Men, Women: A User's Manual*.

Fabien and Ophelie's first child was born in Paris in September 2003.

BATES, Ken

Born: London 4.12.1931

Chelsea's brash, bearded chairman loved to go to war with the journalists who report on his club's affairs. But there was an extra shock in store when he chose a club press conference to annouce that he was splitting up with his wife after falling in love . . . with one of them!

Bates – twice married and father of five children – addressed twenty reporters at the plush Conrad Hotel in Chelsea Harbour two days before the start of the 1992–93 season. Going into the new season, he announced, he had secured a deal that meant Chelsea would be able to stay at their Stamford Bridge home. 'However, there has been a heavy price to pay,' he said. 'The continual publicity has been particularly hard on my wife Pam, whose fierce and unswerving support has been a very significant factor in the outcome. The consequence has been that for some time, by mutual agreement, we have led more separate lives.'

The hacks, expecting a different kind of transfer news, were taken aback. But 60-year-old Bates, reading from a prepared statement, was not finished.

'My wife has been for some time aware that I have been having an on-going relationship with Suzannah, who I believe is known to some of you. Although we have lost something, we continue to be friends and companions, and will continue to be so despite our affair becoming public. Neither Pam, Suzannah nor myself will have any further comment to make.'

Dapper in a blue pinstripe suit, Bates stood up and left, flanked by club officials. The reporters were lost for words.

Bates's new partner was Suzannah Dwyer, 40, a part-time English teacher turned respected football writer from Ruislip, Middlesex, whom he had met when she interviewed him for a magazine.

Dwyer – real name Sylvia Marshall – was still married, to Peter, and had two grown-up children. It later emerged that she had told her building surveyor husband she was leaving only 24 hours before Bates's bombshell announcement.

Pam, contacted at their farm in Beaconsfield, Buckinghamshire, said merely: 'I have got nothing to add.'

Between the lines was an even more amazing tale – Bates's wife

Pam, 62, had told him their marriage was over before he met Suzannah. She was reportedly having an affair of her own. They divorced in 1994, ending an 18-year relationship that had played a pivotal role in Chelsea's history. For it was Pam who persuaded her bored businessman husband to buy the club.

Bates was already married to Teresa, the mother of his five children, when he met Pam on a blind date in Manchester. Romance blossomed and the couple lived in Monte Carlo, where they were married in 1983. As he neared 50, Pam convinced him they should return to Britain so he could at last realise his dream of owning a football club.

He paid just £1 for Chelsea in 1982. It was losing £12,000 a week and heading for Division Three. Twenty-one years later, the club had fielded world greats – including GULLIT, Vialli and Zola – and won two FA Cups, the European Cup-Winners' Cup, Super Cup and Charity Shield. In 2003, Bates sold the club for £140 million to Russian billionaire Roman Abramovich.

Now the 71 year old could plan a long and wealthy retirement with the love of his life – and even afford to make her his third wife. In October 2003, Bates whisked Suzannah, 53, to Venice for a civil ceremony followed by a romantic gondola ride and champagne breakfast. It was a surprise U-turn by the man who once admitted he had twice failed at marriage and quipped, 'As Suzannah would say, why change a winning team?'

BEAGRIE, Peter

Born: Middlesbrough 28.11.1965
Career: Middlesbrough, Sheffield United, Stoke City, Everton, Sunderland, Manchester City, Bradford City, Everton, Wigan Athletic, Scunthorpe United

The talented midfielder became famous for the spectacular somersault he performed whenever he scored. But it was the night the married father-of-three flipped for real and groped two innocent women that he etched his name in soccer's hall of shame.

Manchester City had been on the holiday island of Jersey for a three-day mid-season break in February 1997 to recharge their batteries before their annual relegation battle began in earnest. At 3 p.m. on 25 February, after a round of golf, the players headed for the island's bars. Former Everton hero Beagrie, then 31, and his teammates began a pub crawl that was to lead to disaster.

One eyewitness said: 'The lads were all enjoying themselves and seemed eager to try out as many pubs and bars as possible.'

In the early hours, Beagrie launched his bizarre two-pronged attack on hotel worker Caragh Coburn, 22, barging into the ladies' toilets and urinating in the sink while wearing white knickers over his jeans. Coburn told a court how he groped her breasts and told her she was lovely. Minutes later, at another bar, Beagrie groped her again. Then, she said, he apologised and offered to buy her a drink. When she refused, Beagrie spat twice in her face. Minutes later, outside another club, he assaulted her friend Odette Davidson, 27.

The women, both from Holywood, County Down, reported their ordeal to police and at 4 a.m. Beagrie was arrested at the Grand Hotel. He spent the rest of the day at St Helier police station, where he was also quizzed over allegations that he was drunk and disorderly, before being released on £500 bail. He was charged with three counts of indecent assault.

After phoning his wife in Southport, Merseyside, Beagrie told reporters at Jersey airport: 'This is a nightmare. I am not guilty. This has all got out of control.' Too true.

In August 1997, the case came to court. Teammates Georgi Kinkladze and Kit Symons gave evidence, but had to admit they had drunk so much they could hardly remember the night out. Magistrate Terry Sowden told Beagrie: 'The evidence against you was overwhelming.' The player, now transferred to Bradford City, was found guilty of all three charges, and another charge of common assault. He was put on probation for a year, given 120 hours' community service and ordered to pay his victims £500 each for the sickening attack plus £240 costs. Mr Sowden spared him from prison because it would wreck his marriage and his career.

Caragh's mum Sara said: 'Both girls have had a terrible time. Caragh is still very, very upset and disgusted. The ordeal this man put them through was terrifying.'

BEATTIE, James

Born: Lancaster 27.2.1978

Career: Blackburn Rovers, Southampton

The Saints superstar striker bragged about how amorous women sent him suggestive letters – and he got his blonde lover, Sarah Rendle, to play them out!

Beattie, whose goals fired Southampton to the 2003 FA Cup final against Arsenal, said: 'Girls have sent me suggestive pictures and said what they'd like to do to me and what they'd like me to do to them. I just show them round the lads and stick them on the wall. Then I get Sarah to act them out.' The couple split a year later so that Sarah could concentrate on her TV career.

BECKHAM, David, OBE

Born: Leytonstone 2.5.1975

Career: Manchester United, Preston North End (loan), Real Madrid

Some guys have all the luck . . . David Beckham is captain of England; a £23 million Real Madrid *Galactico*; the world's sexiest man; the face that launched a thousand products; a multi-millionaire; a sarong-wearing gay icon; Britain's favourite dad; the husband of a pop princess. If only he could take penalties!

But when a whirlwind of headlines about TXT sex, hookers and bisexual orgies was unleashed, Posh Spice Victoria BECKHAM almost ended up wearing his Goldenballs, as she called them, for earrings!

In a series of sensational revelations in April 2004, it was alleged that the 28 year old was a secret love god, who had bedded:

● his bisexual former personal assistant Rebecca LOOS regularly in Spain while Victoria and their children were in Britain;

● Australian ex-vice girl Sarah MARBECK four hours after meeting her at a party on a Manchester United pre-season tour;

● vicar's daughter Celina LAURIE as a bouncer guarded his hotel room after a match in Denmark.

The Beckhams dismissed the allegations, implying that they were idle gossip, but for those who believed the hype that neither half of the world's most famous marriage would ever stray, the headlines were like a boot in the face . . . and Becks knew all about that!

Speculation about the Beckhams' five-year marriage was already rife as David settled into Madrid. Of his first 89 days in the Spanish capital, they spent just 35 together as Posh shuttled between London and New York trying to revive a fading music career that now held as much chance of a Number One as Liverpool of a League title. Becks was said to be dismayed at her unwillingness to move the family abroad. She was angry at his partying with his new playboy soccer pals till the early hours when several sexy (and sex-mad) senoritas were said to be targeting him.

Nuria Bermudez, 23, already bragged she had slept with six of his teammates. She even had the club crest tattooed on her midriff, and warned: 'Be scared, Victoria. You should be trembling.' Ana Obregon, TV presenter, actress and ex of Croatian striker Davor Suker, had moved into the same hotel as Becks. Supermodel Esther Canadas was linked with him in Spanish TV reports after attending teammate Ronaldo's 27th birthday party.

Posh and Becks issued a joint statement: 'Our marriage is not in crisis. We are extremely happy together as a family and our only difficulty has been finding a house in Madrid which meets our needs. Since we first met, our careers have always meant we have spent time apart. This is not a reflection on the strength of our marriage and we are very much enjoying our new life in Spain.'

But Posh seemed to have taken her eye off the ball . . . the woman apparently keeping her bed warm was closer to home – his new personal assistant Rebecca Loos, a woman so trusted that her family had even babysat for the Beckhams' children. Sophisticated Loos, Spanish-born English-educated daughter of a Dutch diplomat, had just started work for David's management company SFX. Her task was to help him settle in Spain, translating for him as he house-hunted, socialised and even bought groceries. Thrown together by work, Rebecca Loos and Beckham grew ever closer. 'He's a subtle seducer,' she told the *News of the World*. He would pay her generous compliments. Innocent txt messages between them would turn seriously sexy. When she helped him view houses, he would gently touch her back as he ushered her inside first.

Over a Thai meal with friends, they played Truth or Dare. Becks, she claimed, admitted having sex on an aeroplane but not who with; Rebecca talked about her bisexual fantasies. She said later: 'He loved to hear me talk about all the girlfriends I had and I would tell him in great detail about my lesbian sex.'

Later that night, they went to Madrid's Ananda nightclub and canoodled in a corner. When he suggested sex, she explained, 'I said, "F★★★ off" in a jokey manner.'

But each knew there was a serious sexual spark. 'We gave each other a look and a nod of the head, paid the bill and left. I couldn't wait to be alone with him and I know he felt the same.' They were chauffeur driven to the high-class Santa Mauro hotel where, she claimed, they had sex for the first time.

She told the paper that Beckham was a very generous lover and described their love-making as 'the most explosive sex I have ever had'.

Rebecca was falling in love and they slept together twice more, she revealed. But disaster loomed. Another clubber had photographed the pair together in an alcove of the Ananda on the night Loos claimed they tumbled into bed. When the grainy pictures appeared in the *News of the World*, emphatic denials of any wrongdoing came from all parties. But behind the façade there was blood on the carpet. Posh insisted Becks move to her own management company, 19, and Rebecca eventually lost her £2,000-a-month job. 'Victoria didn't like me from the off,' Rebecca told a friend. 'After she found out that David and I had become close, I didn't stand a chance. I was sacked almost immediately.'

Now Loos rubbed her rival's nose in it. David bedded her, she told newspapers, because he was trapped in a sexless marriage and hated his wife's 'thin, stick-like body'.

'If there hadn't been a gap in that bed, I wouldn't have been in it,' she insisted. 'He did things with me he wouldn't have dared ask his wife for. He told me he likes very curvy women with proper bottoms and hips, which is not like her either. She does have breasts but they aren't real.' Anyway, she adding with scathing irony, 'Posh girls are better at sex.'

She met Beckham just once more for sex. This time, she alleged, lust replaced tenderness. 'It was over very quickly. It was clothes off, get the action done and out. I felt like a whore, really cheap and used.'

Was this the moment a woman scorned by Posh *and* Becks decided to avenge them both? Loos remained in touch with Beckham, but only by X-rated txt sessions around twice a week, and she began storing the messages. The face of Vodafone certainly seemed to make the most of their products.

'Where r u? in ur bedroom?' she claimed he asked her in one message. 'Can just imagine how hot and horny u r,' said another. 'I'm doing something thinking about yr xxxx.'

One came as she visited a museum with her parents. 'I had to go to the ladies to finish the txt session,' she recalled. Becks always instigated the txt sessions, she said. 'He's a married man so I would never be the first person to txt. What if he's sitting at lunch with Victoria?'

But Loos was angered when she heard another girl on the Madrid social circuit claim she was also swapping sex txts with Beckham, and when blonde Swedish model Frida Karlsson claimed she shared 'lingering kisses' with him.

On Sunday, 4 April 2004, the *News of the World* ran the shock headline BECKS' SECRET AFFAIR and detailed Loos's fling with Beckham. The story appeared to come from a friend, but was straight from the horse's mouth.

The world waited for Beckham's denial and for the writ to hit the fan. It didn't.

Instead, came yet another pronouncement from Beckingham Palace: 'During the past few months I have become accustomed to reading more and more ludicrous stories about my private life. What appeared this morning is just one further example. The simple truth is that I am very happily married, have a wonderful wife and two very special kids. There is nothing that any third party can do to change these facts.'

A total denial it was not.

Posh tried harder, swapping her pout for a coathanger grin as the couple played to the cameras at carefully planned photo opportunities in the French Alps, Switzerland, London and Madrid. She reportedly told a friend: 'This girl set out to trap David. She sent him lurid txts, but he never replied. There was no affair. She is a lying cow.'

But Loos's claims were backed by Beckham's former minder, Cuban security expert Delfin Fernandez, 44, who had driven them back to the hotel. 'In public they were always careful not to get too close, but in private they were all over each other like teenagers,' he said. 'David trusted me implicitly and was fine kissing her in front of me. Victoria knew nothing about it.'

A week later, as Posh hoped she had weathered the storm, came a tornado. As well as more damaging revelations from Rebecca, the *News of the World* had unearthed *another* lover.

Former Armani model Sarah Marbeck told how she caught Beckham's gaze as she walked into a party during Manchester United's pre-season tour of the Far East in July 2001. 'He just stood there staring at me,' she said. 'So I went up to him and said "How do you find Singapore weather?" He replied, "It's a bit hot."'

After more scintillating small talk, the on-field pass-master allegedly made his move. 'Look, I don't usually do this, but I'd really like your company tonight. Will you come to my room on your own?'

He left to return to the United stars' hotel. Sarah followed discreetly and four hours after meeting, she claimed, tumbled into his bed at the Shangri-La Hotel. After all-over kisses and a full body massage, he stripped her and they made earth-shattering love.

'It was perfect,' she said. 'Really passionate. I've no idea how long it lasted. When you're in bed with David Beckham you're not looking at the clock.'

She claimed they met occasionally for sex over the next two years, but spent most of their time sex txting.

One of the messages allegedly txtd by David read: 'I cant wait to kiss u head to toe then sit u down and xxxx ur xxxxxxx and xxxx until u are so xxx u cant take any more and I would bend you over and xxxx u so hard :)X,' and he apparently also txtd her his fantasy of bonking on the bonnet of his FERRARI. Embarrassingly, she also claimed that he described the love triangle of Posh, Becks and Sarah as Wendy, Peter Pan and Tinkerbell!

What Becks could not have known was Sarah's grubby past as a hooker in the Far East. She had joined the Boardroom Escorts Agency in Sydney a few months after her first night with Becks. Earlier, in Singapore, she admitted she had worked as a hooker for 'two or three months', before earning enough to fly home. Claims surfaced of her appearance in homemade group-sex porn movies. And one ex-boyfriend, Andreas Markos, 26, claimed she told him she had made up the story for cash. 'The girl is an utter fantasist,' he told *The People*.

Rebecca, too, came under severe scrutiny. As she flew to Britain to launch her own TV career on the back of her new infamy, ex-lovers – male *and* female – emerged. 'The Sleazy Senorita', as she was now dubbed, was a voracious bisexual predator. She admitted she had lost her virginity at 17 and had had 30 partners – '60 per cent men and 40 per cent women'.

Former friends recalled her aggressive sexual past, often complemented by drink and cocaine. 'Rebecca wants to make herself out as a sweet girl who was used and abused by a selfish star,' said one. 'But I find it hard to imagine anyone more manipulative. She is a beautiful girl with a massive sexual appetite who will try it on with anyone she fancies.' A motorcyclist she bedded after admiring his Harley-Davidson in the street and blagging a lift even told his story. Naked pictures of her entwined with a long-term lesbian lover named only as Virginie appeared in papers. And it was reported that she had even txted Beckham while she lay in bed with a lesbian lover – minor TV celebrity Emma Basden, 32, who told reporters: 'There were three of us in the relationship . . . me, Rebecca and David Beckham. She was seeing me at the same time that she was seeing David. She confided in me about the affair.'

Rebecca went on the offensive, telling Sky TV interviewer Kay Burley she knew a secret about the soccer star's body so intimate that only a lover could know. 'If I do ever need to talk about that, it will be in court and not on TV,' she said.

Seven days later, *The People* unleashed its own blonde bombshell. Nursery teacher Celina Laurie, daughter of a teacher father and vicar mother, told how Becks manoeuvred himself behind her in Train nightclub in Aarhus, Denmark, rubbed her back seductively and said: 'I've got a king-sized bed at the hotel. Would you like to join me?'

Minutes later, a security guard ushered her into Room 215 of the Hotel Royal, in Aarhus, where United had just won a pre-season friendly in August 2002.

She was naked within seconds, *The People* reported. 'He performed oral sex almost immediately,' she said. 'He was very unselfish. There was lots of kissing.' After asking the guard to fetch condoms ('I don't normally do this sort of thing,' the star explained sheepishly), they made love for over an hour before falling asleep. 'It was straightforward sex – no crazy positions – but it was lovely,' she added. They had sex again the following morning before she left for home. 'He was still kissing me as I walked through the door,' she said. 'He asked for my number, but I knew he'd never ring me.'

(Shame . . . he'd probably have txtd!)

Celina had two more revelations. Becks, she claimed, totally waxed his Goldenballs, a skinhead style no one had expected, and was very well endowed.

Beckham headed home to Hertfordshire for yet another happy families photocall at Victoria's 30th birthday party, then whisked her very publicly by limo for dinner at the Ritz. Perhaps by now Posh and Becks really were laughing off the whole thing over dessert.

More likely the breadrolls were flying! Because the last time he was accused of seeing other women, fiery Posh had split his lip with a well-aimed punch.

In October 1998, newspapers reported *two* secret alleged relationships after that summer's World Cup, where his red card for an impetuous kick had helped Argentina break English hearts. Defeated and dejected, he made a flying visit to see Posh in America, where the Spice Girls were on tour, then (after conceiving baby Brooklyn in Brooklyn) returned alone to Britain.

Old flame, bar manager Lisa Hames, 19, told how Becks called that July and asked to meet. 'It was fantastic seeing him,' said Lisa, who first met Becks when he was on loan at Preston North End. 'I think he was just looking for some kind of distraction while Posh Spice was away. But we didn't rekindle our sexual relationship.'

Model Emma Ryan told *The Sun* of a month of alleged liaisons that August, including an evening spent in a passionate embrace on a friend's sofa. 'We were kissing and fondling,' she said. 'He squeezed my bum hard and we kissed more.' It was Becks who, apparently, stopped their heavy petting going any further, finally telling the Stockport lass he loved his fiancée and had to leave.

Emma even claimed the playful player had asked her to visit him disguised as a PIZZA delivery boy to fool witnesses, made saucy phone calls (txting was in its infancy) and even suggested a game of strip Scrabble! Emma said: 'He made me feel like a million dollars for a month, but when Victoria came home I never heard from him again. He treated me like a princess and then discarded me.'

The Beckhams' spokesman totally denied any wrongdoing. Pregnant Victoria insisted he had not cheated: 'I've found the person I want to spend the rest of my life with. I trust David 110 per cent.'

She found unlikely allies in David's former girlfriends, who all swore to Becks' mild and caring character. Essex glamour model Leoni Marzell, 18, his girlfriend for a year in 1995, said: 'My dad's a Gunners fanatic and they'd sit for hours discussing their teams over cups of tea. He'd rather talk about Arsenal all night than have sex. But when we did, he was very gentle and considerate.'

Weeks after splitting up with Leoni, Becks met Anna Bartley, 22, a model and former Miss UK, at a Supporters' Club function at Old Trafford. 'I could feel his eyes boring into me. On our first date he took me to a restaurant but said almost nothing. He wasn't great at conversation.' On their third date, he pounced. 'We were in a restaurant when he suddenly kissed me. It was surprising but really nice. He's a great kisser. I had a lovely feeling all through my body down to the soles of my feet. At first I thought he was just being a gentleman because he only ever kissed me. But now I realise he just takes things very slowly.'

David invited her to an after-match party at Old Trafford, then said he couldn't get her a ticket. 'It was at that party he met Posh Spice. After that, things fizzled out,' she said.

Posh and Becks had already spotted each other on TV and told friends about their mutual attraction. When the pop icon and the football genius finally came face to face in the Old Trafford players' lounge in 1996, there was an instant attraction.

In January 1998, they were engaged. The following July, after his epic Treble win with Manchester United, they were married at Luttrellstown Castle, near Dublin. Britain's new royalty sat in giant thrones at the reception. The Beckhams were totally in love, their marriage rock solid, even if her jokes that Becks wore her knickers and that he sashayed round their kitchen saying 'I'm a gay icon!' must have made life difficult for him on the pitch.

But years later, Beckham revealed the painful private truth. Posh had punched him when she read the girls' claims, and split his lip. 'Trying to prove your innocence to someone who was hearing it from everyone else was the hardest thing,' Becks told BBC chat show host

Michael Parkinson. 'The worst thing was seeing how hurt Victoria was.'

Brooklyn was joined by brother Romeo in September 2002. But scandal soon followed. Two months later, the couple sued Internet gossip site Popbitch over scandalous false rumours about their marriage and threatened immediate action against anyone repeating them.

. . . A threat which, tellingly, was never made after the claims of Loos, Marbeck and Laurie 18 months later. But there was the trademark defiance.

'He's done nothing wrong,' Victoria again insisted. 'He's not the sort of man who goes out and gets drunk, has loads of women around him and stays out all night. That's not him. The most important thing through all this is I know the truth. We're just carrying on. I really do believe deep down that I have the most faithful husband I could hope for. He's always faithful and nothing has changed at all. The most important thing is I know the truth and my family know the truth. I don't want to give it any more time than that really. This isn't the first time that allegations have been made. We're just carrying on. David feels the same as me.'

And, with two fingers firmly pointed at Rebecca Loos, she hinted their sex life was perfect.

'Me and David have always been very compatible. We're going to get old together. We have a laugh. We got into bed the other night and he put on the TV, and what's he watching? *Ground Force*! I said to him, "But I heard you're really into porn."'

As season 2003–04 ended, Becks' brilliant career was stuttering and seemingly overshadowed by his public profile. His first season at star-studded Real finished, inexplicably, trophyless. His own promising early-season success trailed away badly and Real fans were left wondering why their £80,000-a-week playmaker was jetting around Europe to save his marriage instead of their season. Some unveiled a banner at Madrid's training complex with the message: 'For you lot, whores and money; for us, indignation and repression.' Were Madrid fans witnessing 'the Beckham Circus' that Sir Alex Ferguson had talked of before Becks was bombed out of Manchester United?

With Posh apparently demanding he return to Britain (and

Chelsea and Arsenal wooing him like upper-class totty in a nightclub), he insisted he would honour his two-year contract with Madrid and that his family would move out there with him. Maybe he realised that, at 29, he was running out of time to get back to his peak before passing it. With just two years before what could be his last World Cup tournament, a new club, new manager, new coaches and new teammates would not help.

What Beckham really needed was a successful Euro 2004. But the pressure appeared to be getting to him. Before the tournament even kicked off, the rattled skipper threatened to boycott newspapers and TV channels he deemed had treated his family badly. 'The way I and my family have been treated is an absolute disgrace, because at the end of the day I'm a nice person and loving husband and father,' he complained. 'I've been called a bad father, I've been called a bad husband and my wife has been called a bad mother. Things always hurt that are said about my family, and for people to call my wife a bad mother is unbelievable. I'm a strong person, I'm a strong family man, I'm a strong husband and a strong father.'

But not, it appeared, a strong enough midfielder to lead England to victory. Poor performances in Portugal – including two critical penalty misses – suggested a loss of concentration. He admitted only a lack of fitness but blamed Real's training regime. His sacked boss at Madrid, Carlos Queiroz, was furious. 'In the last three weeks of the season [Portugal skipper Luis] Figo was at every training session, while you'll have to look at those that David missed for one motive or another. Figo wasn't skiing while his team was still in the Champions League,' said Quieroz, referring to Beckham's dash to Courchevel after the Rebecca Loos revelations, 'and there's the difference – one of them has got to the Euro final and the other didn't. I am not surprised by Beckham's comments.' He added, 'He has always had excuses. When he failed in Korea and when he failed in Portugal, he always had an excuse.'

Booted out by Portugal after his shoot-out penalty reached Row Q of Lisbon's Stadium of Light, Beckham took Victoria to Morocco to celebrate their fifth wedding anniversary. The Beckhams had, it was said, cancelled their plans for a public renewal of their vows. But it did seem more likely they would stay together. Becks had been interviewed by American *Vogue* earlier in the summer. After discussing their plans for the Beckham brand to conquer the US, he was asked about the affairs. Again, there was no direct denial. 'I've learned that sometimes if you respond it gives people more ammunition to come back at you with. People can say what they like,' said the player who didn't like people saying what they liked, 'but me and Victoria will always stay together as husband and wife.'

In September 2004, the Beckhams annouced they were expecting their third child. So it was business as usual.

BECKHAM, Victoria
Born: Hertfordshire 17.4.1974

Posh Spice split her husband David BECKHAM's lip with a punch when newspapers reported his friendships with other women in 1998. God knows what she did when three women claimed full-blown affairs with him amid sensational headlines in April 2004! Victoria publicly insisted her Adonis husband was innocent. But her ferocity when crossed is legendary. When *EastEnders* soap star Tamzin Outhwaite said she'd like to bed Becks, Posh let rip: 'First, I wouldn't say that about a married man. And second . . . as if, love. Third, let me at her.'

See Celina LAURIE, Rebecca LOOS, Sarah MARBECK.

BEHR, Dani (Danielle Lisa)
Born: South Africa 9.7.1975

Huskier than a Norwegian centre-half with laryngitis, kids TV presenter Dani needs only say 'The Word' to bring footballers flocking. So far, three Premiership superstars have fallen for the statuesque blonde nicknamed 'The Mountie' because, like Julian Dicks, she always gets her man.

And when the former *Saturday Show* host revealed her 'most debauched act' ever was sex in an NCP car park ('God, it was really seedy, but great though!'), it sparked a Premiership Whodanit?

Was it . . . Ryan GIGGS?

They dated for eight months in 1994 after Dani interviewed him for her Sunday morning Channel 4 show *Surf Potatoes*. A fortnight after the show, she bumped into him as he holidayed in Marbella, where she was filming. 'It made my trip a little more exciting,' she later confessed. Dani immediately dumped her South American model boyfriend Jairo for the swarthy Red. Each commuted regularly between his home in Worsley, Manchester, and her parents' spacious pad in north London, where she was still living with her three brothers and sisters (Dani once confessed that her most embarrassing moment was when her father walked in as she was having sex with a lover).

Giggs said: 'We instantly liked each other, we met up, got on and we ended up going out with each other.'

A year later the prodigy's form dipped. One Saturday, as Dani looked on from her seat in the stands, one disgruntled fan yelled at her: 'Stop screwing Giggsy. You're screwing up his game.'

United boss Alex FERGUSON told Giggs to concentrate on his work, and he did. Dani insists she was not dumped, but they went their separate ways, and soon afterwards Behr began an affair with her second soccer star lover.

So was it . . . Les FERDINAND?

The £6.5 million centre forward was juggling Dani with two other women – long-term partner Angelea Murray (with whom he had a five-year-old son, Aaron, and would later have another child) and Dutch model Eva Dijkstra, whom he had pulled in a Covent Garden club, The Spot, in February 1995. The next time Eva saw Les, he had Dani on his arm, laughing and giggling. And six months later, after moving from QPR to NEWCASTLE UNITED, he dumped Eva after confessing he had begun an affair with the TV presenter.

As he tried to keep his relationship with Angelea alive, Ferdinand was anxious to keep his trysts with Dani quiet. Photographed leaving London's Royal Lancaster Hotel in October 1996, he exclaimed: 'This is ridiculous. Everyone knows Dani and I are good friends. That's all. Yes, I was there, I stay there now and again.'

But they were – on and off – a couple until October 1998, when Ferdinand returned to Angelea, the mother of his two children, and Dani bumped into an old flame.

So, was it . . . Ryan Giggs?

After a chance meeting at a Boyzone concert in Manchester, Dani and Ryan were spotted snogging at a zoo in Manchester and dining together in London. 'It's definitely back on,' a friend revealed at the time. Giggs had just split from Emma Gardner, who had recently miscarried their child. 'Dani and Ryan are taking it slowly, but both were single and thought "Why not?"' This time the partnership, though intense as ever, was short lived.

Giggs made up with Emma, and Dani declared she was finished with footballers. 'People have a false perception of me being a bimbo who just shags footballers. Now I'd choose to date someone who wasn't a footballer and end this reputation. I don't want to make that hat-trick.'

For a change, she dated . . . another footballer.

So was it . . . Mark BOSNICH?

In September 2000, two months after his marriage ended, they began dating. His career was on the slide after he was shown the door at Manchester United, despite a match-saving Intercontinental Cup performance in Japan. But Bosnich was earning a fortune at star-studded Chelsea. The fling lasted 17 months before ending abruptly as they house-hunted together.

Dani was said to be devastated. 'She honestly thought Mark was the one,' said a friend. 'They got on fantastically well and seemed to have so much in common.'

Bosnich was soon hooked up with troubled supermodel and party animal Sophie Anderton. His own problems – failing to make the first team, failing a drugs test for cocaine, his subsequent stay in the Priory Clinic and an admission that he had tried drugs – would perhaps make Dani count her blessings instead of bemoaning her luck.

Dani, also linked with showbiz stars Sylvester Stallone, Robbie WILLIAMS, Jean-Claude Van Damme and even *EastEnder* Michael Greco, has bemoaned the fate of footballers' partners. 'My advice is never go out with a footballer. It's restricting. They can only go on holiday when the season is over, they play a lot of away matches and they can't go out before a game. There isn't much freedom,' she said.

But don't bet against more soccer conquests, maybe in a parked FERRARI. After all, as she once confessed: 'I'll go into a pub and the only people who talk to me are pissed guys going: "Oi, Dani, fancy a f★★★?"' Which puts half of Britain's professionals in the frame.

BENGAL TIGER
Wild animal that Graeme SOUNESS claimed could not have tamed his first wife Danielle.

BERKOVIC, Eyal

Born: Haifa, Israel, 2.4.1972

Career: Southampton, West Ham United, Celtic, Blackburn Rovers, Manchester City, Portsmouth

The brilliant playmaker was among internationals investigated by the Israeli FA after a sex scandal that followed their 5–0 drubbing by Denmark in a European Championship play-off in 2000. Hookers were said to have visited players at their hotel but charges were never brought after all players denied being involved but, confusingly, apologised as a team for the incident.

BERNARD, Olivier

Born: Paris, France, 14.10.1979

Career: Lyon, Newcastle United, Darlington (loan)

NEWCASTLE UNITED's French international defender faced a three-month investigation by police investigating the gang rape of a 16-year-old girl. In a case with chilling similarities to the alleged GANG RAPE at Grosvenor House Hotel six months later, Bernard and friends were out on the town celebrating in April 2003 – this time a 1–0 local derby win over Sunderland. After boozing in the vibrant Quayside area, the 23 year old and his friends visited the Sea nightclub. The following day, a woman told police at a city-centre police station that she had been raped by Bernard and his friends at a flat in Newcastle in the early hours of Sunday, 27 April. Within hours, police interviewed three men, including Bernard. United boss Sir Bobby ROBSON was informed of the allegation and the arrests. Days later, two more were arrested and questioned. All five were bailed as inquiries continued. In July 2003, Bernard was told the Crown Prosecution Service had decided there was insufficient evidence to proceed and all charges were dropped.

BEST, Callum

Born: San Jose, USA, 6.3.1981

The drop-dead gorgeous son of Soccer Seducer No. 1 George BEST has already carved himself a niche as a young stud. After deciding not to follow in his father's famous bootsteps (despite a real talent for the game), Callum turned to modelling and has ambitions to act.

Already he has had affairs with reality TV floozy Jodie Marsh and model Catalina.

BEST, George

Born: Belfast 22.5.1946

Career: Manchester United, Stockport County, Cork Celtic, Los Angeles Aztecs, Fulham, Fort Lauderdale Strikers, Hibernian, San Jose Earthquakes, Bournemouth

The Belfast Boy had it all – brooding good looks, boyish Irish charm, money, fame and genuine, solid-gold football genius. When the '60s began to swing, George Best, the Beatle-fringed, bed-hopping Manchester United megastar, became the decade's icon.

And, despite four decades of alcoholism that saw the 1968 European Footballer of the Year bankrupted, jailed and just hours from death, his amazing sexual antics still transfix us all.

Best is, quite simply, the greatest soccer sex machine there ever was. In a life of unparalleled debauchery, gorgeous George:

- was SUED for breach of promise by his jilted fianceé;
- DATED two Miss Worlds, several beauty queens and thousands of 'scrubbers';
- BEDDED seven women in one day;
- had a three-in-a-bed with a MOTHER AND HER DAUGHTER;
- CONFESSED his love of 'screwing' while drunk on a live TV chat show;
- ADMITTED he has never been faithful to a woman;
- DUMPED the woman who got him back on his feet for a blonde less than half his age;
- DALLIED with two other women when he hit the bottle again after a life-saving liver transplant;
- MADE one of them pregnant! Then,
- DIVORCED for the second time and . . .
- DATED a woman half his age.

The daddy of all soccer bed-boys had an unlikely start to his sex career. Best was a shy, stick-thin waif at school, teased despite his soccer talent. He said: 'The local bike seemed the obvious one to go for. But I seemed to be the only one who couldn't shag her and it wasn't for the want of trying.'

Instead, Best's first proper girlfriend was a pretty thing called Liz. There was plenty of heavy petting behind the bike sheds, but no sex. 'That was probably the start of it, that thing of me wanting something I couldn't have,' he recalled.

Best famously fled home to Belfast during his first trial at Manchester United. But once he had conquered his homesickness and settled in to the comfortable Chorlton home of redoubtable United landlady Betty Fullaway, his amazing career began in earnest.

When nights on the pull in the quiet Manchester suburb's dance halls, bowling alleys or the local chippy didn't work, Best struck on a new plan and stole the girlfriend of Mrs Fullaway's son Steve.

On the pitch, the gifted winger's skills earned a first-team debut against West Bromwich Albion at the age of 17 in September 1963. He scored his first goal that December and became a first-team regular. For six seasons he was United's top scorer, even though he played from midfield. And, incredibly, he confessed that when he scored in front of the 60,000 Old Trafford faithful he would become physically turned on.

'At moments like that with the crowd cheering I used to get sexually excited, really aroused,' he said. No wonder he was a man possessed – goal after goal was followed by girl after girl, often in the back of one of his white E-type Jaguars or Rolls Royces. 'The girls were mostly young and, like me, still lived at home. So until I got a place of my own, we did what every other young couple did and made the most of the back seat. Mine was just a bit more luxurious than most.'

An unlikely alliance with Manchester City star Mike SUMMERBEE helped too. Summerbee said: 'We used to go Le Phonographe nightclub to sit and gawp at the young ladies – slaver as they went by. George was a bit shy then . . . to be honest, the girls weren't really interested in a skinny lad with a Belfast accent.' But stardom – and Dutch courage from Best's first foray into drinking – brought the birds flocking to the one-bedroom flat they rented together in Crumpsall. 'This was our hideaway, a place we could escape all the madness. And it had a big lounge which doubled up as a bedroom if necessary,' recalled Best.

Best opened two boutiques in Manchester – and not just to make money. 'I think the only reason I opened a boutique was because the flat above was a great knocking shop and a cover from the boss and the club,' he said. 'I suppose I was a bit daft. It's not good for an athlete to spend every afternoon having it away with a woman, every evening drinking and every morning thinking about having it away and drinking.'

As the Beatles and the Stones dominated the charts, the pill liberated women and free love flourished, Best became the embodiment of his age. An amazing virtuoso performance against Benfica in 1966 – and a photo of him arriving back in Britain wearing a sombrero – earned him the nickname 'El Beatle' and made him the most famous face in Britain.

It was, already, the beginning of the end.

United boss Sir Matt Busby – aware the Belfast Boy was the diamond he had searched for since the deaths of his dazzling Babes at Munich in 1958 – trod a precipitous path. Sometimes he indulged the boy wonder. When United clinched the 1967 League title with a thrilling 6–1 victory over West Ham United at Upton Park, Busby even allowed Best to use the team coach to transport a new conquest, a computer programmer called Sonia, back to Manchester.

Sometimes he chided him. Busby went ballistic when he discovered George was seeing a married woman – Dahlia Simmons – after meeting her at Manchester nightclub, Reubens. 'I've dated two Miss Worlds and plenty of absolutely stunning women,' Best said, 'but Dahlia was probably the most beautiful.' They shared what they thought were discreet dates at out-of-the-way restaurants and met at her girlfriends' houses. But news leaked.

'Son,' said Busby. 'It's not for me to interfere, but why this girl? Why someone who's married? There are hundreds of nice single girls out there. Why can't you go out with one of them?'

'I don't know, boss,' replied Best. But he did. 'Dahlia, as forbidden fruit, was irresistible to me.'

He explained: 'Now I was famous, girls were throwing themselves at me. So I would deliberately go for the ones who were supposedly unattainable as a sort of challenge. Pulling girls had become a sport for me and so I wanted to be the best at it.'

Dahlia left her husband for Best but the relationship fizzled out. Best was unwilling to settle down and believed he was untouchable.

He regularly denied tales of late-night debauchery, gambling losses and unseemly womanising. And, with match-winning performances every week, why not believe he could go on for ever?

By 23, he was a European Cup winner, his solo goal early in extra time at Wembley on 29 May 1968 breaking Benfica's will and landing Sir Matt Busby's Holy Grail. That season he was voted European Footballer of the Year.

'There was nowhere else to go but down,' said Best.

Though his pulling partner Mike Summerbee had got married that year, there was no stopping Best in the sex stakes. Summers were spent with up to 20 mates bedding babes in a villa in Majorca. There was just one rule – each would have to shout 'Geronimo' as they climaxed so the rest could applaud. Winters comprised drunken nights at The Brown Bull pub, punctuated by blackouts and one-night stands. The madness had begun.

But a brief encounter at a Danish airport in 1969 as United flew home from a pre-season tour almost tamed him. 'You could say I fell in love with a pair of knockers,' said Best, who signed an autograph for a young blue-eyed blonde, who then vanished into the crowd. Best, for once, didn't get her number. No matter. The wily winger asked the nation's press to find 'My Danish Dream Girl', and succeeded.

Student Eva HARALDSTED, 21, saw the story and sent in a photo. She wasn't the only one. Three others were rejected as frauds by Bestie. Eva visited London and they had dinner at the swish Dell'Aretusa bistro in London's Kings Road. At their hotel later that night, George booked separate rooms. They parted with a handshake rather than sex. But in the early hours a naked Best was apparently seen chasing Eva, who was wearing just her underwear, down a corridor.

Eva persevered. In Manchester, they stepped off their plane to a paparazzi frenzy.

'It was like arriving with a Beatle,' she said. 'All the fans, the adulation, the flashguns. But George was kind, loving, charming and attentive. Within a week he had asked me to marry him. I said yes – it felt so right at the time.'

Despite Busby's concern, the couple moved in together at his digs with Mrs Fullaway before moving to the hideaway flat he had shared with Summerbee. Best was having a £300,000 high-tech mansion built in Cheshire and Eva agreed to set up home with him there.

'We were blissfully happy,' said Eva. 'He was determined it would be the house of my dreams, too, with a Scandinavian-style kitchen. I had no idea until the very end that he thought anything was wrong. It was just before Christmas when a reporter knocked on my door and asked what I thought about George saying he couldn't marry me after all. He had told a newspaper that he was too young to settle down and felt he couldn't be faithful. I confronted him when he got home and he said he couldn't tell me to my face. I still don't know if it was planned or not.'

(Best claims he even bedded the attractive woman journalist sent up to interview him.)

'Meeting someone in a hotel lobby, fancying them like mad and inviting them over for a dirty weekend is not quite the same as courting them for a year or two and deciding to walk down the aisle,' Best later said. Booted out of Best's digs, furious Eva sued the superstar for breach of promise. She won £500 in an out-of-court settlement.

When Best spotted Eva soon after at his favourite nightspot, Blinkers, he commandeered the DJ's turntables and repeatedly played the Beatles' latest single 'Get Back'. A fight ensued on the pavement outside as her new man took exception to the pointed message.

But like so many of the women Best loved and dumped, Eva's bitterness has subsided. 'I didn't regret a single moment of my love affair with George,' she said. 'It was a happy period and a great adventure.'

And, she says, she was the woman who could have tamed George: 'He had left his home at a young age and there was part of him which craved domesticity. If we had stayed together, he would have found that and he would have had firmer foundations. As it was, after we split up, he moved into the house we had planned together and I think he was lonely there. That's where it started to go wrong. He had a lot of hangers-on, people who were only there for him when life was going well. He couldn't see that a lot of his so-called friends were people who were gaining from him. When he was with me, he was happy. He didn't drink very much at all; he was always too busy training. In fact, I never saw him drunk.'

Though he would later lament that it afforded him no privacy, Best's glass house was the perfect pulling palace. Women walked straight into his clutches. 'I had two 16 year olds used to arrive regularly,' Best explained. 'They used to tell their parents they were going to a youth club. You wouldn't believe what they got up to.'

One woman rang his doorbell, explained her car had broken down outside his home and asked if she could call the AA from his phone. Ever the gent, Best agreed. 'I had her on the carpet in the hallway before the AA man arrived. Gave her a quick repair job.'

Easy sex – as well as boozing and gambling – were now replacing football as the daily fix thrill-seeking Best required as United faced the abyss . . . and stepped off.

One married woman told how she met him at a drinks party and spent minutes wondering how to entice him into bed, when a blonde walked up, introduced herself as Julie and asked: 'Would you like a quick f★★★?'

'Certainly,' said Best, who politely offered an 'Excuse me' and departed in her wake.

But not every woman fell for the Best charm – singer Dusty Springfield turned him down. Little did he know she was secretly bisexual and this was not his day.

As United prepared for a clash with bitter rivals Leeds United in the 1970 FA Cup semi-final replay, Best played an energetic game of hide and seek with new United boss Wilf McGuinness and a married woman. It would cost him dearly.

The night before, bored Best had tried his luck with the girl but given up when McGuinness spotted him. Now, with a couple of hours to kick-off, he bumped into the girl again. She asked for an autograph; he asked her for a drink in the bar. She agreed. She was married but lonely. Watchful Wilf, well aware of his number 7's talents, pounced again. Around 20 minutes before the United bus was due to leave for Villa Park, Best made it to her room, only for McGuinness to burst in with a pass key, yelling: 'Get your arse back downstairs. We're leaving in 15 minutes.'

'I'm only chatting,' insisted George as he was frog-marched downstairs to the bar where McGuinness downed a large whisky and told him: 'You'd better play well today.'

As any defender would admit, Best never knew when he was

beaten. As soon as Wilf was out of sight, Best returned: 'This time we both reckoned we'd done enough chatting and we had a quickie before I left.'

A short coach ride later, the usually magnificent Best put in one of his worst United performances ever. One-on-one with the keeper, the knackered Red stumbled over the ball. The flawed genius was now a floored genius, wallowing in the Birmingham mud.

Fans might blame a soggy pitch for his glaring error, but Best knew the truth. 'Their players had got wind of what happened in the hotel and Johnny Giles had a right go at me on the field. I should have made him pay when I had the chance to score the winner, but I fell over the ball. I'd literally screwed up what turned out to be my last chance to reach the FA Cup final,' he admitted years later. 'I played like a big wanker.'

The game ended 0–0 and, after a third titanic struggle, Don Revie's Leeds edged through 1–0. United were out.

McGuinness dropped the United talisman but Busby, still general manager, overruled him. Best played on; McGuinness was fired eight months later. United's new boss Frank O'Farrell fared no better with the rogue Red. Best managed to wake the team hotel in the early hours before an away match when he brought back two girls for a threesome as his roommate tried to sleep. Two other girls were running naked through the hotel trying to find him!

Time was running out for Best at United. Busby said: 'We fined him. We suspended him. What more could we do? We couldn't shoot him. We might have felt like smacking his bottom, as a man might smack his own son's bottom. But this isn't allowed in a player's contract.'

He added: 'George brought great pain but greater rewards to me, as most boys bring great pain and even greater joy to their parents.'

Best's new infamy moved football and footballers from the back pages to the front. And the so-called 'Siege of Noel Street' in January 1971 showed his pulling power with the press. After another bender, Best missed the train to London for United's match with Chelsea. But he had already arranged a post-match date with actress Sinead Cusack. He decided on an awayday anyway, and caught a later train. But when news emerged that he preferred a bunk-up with Sinead instead of a bust-up with Chopper Harris, the quiet Islington street became bedlam, full of press, TV crews and crowds of local kids.

Best recalled: 'When we woke up to a commotion outside one Sunday morning, Sinead looked out of the window . . . and her jaw dropped. "What on earth have you been up to, George?" she said. "I've missed a football match, that's all," I said.'

Best stayed holed up in the flat for three days before being rescued by friends and the police. Questions were later asked in Parliament about the cost of giving George Best a police escort out of the building.

Best relied more and more on his vices to replace the thrill of football. And his vanishing acts – and sexual conquests – became an everyday occurrence.

As well as Sinead, he would bed singer Lynsey de Paul; Juliet Mills, daughter of Sir John; actress Annette Andre; author Pat Booth; Stephanie Harrison, who later married motorcycle racer Barry Sheene; and even *Carry On* star Barbara Windsor.

At least Best had his international career as a distraction from the bad karma back in Manchester. Ever the showman, he would perform exhibition matches in the bedroom with local conquests, watched by giggling teammates crammed into cupboards, behind curtains or even in bushes if it was an outdoor game. 'There was nothing dirty in it,' said Best later with alarming naivety. 'It was just a big laugh for the lads. The girls never knew and I'd have screwed them in any case, so what's the difference?'

The love of his life remained United. But a painful break-up was inevitable.

It began with a trial separation in 1972, in which Best headed to Malaga, announced his retirement and sated his two desires by bedding a barmaid. But a potentially fatal thrombosis struck his right leg and he returned to Manchester in agony for life-saving surgery, rehabilitation and a reunion with United.

But the divorce became official in January 1974. With United staring relegation in the face, manager Tommy DOCHERTY claimed the star turned up for the FA Cup third-round clash with QPR late, drunk and with a girl in tow. 'Total fabrication,' maintains Best. 'I would never insult the team or the fans in that way. He had to find an excuse so he went ahead and made one up. That was it, for me, I didn't even watch the game I was so insulted. I just sat on a bench and sobbed. I knew this time it was really over.'

Best drowned his sorrows in sex. In one 24-hour period he bedded seven different women . . .

- 9 a.m.: Best wakes after spending the night with girl Number 1.
- 1 p.m.: After drinks at the Brown Bull, he pops upstairs for an action-packed hour with girl Number 2, a TV worker lodging there.
- 3.30 p.m.: He waits at the gates for his sixth-form schoolgirl lover, girl Number 3.
- 5 p.m.: She leaves her cousin alone with Best in his flat. She becomes girl Number 4.
- 6 p.m.: A late-afternoon love-in with an occasional partner who is girl Number 5.
- 11 p.m.: He picks up another date for a trip to the casino then it's back to her place, making her girl Number 6, before he heads back to the tables.
- 4.30 a.m.: Best calls in on a casual acquaintance whose boyfriend is away. He stays in girl Number 7's bed until the following lunchtime.

'I was young and fit at the time,' he joked. 'It was just one of those crazy days.'

Best was by now living a dangerous cliché. If he didn't realise he was self-destructing, he was the only one.

But there were other, more immediate dangers of his antics, even though it was before the days of AIDS. Best admits he twice needed treatment for sexually transmitted diseases, once in Spain and once back in London.

Best would have become a father at this time but for the decision of his on-off lover Georgie Ellis to abort their baby. Georgie, whose mother Ruth became the last women to be hanged in Britain in 1955 for murdering her lover David Blakely, said she tried in vain to contact him when she discovered she was pregnant. 'I've never forgiven myself for getting rid of his baby,' she said before her death from cancer in December 2001 aged 50.

Not content with bedding every available woman in Britain, Best began flying in his conquests from around the world and collecting Miss Worlds.

He had already romanced Carolyn Moore, Miss Great Britain. When he walked out on Manchester for Marbella in 1972, he left her behind too. (One night, he boasted, he went out for dinner with Carolyn and eight of her girlfriends – and realised he'd slept with every one of them!)

For a while, Best had dated 1966 Miss UK Jenny Lowe, a former lover of Manchester City coach Malcolm ALLISON. 'She gave me a photo of herself and three other girls who were Miss This or Miss That. Out of the four, I'd slept with three. In my warped mind at the time, the set was not complete until I'd slept with the fourth. It wasn't an easy mission. She was married and didn't sleep around, and it took a lot of hard work and patience, but I succeeded.'

In February 1974, the dazzling new Miss World Marjorie WALLACE, just 19, spent an evening at his Manchester nightclub Slack Alice quaffing champagne and posing for publicity pictures. 'She didn't stay long,' said Best, 'but long enough for me to get her London telephone number.'

George had at last met his match.

Marjorie had celebrated victory by declaring her intention to 'make love to as many men as possible'. In the months following her triumph, she had ditched tennis ace Jimmy Connors and was seeing Welsh crooner Tom Jones while engaged to motor racing driver Peter Revson.

'That didn't put me off,' said Best. 'In fact, if anything, it made her a more attractive catch.'

Their sexual liaison was brief – a two-night stand – and bitter. Best arrived at her flat on a Friday night with an overnight bag. She did not like his presumption of a bed for the night. But she obliged anyway. After sex and a sleep, they spent Saturday in the restaurants and clubs of London. But as they made love in the early hours of night two, Marjorie took a phone call from her fiancé's mother and declared her love for the race ace and told how much she missed him while he was away. Insulted, Best asked her: '"How can you have a conversation like that when you're lying in bed with me?" She asked me who the hell I thought I was to tell her how to behave.'

The following morning she left him in bed and went out.

Such a sharp exit must have been a shock – Best was normally the one doing the loving and leaving. But there was another to come.

After a phone call, apparently to arrange another date, two policemen arrived at Slack Alice. 'They cautioned me and arrested me. I was flabbergasted. "What the hell's going on?" I wondered. Something to do with Marjorie Wallace and some property was all the police could tell me.'

In the early hours, the player was in a police car heading to London with two Scotland Yard detectives. After a spell in Wood Lane police station, Best appeared in Marylebone Magistrates' Court charged with burgling Marjorie Wallace's flat and stealing a mink coat, spirits and a diary. After a five-minute hearing, he was released on bail and returned bemused to Manchester. There was no sign of Miss World. She had apparently gone back to America following the death of Revson in a crash at the South African Grand Prix. When she failed to appear at his hearing on 27 March, all charges were dropped.

She was said to have given George a mark of 3 out of 10 for his performance in bed. 'Three marks is two more than I gave her,' he retorted. After just 104 days, man-mad Marjorie was stripped of her crown for bringing the role into disrepute.

With his United career over, Best headed for America and a starring role with Los Angeles Aztecs. LA, he proclaimed, was 'a sexual paradise for any straight lad, not too ugly and with a British accent'.

In 1976, Best joined the Fort Lauderdale Strikers. At a party at a millionaire neighbour's bachelor pad – where beauties strolled naked round the pool – he met blonde English ex-model Angela MacDonald James, personal assistant to the singer Cher.

Angie said: 'It was love at first sight. He was the sexiest man I'd ever met. He was powerful and fit, and had this wicked sense of humour and that twinkle in his eye. There was just an overwhelming physical attraction between us.'

Too true. He followed her to the spare bedroom and they made love. Best said: 'We came out an hour later looking haggard, and she has the carpet burns on the base of her spine to this day.' Besotted Best quickly proposed marriage and they moved in together against Cher's advice. She even followed him to London, where he enjoyed a vintage season at Fulham. But Bestie's benders continued and Angie moved out. When he drunkenly crashed his car into a lamp-post and needed 57 stitches, she visited him in hospital only to find another woman at his bedside about to perform oral sex. Angie, 25, sought revenge in an unexpected way – humiliating him by becoming a Playboy Bunny. She also began a two-month affair of her own – with West Ham United star Billy JENNINGS – but Best didn't find out. 'I took one look at Bill and thought he was the cutest little thing on the planet,' said Angie.

Then she headed back to America, with Best in hot pursuit. 'He professed undying love and told me he couldn't live without me,' said Angie. 'Stupidly, I believed him.'

On 24 January 1978, the happy couple flew to Las Vegas for a $20 three-minute ceremony at the Candlelight Chapel. Bride and groom arrived late and worse for wear. Best had even forgotten the licence and the ring. And after a boozy reception at Caesar's Palace casino, he headed not for bed but to an all-night bar, arriving home two days later at 4 a.m. It became a constant pattern.

'When I asked George if he had been with a woman, he would never deny it. We both knew where he had been and what he had been up to. George may have rolled in with his pocket full of other women's phone numbers, but the next morning he would be so wonderful to me that I would feel like the only woman in his world,' she said.

And Best loved Angie too. On his sober days, she recalled, he wrote poems to her; but on his drunken days he could be violent to her.

In 1980, Angie discovered that Best had even tried to bed her own sister, Lindy. At one point she laced his tea with sleeping pills to stop him going out drinking. It did not work.

When their son Callum was born in 1981, Best cut the umbilical cord and declared it the greatest moment of his life. But he could not cut out the booze or the women. A month after Callum's birth, Best was even questioned over an alleged attempted rape. A teenage neighbour in San Jose claimed Best had broken into her house in the early hours.

Best was in a rehab clinic when police arrived at their home to question him. When he left the clinic three weeks later, he went to the police. That night, he admitted, he had slept in his car after an almighty drinking session. 'He couldn't have found his way into his own house that night in the state he was in,' said Angie, 'let alone anyone else's. The police admitted to George the description the girl had given of the intruder did not fit him at all. There was no evidence to link George to the alleged crime and the matter was dropped.'

But the flings went on. One night, on his return from a drunken four-day fling with a waitress, Angie stabbed him in the bottom with a carving knife. He returned to Britain alone. But not for long. Mary STAVIN, the sexy Scandinavian Miss World, was living with ex-QPR star Don SHANKS, for whom she had dumped Middlesbrough's Graeme SOUNESS. Within weeks of meeting him, she moved in with Best.

Angie had by now served divorce papers, and was past caring about her husband's infidelity. 'That's typical of you, George,' she joked. 'There was bound to be another woman and being you it had to be Miss World.'

Even by Best's standards, his dalliance with Mary Stavin was the coupling from hell. 'Her public image was of a Miss Goody Two Shoes,' he said. 'But with me at least she wasn't like that. She used to ask me to squeeze her throat while we were making love. And she liked to go to sleep at night with something in her mouth that wasn't her thumb!'

'But,' Best added, 'in all the time we were together, I went with only one other woman, which for me is a record.'

Best and Stavin broke up a year later when the wannabe actress moved out to Los Angeles to try her luck in Hollywood.

Best tried his luck in Blondes, a West End nightclub, where glamour model Angie Lynn was smitten by the Irish rogue's charm. She walked out on *Coronation Street* hunk Chris Quinten for him in June 1984. But the relationship was, in his words, 'warfare'.

One drunken bust-up with Angie in November 1984 landed Best in jail. After a row, he stupidly headed out for a night on the town in his car and was nicked for drink driving outside Buckingham Palace. When he failed to appear in court at 9 a.m. the following day, he was arrested and, after a scuffle, charged with assaulting a policeman. A month later, on 3 December, Bow Street Magistrates sentenced him to three months in prison, as well as a five-year driving ban. When his appeal failed (and after a 'long physical goodbye' the night before, as he put it), Best was banged up.

For the legendary soccer stud, jail was a long, long scoring drought.

On 8 February 1985, he was released. 'As we both headed home, there was only one thought in our minds,' he said. 'We started tearing at each other's clothes as soon as we got through the door, but, as randy as I felt in my head, it wasn't happening physically. Believe it or not, it can even happen to George Best!'

Thankfully, a sunshine holiday in Mauritius did the trick and Best was back bonking for Britain. Another baby Best was on the cards in 1986 until tragedy struck. As his divorce from Angela McDonald James became official, Angie Lynn suffered a miscarriage and the relationship fizzled out.

Best went back to Blondes and found . . . a brunette – dark-haired beauty Mary Shatila. She was with her half-sister Fiona, who advised Mary: 'That's George Best. He's a womaniser and a drunk. Don't go within 100 feet of him.'

Mary remembered: 'Out of the darkness in the smoky nightclub, I saw the most intense pair of blue eyes I have ever seen staring straight at me. George might be an alcoholic but he's still one of the sexiest men alive. The first time we made love I thought I'd died and gone to heaven. I guess he's had lots of practice!'

The couple lived for a while in a flat above the bar they opened, Besties, in Chelsea. 'Occasionally, we'd sneak down in the middle of the night, have some champagne and make love in the bar,' she said. 'He shagged thousands of women, but always made love to me.'

Half-Egyptian, half-Scottish Mary put Best back on his feet, launched him on the lucrative after-dinner speaking circuit and, as his agent, helped end his recent bankruptcy with a money-spinning testimonial match in Belfast.

In return, Best professed undying love for Mary, calling her 'my lover, my friend and my strength' and tried to win back her daughter Layla, six, who had been abducted by her Lebanese father.

But Mary was powerless to help him in 1990 when he appeared on the BBC's primetime Terry Wogan chat show after a session in the green room.

'What about all those women?' Wogan asked.

'Terry, I like screwing, all right?' giggled Best.

Embarrassed, Wogan changed tack. How did George spend his

time nowadays? 'Screwing,' said George with a crazy leer on his face. 'I like screwing.'

The nation squirmed. His descent into disgrace was blindingly obvious, but that incredible football talent had left a legacy of affection for George and he weathered the storm with Mary's help.

But his gratitude would not stretch to being faithful. George cheated on her with various women and she normally forgave him. But in August 1994, Mary received a phone call that changed her life for ever. Best had been spotted at Tramp nightclub with a new young blonde. Now he had called a newspaper to say he was getting married to the girl, Alex Pursey, an air hostess aged just 23. Betrayed, Mary's shock was matched only by her fury, especially when it emerged he had tried to sell the story of his night with Alex to newspapers for a quick £15,000. For Mary, it was the final straw. She moved out, then told her side of the story – how he had slept with 20 other women in their last year together, including the half-sister who had warned her off him, and been mugged of his £6,000 watch by two vice girls in a hotel.

She told him: 'I used to be hurt and annoyed by your womanising, but in the end I realised it was like trying to stop you drinking – pointless. Life with you was one long suicide.'

Best's new blonde Alex read the papers and ignored his calls. But the Virgin air hostess, who had recently split up with Wimbledon defender John Scales after a six-year relationship, finally relented. She insisted he apologise for the newspaper stunt. She said later: 'The truth is that we didn't sleep together at all until about five months after I'd met him. When he told me he loved me, I pointed out that he didn't even know me. And I did think he was a slightly famous man in a nightclub looking for someone to go to bed with. So I didn't go to bed with him. He got my phone number. That's all. I really had known George for quite a time before I went to bed with him. By that time I was sure that it was serious.

'A chemistry just happened between us. I'm terribly attracted to George, more so than I've been to anybody else.'

But Best's propensity for booze, betting and birds ensured it was yet another volcanic partnership.

On 24 July 1995, George Best, 49, married Alex at Chelsea Register Office. It was almost a year after they first met.

He had proposed a week earlier, to make up for his dalliance with another woman, heiress Louisa Banks, 23. Alex revealed: 'George got it into his head that I was seeing other men. When I came back from a flight, I phoned him at 10 p.m. and there was this woman with him. He put her on the phone and she told me to f*** off. I felt absolutely dreadful. I was in tears and didn't speak to him for days. I told him I wasn't going to waste the rest of my life with him. He kept phoning and saying he was sorry, then he phoned to say we were getting married. So I forgave him, as you do.'

She explained: 'I know there have been lots of girls, and I know lots of them were blonde. But I also know that he's only married two of them and that one of them is me. So why should I worry?'

But she admits: 'It's a volatile relationship, very intense. Friends can't believe us. One minute we're at each other's throats and the next we're really lovey-dovey.'

Alex told of a violent bust-up on her birthday a year later. She said: 'George was on a very bad bender and we'd had a row. He went out on the morning of my birthday and didn't come back. I tried to phone him all day. I was absolutely livid. He came home the next day. I said, "How dare you? You haven't even got me a birthday present." We screamed at each other, I lashed out at him, and he hit me. All hell broke loose. He hit me and kicked me about five or six times on the face and the body. He shouldn't have, but it was done through alcohol.'

Police were called but Alex decided not to press charges.

'I chose to forgive him,' she said. 'I would be lying, though, if I said I trusted him. I'm always keeping an eye on him and looking over my shoulder. Women throw themselves at George just because of who he is. I've seen so many of them slip phone numbers in his pocket. I find them and burn them. As far as I know, he hasn't been unfaithful since our marriage, but it would be no surprise if he had been.'

After a successful liver transplant in 2002 and eight months off the booze, Best appeared to have found stability for the first time. The couple even talked of having children. Alex said: 'George would like me to have a baby, but I've told him I need to see he can behave himself first. I don't want to bring a child into the world with an alcoholic father who's falling over all the time.'

We hoped for the best. But the fall was, in hindsight, inevitable. George, now 57, fell off the wagon in style in July 2003 and was linked with a new blonde – 25-year-old crop-haired Paula Shapland. He apparently told her he was bored with Alex and planning a divorce. Alex, 'hurt, betrayed and angry', walked out, declaring their marriage finished. Best complained he had been set up.

He moved in with glamorous divorcee Gina Devivo, though he insisted he was just lodging there. In October, Alex and George were attempting to repair the damage. He had more stomach implants to help him battle the booze. Then Gina claimed she was pregnant with his child – which she later lost. On 24 April 2004, the Bests were granted a divorce at the Family Division of the High Court in London. In written statements, Alex told how she found her husband in another woman's bed the previous 28 November and left him the same day. George admitted adultery and the nine-year marriage ended in just 140 seconds.

Soon, in a TV interview, he confessed he was in love with a married woman who could not be his. In July 2004, 22-year-old Lisa Pesch, a Dutch au pair, told of her own bizarre romance with the drunken icon 36 years her senior.

Best's drinking got worse; his behaviour more and more erratic; his family increasingly worried for his health. With his life – and his body – disintegrating yet again, Best was surely now running out of time to beat his twin demons of wine and women.

Best once admitted: 'Sex and women have been a madness. I have never been faithful to anyone. I find it impossible. It is pure selfish excitement spurred on by boredom and the challenge. And the '60s and '70s were a time when anything went: actresses, waitresses, shop girls, sisters, mother and daughter – at the same time – two in a bed, three in a bed. I even tried to get it together with Brigitte Bardot. The more impossible the conquest the better.'

And he once let slip the secret of his success: 'Don't smoke, don't take drugs and don't be too particular,' Best explained. 'And never make rules – like not sleeping with a friend's wife, married women or girls with big knockers or bandy legs. If they're willing, then they're worthwhile no matter who or what they are.'

Let's hope George one day forgets his own advice. At the moment, he's locked in at the Last Chance Saloon – drinking it dry and pulling all the barmaids.

See STABBING.

BETTER THAN SEX

It's the oldest question in the book. Is scoring a goal better than sex? Yes, yes, oh yes, conclude Arsenal legends Charlie George and Ian WRIGHT, Everton's '70s legend Bob Latchford and even England ace Alan Shearer. 'Goalscoring is better than sex. It's just a tremendous feeling. It's very difficult for me to sit here and explain the adrenalin, the buzz it gives you,' said Shearer. 'Until you've actually done it in front of a crowd of 40,000, you can't know.'

Manchester City's cocky Scouser Robbie FOWLER insists: 'Goals give me a buzz. It's the best feeling in the world, apart from one thing and we all know what that is.' Calm down, Robbie, calm down!

England skipper and global heart-throb David BECKHAM – married to ex-Spice girl Victoria Adams – insists: 'There's no contest. Of course sex is better.' Bet she told him to say that! And Middlesbrough's Dutch star Jimmy Floyd Hasselbaink adds: 'You can never say a goal is better than sex. All the guys who say that are not having proper sex.'

On the other hand, as it were, Ireland's playboy striker Tony CASCARINO, maintains: 'Personally I'd compare it more with masturbation. I've always found sex to be an absolute pleasure, but scoring goals has only ever brought relief.'

BISHOP, Ian

Born: Liverpool 29.5.1965
Career: Everton, Crewe Alexandra, Carlisle United, Bournemouth, Manchester City, West Ham United, Manchester City, Miami Fusion
Notorious for a GAY sex scandal that never happened.

See Trevor MORLEY.

BLACKMAIL

See Martin EDWARDS, Garry FLITCROFT, Mr X.

BLACKMORE, Clayton

Born: Neath 23.9.1964
Career: Manchester United, Middlesbrough, Bristol City (loan), Barnsley, Notts County, Leigh RMI, Bangor City
The curly-permed Red Devil was arrested on false charges of rape during Manchester United's infamous mid-season trip to Bermuda.

American beautician Patricia Savoy, 22, claimed the Welsh international followed her into the toilets of the Oasis disco in the Bermudan capital, Hamilton, and attacked her.

Blackmore – just married – claimed he had been set up, but was arrested and left to languish in a sweltering jail facing a possible ten-year sentence if convicted. United boss Alex FERGUSON said: 'When we were allowed to see Clayton, he broke down in my arms. He convinced us he had been set up by two girls whose evidence was the basis of the charge. We stayed with him, giving comfort, for as long as we could. When he walked away in his prison garb, the dreadful implications of his plight were driven home to us.'

Ferguson phoned the 23-year-old's wife Jackie back in Manchester. 'How do you tell a girl that a rape charge, however concocted, is hanging over her husband?' Fergie said.

United's club secretary Les Olive and solicitor Maurice Watkins worked round the clock and Blackmore was released after 32 hours. Savoy withdrew her statement, saying: 'I want to get on with my life and put this nightmare behind me.' No charges were ever brought.

Four years later, in 1991, Blackmore repaid his boss with a last-second clearance off the line that helped United lift the European Cup-Winners' Cup.

BLOTT, John

Born: Redcar 26.2.1965
Career: Manchester City, Scunthorpe United, Carlisle United, Mansfield Town, Newport County

'Arrogant, egocentric and devoid of remorse' – Mr Justice Hooper wasted few words as he jailed Manchester City keeper-turned-policeman and serial-rapist John Blott.

Blott had excelled as a schoolboy player in his native South Bank, a depressed industrial area of Teesside. At 17, after schools, county, youth and national schoolboy honours, he signed as a pro for Manchester City. A glittering career between the sticks in the wake of Trautmann, Swift and Corrigan beckoned. But two years later, Blott tasted failure.

Without playing a first-team match, City transferred him to lowly Carlisle. There, a wrist injury led to a series of operations.

After two appearances, his contract was cancelled and, after brief spells at other lower-league clubs, he realised his football career was finished. He tried his luck as a PE teacher before joining the police. An able and intelligent student, Blott scored 93 per cent in his final examinations.

His new job as a bobby on the beat gave Blott the perfect chance to snare women. Tall, dark and handsome, and, he believed, irresistible to women, Blott boasted of hundreds of one-night stands with women seduced by his footballer's physique, Armani aftershave and smart uniform.

A woman colleague said: 'He would attend a crime and, if he liked the look of the female victim when he visited her home, he'd leave his notebook behind. Or he'd make another excuse so he could go back by himself and get talking to her.'

Blott also targeted women he worked with. The 22-year-old colleague told how he would fill their conversation with smutty innuendo as they walked the beat. 'He would undress me with his eyes,' she explained. 'He was good looking, but he made my skin creep.'

Blott escaped investigation for five years because his victims were convinced they would never be believed. But justice finally caught up with the rapist cop when one woman confided in a friend and police were alerted.

Leeds Crown Court heard his first victim was just 16 when he pounced in 1993. The girl was out horseriding when 28-year-old Blott, chasing a stolen vehicle, hitched a lift on her horse. He noted her address and later called her, lured her to his home in New Marske, Cleveland, and raped her twice.

His second rape victim was a garage receptionist, aged 18, who agreed to a date with him after his persistent attempts to chat her up. After dinner, he told her he had to get something from his house 20 miles away. At first she waited in the car, but finally she agreed to coffee. Inside, he raped her twice.

Another charge against him came from a 23-year-old tax worker who was kept prisoner in his house for three hours, fondled and threatened with rape then forced to beg on her hands and knees to be taken home.

In May 1998, five years after the first rape, Blott was jailed for ten years. He was given a concurrent ten-year sentence for the second offence and five years for the indecent assault.

He was acquitted of three other indecent assaults, on a trainee policewoman and two nurses, and a further charge of raping a 25-year-old special constable. Three alleged indecent assaults were left on file.

Before his trial, the Richard Gere lookalike boasted: 'The allegations aren't true because I can get plenty of women without forcing myself on them. Women are attracted to me because I'm fit and look good, and that's not a crime.' The truth was very different.

BOSNICH, Mark

Born: Fairfield, Australia, 13.1.1972
Career: Sydney Croatia, Manchester United, Aston Villa, Manchester United, Chelsea

It had all the potential to be the wedding from hell. Instead of waking early to don his best suit, Manchester United goalkeeper Mark Bosnich answered a knock at the door at 7 a.m to police officers who had arrived to arrest him over a fracas in the early hours as his star-studded stag night turned sour. Bosnich, six days after a dream £6 million return to the newly crowned European Champions in June 1999, had been photographed at 1.48 a.m. leaving the Legs Eleven lap dancing club in Birmingham. After a scuffle, a cameraman ended up in the gutter. Bosnich legged it with his camera.

Three hours after his arrest, Bosnich was allowed to leave Sutton Coldfield police station in the West Midlands. A quick change later the ex-Aston Villa star arrived at Coombe Abbey hotel to wed live-in lover, model and promotions girl Sarah Jarrett, 28.

Next, the best man's speech. How Sarah must have squirmed as Dwight YORKE, former Villa striker, current Manchester United Treble-winner and Bosnich's ex porn co-star, rose to say a few well-chosen words about the groom. Thankfully he didn't mention that hilarious night a year earlier when the duo filmed themselves in women's clothing, giving a big thumbs up to a secret camera before a booze-fuelled sex session with four women at Yorke's luxury love palace in Sutton Coldfield. In one scene, Bosnich was seen leaning over as a belt-wielding blonde prepared to spank him.

Clearly not wishing to embarrass the ladies concerned (and wary the incriminating VIDEO might fall into boss Sir Alex FERGUSON's hands), Yorke threw the videos out with his rubbish. Fortunately the video was discovered and sold to the *The Sun* so the world could see perhaps the most thrilling 4–2 performance in football history.

Ferguson took a dim view of the revelations. Bosnich, despite a brilliant display as United won their first World Club Championship in history, was sold to Chelsea, where he again failed to recapture his brilliant form.

Many doubted how long Bosnich's ill-starred marriage would last, though few would have guessed a mere 14 months. 'I did try to be a good wife to Mark,' said Sarah. 'I cooked him the right kind of meals, I made a nice home for him. I was happy to give up my career. I guess people must think that because we were only married for 14 months it couldn't have been serious – but it was. There were no affairs or rows, we just drifted apart.'

Sarah was pregnant when they split, but lost the baby after 12 weeks. By May 2002, the couple were divorced. (But Sarah had not had her fill of football. During a flight from Las Vegas to London after a holiday she met and fell for Simon Jordan, millionaire chairman of Crystal Palace.) 'I have no bad thoughts about Mark,' she said. 'I hope that he is as happy as I am.'

Now 29 and single again, the Chelsea reserve keeper embarked on a fling with husky-voiced TV presenter – and serial soccer groupie – Dani BEHR. But in April 2002, Bosnich gave Dani the boot. Dani was reportedly devastated by the split. She thought he was 'The One'. He clearly thought she was just one more.

Bosnich swapped Dani for model Sophie Anderton, only for it to become another turbulent romance for the man who's dropped more girlfriends than crosses. As he languished in Chelsea's stiffs, with a mere £45,000-a-week wage to keep him happy, he failed a drugs test and was fired, later losing his claim for unfair dismissal. Bosnich maintains his innocence, insisting his drink was spiked with cocaine in a London nightclub, but in March 2003, he was given a six-month ban from football. Soon afterwards, Bosnich confessed he *had* used coke, but only *after* being banned. His career was now dead in the water and his relationship with Sophie ended acrimoniously.

BOWRY, Bobby

Born: Hampstead 19.5.1971

Career: Queens Park Rangers, Crystal Palace, Millwall, Colchester United

Conquest No. 1 of soccer groupie Emma PARRIS.

BOWYER, Lee

Born: London 3.1.1977

Career: Charlton Athletic, Leeds United, West Ham United, Newcastle United

Tearaway midfielder whose bad-boy antics range from smashing up a McDonald's to his trial on assault and affray charges while with Leeds United, after Sarfraz Najeib was victim of a sickening attack. Though Bowyer was cleared, the judge criticised his evidence. Tales of a three-in-a-bed romp with teammate (and co-defendant) Jonathan WOODGATE and serial soccer seducer Emma PADFIELD help make him one of the baddest boys in football.

See GROUP SEX.

BRAMBLE, Titus

Born Ipswich 6.9.1981

Career: Ipswich Town, Colchester United (loan), Newcastle United

The £5 million man-mountain defender risked losing his career when he was arrested over allegations he helped GANG RAPE a 17-year-old girl after a boozy night on the town. She claimed Bramble, fellow footballer Carlton COLE and two other men had attacked her after she consented to sex with one of them – party organiser Nicholas MEIKLE – at a hotel. All four were arrested and questioned. Bramble vehemently denied he had done wrong and in January 2004 – four months after the allegations were made – Crown Prosecution Service lawyers announced there was insufficient evidence to bring a case against the men.

See ROASTING.

BRISSET, Jason

Born Redbridge 7.9.1974

Career: Arsenal, Peterborough, Bournemouth, Walsall, Cheltenham (loan), Leyton Orient, Stevenage Borough

Said to be another conquest of soccer slapper Emma PARRIS.

BROTHEL

After the dressing-room, the soccer love rat's favourite place to get his kit off with the lads. And lasses. Stars across the globe have been caught in them – double-winning Arsenal favourite Peter STOREY was convicted of running one. NEWCASTLE UNITED stars Carl CORT and Craig Bellamy followed the example of club owners Freddy SHEPHERD and Douglas HALL when they visited brothels during an ill-fated booze-up in Spain in 2001. CELTIC stars were embroiled in another Spanish brothel scandal in 1999.

See Wayne ROONEY.

BULLOCK, Tony

Born: Warrington 18.2.1972
Career: Leek County, Barnsley, Macclesfield Town, Lincoln City, Ross County, Dundee United

Dundee United's keeper dropped his trousers during a drinking session to celebrate a Christmas victory and flashed his bullocks at a group of girls. The married father-of-two allegedly simulated a sex act in front of the shocked teenagers outside a nightclub hours after a 3–1 win. The court heard he had been 'drinking heavily'. Thirty-year-old Bullock, a free transfer from Lincoln City, admitted breaching the peace but denied shameless and indecent conduct. His plea was accepted at Inverness Sheriff Court and in October 2001 he was fined £450 – one week's wages. Ross County's chief executive Alistair Kennedy fined him a similar amount, but said: 'He is extremely sorry and deeply embarrassed. He offers his sincere apologies.'

BULSTRODE, David

Queens Park Rangers' controversial chairman found himself a gorgeous blonde mistress to die for – and did! Married Bulstrode, hated by Rangers fans for trying to merge their beloved team with Fulham, died in the arms of former gangster's moll Pearl Read, a woman who had:

- STARRED in peep shows when she was just 17;
- RUN an escort agency for her vice king lover, and was
- CONVICTED of vice charges after his empire collapsed;
- FLASHED her 36D breasts at a posh ball while sitting on Bulstrode's knee;

● POSED in a Wonderbra for a charity's raunchiest ad ever.

No wonder Bulstrode died happy!

Soho 'actress' Pearl had met vice king Joe Wilkins, a pal of the Krays, at 21. When the couple were found guilty of running a brothel, Wilkins was jailed for three years, but Pearl was spared prison. In 1988, he was jailed again for drug smuggling, but by then her life had changed dramatically after meeting the millionaire property magnate, nicknamed 'Bulldozer' as a result of his uncompromising style.

Bulstrode had worked his way up from a junior clerk with Lloyds and by the mid-'80s was chairman of Marler Estates, owners of QPR's, Chelsea's and Fulham's grounds, landing himself a seat on the Fulham board. In May 1987, after Jim Gregory's 22-year reign at QPR ended, Bulstrode became chairman, invested £700,000 and replaced Rangers' infamous plastic pitch with real grass.

While Bulstrode's charity worker wife Sylvia stayed home in Jersey with their two children, Paul and Katrina, he and Pearl flaunted their romance publicly. As photographers took aim at the posh Berkeley Square Society Ball in 1988, Pearl's halterneck top gave way to reveal an ample – and very naked – bust. The picture appeared in papers across the country.

Pearl said: 'It was all so different with David. I saw him almost every day and we were very much in love.' But weeks later, on 1 September, their affair ended. Tragically.

'David was planning to leave his wife as soon as his children were both 18 and we bought a house together,' recalled Pearl. 'The day before we were due to move in, he died. We were both 48. We were in bed in the morning and he hadn't been feeling well. His last words to me were "I think I'll just lay here for a minute" then he let out a little gasp and died from a heart attack. I was devastated, it was the biggest heartbreak of my life, but in the end I had to go on.'

A year later, Pearl fell for ex-showjumper Brian Dye, 52, who had lost his own wife Sue – not to the grim reaper but the grim leaper, moody showjumping champion Harvey Smith. And in 1998, Pearl enjoyed her finest hour. Age Concern chose her as the face – and chest – of a racy new campaign to change people's perceptions of old people. With an Eva Herzigova-style Wonderbra making the most of her 34–25–36 size 10 figure, the 56-year-old beauty appeared with the slogan: 'The first thing some people notice about her is her age.' Pearl, never a shrinking violet, made the most of her new fame. 'I am a mature, sensuous woman having the best sex I have ever had in my life,' she said, a boast that must have had Bulstrode turning in his grave.

C

CAMPBELL, Kevin
Born: Lambeth 4.2.1970
Career: Arsenal, Leyton Orient (loan), Leicester City (loan), Nottingham Forest, Trabzonspor, Everton

The veteran striker dumped his girlfriend when he turned on a porn movie for a quiet night in – and spotted *her* bonking men *and* women. Everton skipper Campbell had met the girl, Lisa, at a topless beauty contest. But the no-holds-barred action was too much for him to take and the relationship ended.

● In 1995, Campbell was charged with indecent assault after a night out at The Ritzy in Nottingham. Campbell, 26, walked into a police station voluntarily after a 21-year-old woman told police she had been attacked. He was bailed to appear in court days later but on 25 July the complaint was dropped and Campbell was in the clear.

CAMPBELL, Sol
Born: Newham 18.9.1974
Career: Tottenham Hotspur, Arsenal

It's a hell of a way to convince the world you're not GAY . . . but Arsenal and England's defensive giant will probably look back at the day a DNA test proved he was a secret dad as a turning point in his life.

Campbell had denied being the father of tiny Joseph Jeremiah

Tyler-Campbell, born in April 2004. But two months later, tests proved he *was* the father. He would have to prise open his wallet to help pay for the child's upbringing. But at least he could put behind him the wicked whispering campaign about his sexuality that began when he moved from Spurs to Arsenal three years earlier.

The star had hit back at 'bitter, twisted, jealous liars' in a special interview about the rumours with the *Daily Mirror*. 'There are people who have made it their goal to make my life difficult,' he said. 'I couldn't believe how jealous, bitter and vindictive those people were. They tried to drag me into the gutter with their lies. What's even sadder is that some people with decent minds actually believe them. But no more are they going to hold me in bondage. Their lies don't really hurt me, but when it starts affecting my family, that's when it moves on to a different level. I want my family name back for my mother and father. Dispelling these lies means a hell of a lot to me.'

Campbell played 315 times for Spurs and even lifted their first trophy in eight years, the Worthington Cup, in 1999. He'd been an England hero in two World Cups. He'd never even said a bad word about Spurs since his short move across north London on a Bosman free transfer. So why had he been targeted? 'Because people haven't seen me in the papers with women, they assume things,' he explained. 'I am also quite shy when it comes to women. It goes back to my childhood. I wouldn't walk past my mum and dad's house with a girl, so I used to do it on the quiet.'

Sol revealed the three 'real' relationships of his life: Donna, they were just sweet 16; Dee, whom he courted for 18 months; and Michelle, a three-year courtship.

The handsome 6 ft 2 in. tall, muscle-bound, working-class millionaire revealed that, although he was happy with his bachelor lifestyle for now, marriage was on the agenda. He said: 'If I hadn't been a footballer, I'd probably be settled down with a woman in east London today. But it's very difficult to find the right woman. I'm like 90 per cent of footballers. When we meet a woman, we are thinking, "Are they just after me for the money?" You get suspicious of strangers. You really have to think, "What's their agenda, do they really want to know me?" It's made me even more wary than I naturally am.'

But not too wary . . . 'Look, I see girls for a few months at a time, but undercover. If my family saw me in the papers with a different girl every week, they'd say, "What's going on here?" I'm just happy dating and trying to find the one who is perfect for me. When I do live with a woman, it will have to be the right one. But when I come to the end of my career, when my focus is on something else, I'll look at life in a different way. I want kids. I want a happy family. I want to create a kind of dynasty.'

All very reassuring for England managers desperate for a long line of fearless, goalscoring centre-backs, but less so for the woman pictured in the paper and described as his 'current girlfriend', estate agent Theresa Lartey, 27. 'I'm very fond of her,' he said. 'We have good conversations. It's going OK. We're taking it nice and easy.'

To bolster the defence, so to speak, of his heterosexuality, Sol dropped the names of beauties he had, and sometimes hadn't, had relationships with . . .

- Singer Christina Milian: He clocked her in a restaurant and, on a serviette, wrote: 'To the Lady in Red, give me a call' and asked the waiter to give it to her. 'Three days later it's in the papers that she snubbed me for being too cool,' he said. 'It's just stupid.'
- Model Gabrielle Richens: 'She just wants to have fun, be free and single, whereas I'm looking for someone who wants to settle down.'
- Bond girl Helena Tepper: She claimed he 'pushed all the right buttons in bed'. Sol was touched by her generosity. 'She's cool — a nice girl.'
- Spice Girl Mel C: 'I asked a friend to get in contact with her. I wanted her number. She didn't get back to me.'
- Lisa, a dancer, on whom he reportedly cheated while on holiday: 'I was on holiday in Rome. I met a young lady. We went out for dinner. A few things happened and we went to a bar. I should have cooled things off with Lisa before I went on holiday.'

But Sol had another couple of women up his sleeve.

Teddy Sheringham was said to be unamused when his ex, Nicola Smith, was spotted walking out with Sol, his former teammate. The night before Arsenal's derby clash with Spurs in December 2002, even Arsenal boss Arsène WENGER was worried, saying: 'It is dangerous when two players develop a feud in this way.'

But the most significant was his long-term on-off lover, former

Miss Wales Tazmin Proctor, who fell for him aged just 18. They met at London's Emporium nightclub in 1997. Sol sat next to her, said he was in banking and chatted for hours. It was months later that he confessed he was really a footballer. 'He said he often lied to girls about what he did because he was frightened they'd only like him for his money or for the fact he was a famous footballer,' she said later.

The couple were loosely attached for six years. 'In between, there would be long gaps apart if we were seeing other people. We never fell out or argued. I always waited for Sol to call.' By 2001, they were becoming closer and viewing houses together. Sol even referred to her as 'my partner' and they appeared close on a DVD – *Sol Man* – charting his career so far.

Tazmin gave fascinating insights into his closely guarded secret life. 'He was really upset at the rumours he was gay. Ultimately, he shrugged them off saying if he'd been married there'd be rumours he was having affairs. But it did bother him.' And, she revealed, he was also the ultimate pro. 'Before a match he'd turn off his mobile phone for a couple of days. He didn't want to be in touch with people, and love-making would be out of the question. He just lives for football.'

But the relationship ended abruptly and in mystifying circumstances. Tazmin later told the *Mail on Sunday* how, in the summer of 2003, Sol asked her to have unprotected sex as a sign of her commitment. She declined. Soon Campbell ended the affair.

Perhaps the soccer star had other things on his mind. For there was yet another romance he had kept very quiet indeed . . .

Businesswoman Janet Tyler met the footballer in May 2002 at a Soho restaurant. He took her number and, after returning from the World Cup that summer, rang her. By November, she said, they were lovers. It was far from a normal relationship – many of Campbell's visits to her home, just ten minutes from his Hertfordshire mansion, would be sudden, unannounced and in the early hours.

Around Christmas 2003, she broke the news that she was pregnant. Sources said Campbell was 'not very happy' and stopped seeing her. The £100,000-a-week star was said to have offered a 'derisory' out-of-court settlement with no admission of paternity, but wanted nothing to do with the child when it was born.

On 12 April 2004, Janet, 33, gave birth to Joseph, who looked the spit of his dad. Sol, now dating millionaire high-society interior designer Kelly Hoppen, 44, insisted it was not his child and took a DNA test to prove it. On the eve of England's Euro 2004 opener with France in Lisbon, the result was announced.

He *was* the father. Campbell's solicitor Bon Battu said: 'We have received the results of DNA tests and I can confirm Sol is the father. I am positive my client will wish to honour and fulfil his legal and financial obligations.'

But not his emotional ones.

Janet believed he had not even looked at pictures of the baby that she had posted to him. And she said Campbell had wanted her to have an abortion. 'He made me choose between him and the baby,' she told the *Mail on Sunday*. 'He told me in no uncertain terms that if I went through with the pregnancy, he would not have anything to do with me, but that if I was to get rid of it, things would be very different. It wasn't an option and I just thank my lucky stars I wasn't bullied into a situation I didn't want, because otherwise I wouldn't have this beautiful little boy.'

With Janet busy changing nappies and Kelly supporting him in Portugal, Sol concentrated on his football and was one of England's few stars in a disappointing tournament. Though they were said to have split up soon afterwards, there could be no more questioning of his sexuality. The man who once said he wanted to create a 'dynasty' now had one. Reluctantly.

'I can provide Joseph with all the love and care he needs,' said little Joseph's mum. 'The only thing I can't do is give him a father. That's up to Sol.'

CANTONA, Eric
Born: Paris, France, 24.5.1966
Career: Auxerre, Marseille, Bordeaux, Marseille, Nimes, Montpellier, Leeds United, Manchester United

Ooh, aah, Casanova! Manchester United's magnificent number 7 was the Gallic genius who brought the League title to Old Trafford after 26 barren years. The swarthy hunk could turn matches on their head with one moment of magic . . . and turn women on with one brooding look.

When he left deadly rivals Leeds United to join Alex FERGUSON's title wannabes for a cut-price £1.2 million, there were unfounded rumours that he had been bombed out for having an affair with Leslie ASH, the actress wife of the club's centre-forward Lee CHAPMAN. She denied an affair.

Until then Cantona had enjoyed a reputation as a loyal family man – a devoted husband of teacher wife Isabella and young son Rafael. Shunning the fleshpots of Manchester for a quiet life at home in his understated semi-detached house added to his homely image. When an ITV camera crew filmed his wife, pregnant with their second child – a girl, Josephine – on holiday in 1996, he was so incensed that he lashed out, narrowly escaping criminal action to add to his conviction, and nine-month ban, for kicking a yob at Crystal Palace months earlier.

But there appear to be two sides to 'Eric the King', as they called him at Old Trafford.

Playboy model and TV presenter Gabrielle Richens claimed she had an affair with the French ace in June 2001 after meeting him as he starred in a beach soccer tournament in London. Gabrielle said: 'I was seeing him for a while. I was introduced to him by one of my girlfriends. I'd go and visit him sometimes. He was fun – French guys know how to have fun. That's what I loved about him. He's very much into his poetry and art. He's a very intelligent man and I love intelligent men. He's great.'

Though he was married, Gabrielle insisted: 'In France there is a different attitude to these things. Lots of public figures have mistresses.'

Which may account for his pursuit of a blonde beauty while on a family holiday in Majorca the following summer . . .

Eric, now a portly 36, was spotted stroking the neck of a blonde tourist in a swanky seafront bar – hours after frolicking with his family on the beach. Cantona, in town to play another beach soccer tournament, saw the beauty in Tito's, in Palma. An onlooker said: 'Eric's mate went for a dark-haired girl and Eric homed in on her blonde friend. They just talked at first, then, after a while, Eric started stroking her neck and the back of her hair. They had a dance and it was very intimate, they even kissed once or twice. Maybe it's what you'd expect from a Frenchman . . . '

And the memoirs of former Manchester United security chief

Ned Kelly cast more light on the French idol's exotic love life. Kelly, the former SAS man who guarded him after his Kung Fu madness at Selhurst Park, told how Cantona revelled in an orgy on a circular bed at a Paris brothel in 1997 while other revellers looked on. He also apparently enjoyed spanking sessions and even regularly bedded a Manchester United teammate's wife in Kelly's flat, which he borrowed for the secret assignations, according to Kelly. 'To be fair, Eric rarely played away during his time in the UK,' said Kelly in *Manchester United: The Untold Story*. 'But once Eric was in Europe, the gloves – or should it be the pants – were off.' Cantona refused to confirm or deny the allegations.

CARDIFF CITY

The Welsh club's official chaplain was jailed in October 2001 for a total of eight years for sex offences against young boys. Perverted Father Joe Jordan (no relation to the toothless Scotland centre-forward) had groomed two of the three youngsters, aged nine to eleven, by taking them to soccer matches, Cardiff Crown Court was told. He was trapped when police, alerted by worried parents, found pictures of young boys in a desk drawer of his Cardiff home. The indecent assaults had happened in the 1980s when he was a teacher.

CARRAGHER, Jamie

Born: Liverpool 28.1.1978
Career: Liverpool

Liverpool's midfield starlet Jamie Carragher is infamous for his naked antics with fresh cream and a stripper at the players' outrageous 1998 Christmas party. After helping himself to lager at the free bar, Carragher, the club's Young Player of the Year a season earlier, whipped off his hunchback of Notre Dame outfit so the stripper could squirt cream on his chest and private parts before licking it off. As she played with a sex toy, Carragher, just 20, took centre stage on all fours demanding to help. In a reversal of roles, he picked up the stripper, who had been dressed as a fireman, and spun her drunkenly in the air. Later, Carragher flashed his tackle as a comedian struggled to tell his gags. After a beer break, the girls returned and Carragher and three other guests cavorted naked with them on the dance floor. Finally, one of them performed a sex act on the Premiership star, as his Liverpool teammates looked on in horror. Amazingly, just days after the party at Liverpool's Pen and Wig bar, Carragher managed to score on the pitch instead. Once again he was the Crème de la Prem.

CASCARINO, Tony
Born Orpington 1.9.1962
Career: Gillingham, Millwall, Aston Villa, Celtic, Chelsea, Olympique Marseille, Nancy, Red Star Paris

Ireland's English World Cup hero led an amazing double life for two years as he lived with his wife and two children – and fathered a child with his French lover. The striker continually lied his way out of trouble, even when his wife found a fax his girlfriend sent of her ante-natal scan!

Cascarino admitted a string of one-night stands in his memoir *Full Time: The Secret Life of Tony Cascarino*. His first was just six weeks before his wedding to Sarah Boost, whom he had met at a pub disco in Eltham, south London. After celebrating his first international goal, against Poland, Millwall ace Cascarino shared a taxi with a woman he didn't know, who asked: 'Your place or mine?' He woke at 6.30 a.m. in a house in Dublin's sprawling southern suburbs and dashed back to the team hotel just in time to avoid disciplinary action.

The marriage went ahead in Chislehurst, Kent, in July 1988. But within a year – and just four months before the birth of his first son Michael – he had cheated again, after another international in Dublin.

It would not be the last time. As the boys in Green returned in triumph from Italia '90 – where they had reached the quarter-finals under talismanic boss Jack Charlton – the Republic's female population went mad for their warrior heroes. There were scoring opportunities even the often-hapless Cascarino could not miss. 'I tried to stay onside but more often than not succumbed,' Cascarino recalled. 'They just wanted to be straddled by one of the champions.'

By 1994, Cascarino was, he admitted, 'cheating on Sarah at every opportunity'. And for an international footballer at the World Cup, the consequences of being discovered were massive. But Cascarino carried on carrying-on. In Orlando he chatted up one girl then smuggled another back to the team's hotel. All hell broke loose. Security guards and police officers checked the hotel top to bottom for an 'intruder' spotted on CCTV cameras. She was never found. Boss Jack Charlton was furious the following morning and, when Cas confessed, threatened to send his striker home in disgrace. It could have ended his marriage and his international career.

As the marriage struggled – thanks in part to the added pressure of his nightmare goalscoring form through big-money moves to Aston Villa, CELTIC and Chelsea – Cascarino began having vivid dreams about a mystery woman. Incredibly, the dream was about to come true thanks to a match-fixing scandal at Olympique Marseille.

The 1993 European Champions had been demoted and forced to rebuild. The search for cut-price talent handed Chelsea's last-choice striker a dream move. Days before his Olympique debut in August 1994 – a goalscoring start against Le Mans – Sarah returned to England to prepare for the permanent move abroad with their children, Michael and Teddy. After the game, as he dined alone at a seafront hotel, he met the woman of his dreams – Virginie Masson, 20, a law student. They swapped addresses and a fortnight later he visited her in Nice. 'The attraction was more than physical,' said Cascarino. 'There was something about Virginia [as he called her] I had never encountered in a woman before.'

When she found out he was married, Virginie tried to stop the affair. But Cascarino, now enjoying the hottest form of his career, was determined to win her. Virginie demanded he do the decent thing – tell Sarah and leave. He agreed, then, not for the first time, lost his nerve. Cas did confess his affair but when Sarah left with their children he begged her to return and promised to end it.

It was yet another lie.

Instead he began a double life, seeing Virginie before and after training and matches. That November she became pregnant, but left to be cared for by her family. In March, she faxed the result of a scan to him in a Dublin hotel where he was preparing for a European Championship qualifier. After showing it to best friend and teammate Andy Townsend, he rolled it into a ball and put it in the bin.

After dinner, Sarah borrowed the room key and left. When she returned, she was holding the fax. Cascarino lied again. It was from a crazed stalker fan, he insisted. Sarah, amazingly, believed it. 'I was a total shit,' he admitted.

In August 1995, Maeva was born in Nice. Two days later the absent father saw her for the first time. 'I took her in my arms and touched her little fingers. But the moment was tarnished by the guilt I was feeling inside.'

For a year Cascarino split his time between his two families. Finally, when Virginie could take no more, he confessed the whole truth to Sarah. When she took their children to school, he scrawled a note and walked away. 'If there was one day I could change it's that one,' he recalled. 'Sarah deserved better. It was a spineless way to go.'

In June 2000, Cascarino, the Londoner with an Italian name, Irish passport and French daughter, married Virginie. Within a month of the new season the 37 year old finally quit the game that had brought them together yet caused such pain.

CELTIC

The Scottish giants soon regretted sending their players on a mid-season break to sunny Marbella in January 1999. The players enjoyed a pub crawl to toast the birthday of centre-forward Tommy Johnson and, after closing time, allegedly found themselves in the exceptionally low rent Number One club, a dingy bordello in the basement of a rundown villa. Most of the players left soon after, but four – Jackie McNamara, Stewart Kerr, David Hannah and Jonathan Gould – were said to have stayed on to celebrate a little more.

It was in the early hours that prostitute Camilla Erradi, 35, attached herself to the party. She claimed to have struck up a special friendship with 24-year-old Scotland international McNamara. Events became hazy. At 5 a.m., Spanish police were said to have arrived at the BROTHEL amid reports that the players were refusing to settle their bill and leave. But the bar manager later insisted the players had never even visited the bar. A club spokesman backed him: 'The players have informed us that not only did they not meet this woman, they did not even enter the club.'

Keeper Kerr, 24, said: 'It's a total load of rubbish.' McNamara's wife Samantha added: 'I have spoken to Jackie about this and I am sure that it was all perfectly innocent. He never spoke to any prostitute. I trust Jackie and I'm sure nothing happened. None of the Celtic players would do anything out there that would get them into any trouble because they know that the eyes of the world are on them.' Fair enough, then.

CHANDLER, Dean
Born: Ilford 6.5.1976
Career: Charlton Athletic, Torquay United (loan), Lincoln City, Yeovil, Slough, Yeovil, Slough, Woking, Ford United

Soccer starlet Dean Chandler earned infamy when he became only the second player to fail a random drug test – then wrote another sordid chapter as defendant in a high-profile 'Sleeping Beauty' rape trial.

The hugely promising CHARLTON ATHLETIC youngster – together with Addicks teammate Lee BOWYER – was suspended for smoking cannabis. Though Bowyer would go on to achieve notoriety thanks to sex revelations and a high-profile court case for affray before he was cleared, he became a fully fledged Premiership star and England international. Chandler's career just went downhill.

Months after failing the drug tests, Chandler stood trial at the Old Bailey for rape, a crime fuelled, the prosecution claimed, by drugs and booze. The 19-year-old admitted smoking cannabis and drinking six pints of lager and two bottles of beer during a party at a woman friend's flat before slipping into her bed in the early hours of 3 December 1994. The woman, a care worker, claimed she woke to find Chandler on top of her having sex with her. She pushed him off, she told the court, and alerted friends who found him pretending to be asleep on her flatmate's bedroom floor. Chandler told the court he had regularly had sex with the woman and had slipped into her bed because he could not find a spare duvet.

A jury heard the victim was so traumatised she scrubbed her body in a boiling hot bath. Chandler maintained she had consented to sex and added: 'I did not force myself on her. She had a half smile on her face.'

On 14 July 1995, a jury failed to agree a verdict. A retrial was ordered. Three months later, on 10 October 1995, Chandler was cleared. Charlton Athletic director Jonathan Fuller said afterwards: 'Now he can concentrate on a promising football career.' But after just one start for Charlton, he was loaned to lowly Torquay United then given a free transfer to Lincoln, before various lower-league moves. It should all have been so different.

CHANTS

Terrace wits have never been slow to seize on opposing players' public infidelities and give them 90 minutes of humiliation. Generations of players have suffered the classic chorus reprised most recently when Blackburn Rovers – skippered by double love rat Garry FLITCROFT – played Liverpool in March 2002:

> Garry Flitcroft,
> Garry Flitcroft,
> Does your missus know you're here?

Bolton Wanderers' Dean HOLDSWORTH received a bigger than ample share of abuse when the tabloids revealed his fling with vast-chested porn model Linsey Dawn McKenzie. The fans' verdict on his lover, to the tune of Big Ben's bongs:

> Shit face, Big Tits
> Shit face, Big Tits.

QPR's '70s legend Stan Bowles was on the receiving end when his wife was said to have played away:

> Stanley Bowles,
> Stanley Bowles,
> Does your wife give Green Shield stamps?

Manchester United boss Tommy DOCHERTY did not escape lightly when he left his wife – and lost his job – over an affair with club physio Laurie Brown's wife Mary. Choruses of:

> Who's up Mary Brown?
> Who's up Mary Brown?

Tommy Tommy Docherty?
Tommy Tommy Docherty?
Tommy's up Mary Brown.

cheered up dark winter afternoons around grounds nationwide as the Doc managed new club Derby County.

And the '70s wouldn't have been the '70s without this terrace eulogy to LEICESTER CITY's sex-mad striker Frank WORTHINGTON:

Ooooh, w★★★er, w★★★er . . . w★★★er w★★★er w★★★er w★★★er
Worthington.

Arsenal fans lauded their 1998 World Cup-winning midfielder Emmanuel Petit with:

He's blond,
He's quick,
His name's a porno flick,
Emmanuel, Emmanuel.

See Leslie ASH, Eric CANTONA, Lee CHAPMAN.

CHAPMAN, Lee
Born: Lincoln 5.12.1959
Career: Stoke City, Plymouth Argyle (loan), Arsenal, Sunderland, Sheffield Wednesday, Niort (France), Nottingham Forest, Leeds United, Portsmouth, West Ham United, Southend United (loan), Ipswich Town, Leeds United, Swansea City

The one-time title-winning striker's marriage to TV beauty Leslie ASH has been studded by sexual controversy – culminating in her battle to walk again after an apparently over-vigorous sex session on a new mattress went catastrophically wrong.

Building workers had called an ambulance after seeing Leslie call for help from the balcony of their London riverside flat around 8 a.m. Police turned up, too, and within minutes Chapman was arrested and led away in handcuffs. Leslie was taken to hospital with a punctured lung and broken rib.

In hospital, despite her pain, she protested her husband's

innocence and blamed the bed: 'We were having a good time and I slid off the bed and put out a hand to save myself, missed and ended up between the bedside table and the bed. It was a total misunderstanding. Lee didn't do this. We were making love and this happens. How embarrassing is that?'

Slightly less embarrassing than talking about it, probably.

Chapman was released without charge. Police said: 'We are not taking any action. Mrs Ash has asked us not to.'

Chapman insisted his wife would soon be out of hospital. And she was. But she had been infected with the hospital bug MSSA and, two days after her release, she was rushed back to hospital in agony, suddenly facing a battle to ever walk again.

Suspicion, not for the first time, haunted the former soccer hard man.

Leslie's sister Debbie Ash accused him of a violent assault two years earlier when she tried to break up an argument between the couple. Chapman was arrested in June 2004 and released on bail as police investigated Debbie's allegation.

In 1997, after ten years of marriage, Leslie won a court order to keep Lee away after a violent argument outside London's Groucho Club. Leslie fled to the home of her friend and TV co-star Caroline Quentin, but the following morning a drunken Chapman, then playing for Nottingham Forest, arrived in a taxi, smashed the door down and was arrested by police. Charges were later dropped when he agreed to attend counselling to curb his temper. Chapman explained: 'We're incredibly passionate. We have had explosive rows in public places because neither of us will budge.'

After another almighty humdinger on holiday in Ibiza in 1995, Lee stormed off and ended up in bed with holidaymaker Cheryl Roberts, 26, a model from Leeds. The centre-forward claimed he'd blacked out and begged furious Leslie for another chance. He got it.

And three years before that, Manchester United fans had celebrated the arrival of their new talisman Eric CANTONA by chanting: 'He's French, He's flash, he's shagging Leslie Ash, Cantona, Cantonaaaa!

Not a pleasant thing for Chapman to hear about his teammate and the woman expecting his baby. The couple – and Cantona himself – said nothing about the false rumours for a decade, until

Leslie herself broke the silence. 'It was lies and garbage,' she insisted. 'It really annoyed me, because it wasn't true. Those sorts of things upset you and you have to rise above it, just ignore it. People have been horrible to Lee and me, but I know it's only because they are jealous. And they've got something to be jealous about, because I am having a fantastic life, earning loads of money, and Lee and I are very happy.'

Years later, when the actress endured public humiliation after botched plastic surgery led to her infamous 'Trout Pout', loyal Chapman was her staunchest supporter. 'Until I met Leslie I'd never even had a steady girlfriend,' he said. 'I always wanted a long-term relationship, but I just played the field with one-night stands, which I'm not proud of.'

In July 2004, as Leslie took her first steps, the couple were reportedly preparing legal action against the hospital where she was infected.

The bed-makers could sleep easy . . . for now.

CHARLTON ATHLETIC

The Addicks fired an office worker for allegedly having affairs with four players. 'She was a sex Addick' quipped the *News of the World* about Jane Playford, 30, an administrator in the Premiership side's community development office. An £8,000 settlement with the club in August 2000 meant she could not discuss her sacking for improper behaviour, but she did tell a friend: 'I only had one proper relationship, but the club alleged other things. I had flings with three other players, but as far as I know they were single like me, so where's the problem?'

Jane apparently notched her first player on a club night out. He said he was single and they went for dinner. Only later, after a 'serious' relationship, did she discover he was married. A club insider said: 'Jane is the talk of the club. She's a very attractive girl who catches the eye of all the players.'

Final score: Charlton Athletic 1 Sexually Athletic 4.

COLE, Andrew

Born: Nottingham 15.10.1971
Career: Arsenal, Fulham, Bristol City, Newcastle United, Manchester
United, Blackburn Rovers, Fulham

God-fearing family man Andy Cole let his standards – and his
trousers – slip when he enjoyed a three-in-a-bed romp with a
teammate.

The man who once said: 'I'm very religious. Everything in my life
used to be football. Now my family take priority. I thank God above
for what I am' then enjoyed a session with fellow Red Devil Dwight
YORKE and an 18-year-old fan. And it wasn't his first offence, for
Cole was apparently already in the middle of a four-year affair with
a woman he seduced at his granddad's funeral!

Andy – or Andrew as he prefers to be called – was 19 and just
another Arsenal wannabe when he fell for Shirley Dewar, the woman
he would later marry, at the wedding of teammate Kevin
CAMPBELL's brother.

Shirley, sweet 16, said: 'I had seen him across the room but didn't
pay much attention. I knew he was a footballer but I didn't really
know much about the game so I wasn't that impressed – plus I was
wearing a black mini dress and I knew he was looking at me.' After
dancing they swapped phone numbers and soon became an item.

After failing to make the first team at Arsenal, Cole had to move
to Bristol City. But his fighting spirit and self-belief helped him
survive and his goals made him NEWCASTLE UNITED's record £1.5
million buy. He scored 68 goals in 84 appearances, firing them into
the Premiership and earning cult status at St James's Park. Then, in
January 1995, Alex FERGUSON stunned the football world with a
record-shattering £7 million swoop.

Cole's arrival at Old Trafford coincided with Shirley's news that
she was pregnant. The couple were still apart – he struggling to
make an initial impact in Manchester, she completing an HND
course in computers at a college near her south London home. They
delayed wedding plans, but Shirley insisted: 'I know it's easy for
someone in Andrew's position to get carried away with the adulation
and girls hanging around. But our relationship is based on trust.'

In April 1995, their son Devante was born, but Cole's pride at
being a dad could not stop him falling into temptation. At his

grandfather's funeral in his home town of Nottingham in May 1997, the soccer ace – now scoring freely at United – spotted legal executive Anne Boriel. 'As I walked into the church our eyes locked,' claimed the mum of one. 'When it was time to go back to London, he was waiting with his chauffeur-driven car and asked if I'd travel back with him. I was amazed.'

Cole began calling her up to 15 times a day. 'He admitted he was in a relationship and had a little boy,' Anne added. 'He said he wasn't happy. He started to call me "babes" or "darling" but I always called him Andrew.'

Weeks later they slept together for the first time, at her council flat in Tottenham, a corner kick away from Spurs' White Hart Lane ground. They would later make love in more salubrious surroundings at some of the capital's finest hotels, thanks to Cole's millions. And, amazingly, in his parents' house in Nottingham.

'At first we had separate bedrooms,' she explained, 'but as time went on we'd share the same bedroom. After going there over a period of time I started to call them Mum and Dad instead of Mr and Mrs Cole. My son also stayed there a couple of times and called them Nanna and Grandad.'

But when Shirley *and* Annie weren't looking, Cole was pursuing a sexual treble to match his club's quest for trophies. After flying home from a European tie with Inter Milan, Cole and pal Dwight Yorke ended up in bed with Yorke's 18-year-old admirer Nikki Kilroy, who collected them from Manchester Airport at 3 a.m.

The two footballers plied the teenager with wine and played spin the bottle. Then, after carrying her upstairs, they both had sex with her, Yorke instructing Cole to 'take over' when he had finished. When Andy dressed and left, Yorke carried on.

Why the sharp exit from Cole? Was it guilt at cheating on his wife and child; or that the plane bringing the players' families back from Milan was due any minute? Nikki said: 'I had no idea Andy had a steady girlfriend and a child. I couldn't believe it when Dwight told me because Andy didn't show any sign of guilt. What a nerve!'

Cole's relationship with Yorke emerged as newspapers investigated the 'ManUge a Trois'. In a telephone conversation following their threesome, Yorke told Nikki: 'To be quite honest Coley surprised me. We've been out many a time – there are always ladies floating around but he's never took any interest. But once he's had a few drinks he's like a different person.' Yorke said he would ask Cole about an action replay. 'I'll ask him. But he's a family man,' said Yorke. 'He's not totally committed though, is he, or he would have married his missus.' He added: 'Me and Coley always talk in the showers. We got all excited, man. But he's not a single man like me who can do everything. He's got to plan his time.' In another phone call, taped by *News of the World* investigators, Cole told Nikki their threesome had been 'beautiful, beautiful'.

Cole and Shirley were said to have grown closer – once she had forgiven him. But incredibly, around Christmas 1999 – after his goals had helped win a historic European Cup, Premiership and FA Cup Treble – Anne claimed he had proposed marriage.

As they partied at London's trendy Ten Rooms, she claimed, Cole said: 'If I asked you to marry me what would you say?' Anne said: 'I laughed. He never promised to leave Shirley but he always said the reason he stayed in the relationship was because of his son.'

Then Cole dropped a bizarre new bombshell. 'He called me and asked me to meet him in Nottingham,' said Anne later. 'I went up there and we made love in his parents' house. Afterwards he said, "I've got something to tell you. She's pregnant." I was crying. He kept saying he was sorry.'

Meanwhile, back in Manchester the player was trying to smooth things over with Shirley. An Old Trafford insider explained: 'These days Andy is introducing Shirley as his fiancée. They are totally dedicated to each other and their little boy Devante.'

Finally, in June 2001, soon after the birth of his second child, a daughter, the affair with Anne ended. She claimed his advisers offered her £275,000 to sign a confidentiality agreement about their affair. But Anne revealed how the Red was insecure about his tackle . . .

'He wanted me to reassure him he was adequate. I said to him, "You're fine, you satisfy me." It did go on for months, though.'

Early in 2002, with new striker Ruud Van Nistelrooy firing on all cylinders, Cole followed Yorke out of Old Trafford for a reunion at Blackburn Rovers, already infamous for the GROUP SEX antics of skipper Garry FLITCROFT and winger Craig HIGNETT.

COLE, Ashley

Born: Stepney 20.12.1980

Career: Arsenal, Crystal Palace (loan)

Arsenal and England's boy wonder full-back joined a long list of Highbury bed boys when he cheated on his girlfriend with a model – then booted her out of bed so his mum wouldn't find out.

Cole chatted up Laura Key at London's Emporium nightclub, asked for her phone number and offered to 'peel down my top, start with my boobs and lick me all over'. Laura recalled: 'I have to admit it sounded good. We didn't get a chance that night but from then on he'd ring me or TXT up to 20 times a day.'

Cole soon lured Laura, but proved himself a cut-price Casanova. He offered to pick her up in his sporty Audi TT car and take her for a Chinese feast. But, she told the *News of the World*: 'I thought we were going to go somewhere romantic. But he drove me straight to his local Chinese takeaway in the East End, pulled up outside the door and asked me to go and pick up a takeaway that we could have in his place. I couldn't believe it. I thought, "Here's this millionaire footballer and I'm paying £20 for crispy chilli beef, sweet and sour chicken, boiled rice and prawn crackers!"'

Back at his Limehouse penthouse, Cole – 5 ft 8 in. tall and a muscular 10 st. 8 lb – made his play. Laura said: 'I fancied him like crazy – he has a beautiful bum. We sat there slurping curry sauce and watching a porn video. It was really filthy. After we'd finished watching, he took me to bed.'

Cole, famed for his crunching tackle and ball-playing ability, was, she reported, a considerate and expert lover. The part-time *Playboy* TV presenter said: 'He gave me oral sex for ages. He spent hours pleasuring me with just about every movable part of his body. And he's got thighs like tree trunks.' Grateful Laura even offered the Arsenal ace a three-in-a-bed session alongside her best friend. Cole said thanks but no thanks. Laura said: 'I thought it would be such a turn on but Ashley just wanted to concentrate on me.'

But there was someone else on amorous Ashley's mind . . .

Eventually he came clean to Laura and told her he had a long-term girlfriend, Emma. 'Ashley said he wanted me to be his girlfriend as long as Emma didn't find out,' said Laura. 'He said I was special. But his mum liked her and he said there'd be hell to pay if she found out. So he made sure I left before his mum came round to do his cleaning.'

But once they overslept. 'We'd been lying in bed after an amazing night and I was thinking of breakfast when Ashley sprang up and said, "Oh, my God, it's almost seven, my mum'll be round soon!"' said Laura. 'Before I knew it, I was standing there scrabbling for my bra and knickers and asking Ashley where he'd thrown them. I just had time to put my dress on with nothing underneath, stuff my undies in my handbag and get out through the door. I took a Tube home to Brixton and by now it was rush hour – I was sitting in this really short dress with my legs together so no one would see that I had nothing on underneath.'

With Cole anxious not to blot his copybook before the World Cup finals or to lose his other, real, girlfriend, there was little future for their secret relationship. 'I wanted someone I could be seen openly with,' said Laura. 'So we eventually split up.'

COLE, Carlton
Born: Surrey 12.11.1983
Career: Chelsea, Wolves (loan), Charlton Athletic (loan), Aston Villa

If the brilliant young striker had learned the lesson from his part in the ROASTING orgy that went disastrously wrong, it didn't show. Weeks after GANG RAPE charges were dropped after the alleged attack at London's Grosvenor House Hotel, Cole – on loan at CHARLTON ATHLETIC – and two friends reportedly had another GROUP SEX session with a teenage girl at his flat. Bank clerk Sharon Miller, 18, met Cole and his pals, including Spurs defender Anthony Gardner, in Faces nightclub, Ilford, and agreed to return to Gardner's flat for a drink. Instead, she claimed, Cole drove her and his two friends to his own flat in Eltham, south-east London, joked about how he had 'got done for roasting' then told her: 'Get your knickers off.'

Sharon said: 'From that moment it was just a blur. The sex just sort of happened. I'd have been happy to sleep with my guy. But as we began to kiss, the others joined in groping. In the end, they all got me to perform oral sex. At one point I was doing that to Carlton while someone else was having full sex with me. I know people will say I only have myself to blame. Yes, I was stupid but I'm not a slut.'

See Titus BRAMBLE, Kieron DYER, Nicholas MEIKLE.

COLLEY-MOORE, Steve

Born: Barbados 1943 (Stanley Collymore)

The father of DOGGING soccer star Stan COLLYMORE went on the run after being found guilty of flashing at a teenager opposite his 16th-floor council flat.

Jobless Colley-Moore, who had changed his name from Stanley Collymore to avoid being linked with his son, repeatedly strolled round his flat naked before performing indecent acts at the window. Neighbour Sharon Buckland, 19, said: 'I was disgusted. He didn't care if I could see him. I could feel him looking at me and watching to see if I was paying attention to him.'

When police staked out the flats, in Swindon, Wiltshire, they caught him in the act and arrested him. Colley-Moore was given bail but, after initially pleading not guilty in court, did a runner and was convicted of two charges of indecent exposure in his absence.

Collymore, then playing for Aston Villa as his career imploded, had not seen his father since he walked out on their family some 20 years earlier. Collymore Senior had gone back to his Barbados home before returning to Britain.

Sharon said after the case: 'I was very frightened living next to this man. He was a bully and tried to intimidate me.'

COLLYMORE, Stan

Born: Stone 22.1.1971

Career: Walsall Wolves, Stafford Rangers, Crystal Palace, Southend United, Nottingham Forest, Liverpool, Aston Villa, Fulham (loan), Leicester City, Bradford City, Real Oviedo

When Stan 'The Man' Collymore was exposed for his addiction to 'DOGGING' – where strangers watch each other have sex in parked cars – it was the humiliating climax to a career dogged, appropriately, by controversy.

The brilliant former £8.5 million England striker admitted he had been hooked on the kinky car escapades for years and begged his disgusted wife for forgiveness. Not for the first time was Stan pleading for mercy.

Before throwing away his brilliant career, the big-headed bully-boy:
● was CLEARED of assaulting Michelle Green, the mother of his child, then . . .

- BEAT UP his celebrity lover Ulrika JONSSON in a Paris bar;
- was QUESTIONED over an attack on girlfriend Estelle and a man she met in a nightclub;
- regularly ASSAULTED a previous girlfriend Lotta Farley.

Collymore was already known as an unstable and egotistical star. Liverpool had sold him to Aston Villa after he criticised their tactics, then failed to deliver the goals. But a high-profile romance with TV presenter Ulrika Jonsson meant he was regularly in the headlines. When he appeared in court accused of assaulting ex-girlfriend Michelle Green, Ulrika was by his side. He was cleared and Ulrika said she stood by her man. But at that summer's World Cup she saw another side of him.

In The Auld Alliance pub in Paris, 500 Scotland fans party before their opening clash with Brazil. To escape the crush, Ulrika gets behind the bar and, for fun, helps pull pints with other celebrities. The fans chant: 'There's only one Ulrika!' as she sinks a pint in one.

Shaven-headed Collymore – 6 ft 3 in. tall and 14 st. – arrives and is not amused. Martin Geissler, a Scotland fan and TV reporter says: 'Everybody was happy. Then Collymore arrived. He came in a back door and went straight to Ulrika. I think he'd been hit by some of the beer. He said to Ulrika, "We're leaving." She said "No." He said, "Yes, we're leaving." She said "No" again, more forcefully. Collymore tried to grab her. She broke free. He dragged her out of the bar into a room where I was. Ulrika hit her head on the door on the way in. Collymore pushed her right into the middle of us. Then Ulrika fell. A couple of people tried to get between them. Collymore was lashing out with his feet, aiming kicks at Ulrika's head. She was screaming and very upset and seemed to be in pain.'

Bar manager Danny Farmer adds: 'He was like a deranged animal. He jumped out of nowhere as Ulrika was drinking beer, like he was some kind of mad stalker. There was real anger in his face and his eyes were staring as he hit her.

'Ulrika flashed past me and hit the deck. Then Collymore lashed out with his hands and feet. Ulrika was screaming for him to stop but he kept on hitting and slapping her and grabbing her hair. At one point he shouted her name.

'I grabbed him by the arm with two or three other lads. But one of them had to headbutt him to get him out of the door. When he got outside, he was trying to make excuses by saying, "You know what it's like – we all have rows with our girlfriends." But there's no excuse for what he did.'

Collymore walks away alone. Minutes later a chauffeur-driven car arrives to take Ulrika away. A day later they both return to England. In a minute of madness Collymore, 26, had changed their lives for ever.

The player issued a statement apologising for his 'reprehensible actions': 'A stupid and silly argument had developed throughout the day between myself and Ulrika, someone who I have realised for some time is very special to me,' he said. 'In a fit of petulant temper I struck out at the girl I love and immediately regretted my actions but it was too late. I could hide behind a façade of excuses and no comments, but petulance, jealousy and possibly having too much to drink are the real reasons behind this regrettable and avoidable incident.

'I now have to look long and hard in the mirror. I hope to be able to sort out this undignified mess with some semblance of dignity, in private, and with the person who matters most of all – Ulrika.'

Ulrika had an announcement of her own: 'I'd like everyone to know that I'm fine and I can confirm that my relationship with Stan Collymore is now over.'

She had already tasted his temper. Once he locked her sobbing out of his house in the middle of the night in her underwear. Another time he shredded her clothes. The Paris assault was the final straw, though she decided not to press charges. Later Ulrika revealed: 'Stan was very abusive verbally and emotionally and that extended into the bedroom. He had to have a psychological power over me.'

Another victim of Collymore's violent streak came forward. Lotta Farley, 25, told how she had been kicked and beaten during their five-year relationship. 'I want every woman in Britain to know what he's like,' she told the *News of the World*. Michelle, whose assault allegation had not been believed, said: 'Frankly, I'm not surprised that someone has found themselves on the receiving end of something like this.'

Collymore's fragile reputation was now in ruins. Football fans reviled him. His sponsors, Diadora, ended their contract. Collymore lay low with another celebrity shoulder to cry on – he holidayed with old flame Davina McCall, the *Big Brother* host.

Amid the backlash, Collymore says he contemplated suicide but sought help for depression at the Priory Clinic in London. After cognitive behavioural therapy, in which patients study which events trigger their depression, he reflected on the Ulrika incident: 'If you take Paris out of the equation and we had met now, I wouldn't have gone into a relationship. It would have been more of a friendship. Because of our insecurities, when they come together, they come together in a big way. To me, she will always be very special and I know for a fact that I will be for her.'

Mr Modesty's football career was now firmly on the slide too. When he announced he was suffering from depression, Aston Villa manager John Gregory said: 'I find it difficult to understand how anyone in Stan's position, with the talent and the money he has, is stressed. I wonder how a 29 year old at Rochdale, in the last three months of his contract, with a marriage and three kids, copes with stress. I wonder what he'd be thinking, looking at this.'

Collymore tried to rebuild his career on loan at Fulham, where he denied reports he had shown nude photos of Ulrika to his new teammates.

In August 1999, he was quizzed by police over an alleged attack on his new girlfriend Estelle Williams and the man she was leaving a nightclub with. Estelle, who had once been Collymore's cleaner, decided not to press charges.

Free transfers to LEICESTER CITY (where he was disciplined over incidents on a club trip to Spain), Bradford City and Oviedo failed to reignite the former £8.5 million British transfer record holder. Finally, in March 2001, he walked out on the Spanish side and announced his retirement aged just 30. Months later Estelle, 28, gave birth to his second child, Mia.

After a break to 'let my brain cool down', Collymore began a new career as a pundit, working mainly on BBC Radio Five Live. Clever and intuitive, he was even tipped to be a guest on Question Time, and expressed an interest in acting. Then Stan hit the self-destruct button once more.

On Sunday, 29 February 2004, Collymore was prowling a woodland car park in Cannock Chase, Staffordshire, where he struck up a conversation with a man and woman in a parked car, posing as a married couple and apparently interested in trying casual sex with strangers. 'Are you playing this evening?' he asked matter-of-factly. In fact, they were working. As reporters from *The Sun*.

After discussing dogging (he even described his first experience, saying, 'I pulled up next to a car and there were two guys in the front, two girls in the back. I got out and stood there, and before you knew it everything was going off'), swapping phone numbers and offering to 'hook up' some time soon, he left in his Range Rover – with personalised plates.

The following day, he TXTed to invite the 'couple' to another dogging session, before they announced who they really were. He reportedly fell silent and switched off his phone.

Later, Collymore admitted everything. He claimed depression and 'self-destructive curiosity' fuelled his bizarre fetish, which he had discovered while surfing the Internet.

'What I have done is disgusting and I'm so ashamed, but I'm only human. I can only beg for forgiveness. Over the last couple of years I have been to dogging sites maybe a dozen to 15 times and, yes, I have taken part and had sex during them. My only hope is that the people I know and love can find it in their hearts to forgive me. Estelle is furious but absolutely calm. I can't believe I've caused her all this hurt.'

His agent Simon Kennedy said: 'I hope the public realise that Stan has made mistakes but that fundamentally he is not a bad egg and he is not an evil individual.'

But the BBC insisted: 'We have no plans to use him in the near future.'

Collymore now admitted he had been treated at Sex and Love Addicts Anonymous. But he explained: 'The sex part of it was 1 per cent – the buzz of it is the danger of being there. And to be perfectly honest, why I went is nobody else's business but mine. But I suppose in a way it was a bit of a relief to be discovered because it means I can deal with it and get on.

'At the beginning of that week,' he explained to *The Observer*, 'there was something private to me that most people with normal functioning mental health would probably have been able to cope with. But this thing happened – I don't want to say what – on the

Tuesday, and by the Saturday I was like a cat on a hot tin roof. And I found myself going back to this place [Cannock Chase]. Nothing happened there. And even in the past when it has, the sex was never the point. It's the escape or whatever. It's probably happened to me a dozen times in the last couple of years that I've gone up to this place, and each time it coincided with this problem in my life.'

He added: 'I've got to make amends to my family. I've explained to friends, you know, I'm not bad, evil or a freak. Everyone, I think, has some of these kinds of problems. It's just that mine manifests itself in this particular way.'

Collymore checked into the Priory Clinic in south-west London once more.

Collymore admits his own childhood holds the key to his troubles. 'My mum and dad split up when I was young,' he once said. 'That was a very abusive relationship.' Friends pray he will get his head together before inflicting more pain on the ones he loves.

• Collymore professed his abilities as a soccer stud in his early days at Crystal Palace. Coach Alan Smith said: 'On one trip he said he was a ladies man, I think he called himself an "International Lover". He got slaughtered.'

See Steve COLLEY-MOORE.

CONDOMS

Blackpool midfielder Gary Brabin put the Mates into 'teammates' as he lined up for the annual pre-season photo. The prankster placed a condom on Marvin Bryan's shoulder as the snapper clicked away. When it appeared in the local paper, club bosses hit the roof, fining Brabin £2,000 and giving him a severe bollocking. 'He's feeling a bit of a plonker,' said one witty player.

CORT, Carl

Born: Bermondsey 1.11.1977
Career: Wimbledon, Lincoln City (loan), Newcastle United, Wolves

NEWCASTLE UNITED's new £7 million signing limbered up for his wedding by bedding a topless model one week before the big day. Cort romped with Rachel Collins 'in three or four positions', and even enjoyed slapping the bottom of his bedmate. At least the striker had the decency to regret his shameful antics. He confessed:

'I wish I'd never done it. I love my wife. It was a massive mistake.'
And by November he had almost cleaned up his act. With Toon
teammates Craig Bellamy, Kieron DYER and Stephen Griffin, Cort
snubbed a dinner for club chairman Sir John Hall and headed for the
sleazier bars of Marbella, where the club was on an early-season
break. Cort, like the others, looked but didn't touch as a parade of
high-class hookers offered their services till dawn.

CORTISONE

The painkiller used to keep the stars on the pitch when the magic
sponge fails is said to have a heartbreaking side effect. Southampton
legend Jim Steele claims he was made infertile by the drug. Steele,
Man of the Match in Saints' 1976 FA Cup victory over Manchester
United, endured two years of fertility treatment after marrying
second wife Cathy, only to discover he could never father a child. He
said: 'When I was at Southampton, I was given cortisone injections
in my groin every week for a year. Now doctors say that is what has
caused the trouble. I felt pretty low for a couple of months. I would
have loved to have been a father.' Soon after the discovery, in 1994,
Steele split from his wife.

CRAWFORD, Michael, OBE

Born: Salisbury 19.1.1942
Star of classic TV sitcom *Some Mothers Do 'Ave 'Em* lost his first wife
to hard-drinking Chelsea striker Tommy BALDWIN in 1974.

CROSS-DRESSING

See Mark BOSNICH, Tony POWELL, Pat VAN DEN HAUWE, Dwight
YORKE.

CURCIC, Sasa

Born: Belgrade, Yugoslavia, 14.2.1972
Career: Partizan Belgrade, Bolton Wanderers, Aston Villa, Crystal
Palace, New Jersey MetroStars, Cheltenham, Motherwell
And they said Eric CANTONA was a sardine short of a trawler! Sasa,
the enigmatic Serbian sorcerer, fell out of love with football and in love,
he said, with sex. As his career hit the buffers, Palace poser Sasa (who
had campaigned against UN bombings in the Balkans) issued the

following statement on why he was apparently forsaking the game at just 28.

'I have given up football because of sex. I would not sign for another club, not even if I was offered $15 million. However, it would be different if they were to instead offer me 15 different women from all around the world. I would tell the club chairman, "Please let me make these women happy – I will satisfy them like they have never been satisfied before." There is a world of difference between football and sex – no question about that. I can't achieve an orgasm by looking at a teammate, but it would be a totally different matter with Cindy Crawford.'

Yeees.

Far from giving up the game, the rebel without a clue attempted to revive his career in the US with MetroStars, at Cheltenham Town reserves and Tranmere Rovers, where boss John Aldridge even cut his trial short. A comeback for Aston Villa's former £4 million record signing was now, like those 15 fantasy women, just a dream.

DEAYTON, Angus
Born: London 6.1.1956

The celebrity Manchester United fan and *Have I Got News For You* host's TV career came to a shuddering halt as he celebrated a United win.

After watching the Reds beat Charlton at Old Trafford in May 2002, dirty Deayton should have got his head down before heading to David BECKHAM's pre-World Cup party for England in Hertfordshire the following morning. Instead he called up a blonde he had met in the city's Sugar Lounge bar and invited her to his room. Caroline MARTIN arrived at the Malmaison Hotel at midnight and knocked on the door of his room. A bottle of pink champagne was on ice. After talking into the early hours (he claimed he was single when in fact he had a long-term partner Lise Meyer and a child), they went to bed and, said Caroline, had sex 'three or four times'.

Days later they met at a hotel in London, where Deayton produced a wrap of cocaine and snorted it through a £20 note before they had sex again.

What he didn't know was that Caroline was an escort girl who counted United chief Martin EDWARDS among her clients, as well as servicing Fabian BARTHEZ and Dwight YORKE during her nights off (and without telling them her real job). Oh, and that the following week the story of his sleazy deeds would be splashed all over the *News of the World*. The revelations would cost his job, bring him national humiliation and even keep him off TV for a while.

DELL'OLIO, Nancy

Fiery Italian partner of England boss Sven-Göran ERIKSSON who beat off TV star Ulrika JONSSON's attempts to lure him away. Nancy finally gave Sven the push after it was revealed in August 2004 that he had been having an affair with FA secretary Faria ALAM.

DENNIS, Mark

Born: Lambeth 2.5.1961
Career: Birmingham City, Southampton, Queens Park Rangers, Crystal Palace

Tough-tackling Mark Dennis revelled in his reputation as the wildest man in football – until he was accused of indecent assault and had to convince a jury of his innocence.

Dennis, sent off 12 times in his career, was accused of grabbing a 15-year-old schoolgirl's breast outside a McDonald's restaurant in busy Mitcham, Surrey, in August 1991. Allegedly drunk, and wearing shorts and a T-shirt, Dennis, then 31, asked her repeatedly: 'Am I good enough?' The girl, who could not be named for legal reasons, told Kingston Crown Court: 'I could see a man coming towards us, he was walking all over the road and the pavement. He grabbed hold of my shoulder and pulled me towards him. He asked me if he was good enough, he asked me about six times. He was drunk. I just kept saying, "I don't know you." He touched my left breast. He was feeling around with one hand and pushing himself against me down below as well. I did not like what he was doing. He asked me if he was good looking. I said, "I don't know you."'

When the attacker walked away, the girl called the police and rang her family. An hour later, her brother found Dennis on Mitcham Common doing press-ups and squat thrusts with his shorts and underpants round his ankles. Dennis was arrested moments later after the brother alerted police. A police doctor decided Dennis was too drunk to be questioned. Hours later, after sobering up, he agreed to line up for an identity parade, but it was scrapped because he came face to face with the victim in a corridor.

Dennis, who denied indecent assault, did not give evidence at his trial 13 months later, leaving unsolved the mystery of his half-naked press-ups. But the brother told the court: 'When we got close, he stood up and pulled up his pants and shorts. I recognised him. I said, "You are Mark Dennis the footballer." He said, "Yes, that's right, what are you going to do about it?"' But Dennis's barrister Bill Glossop told the jury the brother could well be the person who phoned two national newspapers and tried to sell the story.

The temperamental Dennis had to wait only five minutes before the jury of six men and six women returned their verdict: not guilty. The star clenched his fist, punched the air and grunted 'Yeah!' in celebration of the most crucial victory of his controversial career.

DESAILLY, Marcel

Born: Accra, Ghana, 7.9.1968
Career: Nantes, Olympique Marseille, AC Milan, Chelsea
France's World Cup-winning defender cried foul when he was ordered to pay £100,000 to a daughter he denied was his.

Desailly – dubbed 'The Rock' due to his brilliance for club and country – was said to have fathered 12-year-old Aida during a four-year fling with Helene Mendy in his early days at Nantes and Olympique Marseille.

Senegalese-born Helene, 33, said: 'We started our relationship by post and telephone, and a year later he invited me to Marseille where he had come to play with Nantes. We became intimate on 20

October 1989 at the team hotel [she recalled with impressive detail].
Aida was born on 12 July 1990. We saw each other regularly but after
he won the European Cup with Marseille in 1993 he would no longer
talk to me. He refused to recognise Aida because he said I had
betrayed him. But that is not true. I warned him I was not taking
contraceptives.'

Desailly, now married with three children and living a millionaire
life in leafy Surrey after a £4.5 million move from Italy, always
refused to take DNA or blood tests. He even threatened to sue
jobless Helene for defamation. But in November 2002, her testimony
persuaded a court in Toulon, France, to rule he should pay £45,000
in back-dated maintenance, plus £800 a month until Aida's 18th
birthday. Desailly's lawyer said: 'He still contests paternity. We
believe he is the victim of a plot.'

DIBBLE, Andy
Born: Cwmbran 8.5.1965
Career: Cardiff City, Luton Town, Sunderland (loan), Huddersfield Town
(loan), Manchester City, Aberdeen (loan), Middlesbrough (loan), Bolton
Wanderers (loan), West Bromwich Albion (loan), Oldham Athletic
(loan), Sheffield United, Rangers, Sheffield United, Luton Town,
Middlesbrough, Altrincham, Barry Town, Hartlepool United, Carlisle
United, Stockport County, Wrexham

The colourful Welsh international keeper found himself woefully
short of cover when his afternoon romp with a brunette was
interrupted by her husband!

Paul Williams returned early to his three-bedroom semi in Belle
Vue, Manchester, to find the naked goalie standing on the landing
with just his hands covering his tackle. Williams' wife Adele was in
the background. He explained: 'I came home and saw some bloke's
underpants and trousers lying in the lounge. I heard some
whispering so I went upstairs. Then I saw Dibble. I was almost
speechless. I couldn't believe it when I saw Dibble on my landing,
hiding his privates with his hands. Dibble said, "It's not what you
think", but I called him a lying bastard and we shouted at each
other. I stormed out, rang from a call box, and told Adele to get him
out of the house.'

Adele had met the lanky keeper when she began a new job as a receptionist at Manchester City's Maine Road ground. But their afternoon love-in in 1996 was to end her marriage. Paul added: 'It could never be the same between us after that. They denied anything was going on but any husband would have his suspicions. I couldn't get the image of Dibble standing there out of my mind. We tried to patch things up but I was suspicious. It all came to a head again when I accidentally pressed the redial button on our phone and heard Dibble answer. I also rang Dibble's wife [Jacinta] and she was in tears. She asked if I knew she was pregnant and I said I was sorry.'

Dibble served 16 clubs in a 20-year career. The undoubted highlight was his Wembley penalty save at 2–1 down that helped Luton Town beat Arsenal in the 1988 Littlewoods Cup. His lowest – and most bizarre – was the serious burns he suffered when he dived on penalty area lines that had been wrongly treated with hydrated lime, while playing for Barry Town in 1999.

But his favourite football memory remains a loan spell at Rangers in 1997 – where partners in crime included soccer love rats Paul GASCOIGNE, Andy GORAM and Ally McCOIST. Memorable is an understatement. 'Team spirit was great,' he recalls cryptically. 'My wife says I never came down from Glasgow to visit her.'

Dibble had already got away with straying. He was named as the star sex performer in soccer groupie Sarah MOORE's sex marathon with seven players at the PFA's annual awards bash in March 1993. And he cheated on his air stewardess wife Jacinta again in 1994 with a waitress.

But in 1997, his penchant for playing away would backfire when, along with two friends, he was accused of a sex assault on a woman. Charges were finally dropped a week before the trial and after nine agonising months in February 1997. 'I've been through murder,' Dibble said afterwards. 'I have had these rapist chants for the last nine months. It is not very nice being called a rapist when you've not done anything like that.'

See GROUP SEX.

DICKOV, Paul

Born: Glasgow, 1.11.1972

Career: Arsenal, Luton Town (loan), Brighton (loan), Manchester City, Leicester City, Blackburn Rovers

Accused of rape after a night on the lash in LA MANGA with his LEICESTER CITY teammates. Striker Dickov and teammates Keith GILLESPIE and Frank SINCLAIR spent a week in jail and months on bail before all charges were dropped.

DIVORCE

They might find fame and fortune, but the one thing professional footballers seldom seem to find is a happy marriage. One in ten footballers divorce before reaching their late 20s. A survey of 4,000 players revealed the staggering cost of football to family life. The research found that 50 per cent of British footballers are married, 39 per cent are single and 9 per cent divorced or separated. And however much they might blame family breakdown on living away from home, constant travelling to away games and internationals or the intermittent uprooting to new clubs in Britain or abroad, the truth is they've often only got themselves to blame. Because, let's face it, when you're young, famous, fit and rich, you're never going to have problems pulling.

Eighty per cent say they have been targeted by gold-diggers, and clearly an awful lot give in! Divorce lawyer Henry Brookman, who commissioned the research in 2002, said: 'There clearly are special factors such as money, the media, the high life and players being the target of the temptation that goes with that. Most auditors don't have to ask hotel security staff to order young women away from their hotel doors, do they?'

And it's not just the pros whose marriages can be torn asunder. Joanne Bradley, of Manston, Kent, divorced husband Neil because of his obsession with Norwich City in 2002. His crimes against marital harmony included:

- PAINTING their bedroom yellow and green while she was away;
- WHISKING her off for a romantic break in Norfolk – to watch the Canaries train;
- BUYING her Norwich City knickers for their wedding anniversary.

Joanne, 36, said: 'Our son Lee doesn't support Norwich but Neil bought him every club hat, shirt, scarf, mug and duvet.'

DOCHERTY, Tommy

Born: Glasgow 24.8.1928

Career: Player – Celtic, Preston North End, Arsenal, Chelsea. Manager – Chelsea, Rotherham, Queens Park Rangers, Aston Villa, Scotland, Manchester United, Derby County, Queens Park Rangers, Preston North End, Wolverhampton Wanderers

The fast-talking, wise-cracking Scotsman known as 'The Doc' was on the brink of greatness with his swashbuckling Manchester United side, but instead he hit the top of the love-rats' league for his affair with the club physio's wife.

United had won the FA Cup against mighty Liverpool only two months earlier in May 1977 – the fallen giants' first honour in nine turbulent years since their historic European Cup win. The Doc, once a fiery midfielder, had built a team in his own style. He had replaced, by hook, and often by crook, the Reds' holy trinity of BEST, Law and Charlton with Hill, Coppell and Pearson and, despite a season in the Second Division, transformed the club's fortunes.

'I was fired for falling in love,' was the Doc's furious response to his dismissal for breach of contract. But the truth had, like many of Docherty's claims, been given a free transfer.

It was claimed that he had ordered physio Laurie Brown to attend away games and carry out extra physio sessions on his days off in order to carry on the affair with Brown's wife, Mary, behind his back. Father-of-four Docherty's own 25-year marriage to Agnes ended. Mary Brown, a mother of two young children, left her husband.

The Doc moved on with diminishing success. He found new notoriety when he sued star winger Willie Morgan for libel, then suddenly withdrew the case. A judge decided he had lied in the dock and he was charged with perjury before being cleared in 1981.

Thirty years later Docherty and Mary are still together and it is clear that they were indeed in love. But the pain of his marriage split remains – especially for his three children. The Doc, now an entertaining after-dinner speaker, says: 'When I was sacked, Manchester United lost but I won. Mary is the best thing that ever happened to me. We'd been going for a year and a half, but there was nothing unclean or tacky about it. With the greatest respect, we were both just bored with our marriages. I didn't know if our love would last – I wasn't sure initially – but at the time it was lovely and now we couldn't be happier. At the start, it was a fresh face, a bit of fun and laughter, but it just grew and grew until we just didn't want to be away from each other. I know there were people hurt when we did what we did, but you only get one life. We did what we thought was best for us.

'But I'm still paying for it. Three of my kids from my first marriage to Agnes don't even speak to me. There is no contact at all, no cards, no calls, no presents. It was a heartbreak at first, but now it doesn't even bother me. Ironically, those three have been married and divorced themselves. I think if they came back and said we should start from scratch, I wouldn't do it. No, not now.'

When Agnes died in 2002, she banned him from the funeral. 'We were together for 20 years,' said Docherty. 'But Agnes had it in her will that I shouldn't attend. I wanted to go, but I felt there would be a scene with the family, and in a way it was a blessing that she helped me. But I paid my respects elsewhere. She was a nice lady. God rest her soul. It was a very, very sad time.'

Some said his teams were more cavalier than cunning. But his two-timing tactical awareness made Thomas Henderson Docherty the maestro of soccer marriage-wreckers.

DODDS, Billy

Born: New Cumnock 5.2.1969
Career: Chelsea, Partick Thistle, Dundee, St Johnstone, Aberdeen, Dundee United, Rangers, Dundee United

The Rangers and Scotland star found himself on the front pages when his perverted father-in-law was jailed for nine years for abusing girls. Builder Ewan McGillvray, 59, molested kids aged between four and 13 for some 25 years, often using his position as a trusted athletics coach to snare them. He was convicted of five charges of indecent behaviour, but cleared of the attempted rape of a 12-year-old girl.

DOGGING

Dubious open-air sex-thrill enjoyed by ex-England ace Stan COLLYMORE.

DOUVALL, Alicia

Ever-present on the footballer party circuit, the silicone enhanced 32FF blonde lapdancer, porn star and sometime singer revels in her role as bed-partner to the stars. She counts Dwight YORKE, Fabien BARTHEZ and Celestine BABAYARO among her conquests and is always on the lookout for more.

Douvall pulled down her straining top to give Arsenal's Double-winning players two more massive cups as they celebrated the title-clinching victory over Manchester United at London's Chinawhite club in May 2002. Alongside her was fellow porn model Linsey Dawn McKenzie, one-time illicit lover of Bolton Wanderers striker Dean HOLDSWORTH. 'They literally threw themselves at every football player in the club,' said one onlooker. 'But, fortunately, they were turned down every time.'

DREYER, John

Born: Alnwick 11.6.1963
Career: Oxford United, Torquay United (loan), Fulham (loan), Luton Town, Stoke City, Bolton Wanderers, Bradford City, Cambridge United
Dreyer copped a £200 fine for picking up a prostitute yards from his side Luton Town's ground. The big defender was followed by an undercover police squad as he KERB-CRAWLED in his car and picked up the blonde by the side of the road. After stopping in a quiet shopping centre car park, the lights went out and the cops pounced. Dreyer's lawyer announced in court his client was 'deeply sorry' for his actions. Coincidentally Luton Town boss David PLEAT had been cautioned for kerb-crawling a couple of years earlier.

Dreyer appeared to have learned his lesson after his 1987 offence and became one of the Bradford City heroes who helped their brave club beat the drop in an epic 1999–2000 Premiership campaign.

DUBERRY, Michael

Born: Enfield 14.10.1975

Career: Chelsea, Bournemouth (loan), Leeds United

When football goes on trial one day for bringing Britain into disrepute, Leeds United's defensive powerhouse could well be called as a witness.

Duberry has already figured in two major cases – in one he admitted lying to police to keep his teammates out of trouble after a man lay brutally beaten in a gutter, though he later told the truth in court. When the dust settled, Leeds teammate Jonathan WOODGATE was found guilty of affray, Lee BOWYER was cleared of assaulting Safraz Najeib and Duberry's reputation was damaged.

In the next, he admitted a six-hour drinking session with Rio FERDINAND and a Yorkshire gangland villain. But he denied cornering a woman in a nightclub toilet and putting his hand up her skirt minutes before a rapist attacked her at gunpoint.

As the 22 year old left the Hi-Fi club in Leeds, evil Martin Luther King pulled her by her hair into his BMW, took her to a quiet lane, stripped her at gunpoint and assaulted her, saying: 'It's not me doing this to you – it's Michael and Rio.'

Both players gave evidence at the trial of King, 33, an associate of the wealthy drug dealer, named only as Reds, they were partying with.

Duberry, 27, denied assaulting the woman in a toilet cubicle, saying: 'It never happened. I wasn't misbehaving.' And he denied his pal Rio threatened to have her beaten her up when she refused their advances. Duberry insisted: 'If anything like that happened, I would know.'

In May 2003, at Leeds Crown Court, convicted rapist King was found guilty of indecent assault and attempted rape of the woman. He received two life sentences.

The woman wanted both footballers to face criminal charges, but Judge Scott Wolstenholme announced there was no evidence they were involved in the rape.

● Duberry appeared fleetingly in the notorious AYIA NAPA soccer sex VIDEO. The then-Chelsea star was seen drinking alongside his bad-boy pals but was not involved in sex scenes.

DUBLIN, Dion

Born: Leicester 22.4.1969

Career: Norwich City, Cambridge United, Manchester United, Coventry City, Aston Villa, Millwall (loan), Leicester City

Sax-mad England striker Dion Dublin fathered a love child with his married girlfriend, leaving her unsuspecting husband gobsmacked.

Dion's days as a Premiership hitman were still just a dream when he met Cambridge housewife Beverley Murray soon after signing for the local side from Norwich City. And when Beverley gave birth in October 1989, no one was more shocked than her husband James. 'He knew nothing about the affair,' a friend told *The People* newspaper, 'and, as Dion is black, it was a hell of a shock when the baby was born.' After the affair, the teenaged Dublin fell for Louisa Howlett, daughter of a former Cambridge director, and they later wed. Beverley was left to bring up the child, Adam, with James.

When the secret was revealed in 1992, as Dion began his short spell at mighty Manchester United, Beverley, 30, said: 'My relationship with Dion is in the past and my husband obviously knows all about it. Of course he was absolutely outraged at the time. It was very difficult but he has stood by me and we've both put what happened behind us. Adam is now part of our family, though it's no secret around here who his father is.' Dion added: 'I don't want to talk about anything that happened while I was at Cambridge. I'm too busy.'

DYER, Kieron

Born: Ipswich 29.12.1978

Career: Ipswich Town, Newcastle United

After starring in a home-made sex movie while on holiday in AYIA NAPA, Cyprus, the all-action midfielder vowed to clean up his lifestyle.

Dyer, Rio FERDINAND and Frank LAMPARD had picked up women who would subsequently appear in a sordid sunshine sex flick. Days later in July 2000, after NEWCASTLE UNITED boss Sir Bobby ROBSON had ordered him to move out of Newcastle's vibrant Quayside quarter and temptation's way, he announced the end of his nightclub and booze days . . . and was glassed in a disco in his home town of Ipswich, needing stitches in his face.

Next, he crashed his car on the way to training in Newcastle and was later banned for two months and fined £1,000 for doing 104 mph on the A1 in Durham. A month later, he was seen clubbing with new girlfriend, Page 3 girl LEILANI, and a month after that, he grabbed the headlines again after a marathon bar crawl during an early-season club trip to Marbella.

With teammates Carl CORT, Craig Bellamy and Stephen Griffin, he snubbed a dinner in honour of club chairman Sir John Hall and headed for the bars and strip clubs of the Spanish resort. Through the night, the foursome eyed up a bevy of strippers and vice girls, but, thankfully, kept their tackle in their shorts.

Dyer later said of the Ayia Napa video: 'I was young and I think to become a better person you have to make mistakes. I looked at the front page of the *News of the World* and cringed because it was a silly thing to do. The chairman and Bobby Robson really told me off for that. I should be thankful to them because, hopefully, when I look back over a long and successful career I'll know it was down to the sort of advice they've given me.'

Maybe it was his previous bad-boy image that dragged him into the ROASTING scandal in September 2003, when his name mistakenly emerged during a police investigation into an alleged GANG RAPE by soccer stars at a London hotel. The millionaire Newcastle United star was wrongly said to have booked £400-a-night rooms there for friends after the club's Friday night Premiership defeat by Arsenal. In one of the rooms, the 17-year-old accuser said she was attacked after returning from a nightclub. Charges against all four men involved – Dyer's Newcastle teammate Titus BRAMBLE, Charlton striker Carlton COLE, party organiser Nicholas MEIKLE and Meikle's friend Jason Edwards – were later dropped because of insufficient evidence. Witnesses insisted Dyer was not involved in the orgy and police later confirmed that he was indeed elsewhere at the time.

See VIDEO.

EBDEN, Brian

Struggling soccer club owner whose girlfriend Nadia ABRAHAMS accused Manchester United boss Sir Alex FERGUSON of a sex assault as she drove him back to his hotel from a Cape Town nightclub. Charges were never brought, but Ebden sold their story for £75,000 to two British papers.

EDWARDS, Martin

Born: Manchester 24.7.1945

Maybe he was missing the limelight after stepping down as chairman and chief executive of mighty Manchester United. But for multi-millionaire Martin Edwards, 57, to walk calmly past the reception desk at elegant Mottram Hall health club, enter the ladies' toilets and peer under the door of an engaged cubicle was an act of folly almost unparalleled in the annals of soccer sex pests. Even though Edwards had played away from Brazil to Bramhall and back, United fans were gobsmacked by the chairman's bizarre behaviour. But at Old Trafford, his sordid fetish was a standing – or crouching – joke. United security chief Ned Kelly would later reveal he had been detailed to keep Edwards away from the ladies' toilets at charity bashes as early as 1998. 'The chairman's fetish was a source of amusement to the players but undeniably embarrassing,' Kelly revealed in his book, *Manchester United: The Untold Story.*

Incredibly, Susan, his wife of 30 years and mother of his grown-up children, stood by him. But then she is used to Edwards' bizarre behaviour . . .

In 1990, he romanced former model Caroline Wyke, 26, who

allegedly demanded £100,000 to keep their relationship a secret. *The People* newspaper ran the story of his dangerous relationship with Wyke under the headline MAN UTD SEX CASH & BLACKMAIL SENSATION. Wyke had kept a detailed diary of her meetings with Edwards. She said: 'I spent a couple of nights in hotels with him but mostly we had dinner. We talked a lot about his wife, Sue.' After realising how much a divorce would cost the United chief, she wrote asking for £100,000 as payment for not talking about the affair with newspapers. She didn't get it. But the lurid publicity hurt. And it was merely a taste of things to come.

That same year he bedded BBC newsgirl Lynette Lithgow at posh hotels in London. But he told friends rising star Lynette was falling in love with him and ended their relationship. (Tragically the TV beauty was murdered 11 years later on a Caribbean island. Two men were sentenced to death in July 2004 for her killing.)

In March 1994, blonde receptionist Debbie Miller told of her five-month affair with the man she described as a 'gorilla' because of his hairy back. Debbie, 28, told of all-night sex, thanks to his 'terrific stamina' after drinking champagne in the bath. 'He's a wonderful lover but very straight. I wanted him to be a little more rough,' said Debbie, 'but he was always gentle. He's definitely not kinky.'

After sex, she reported, he would get his silk pyjamas out of an overnight bag and jump on them to fool his wife that he had used them. She decided to dump him when he only handed her £100 for a birthday present. Confronted, Edwards said: 'I confirm I know Debbie but I never talk about my private life.'

In 2000, as United played in the first World Club Championship tournament in Rio de Janeiro, Edwards picked up prostitute Maria Elves, 35, in a club and, she said, paid her £120 for sex at his hotel. He had spent a boozy day sipping cocktails by the hotel pool and a night touring the seamier fleshpots of Rio. As United's stars had an early night before a vital game against Vasco da Gama, Edwards and a group of friends visited the Hipopamus club, famed for its high-class hookers, then the Centaurus strip club before dancing at the Help disco, an infamous pick-up joint for prostitutes. After three hours, he left in a taxi with stunning Maria and a pal following in another cab with a friend of Edwards. Once in room 1616, Maria told

The Mirror, 'it took four hours to make love and in the end it wasn't very good. I used every trick I knew. I gave him a normal massage and then gave him a massage with my hair, trying to get him to relax. At first he was just very nervous about the papers and he paced around his room. Then he blamed alcohol and said he had drunk too much. He always came up with an excuse, but it was very embarrassing for me. I thought I had tried every fantasy I could dream of and it still didn't work.'

The following morning Edwards refused to let her leave for her part-time job as a dental surgery receptionist in case she was spotted leaving his room by players heading for breakfast. Finally he smuggled her into the corridor, down a fire exit, into a service lift and then out through a tradesmen's entrance. After handing her £120 and £20 for a taxi, and inviting her to the game, she left. Maria explained: 'He rang me a couple of times on the mobile asking for me to go back to the hotel. It was like he couldn't help himself.'

Edwards later denied the liaison, insisting: 'I have not had sexual relations with a girl called Maria Alvarez.' His mispronunciation of her name was lost on no one.

Prostitute Caroline MARTIN – later to bed celebrity Red fan Angus DEAYTON – revealed her fling with Edwards in 2001. He had hired her through a Manchester escort agency for £130 an hour and they met at the city's Pelican Inn hotel, the *News of the World* reported. 'He was well dressed, carrying a bottle of wine and said his name was Mike Edwards. But when he kissed me, I reeled from his exceptionally bad breath,' she revealed.

After pouring a glass of wine and undressing, the tycoon removed his clothes and folded them up meticulously before slipping between the sheets. Caroline stripped, then they performed oral sex on each other. She claimed she faked her orgasms to shorten the ordeal, but Edwards was clearly impressed. He arranged another session, this time at a cottage in Bramhall, Cheshire – some five miles away from his family's £1 million mansion at Wilmslow – and continued seeing the vice girl for around ten months.

'I was sworn to secrecy, as he was such a good customer,' she added. 'The boss told me he had bought the cottage specifically to use for sex with prostitutes. Over the next ten months the routine was always the same, with him booking me every two weeks or so.'

Playing Away

It was United fan and Independent Supporters' Club spokesman Andy Walsh who summed up Edwards best: 'Martin Edwards goes around the world laying it about. That's not news — that's to be expected!' The chairman who made United the biggest club in the world, and helped decide the fates of errant managers Tommy DOCHERTY and Sir Alex FERGUSON, had also brought it more shame than the baddest of its bad boy stars could ever have managed.

ERIKSSON, Sven-Göran
Born: Sunne, Sweden, 5.2.1948
Career: Manager — Degerfors, IFK Gothenburg, Benfica, Roma, Fiorentina, Benfica, Sampdoria, Lazio, England

Beware the Svengali stare of Sven-Göran Eriksson. Despite the air of a rather dull insurance salesman, England's cerebral Swedish soccer boss is a 'Master of Love-making' who can pull with just one devastating look from his bespectacled blue eyes.

The unlikely love god has enjoyed a series of lust-filled liaisons despite the ferocious man-marking of his long-term partner Nancy DELL'OLIO, but has *twice* risked his £4 million-a-year job over them.

First, as England prepared for the 2002 World Cup, his fling with *Shooting Stars* host Ulrika JONSSON was revealed to a stunned public. Nancy, a fiery Italian, launched a very public battle to win him back. And succeeded.

Two years later, as England reeled from defeat in Euro 2004, it emerged that in the run-up to the tournament Sven had been romancing 38-year-old FA secretary Faria ALAM — who had already slept with his boss, chief executive Mark PALIOS.

This time Nancy dumped him — which was the least of his worries as he ended up at the centre of the greatest scandal in the history of the FOOTBALL ASSOCIATION.

The FA had at first denied any relationship between Sven and Alam, then backtracked. Someone had lied, and the finger of suspicion was pointed at Sven. But within days it emerged that an FA spokesman had offered to dish the dirt on Sven if the chief executive's name was kept out of the story. Palios resigned within hours of the skulduggery being exposed. Sven kept his cool, and transformed looming defeat into the greatest victory of his England career . . .

1–0: His boardroom rival Palios is gone.

2–0: He wins public sympathy over the FA's backstabbing plot.

3–0: His £4 million a year job is safe.

4–0: Nancy is history and Sven, at last, is single.

5–0: Faria tells the world he's a superstud in bed.

If only his results on the pitch were as good! Instead he had enjoyed, as they say, a game of two very different other halves.

Father-of-two Sven, 56, had been with Italian lawyer Nancy since 1998, three years before his appointment as England boss in January 2001. They met at the exclusive Terme di Saturnia Spa in Tuscany. Both were married, Nancy, known as '*La Dama Nera*' – the Dark Lady – to a fellow lawyer, Giancarlo Mazza. To complicate matters, Mazza was also a director of Sven's club Lazio, which he would later guide to the Scudetto, the Italian League title. It was a very messy love affair indeed. But Sven, determined yet pragmatic, had the perfect game plan. He took the cuckolded husband for a civilised lunch and broke the news. Nancy's husband agreed to a transfer.

Eriksson's appointment as the first foreigner to manage England was hugely controversial, but his dignified air and his transformation of the team from bottom of their World Cup qualifying group under Kevin Keegan to qualification via an epic 5–1 victory in Germany earned him cult status. Who could doubt his passion now?

Certainly not mother-of-two Ulrika Jonsson, the blonde former TV weathergirl turned tabloid icon thanks to her sexy roles in *Gladiators* and *Shooting Stars* and her lurid love life.

Sven and Ulrika were introduced at a party by Tony Blair's spin doctor Alastair Campbell in December 2001. As Sven walked past, Campbell told Ulrika: 'Here's another Swede for you to talk to.'

Ulrika the manhunter became Ulrika the autograph hunter. As a wary Nancy looked on, Sven signed, and, in Swedish, asked for her phone number. What an operator. Ulrika obliged as Nancy watched, instantly aware of the frisson. 'She gave me a cold, false smile,' Ulrika recalled later. 'It said, "This is my territory, keep away."'

Ulrika got the hint . . . and ignored it. For four months, they enjoyed secret meetings without the knowledge of 'the Italian' or 'the Third Party', as Sven referred to Nancy. Sven would visit Ulrika's rambling £850,000 hillside home in Cookham Dean,

Berkshire, on his journeys between matches scouting. One day he arrived with more champagne for lunch. 'As I turned to open the fridge,' Ulrika said, 'I felt his hand on my neck as he turned me around and kissed me . . . I reciprocated without needing to think about it.'

Ulrika visited his villa in Portugal – bought when he managed Benfica – for a whirlwind liaison. At the villa, they had sex for the first time. Back home, Sven even became close to Ulrika's children, Cameron, eight, and seventeen-month-old Bo, and her mother Gun Brodie, and began to play a major role in Ulrika's life. The smitten boss even suggested they set up a secret love nest. Ulrika said: 'He wanted to get a place for me in north London where we could meet. I said, "Are you mad?" Even if we'd arrived separately somebody would have seen us.' (Actually someone *had* seen them. Ulrika's housemaid spotted the diminutive manager's stack-heeled shoes placed neatly outside the bedroom as they made love inside.)

But his dream was about to be shattered. In April 2002, with the World Cup less than two months away, the extraordinary love story appeared on the front page of the *Daily Mirror*, now committed to serious journalism but unable to resist the ultimate tabloid tale of TV, soccer *and* sex. SVENSATIONAL! said the headline. And it was.

Nancy joined battle. They were formidable opponents . . .

Nancy: 37 (but rumoured to be 43). A brainy raven-haired beauty with independent wealth thanks to her legal career, and a flamboyant taste in clothes. Her ambition was fired by a hot-blooded Italian temperament.

Ulrika: 34. A sexed-up blonde Swedish siren, made rich by her successful TV career, who counted Prince Edward, pop star Mick Hucknall, Chris Evans, two muscle-bound Gladiators, various TV workers, and footballers Stan COLLYMORE and Les FERDINAND among her conquests.

Besieged by news teams outside her £3 million Regent's Park mansion, Nancy said of Ulrika: 'Poor girl . . . she is nothing. Why would I still be with Sven if this was true? I am very angry. Where has this rubbish come from? There is nothing for me to worry about or talk about.'

Asked if she was still with Sven, she replied: 'We live in the same house, don't we?'

Frosty Ulrika declared: 'I'm not going to talk about it. I won't talk about it today, tomorrow or ever.' Which wasn't quite true, considering she would publish her memoirs months later.

Two days later, Nancy showed off a large diamond ring on her engagement finger after a public dinner date at Knightsbridge's San Lorenzo restaurant. Earlier that day, Sven and Ulrika had been at the same football match, Chelsea v. Manchester United at Stamford Bridge, but sat on opposite sides of the stadium. Sven was subdued. United fan Ulrika, accompanied by fellow celebrity Red Angus DEAYTON, was animated as she cheered her boys to a 3–0 win.

A week later Ulrika said: 'I am no longer part of this relationship.' In fact, she later admitted, she and Sven were still secretly phoning and TXTing. And she was still expecting him to finish with Nancy.

But the Italian determined to outfox foxy Ulrika. She stole the front pages by wearing a skintight scarlet sequinned catsuit to another Downing Street reception, then chose a racy black basque for an England players' bash: just the outfits to show what their manager would be walking out on.

Sven was caught in the crossfire, but insisted his private life was just that – private.

From Stockport to Stockholm, soccer fans lapped up the news. In Sweden – England's first opponents – coverage reached fever pitch.

'In Sweden, Svennis is huge,' said a spokesman for *Expressen*, with punintentional humour. Only an injury to David BECKHAM's left foot took the spotlight off Sven as the tournament drew closer.

A draw with Sweden, a famous victory over Argentina and a point against Nigeria saw England through to the second phase. Beating Denmark set up an epic quarter-final with Brazil, and, thanks to Ronaldinho's freak winner, World Cup agony. Game over. Now it was time to settle his future and, Ulrika hoped, dump Nancy.

But suddenly he changed his tactics.

Sven's last call to Ulrika came on the morning of the Sweden game. 'He left a jolly message on my mobile and since then, nothing,' said Ulrika. 'I really believed I'd get another call because he was insistent to me that his relationship with Nancy would end.'

Sven had also, she heard, had other affairs during his years with Nancy. When she confronted him, he said, 'Yes, of course.'

'Being with Nancy was not the life that he wanted,' said Ulrika. 'I can only believe what people say, that he's frightened of her.'

Ulrika said: 'I don't look back on the affair with any longing, but I do have moments when I think, "Well, it's a great shame." I was on the verge of falling in love with him.'

In October, after her book *Honest* was published, she said: 'I know he still wants to leave Nancy. If he does find the courage to leave, then I hope he calls me. I am still interested.'

The call never came. But then he was a little tied up.

While romancing Ulrika and cheating on Nancy, he had met blonde sales promotions girl Jayne Connery, who had fallen for Sven's hypnotic stare as he signed autographs at a Chelsea game.

Jayne, 35, and – like Ulrika – blonde, said: 'Without sounding soppy, everyone flocked around him but our eyes locked. I was standing at the bar and he smiled at me. It was complete and utter blinding chemistry. We continued making eye contact while he signed autographs and eventually I leaned over and cheekily said, "Would you like my autograph, Sven?" He laughed and I thought, "Something's going to happen." As soon as he had my mobile number, I was like jelly wondering if the call would come. When it did the following day, I was trembling like a leaf. But I had no idea he was living with a woman.'

Their first date was at an airport coffee bar, where 'he touched my hair as if it was gold dust. We both knew it was a sexual attraction.'

Twice-married Jayne explained: 'What's overpoweringly attractive about Sven is that he focuses on you 100 per cent. He looks straight into your eyes while he's talking. He makes you feel wonderful, like you are the only woman in his world. It's devastating. He made me melt.'

The would-be lovers never actually slept together – despite kissing and hand-holding.

But when news of his affair with Ulrika broke, his phone calls to her home in Aylesbury, Buckinghamshire, stopped and his phone number changed. 'Looking back, I suppose I was taken for a bit of a fool,' said Jayne. 'Maybe he isn't the gentleman we all thought he was.'

The following summer, after causing a storm with allegations that she was date-raped by a TV celebrity, Ulrika married a contestant on her dating show *Mr Right* – toff Lance Gerrard Wright.

Despite his apparent domestic hell, Sven stayed with Nancy. She even told TV's Jonathan Ross they kept fit with regular sex, and were contemplating starting a family.

This was clearly news to Sven. At the same time, he was pursuing another woman (after flirting with Chelsea and securing a massive new pay deal).

At Christmas 2003, the England manager introduced himself to the new employee in the FA's offices, secretary Faria Alam. It was not their first meeting – two years earlier those deadly eyes locked with hers as he walked past her in a restaurant. 'He stared at me with the kind of look which takes you away,' she said, and resolved to meet him one day.

Soon he took her for a meal, but she turned down his persistent advances. Sven did not know she was seeing his boss Mark Palios. After seven months of flirting and playing footsie at banquets (at one dinner the two suitors sat either side of their prey), and almost daily phone calls from England's Euro 2004 training camp, she relented.

After England's exit, she agreed to fly to Sweden to stay at his home. He cooked dinner – salmon and champagne – rinsed the dishes and loaded the washing machine before taking her to bed.

'He was a master in the art of love-making,' Faria told the *Mail on Sunday*. 'After he'd filled the dishwasher, he led me up the stairs to his bedroom where he picked me up in his arms and gently laid me down on his huge four-poster bed. He peeled off my jeans, unclipped my bra and started kissing my breasts then told me, "You are incredibly beautiful." He stroked my back, ran his fingers through my hair, we made passionate love and it was beautiful. At the height of passion, he bit my shoulder. It was the best sex of my life.'

Afterwards, Sven – who admitted to her he had not had sex for a year – put on his blue cotton pyjamas and they slept. The following morning, there was an action replay – astonishingly, this time Sven took a call from Nancy, who yelled down the phone as Faria continued.

Twenty-four hours later, Faria woke the boss with a 'Special Present', oral sex apparently perfected on an 8 in.-long candle! 'I gave him one of my deep throat jobs and he suddenly shouted out, "Oh my God. What are you doing to me?"'

Well, if he didn't know by now . . .

Later the same day, Faria revealed, Sven took her – literally – on a guided tour of his pad and tackled her from behind as they mounted the stairs. 'He pulled me back to him and tore off my jeans,' she said. 'I was taken aback by his desire.' The encounter left her with grazed knees.

Faria returned to England in love, she claimed, and ready to continue the affair. But she began to boast about both affairs in e-mails to a friend. Newspapers heard whispers and began to dig for more. The FA's inept response to press inquiries sparked the greatest scandal in its 140-year history and three weeks of damaging headlines.

Sunday, July 18 2004
The *News of the World* reveals Sven has had an affair with an FA secretary but does not name Faria Alam.

Monday, 19 July
Gossip points to Faria, but sources close to the England manager insist: 'It's simply not true. Sven, Nancy and the other woman concerned are extremely pissed off.'

Tuesday, 20 July
Instead of simply refusing to comment on a private matter, the FA puts out a statement from Faria's lawyers saying there was 'no truth whatsoever in the suggestion that our client and Mr Eriksson are having, or have had, a sexual relationship'.

Wednesday, 21 July
Furious Nancy, on holiday in Italy, decides there's no smoke without fire and announces a trial separation.

Saturday, 24 July
The *News of the World* presents its evidence to the FA and at last Faria admits the truth. An FA official reveals: 'She swore black and

blue she was not the person having an affair with Sven and only when shown the proof did she change her tune.'

Sunday, 25 July

The paper publishes Faria's e-mails to a friend boasting of her affair. Suddenly the FA is forced to retract the statement. 'Having made further inquiries, we can confirm that a relationship did take place.' Crucially, the FA also admits Faria had a fling with chief executive Mark Palios too.

Monday, 26 July

The FA, embarrassed at its massive own goal, announces an inquiry into how the misleading statements were issued.

Thursday, 29 July

As calls for his sacking grow, Eriksson insists he had not lied: 'I have at no time either categorically confirmed or denied any relationship with Ms Faria Alam.'

Sunday, 1 August

The *News of the World* prints a transcript of off-the-record phone calls from FA communications chief Colin Gibson. In them, he offers to give every detail of the manager's affair in return for their leaving Palios's name out. At 6 p.m. Palios quits, but insists: 'I do not accept I have been guilty of any wrongdoing.' Gibson says he was 'uncomfortable' at offering the deal and insists: 'I simply did what I was asked.'

Wednesday, 4 August

The board meets at London's Leonard Hotel for a crisis summit. After hearing results of an independent investigation, it announces boss Sven has 'no case to answer'. Gibson's resignation is accepted; Faria's position is unclear. It admits: 'This entire episode has been regrettable for the reputation of football in this country but the board remain determined to restore the highest standards.'

Thursday, 5 August

Faria returns from holiday and hands in her notice on her £35,000-

a-year job. She signs a deal with PR king Max Clifford and prepares to sell her story to newspapers and TV stations.

Sunday, 8 August

Faria's story appears in the *News of the World* and *Mail on Sunday*. As well as detailing her sex romps with both men in vivid detail, Faria tells how Palios believed Sven's eye for the ladies would interfere with his job and how she was put under pressure to lie about her affair. Cruelly, she says Nancy looks like a 'drag queen' and that Sven had called her 'Mad, absolutely mad' as he regularly dodged the plates she threw at him!

But if Sven cringed at Faria's intimate revelations, at least he could purr with pleasure at her compliments. Maybe his England players might learn a trick or two off him!

With no more names dragged into the scandal, and no evidence that Sven had misused his position, he could prepare for the World Cup qualification campaign. And pray for victory.

Shrewd observers believe the libidinous manager will get the chop as soon as England fail, and results – not affairs – can be blamed.

See FERRARI.

EROTOMANIA

See Mr X.

F

FASHANU, John

Born: Kensington 18.9.1962

Career: Norwich City, Crystal Palace (loan), Lincoln City, Millwall, Wimbedon, Aston Villa

The King of Wimbledon's Cup-winning Crazy Gang has led an amazing double life as a philanthropist and philanderer.

He scaled the heights with a giant-killing FA Cup victory over mighty Liverpool in 1988, then plunged the depths with match-fixing allegations in the 1990s. And in his spare time the self-styled family man, charity worker and global businessman:

- CHEATED on his pregnant girlfriend with a shopworker;
- KEPT the secret lover for ten years then . . .
- BONKED another lodger who moved in with her;
- SLEPT with both behind his new fiancée's back, and;
- CONSPIRED with his teammates to give him alibis for his other affairs.

Fash the Pash's secrets were exposed as he faced match-fixing charges alongside Bruce GROBBELAAR and Hans SEGERS. The Aston Villa striker and popular host of ITV's *Gladiators* show married his pregnant girlfriend Melissa Kassa-Mapsi in Dakar, Senegal, in March 1995, just weeks before the trial (Melissa, 26, had also been arrested but charges of conspiracy against her were dropped).

Newspapers soon revealed his ten-year on–off affair with Niki Thompson, 29, and his liaisons with Swedish Anna Odell, 22, the woman who lived with Niki in a £500,000 house rented from Fashanu. The housemates knew he was bedding them behind the back of his fiancée Melissa – but not that he was bedding both of them *and* another girl.

Niki had been a long-term fixture for Fashanu. She was an 18-year-old shopworker when they met. He was a 22 year old discarded by Norwich City and trying his luck with Lincoln City.

Niki said: 'He was going out with my manageress, but as soon as he saw me he started chatting me up. He said I looked beautiful and asked for my phone number.'

Back at his one-bedroom flat Fash got straight down to business. 'Afterwards he got straight out of bed and said we had to go. I did feel used. But I was overwhelmed by his looks, beautiful body and personality.'

When Fashanu moved to Millwall a year later, they stayed in touch. She was a very interested spectator when Millwall travelled to Lincoln City, and won 1–0. 'After the match,' Niki said, 'John took me down an alley behind the stadium and had sex with me. I felt so dreadful afterwards and I started to cry. But I loved him and would do anything for him. And he knew it.'

Fashanu had begun dating Spanish model Marisol Acuna in 1980, but, says Niki, still continued to see her, including one afternoon as he recovered from an injury in hospital.

Niki said: 'When I turned up at his private room, Marisol was there. I made my excuses and left. An hour later I rang him and he said, "You did well, darling. Come back over." When I arrived, he was feeling really randy and we had sex. I was paranoid that someone might come in. But John didn't give a damn.'

The affair continued even when Marisol became pregnant then had their daughter, Amal, in 1990. But Marisol had her suspicions. The couple twice cancelled their wedding, and finally, in 1991, they split over his affair with the wife of a business partner. Marisol said: 'John was kind, generous, romantic, a good father and a great lover. He had money, good looks and charisma and he had women literally falling at his feet. I saw what they were like when I went out with him. They'd thrust pieces of paper into his hand with their addresses and phone numbers on them in front of me. Looking back, I think he probably did cheat on me more than once but I still believe John really did love me.'

When Marisol confronted him, Fash denied everything but

moved out that night. 'Something broke in my heart,' she said. 'Even though I was still in love with him I couldn't trust him any more. If you put a plate of caviar in front of someone who loves caviar, they will eat it, won't they?'

One of the affairs was with old flame Niki, whom he installed in a friend's London flat, bedding her regularly in his own apartment downstairs. During this time he also met wife-to-be Melissa, daughter of a wealthy diplomat from Gabon. Then, says Niki: 'One day, a new girl, Anna, arrived at the house. She said she was a friend of John's. I feared the worst and I was right. I later found he was sleeping with Anna *and* me *and* Melissa *and* a girl called Chantel.'

Fash had pulled Anna on Wimbledon's summer tour of Sweden. She said: 'He was an incredible charmer. He invited me up to his room and we made passionate love. Then he invited me to London. I was drawn like a magnet. When I arrived, he went straight to the point, took me into his bedroom and had his way. It wasn't love-making. I left in tears and went back to Sweden but he asked me to come back. He'd said he hadn't been with a girl for over four months. Incredibly, I believed him.' The *Gladiators* host even bonked Anna backstage as he filmed the show at Wembley Arena.

Anna added: 'I later met Melissa, the real love of his life. She was really nice. But once while she was in the penthouse we had sex on the staircase. He just didn't seem to care.'

Fashanu even let Anna stay with them for a month. 'Melissa didn't seem to mind,' claimed Anna. 'I slept in a spare room on an inflatable mattress. But one night John sneaked in and we had sex. When I think what he's done to us, it makes me feel sick. To have three women on the go at once is bad enough. But to put two lovers up in the same house, when they had no idea he was sleeping with both of them, is beyond belief.'

Niki agreed: 'Anna and I were both passionately in love with him but all along he looked upon us as his sex toys to pick up and drop at his pleasure. He has an incredible hold over women, an insatiable appetite for sex, not love-making, just raw sex!'

Fashanu once bragged: 'I always try and stay well clear of problematic women.' Now Niki and Anna steered clear of *him* and moved out.

Fashanu confirmed he had slept with the girls in taped phone calls to Niki. He said: 'We had a good friendship. OK, once in a while I slept with you. Anna, when she didn't have somebody there, when I wasn't going out with Melissa, once in a while. I told Melissa that Anna's a good friend. No problem at all.'

And that was all *before* the match-fixing trial even began . . .

Winchester Crown Court heard how Fashanu had arranged with former Wimbledon teammate Hans Segers that they would cover for each other if their partners rang. Segers said: 'I asked John quite a few times to cover for me.' In return, he explained, he had done 'quite a few favours' for Fashanu while the England striker carried on with a 'quite well-known pop singer'.

Was this sex-addict singer Sinitta? The self-confessed maneater – whose hits included 'So Macho' and 'Toy Boy' – once boasted of having sex every single day, and claimed David Essex and Brad Pitt as former conquests. Fashanu later counted her among his.

Fashanu's business partner Glyn Mason also revealed he was an 'alibi' for the affairs, and confessed he 'could not keep up' with the player's love life.

Fashanu preferred not to take the stand. And, after a retrial, all three footballers, plus businessman Heng Suan Lim, 31, were cleared. Fash, however, was ordered to pay his own £650,000 costs after the judge said he 'brought suspicion on himself'. Grobbelaar sued the newspaper that had broken the story for libel, with disastrous consequences.

A few months after the trial ended, Melissa gave birth to Amir. Their second son, Akim, was born two years later in 1998. In the years since his court victory, Fashanu has rebuilt his business career, becoming Nigeria's Sports Ambassador, and a UNICEF representative and sports agent.

In April 2003, he even relaunched his TV career on reality show *I'm A Celebrity, Get Me Out Of Here!* alongside beauties Danniella WESTBROOK and Catalina. In July 2003, he denied new allegations of match-fixing after an undercover sting by the *News of the World*.

● Fashanu was grief-stricken when an ex-girlfriend was murdered by a stalker. Beautiful Joan Francisco, a gynaecologist who dated Fash in the early '90s, was strangled with a vacuum cleaner flex at her St John's Wood flat on Boxing Day 1994. Prime suspect Anthony Diedrick, her ex-lover, was never charged because of

insufficient evidence. But in 1998 a civil court ordered him to pay
£50,000 damages to Joan's family. Mr Justice Allott told Diedrick:
'I find assault and battery, in effect murder, to have been proved.'

FASHANU, Justin

Born: Barking 19.2.1961; Died: 2.5.1998
Career: Norwich City, Nottingham Forest, Southampton, Notts County,
Brighton and Hove Albion, Manchester City, West Ham United, Leyton
Orient, Torquay United, Airdrieonians, Heart of Midlothian
Carrow Road, Norwich, February 1980
With his back to goal and a defender at his back, little-known Justin
Fashanu, 19, flicks the ball to his right, swivels and thunders a
swirling, curving, 30-yard left-foot volley past Liverpool and
England keeper Ray Clemence. The youngster turns and walks away
with a modest smile and an understated wag of his finger after his
'Goal of the Season'.

Shoreditch, east London, May 1998
Justin Fashanu, 37, spends six hours at Chariots Roman Spa – a GAY
bath house in London's Whitechapel. Some say he is agitated, others
happy, as he uses the spa's saunas, pool and steam room. At 8 p.m.
he leaves. Sixteen hours later his body is discovered hanging from
the rafters of a lock-up garage in a railway arch opposite.

If Fashanu's suicide had been the final act of a famous ex-footballer
facing 40 and an empty future, it would not be the first, or probably,
the last. But Fashanu died for an appallingly different reason.

Ellicott City, Maryland, April 1998
Justin Fashanu, Maryland Mania coach, offers joints and beers to six
youngsters at a party in his home in Ellicott City, not far from
Washington DC. All the youths were under the legal drinking age of
21. One boy, DJ, aged 17, later claims: 'I walked into a bedroom to
call my girlfriend and Justin followed. While I was talking to Laura,
he reached around and started fondling me. I got up, turned around
and told Justin I wasn't gay and I preferred women. He said he was
sorry and "nothing would happen again. Can we let the night go on
as it was?" I said that was fine by me. We were still drinking,

dancing, having a good time. About midnight I fell asleep on the couch. The next thing I remember is waking up in the bedroom with him. I looked down and my clothing wasn't on me and Justin was performing oral sex on me. I got my clothes and left.'

Fashanu's deadly downfall had begun.

DJ alerted police and Fashanu went voluntarily to a police station to deny the allegations and was released. But when officers arrived at his home the next day to do forensic tests, he had fled to England. Medical examinations were said to have shown signs of a sexual assault on DJ and, on 3 April, Fashanu was charged in his absence with second-degree sexual assault, first-degree assault and second-degree assault. The sex offence alone carried a maximum 20-year jail sentence.

When British papers carried the story, Fashanu convinced himself police would be hunting for him in London. He believed, too, that he would then be found guilty if the case went to court. So Fashanu took his own life first. In a three-page suicide note left in his Filofax, the fallen star wrote:

> Well, if anyone finds this note, hopefully I won't be around to see it. But let's begin at the beginning. What a start, everything going so well then I felt I was abandoned, left alone, without anybody to turn to.
>
> Being gay and a personality is so hard but everybody has it hard at the moment so I can't complain about that.
>
> I want to say I didn't sexually assault the young boy. He willingly had sex with me and then the next day asked for money. When I said no, he said 'you wait and see'.
>
> If that is the case, I hear you say, why did I run? Well, justice isn't always fair. I felt I wouldn't get a fair trial because of my homosexuality.
>
> Silly thing really but you know what happens when you panic. I want to die rather than put my friends and family through any more unhappiness!
>
> I wish I was more of a good son, brother, uncle and friend. But I tried my best. This seems to be a really hard world. I hope the Jesus I love welcomes me home. I will at last find peace.

Ironically, Fashanu's inquest was told British police had no warrant for his arrest. DC Andrew Ormison said: 'At the time, there was no request from any other agency to seek the whereabouts or the arrest of Justin Fashanu.'

Coroner Dr Stephen Chan said: 'This was a very tragic end for a man who had become a fallen hero, but in the eyes of many, a man who succeeded in life against tremendous odds.'

The seeds of self-destruction and the signposts to disaster are now clear. In a blur of half-truths and blatant lies Fashanu:

- CRUISED gay bars and clubs in secret;
- SUED *The People* newspaper over gay rumours in 1982 and won; then . . .
- ADMITTED it was true eight years later;
- CLAIMED one in four footballers was gay;
- BRAGGED of a straight affair with *Coronation Street* TV star Julie Goodyear;
- BOASTED of three-in-a-bed gay affairs with two Government ministers to try and scam newspapers for £300,000;
- TIPPED OFF police he had information on the kinky sex death of a Tory MP;
- CONFESSED it was all a lie and lost his job;
- FLED to America where he boasted of his deep faith in God, yet
- TRAWLED notorious hardcore gay clubs.

It was a downward spiral as spectacular as his rise to fame from the toughest of starts in life.

Justin and his brother John, aged just six and five, had been handed by their mother Pearl to a Barnardo's home when their lawyer father returned to Nigeria and she felt she could not cope. Eventually, the boys were adopted by Betty and Alf Jackson and grew up comfortably in the quiet Norfolk village of Shropham. Both boys showed promise at football and were spotted by famed Norwich City scout Ronnie Brookes. Justin showed most potential – his goals earned a £1 million move to Brian Clough's Nottingham Forest. 'That move was the biggest mistake of my life,' said Fashanu.

A born-again Christian, he became troubled by his church's attitude to sex outside marriage. 'I stopped having sex with my girlfriend and that's when I started to have homosexual feelings.' He regularly visited Nottingham's homosexual clubs. Clough found out, and suspended him after asking him:

'Where do you go if you want a loaf of bread?'

'A baker's, I suppose.'

'Where do you go if you want a leg of lamb?'

'A butcher's.'

'So why do you keep going to that bloody poofs' club?'

When he still turned up for training, a police officer ejected him from the premises. Within a year he was handed to Notts County for just £150,000. After a good start, he gashed his knee on the pitch, mud entered the wound and blood poisoning set in. His days at the top were effectively finished. He tried coaching in Canada and America, and bought a gay bar to earn money for £200,000 surgery to fix his leg.

In 1990, during a failed comeback bid, he finally admitted what had been common currency in dressing-rooms – he was gay. With his career ebbing away and desperate for cash, Fashanu began milking the tabloids. He sold the story that he was gay to *The Sun* for £20,000, confessing that he had first had sex with a man in early 1982. (In July 1982, he had successfully sued *The People* over a similar story.)

His brother John, by now a wealthy soccer star with Wimbledon and England, said: 'I tried to talk him out of the articles, saying if he was doing it for the money, I could help. I told him it would ruin his career.' It caused a rift. Soon Justin told the papers he was heterosexual again, and had enjoyed a straight affair with Julie Goodyear, brassy barmaid Bet Gilroy in *Coronation Street*. He said he dumped the soap star because she was too old to have his children. Julie insisted she was just a friend and said: 'He told a lot of lies about me for money.'

In a sordid bid for a final massive payday, Fashanu contacted the *News of the World* claiming he had bedded two gay Tory government ministers, enjoyed three-in-a-bed sex sessions with one, and, he bragged, even sat in the Speaker's chair at the House of Commons after one night-time liaison.

'This is the story of the century,' said Fashanu, 'but it will end my career.'

His agent demanded £320,000. The paper refused. Instead, for just £1,000 up front with £300,000 on publication, they revealed the tale to the rival *People*. The paper could find no evidence and smelt a rat.

Instead of reporting his allegations, *The People* exposed Fashanu for peddling lies. A disastrous chain of events began. First he denied ever speaking to the paper and complained to the Press Complaints Commission. Then Hardie called police investigating the death of Tory MP Stephen Milligan, who was found at his home suffocated in bondage gear and with an orange in his mouth. He claimed Fashanu had information to help their inquiries. Officers interviewed the footballer and quickly announced he was a time-waster who knew nothing about the case. The following day Fashanu admitted making the story up in a bid to get more money from the papers. His bosses at Scottish side Hearts fired him instantly for 'conduct unbecoming a professional footballer' and in February 1995 he left the country.

After a series of short-term positions, he accepted the £50,000-a-year coaching job with Maryland Mania. Again he explored the thriving and often dangerous gay scene. In nearby Washington DC he was a regular face in the low-rent homosexual bars of Dupont Circle, including Mr P's, popular with young, adventurous gay men, and Trio. But at the same time he worshipped regularly at Columbia's Bridgeway Community Church.

Fashanu was a man in torment and, after his ill-judged drinking and sex session with boys on 25 March 1998, found himself in the middle of a scandal that, for once, was real. Within five weeks he was dead.

FERDINAND, Les

Born: Acton 8.12.1966

Career: Hayes, Queens Park Rangers, Besiktas (loan), Brentford (loan), Newcastle United, Tottenham Hotspur, West Ham United, Leicester City

It wasn't just in front of goal that Lusty Les rewrote the scoring record books. He promised to marry his stunning model mistress then dumped her twice – for a TV presenter and then for the mother of his children.

The muscular number 9 enjoyed a seven-month fling with Dutch *Vogue* model Eva Dijkstra, then told her he was also sleeping with

Dani BEHR. Les told both his mistresses he lived with his 'friend' Angelea only for the sake of their eight-year-old son. Then he got her pregnant again . . .

Eva met Les at The Spot bar in London's Covent Garden, where the QPR star was partying with friends in February 1995. 'I'll never forget my first glimpse of him,' said swooning Eva. 'He was wearing a baseball hat, a beige linen shirt and slacks. He looked gorgeous. I went over and said hello. Ten minutes later, Les came over. I didn't have a clue who he was. All I knew was I'd met a man I really fancied and I could tell he liked me too.'

Eva should have smelt a rat when she invited him to a party days later and he turned up with blonde TV host Dani Behr. 'They were giggling together all night long,' said Eva.

A week later she saw Les again at The Spot. He got her phone number and arranged a dinner date. After a Chinese, Les dropped her off at her flat and gave her a kiss on the cheek. 'He behaved like the perfect gentleman,' said Eva, 'and I was dazzled. I told Les I had been hurt by men. He took my hand, gazed at me with his deep brown eyes and said, "Don't just listen to what I say, listen to what I do. I won't be like all the rest. Just wait and see – I'll show you."'

Next Eva missed clue No. 2: Les explained that he lived with 'friend' Angelea Murray, who was the mother of his son. 'Les told me that he and Angelea only lived together for the sake of their son. I believed him.'

After 'the longest, most passionate, intense kiss I've ever shared' and saucy games with raspberry jelly, Eva finally bedded the striker at her flat – well, they couldn't go to his gaff, could they? 'Les whispered "Shall we go into the bedroom?" I said, "I'm not ready for sex", but as he led me by the hand we knew what was going to happen.' Mutual naked champagne-licking, to be precise. 'Finally, he pulled me to him and we made love,' said Eva. 'As he started to make love to me, Les whispered "I've been dreaming of this moment."'

A torrid, passionate affair began, with sex at every opportunity, especially after Les had argued with Angelea. Eva said: 'I would run him a deep, hot bath and wash him like a baby – shampooing his hair, massaging his shoulders and then soaping his whole body. I told him everything would be OK, I'd make love to him – and then kiss and cuddle him as he slept.' When Ferdinand moved to NEWCASTLE UNITED for £6.5 million, the affair continued.

Clue No. 3: Eva sees a magazine article in which he boasts of his so-called ex: 'Angelea has a great body and knows how to be extremely desirable in bed.' He told Eva it had been written a year before.

By April, Les had proposed marriage. Eva recalled: 'He said casually, "You know I'm going to marry you one day." Then he said, "I want to go to Holland for the weekend so I can ask your dad for your hand in marriage."'

Now this was a surprise. Les had so far evaded commitment like he muscled past centre-halves each Saturday. The proposal, you've probably guessed, was followed by passionate sex.

Clue No. 4: The trip to Holland was cancelled because 'Les couldn't make it.' In June, he set off for the West Indies on Newcastle's pre-season tour. He said farewell with a no-holds-barred romp in her bathroom as members of her family waited in the lounge.

But in August 1995, hours after yet another athletic hotel room romp, Les confessed over the phone that he was seeing Dani Behr. 'He said: "I've been seeing someone else, but only for a while. I was going to tell you before we slept together." Something made me ask, "Is it Dani Behr?"' said Eva. 'I asked if he was in love with her and he said: "We're just having sex. There's no hassle. It's cool." Then he added: "Do you still want to do the bed business, or shall we leave that out?"'

Eva agreed one last meeting at a posh hotel in Northumberland. Ferdinand arrived after 11 p.m., stripped naked and lay on the bed . . . to check the football scores. Eva said: 'That was typical. He loved sex, but he always checked the football results on Teletext first.' She added: 'He never intended splitting up with Angelea and strung me along from the start.'

Furious Eva took her revenge by selling her story to *The Sun*. Cornered, love rat Les insisted: 'Eva is a jealous girl. She will do anything now to make up any stories she likes. I'm a good friend of Dani Behr but it doesn't mean I'm having a relationship with her. Allegations about my private life will not affect my game.'

Over Eva, Les banged in 29 goals for Newcastle United to become

PFA Player of the Year. On his nights off he wined and dined Dani, while keeping poor Angelea in the dark. When he was snapped leaving London's Royal Lancaster Hotel after a night with the presenter in October 1996, Les reprised the 'just good friends' line. In fact, Dani remained Les's lover for another two years despite a series of fallings out. In January 1998, Dani described them as 'completely together and very happy'. But by October they had split for good. She swapped Ferdy for another of her on–off footballer fellas – Manchester United ace Ryan GIGGS.

Les did the decent thing when 'friend' Angelea became pregnant with his second child and returned to his family.

● In the mid-1990s, Les even found time for a secret affair with *Shooting Stars* beauty Ulrika JONSSON. 'They somehow managed to keep the whole thing hush-hush,' a friend said. 'They didn't want prying eyes watching.' Les was identified as the Swede's secret third soccer star alongside Sven-Göran ERIKSSON and Stan COLLYMORE.

FERDINAND, Rio
Born: Peckham 7.11.1978
Career: West Ham United, Bournemouth (loan), Leeds United, Manchester United

When the world's most expensive defender forgot to take a drug test in October 2003, he sparked a strike threat by his England teammates, was banned from football for nine months, arguably cost his club the title and missed the Euro 2004 tournament. But it wasn't the first time the cultured Manchester United centre-back had made an error of judgement . . .

● At 18, Rio celebrated his first England call-up with a boozy night out, then was caught drink-driving. It cost him his England debut.

● At 19, Shera Rosun, a Heathrow Airport worker, told how she had become pregnant with Rio's child and how he begged her to have an abortion.

● At 22, he was filmed having consensual sex during a boozy holiday in AYIA NAPA.

● At 24, he was questioned in court over a six-hour drinking session with an underworld crime boss that ended in a 22-year-old woman being attacked by a rapist at gunpoint. The judge made it clear that Ferdinand had committed no offence.

Sir Alex Ferguson had bought the Leeds United ace for £30 million on the back of his mature performances as England reached the World Cup quarter-finals in 2002. If only he had been so cool off the park. After his seedy shenanigans in the Ayia Napa VIDEO (slurring his speech as he told the cameraman: 'I'm out of my nut but I know I could get through the whole day again. The way I'm feeling at the moment, I could be in the swimming pool'), the prodigiously talented successor to Bobby Moore at the heart of England and West Ham's defence explained: 'I thank God it happened, to be honest. It made me realise early that you have responsibilities as a professional footballer. You can't go around doing silly things and putting yourself in situations where you are going to get into trouble. Things happen for a reason and I'm just happy that something good came from it.'

Wise words. But had he really learned?

At Leeds Crown Court in May 2003, another example of his naivety was revealed. Rio had spent six hours drinking with underworld crime boss Michael Archibald – known as Reds for the red BMW, registration RED9, he drove – in January 2002. At Hi Fi nightclub in Leeds, Reds was said to have provided a woman each for Rio and his Leeds United teammate Michael DUBERRY. As he knocked back vodka and Baileys drinks in the club, Ferdinand was alleged to have pawed several women by running his hands down their faces and over their bodies. He also found time to ring his longtime girlfriend Rebecca Ellison on his mobile phone. The two footballers then hung around in a corridor near the ladies' toilets so women would have to brush past them. At 2.15 a.m., they allegedly pursued one woman inside, and in a cubicle, the court heard, Duberry put his hand up a woman's skirt and touched her knickers.

When she rejected the players' advances, she alleged Ferdinand told her: 'If I don't slap you up, then I'll get someone else to.'

After their nightclub escapade, the court heard, Reds drove Ferdinand, Duberry and two women back to the Oulton Hall hotel where he was staying. They drank champagne into the early hours in a room there.

Meanwhile, as she walked home from the club, the 22-year-old was grabbed by Reds' associate Martin Luther King, 33. He dragged her into his car, drove her to a secluded lane, partially stripped her at gunpoint and sexually assaulted her.

Prosecutor Richard Newbury suggested Ferdinand's friend Reds had overheard his conversation with the woman and acted on it. 'No,' said Ferdinand.

'I'm not suggesting necessarily you instructed anyone to go and smack this girl up,' said Mr Newbury. 'It would have been sufficient that Reds or his friend in the car had seen this incident.'

'No,' said Rio.

'Did you know Reds has a history of serious criminal convictions?'

'No,' said Rio.

'For drug dealing,' said Mr Newbury, 'you've not heard of that?'

'No,' said Rio.

'And for violence?'

'No.'

'Were you not worried about being in this man's company, about taking a lift from him?'

'No,' said Ferdinand.

Ferdinand and Duberry both insisted they only knew Reds because he was a football fan. Both denied being drunk and denied ever meeting King.

Mr Newbury questioned Ferdinand about his own actions. 'I suggest a guard told you females were complaining you had been touching them up.'

'No,' said Rio.

Mr Newbury suggested Ferdinand had touched women's faces while dancing before 'sliding his hand down'; Ferdinand denied it.

Mr Newbury said: 'For some of the females, the complaints were of indecent assaults.'

'No,' the star repeated, though he admitted a bouncer had asked him to 'chill out'.

On 22 May 2003, evil Martin Luther King was found guilty of indecent assault and attempted rape, and given two life sentences. He had committed the crime while on bail accused of raping a 17 year old, and had been found guilty of rape, attempted rape and indecent assault at earlier trials. Reds would soon go to jail, too. In

September 2003, after a two-year undercover police operation, Michael Archibald, 37, pleaded guilty to supplying drugs and possessing guns and ammunition and was sentenced to 11 years in prison.

Rio's punishment for crimes against common sense was a public airing of his dodgy friendship and an unfortunate penchant for women and drinking (he admitted two serious sessions a week if there was no midweek game).

● Rio revealed his caring, sharing side in an interview with *FHM* magazine in 2003 . . . not! By the time he's 50, he joked: 'I'll be sitting on a beach with the boys, having a laugh and leaving the wife at home. Then I'll come back, go out and see my mates and leave the wife at home again!'

FERGUSON, Sir Alex
Born: Govan 31.12.1941
Career: Player – Queens Park, St Johnstone, Dunfermline, Rangers, Falkirk. Manager – East Stirling, St Mirren, Aberdeen, Manchester United

British football's greatest ever boss keeps an iron grip on his players – from GIGGS, YORKE and BECKHAM to McGRATH, BLACKMORE and BOSNICH, disciplinarian Fergie has shepherded his fledglings through a series of controversies. But the night he accepted a lift from a 21-year-old South African beauty he had never met before, *he* became the story. Nadia ABRAHAMS accused him of indecent assault during the short ride to his hotel. Fergie totally denied the allegations and was cleared of any wrongdoing. But not before his worst week ever . . .

Wednesday, 8 October 2002
Sir Alex – married for 36 years – flies to Cape Town with wife Cathy for a series of official engagements. United were considering a link-up with a local youth academy; Cathy plans to visit their son who had moved there with his new wife.

Thursday, 9 October
Fergie inspects the academy, then meets lawyer friend Alex Abercrombie before attending a South African FA reception.

Afterwards, the party of 17 heads for the lively Manenberg jazz club on the Cape Town waterfront. Wine buff Fergie signs autographs and enjoys glasses of fine Vergelegen Cabernet Sauvignon. Elsewhere in the club, Nadia Abrahams, a computer programmer, is said by friends to be drinking heavily after a row with her boyfriend. At some point in the evening she gets Fergie's autograph and they chat.

Friday, 10 October
In the early hours she drives Sir Alex back to his hotel, Camps Bay, two miles away, in her ageing Honda hatchback.

8.15 a.m.: Fergie is woken in his room at the Bay Hotel by a phone call. Nadia's boyfriend, Brian EBDEN, 46 – married four times, with a string of debts and the owner of ailing Mother City Football Club – says: 'I phoned Ferguson. I asked him, "What gives you the right to mess around with my fiancée?" Ferguson denied everything categorically and said Nadia was drunk. I said if she was drunk – which I know she wasn't – why did he get in the car with her? He rang off. Had he apologised and said he'd been drinking and was very, very sorry, then at worst we'd have accepted that. But he didn't. I want justice.'

Ebden has secretly taped their conversation. Evidence, perhaps, of the failed businessman's plot to sell the tape, or of a sensible attempt to collect evidence?

10 a.m.: Ebden takes his fiancée to the Camps Bay police station where she makes a formal complaint of 'improper sexual behaviour'. A police source later recalled: 'When Abrahams gave her statement there was concern she was the worse for drink. We are obliged to investigate but are also looking at the possibility this was fabricated and an attempt to extort money.'

Saturday, 12 October
Fergie releases a categorical denial: 'At the end of the evening arrangements were made for lifts back to the hotel, at which time a young lady who had been talking to myself and members of our party suggested that she could drop me back at my hotel since it was on her way home.

'In retrospect, clearly it would have been better if I had travelled back with members of the party who were already known to me. But I had no reason to expect that it would lead to her and her boyfriend making false claims to the police and then selling their story to British newspapers. There is, however, no story to tell beyond the fact that she gave me a lift back to my hotel, which was only ten minutes away.'

Police officers visit the club to question staff and regulars.

Saturday, 12 October

Ebden faxes British newspapers offering an exclusive interview with Nadia for £75,000. Fleet Street is in a quandary. The sceptical *News of the World* turns Ebden down. The *Mail on Sunday* and *Sunday Mirror* split the £75,000 cost.

Manchester United back their boss. A spokesman says: 'We are confident his conduct has been professional as always.'

Police in Cape Town have still not passed the official police file to the Director of Public Prosecutions.

Sunday, 13 October

Nadia Abrahams' claims fill the news pages of the two tabloids. And a timetable of the evening emerges.

11.20 p.m.: She arrives at the club and chats with co-owner Dmitri Jegels, a friend of Brian's. 'I chatted with Dmitri about some problems I was having with Brian. He was very sympathetic,' she tells the *Mail on Sunday*.

When word was spread that Sir Alex was in the club, Abrahams approached him for an autograph. 'He seemed pleasant. At one point he put his arm round me, but I didn't get the impression he was trying to hit on me.' But later she claimed: 'I felt uncomfortable, not with what he was saying, but because he was giving me so much attention. The whole thing left me feeling confused and physically sick.'

But club bouncer Mark Hanekom, minding Fergie for the evening, saw events very differently.

Nadia, he said, was wearing tight jeans and a slinky black top. He said: 'The girl went over to Sir Alex, asked for his autograph and made some small talk. He went to the bar where she engaged him in conversation. They chatted at the bar but that was all. She became very flirtatious and some of the other members of the party became uncomfortable. She was definitely zooming in on Sir Alex.'

1.15 a.m.: Fergie leaves the Manenburg with Alex Abercrombie.

1.45 a.m.: Jegels gives Nadia a lift to her car, a blue Honda Ballade, parked a couple of miles away in Greenpoint, a down-at-heel suburb of the city outside another club, the Bossa Nova.

2 a.m.: 'I said goodbye to Dmitri,' Nadia claimed. 'As I got in the car, my cellphone rang and the voice said "Hi, it's Alex. Are you at the car yet?" I said yes and suddenly this dark-coloured jeep pulled up alongside me and the phone went dead. Alex got out of the jeep and quickly got in the front of my car. I shouted at him what was he doing and why the jeep had dropped him and then sped off. He just asked for a lift to his hotel. It was frightening. I didn't know this guy. He could have done anything to me. I decided to drive him just to get rid of him. I honestly did not know what to do.

'On the way,' she alleged, 'he kept putting his hand on my inner thigh. He kept going on about the night still being young and that it didn't have to end. It was sickening. I kept pushing his hand away and saying that I was involved with someone, but he wouldn't listen. He kept asking me back to his hotel for a coffee. I was driving fast so I could get rid of him sooner.'

Then, she claimed, they had a lucky escape.

'Because of the speed, I hit the kerb which punctured my tyres. But he didn't seem to care. When we got to his hotel, he turned and looked at me and asked me again. He said, "You were the sexiest girl there. Let's go to my hotel room for a coffee." He said he was leaving Cape Town at 2 p.m. and suggested we spend some time together the next day. I agreed just so he would leave me alone. Then he went inside the hotel.'

Nadia claimed she drove another mile and a half before phoning Ebden, who collected her. She added: 'I don't know how Alex Ferguson got my number. I didn't give it to him, someone at the club must have. And I can only assume he knew where my car was parked because he must have overheard me talking.'

Fergie's friend Alex Abercrombie gave police a very different account in his affidavit, the *Mail on Sunday* reported. He intended to drive Fergie back to the hotel but the boss told him Nadia 'seemed a decent person and there could be no harm done'. He drove the boss to where her car was parked. But Fergie was surprised by the distance and, as she had not arrived, phoned her to say he would get a lift with Abercrombie after all. 'When he rang off he told me she had asked me to wait,' Abercrombie said. 'Then she arrived with Dmitri. She got into her car and drove off with Dmitri behind her. Sir Alex phoned her again and after he rang off said she was turning back but did not want Dmitri to see her. She then came back and Sir Alex walked to the front side passenger door. I was parked behind the complainant's [Abrahams'] vehicle and I saw her reach over to the passenger door. She either unlocked the door or opened it. Sir Alex then got in. The complainant made a U-turn and we waved at each other. She drove off at high speed and the car wheels spun as she changed to second gear. I assumed that she was travelling fast to get away from Dmitri.'

Fergie seemed to be an innocent victim in a battle between Nadia, Dmitri and Ebden. Did they almost crash because of Fergie's alleged groping? Or because of the booze she had consumed – and the fact she had never passed a driving test?

That afternoon, South African police announce the case has been dropped. A spokesman for the public prosecutions office hints she may face prosecution and confirms: 'We feel our time and everybody else's has been wasted. There are no grounds for prosecution.'

Sir Alex says: 'I welcome the decision. I am extremely appreciative of this swift but no doubt thorough and decisive investigation.'

Monday, 14 October
The Mirror – a seasoned critic of the United boss – runs the headline RIDICULOUS and points out Fergie's folly: 'Isn't it ridiculous to go off with a girl of 21?' it says. 'Questions were still being asked over whether he was foolish to take a lift alone with the woman.'

Cape Town police announce they will not be charging Nadia Abrahams with wasting police time.

Tuesday, 15 October

Abrahams' boyfriend Ebden says she'll sue Sir Alex for damages, adding: 'The suggestion I set this up to make money is putrid, it's disgusting.' But Ebden is forced to admit he is being chased for £112,000 by creditors after his advertising company ACMP was put in receivership two years earlier. Alex Abercrombie says: 'We believe that may have influenced his decision to encourage Nadia to make false allegations.'

Fergie and his wife fly back to Heathrow. 'I'm relieved it's all behind me. It was a bit of an experience,' he tells waiting reporters. Alex Abercrombie says Fergie is considering suing for defamation.

Wednesday, 16 October

MPs table an early day motion in the House of Commons attacking the *Mail On Sunday* and the *Daily Mail* 'for paying up to £100,000 to Nadia Abrahams and Brian Ebden for what has been shown to be a fabricated story about Sir Alex Ferguson and which at the time was the subject of a police inquiry'.

Thursday, 17 October

Abrahams is lying low. Her relatives appeal for her to come home. Ebden denies keeping her a virtual prisoner. 'Nadia wants to remain out of the spotlight at the moment,' he says.

Sunday, 20 October

A new witness has come forward, the *Mail on Sunday* reports, to back Nadia's story. Thomas Makhubele, 32, a security guard at the Bay Hotel, claimed he watched the couple for ten minutes around 3 a.m. as they sat alone together in a car. But he was adamant no assault had taken place.

The scandal died down, but Abrahams and Ebden are clearly enjoying their cash. In November, they are spotted driving swanky new cars. Hers: an MG convertible with the number plate NADIA1. His: a BMW X5 with the plate MCFC (not to taunt Fergie but the initials of Mother City FC).

Fergie had come through with his reputation intact – even if his judgment was in doubt. And, after a strife-torn season, an eighth

Premiership title arrived the following May. But, interestingly, it was not the first time the boss had been the subject of similar sensational – but unsubstantiated – talk.

Soon after joining Manchester United from all-conquering Aberdeen in 1986, newspapers reported that Ferguson had had an affair with Deirdre McHARDY, a waitress he had met at a charity bash. They were said to have met once or twice a week at a flat near the club's Pittodrie ground. 'There was no deep, burning passionate love affair,' Deirdre claimed. 'But there was affection between us – intimate affection.' Deirdre also revealed: 'Alex talked about his wife. He said she was a lovely woman.' United chairman Martin EDWARDS swiftly announced that Ferguson had denied the affair and that his job was safe.

Fergie avoided a similar fate to his United predecessor Tommy DOCHERTY. Four years later Fergie landed his first trophy. Then rewrote football history.

FERRARI

Nickname of Faria ALAM, the racy secretary whose affairs with England boss Sven-Göran ERIKSSON and chief executive Mark PALIOS sparked a crisis at the FA in July 2004. Also, luxury Italian sports car over the bonnet of which David BECKHAM was alleged to have fantasised about bonking Aussie model Sarah MARBECK.

FISH

Dubious culinary excuse used by various soccer love rats to disappear for secret trysts. England boss Sven-Göran ERIKSSON first seduced FA secretary Faria ALAM by cooking her salmon at his Swedish home in July 2004.

See Malcolm ALLISON, Andy GORAM.

FLITCROFT, Garry

Born: Bolton 6.11.1972
Career: Manchester City, Bury, Blackburn Rovers

'Who's Garry Flitcroft?' asked millions of newspaper readers when the daftest love rat of the lot was finally named after a year-long legal war. Blackburn Rovers' skipper was revealed as a two-timer who cheated on his childhood sweetheart and their new baby with not one, not two, but three other women – then lost a fortune trying to keep it secret. The once unknown defender was now a household name for all the wrong reasons.

But it wasn't the first time the question 'Who's Garry Flitcroft?' had been heard. When executives on *The People* newspaper were offered the tale of the relative unknown's dalliance with a lapdancer in April 2001, editor Neil Wallis was unimpressed by the subject's low calibre. The story was spiked.

But you get nowhere on Fleet Street without persistence. When journalists discovered he had also had a fling with a nanny, the story was prepared for a spread inside the paper. But don't hold the front page!

Most soccer love rats would denounce the story as lies to their wife, begin legal action to prove their innocence, then quietly drop it when the fuss died down. But when Flitcroft was contacted to give his side of the story, he chose a different tactic and called in the lawyers. On 27 April 2001, they won an injunction banning publication. The *People*'s legal eagles fought it tenaciously, realising this was now a battle for the very freedom of the press.

Six months later, Mr Justice Jack upheld the injunction, deciding that a sexual relationship between two people was confidential. Flitcroft's lawyers had also successfully invoked the European Convention on Human Rights, newly enshrined in English law, claiming his right to privacy. The judge rejected the paper's argument that there was public interest in what he described as 'salacious details'.

But *The People* fought back. On 11 November 2001, it ran the story minus the names of the player and his conquests, branded the ruling a 'Love Rat's Charter' and appealed. In January, Lord Woolf, the Lord Chief Justice, made history. He ruled there was public interest in footballers' off-field behaviour, that press freedom was crucial, and that what a newspaper reported was down to what its readers wanted to read. He overturned Jack's ruling and gave Flitcroft's lawyers one chance to appeal. They tried . . . and failed.

Lord Woolf made a devastating denouncement of Flitcroft. Far from trying to protect his family from the publicity, he was negotiating to sell his story to a rival paper. And, he said, Flitcroft had lied to his wife: 'One reason the court was prepared to grant a stay was because . . . Flitcroft was anxious to protect his wife and child. He has now said something to his wife, but apparently not the full story.'

At midnight on Friday, 29 March 2002, Flitcroft's name, his story and the identities of Miss C and Miss D could, at last, be published. Miss D was lapdancer Pamela James. She had performed for the £15,000-a-week footballer at the Fantasy Bar, a topless club in Manchester, in November 1999 as he celebrated his birthday with teammates. As the 34C–23–34 blonde writhed on his lap and perched on his knee in her black-tasselled bikini and high heels, Flitcroft tossed her a £50 note for 30 minutes' dancing. Two weeks later, the wild Rover returned for the club's Christmas party and they swapped phone numbers. 'There was a real sexual chemistry,' the former air hostess told *The People*.

After pub lunches, passionate kisses and swapping Christmas gifts, they finally made love at her flat. It turned out to be a three-hour marathon, with stops only for refreshing glugs of champagne. Pamela told the paper: 'He knew all the moves and was an unselfish lover. That evening we had sex for three hours. When he got home, he TXTed me to say, "I'm in bed and am going to have nice dreams of you." I was falling in love with him.'

Soon Flitcroft revealed his penchant for naughty sex. 'He talked dirty to me as we made love and told me his rudest fantasies,' said Pamela. 'His favourite was for people to watch us. He would pop me on the window sill, open the blinds and make love to me. Once we had sex in a corridor outside our hotel room. We were very noisy and someone came out of their room next door, saw what we were up to and ran back in. Garry loved that. It was X-rated stuff. He was always fantasising about having sex in the open air.'

At a party, she revealed, 'We had a magnum of champagne in our room then before we went downstairs he told me to take my knickers off,' Pamela recalled. 'Garry got really excited seeing me mingle with people with no underwear on.'

Then Flitcroft broke unexpected news. 'He told me in a txt message he was married but getting a divorce,' said Pamela. 'He hoped I'd wait for him.' After initial doubts, she did, and even met his parents. But in June 2000, one of his friends asked: 'Have you got any mates for me?' Pamela said: 'I realised that to his pals I was just his bit on the side. He would never leave his wife.' Pamela moved to Perth, Australia.

Flitcroft immediately brought on a sub, Miss C – another blonde beauty, single mum and nursery nurse Helen Hammonds, 23. They had met in a Cheshire bar and once more he had said he was single. He even proposed marriage. Helen said: 'He said he lived on his own with a dog. He used me, stringing me along with promises that we'd be together for ever. I thought we had a real bond, but all he was interested in was getting me into bed.'

The player later claimed she had blackmailed him for £3,000 for breast surgery. Helen denied it. 'Other young women need to be warned about him,' she said. 'He is a coward, a rat and a manipulator – a sexual predator who used his wealth, fame and position to seduce me. If I was his wife,' she added venomously, 'I wouldn't stand by him.'

The tide of publicity that Saturday made Flitcroft famous at last. A 2–1 defeat at LEICESTER CITY, whose fans sang 'Does Your Missus Know You're Here?', didn't help. And one week later, new allegations of a three-in-a-bed sex assault on a drunken girl rocked Flitcroft and his club.

In December 2001, at the height of his battle to stay out of the papers, Flitcroft spotted fashion student Claire Nash at Manchester's Tiger Tiger Bar, where Rovers were again pulling crackers at their Christmas party. Claire, who had already shared drinks with a girlfriend, was beckoned over to the stars' VIP area by the handsome six-footer. She explained: 'I told him I'd lost my friend. He seemed nice and I thought he was trying to help me. I was enjoying myself and the drinks flowed. That's where the evening ends for me.' She woke in a hotel room at Blackburn's Brockhall training complex. She was, *The People* reported, naked, bruised and confused. Flitcroft was in the room with divorced teammate Craig HIGNETT.

Claire recalled: 'Flitcroft was pulling his trousers on. Hignett had just got out of the shower. I felt dazed and confused – I didn't know who these people were or where I was. I realised I had no clothes on and I started to shake and felt sick. I asked Flitcroft where I was and how I was going to get home. He said "I've left you some money –

you can get to Birmingham and back on that." He was gesturing to a pile of £20 notes. I felt like a whore. I couldn't believe what was happening to me. He left me £60 and went. Hignett never spoke and wouldn't even look me in the eye.

'My body felt bruised and stiff. I inspected myself and I had cuts and a carpet burn on my shoulder. I knew I'd been violated. I could feel that someone had been playing about with my body but to my horror I couldn't remember it.'

Claire dressed hurriedly and went to reception to call the police. While she visited a rape suite and was checked by a police doctor, Flitcroft and Hignett visited Blackburn police station voluntarily to give statements

A picture of Claire's lost night emerged later. She explained: 'Flitcroft and Hignett admitted to police they both had sex with me but were insistent I consented. I knew I had been in no fit state to stop anyone from doing what they wanted with me but my lack of memory meant I didn't have a leg to stand on.' She added: 'I have had panic attacks and even thought of killing myself. It makes me sick to think they both had sex with me and I was too drunk to know. They used and abused me.'

Police later told Claire there was not enough evidence to prosecute. Flitcroft's spokesman confirmed: 'This incident was fully investigated by the police and both men were exonerated of any wrongdoing.'

Flitcroft's innocent, and largely forgotten, victims in all this were his wife Karen – his childhood sweetheart – and their child Millie, born as he fought his legal battle. In May 2002, a month after his public humiliation, Flitcroft announced he had patched up the marriage. 'Everything's all right at home,' he announced. 'The last month has been difficult for me and my family but the fans have helped me through.'

He had survived public shame and private grief. Now, it seemed, the millionaire footballer would escape serious financial penalty. He had been ordered to pay 60 per cent of the legal costs, around £200,000. But, in a move that enraged many footballers' wives, his union – the PFA – paid half the bill.

The *People*'s editor was triumphant. 'Early on in this saga,' said Wallis, 'his lawyer looked him in the eye and said, "Garry, don't do this. Go home, tell your wife, say you're sorry, take the knocks and get on with life because within weeks it will be forgotten." By launching his privacy action, Flitcroft made himself a laughing stock and will forever get taunts from the terraces.'

FOOTBALL ASSOCIATION
Secretary Faria ALAM's flings with England coach Sven-Göran ERIKSSON and chief executive Mark PALIOS led to resignations and a bloody crisis at the very heart of English football's ruling body in July/August 2004. Alam alleged the Soho Square HQ was a bearpit of testosterone-fuelled rivalry. 'They surround themselves with the prettiest girls and like to argue over who has the best-looking PA. Once they have decided, they all vie for her. It is unprofessional but it's the nature of the big beasts at the FA.'

FOWLER, Robbie
Born: Liverpool 9.4.1975
Career: Liverpool, Leeds United, Manchester City
The Scouse Scallywag was destined to become Anfield's greatest striker – but he blew his place in history when he dabbled in politics! Already notorious for pretending to snort 'coke' off the pitch markings and being the first player charged by the FA for making false gay taunts after insulting Chelsea's Graeme LE SAUX in March 1999, he enraged the local MP by having a threesome with his daughter.

In 1996, Fowler was in Liverpool's Rosie O'Grady's nightclub, celebrating two goals against Nottingham Forest, when he chatted up university dropout Amy Kilfoyle, 20, and her best mate. Amy, who had left a politics course at Glasgow University, said: 'He was good company and very chatty. He said he'd heard of my dad, who's the local MP. Robbie invited a group of us back to his house for a drink. At 4 a.m. the others left, leaving just me and my friend with Robbie and his mate who'd fallen asleep on the couch.

'Robbie asked both of us to join in sex games. My friend wasn't up for that, although I was a bit drunk and might have. Then Robbie asked me to satisfy him. He was sat on the sofa with his mate beside him when he undressed and said, "Well, come on then!" I was standing up and I did. Then Robbie asked my friend to do it and she did too. Incredibly, Robbie's mate slept through it all. Robbie then slipped off my black hipster jeans and began kissing me all over. My friend left the room for a minute, but when she came back and saw us, Robbie took her into the kitchen. She said she satisfied him again.'

After her pal left in a taxi, romantic Robbie led Amy to the kitchen! 'He told me to lie down on the floor. We had sex right there. It wasn't the best sex I've ever had,' she revealed, 'but it was Robbie Fowler – and I wasn't going to pass!' (Just like any good goalscorer!)

'It was an unbelievable night,' Amy said. 'There I was with a bloke thousands of girls fancied, having a great time with my best pal. I'll remember it for the rest of my life – and I bet he will too!'

Maybe not, Amy. When reporters tracked Robbie down before an England match, he said: 'My nan will kill me for this . . . what were the girls' names?'

Amy's dad Peter Kilfoyle – MP for Walton and a Labour hero for defeating the Militant Tendency in the 1980s – was sickened by the revelations in, of all papers, *The Sun*. A picture of his daughter clad only in a Liverpool shirt on the front page of a paper still reviled on Merseyside for its coverage of the Hillsborough disaster added to his humiliation. He claimed she was 'emotionally fragile' and had been used by the paper.

But Robbie's nan Mary Ryder, 72, was not about to admonish her boy. 'He's a single lad. And if it's handed to you on a plate you're going to take it, aren't you?'

A football magazine once asked Fowler: 'Who have you learnt the most from?'

'John C. Holmes,' he replied. Holmes wasn't a coach or childhood soccer hero but a porn star dubbed 'The King', who had made more than 300 hardcore sex movies.

Two Spice Girls, at least, may never know what they missed. Fowler dated Spice Girl Emma Bunton, who even watched him in action – on the pitch – before apparently deciding his bad-boy image was bad for hers. A rumoured romance with her pal Sporty Spice Melanie Chisholm – a Scouser and Liverpool fan – also came to nothing.

When Fowler married Kerry, the mother of his children, at romantic Duns Castle in the Scottish borders, Liverpool fans – and the club's boss – prayed he would regain his Anfield crown. But persistent injuries and a training ground bust-up with coach Phil Thompson pushed him closer to the door marked exit. In September 2001, manager Gérard Houllier said: 'Robbie has matured a lot and has now married and has two children. He's a great guy and has probably put some daft years behind him. At 26, he has got a lot more to offer at Liverpool Football Club.' Two months later Fowler made a £6 million move to Leeds United. Within months he was at Manchester City, attempting to resurrect a career in crisis.

FRIENDS REUNITED
England keeper David JAMES had secret dates with a childhood sweetheart he met again on the cult website.

G

GANG RAPE
See LEICESTER CITY, ROASTING.

GARDNER, Dave
Born: Salford 17.9.1976
Career: Manchester United, Wrexham, Stalybridge, Morecambe, Leigh RMI
One-time best mate of Manchester United ace Ryan GIGGS and David BECKHAM, the football agent and former United youth player married Giggs' ex, actress Davinia TAYLOR in 2003. Giggs had just left Gardner's sister Emma, who had miscarried Giggs' baby. The love tangle was said to have caused a dressing-room rift that threatened United's title challenge.

GASCOIGNE, Paul

Born: Gateshead 27.5.1967

Career: Newcastle United, Tottenham Hotspur, Lazio, Rangers, Middlesbrough, Burnley, Everton, Gansu Tianma, Boston United

Only one thing prevented Paul Gascoigne from becoming the greatest footballer ever – Paul Gascoigne.

When he returned from Italia '90 sporting a pair of oversized plastic breasts, the stunt was forgiven as mere youthful exuberance. The chunky NEWCASTLE UNITED prodigy had already endeared himself to the nation with his explosive genius – surging and dancing through packed back fours with the ball seemingly stuck to his feet . . . then sobbing bitter tears when a yellow card against Germany ruled him out of a possible World Cup final appearance.

But Gazza was the Geordie boy who would never grow up. And in a haze of lurid headlines, the booze-guzzling, binge-eating midfielder:

● CONFESSED he was a jealous bully who beat up girlfriend Sheryl if she looked at other men;

● ATTACKED his new bride in a drunken rage and admitted 'I'm a disgrace';

● BEDDED a woman old enough to be his mother;

● SHARED a PIZZA waitress lover with Rudd GULLIT;

● THREATENED suicide when Sheryl refused to take him back.

When Gazza married blonde divorcee Sheryl Kyle, 30, in a lavish ceremony in a Jacobean-style mansion in Hertfordshire on 1 July 1996, *Hello!* magazine paid £150,000 for the wedding photos. That they had even married was a shock. The couple had reportedly split up and been reunited six times already since meeting in 1991, the year he injured himself in the FA Cup final. He was sidelined for 18 months before a £5 million move to Lazio, and, with little to occupy his time, Gazza hit the bottle – and Sheryl. After one violent bust-up he publicly admitted attacking Sheryl and apologised. Sheryl foolishly took him back.

After their wedding (a bash even more over the top than that tackle) the Clown Prince of British football appeared now to be the mature, doting dad to their four-month-old baby Regan and Sheryl's two children Bianca and Mason. But as soon as the ceremony was over the drinking began again.

In October – just four months after the ceremony – Sheryl was pictured leaving the Gleneagles Hotel in Perthshire with cuts and bruises to her face and three dislocated fingers. Drunken Gazza, based there while playing for Rangers, had beaten her up again.

Sheryl realised there was no hope, despite Gazza's public apology, and began divorce proceedings. 'We never really got back together again after Gleneagles,' said Sheryl, 'and once we had definitely split up Paul started drinking more and more.'

Women's groups demanded Gazza be dropped from the England team. 'We don't want a wife-beater to be an ambassador of our country,' said Julie Bindel of Justice for Women. 'It gives the impression that beating your wife is irrelevant compared to winning a match. I'm not interested in helping Gascoigne. Wife beating is a crime. I want him imprisoned. You don't talk about helping a robber or a rapist.'

England boss Glenn HODDLE insisted: 'There is no way I'd be backing a wife-beater. I'm actually trying my hardest to make sure there will be one less in the future. What a great example to youngsters it would be if he can change. I honestly believe he can.'

Parted from his family, Gazza didn't wait long for female company. Pub landlady and former model Irene Dunford sent him a nude photo and her phone number soon afterwards. Blonde Irene, manager of a pub in Chelsea, finally met Gazza at his friend Chris Evans's mansion in Notting Hill. But when he saw her black leather outfit, Gazza, 30, must have taken his eye off the ball. Irene was 52 – old enough to be his mum!

She said: 'Paul kept guessing my age and I kept saying "Higher, higher" and then he got to 35. I wasn't going to deny it.'

On their second date they slept together. 'I had obviously heard all the stories about him beating up his wife but he was always the perfect gentleman with me.'

Irene, a former lover of Frank Sinatra, George BEST and the randy Marquess of Bath, admired his 'chiselled looks, fun personality and superb body'.

When the story of their romps broke, Gazza denied everything, fearing news of his assignation would affect visiting rights to his son Regan and cost him millions in a messy divorce from Sheryl. Therefore, when Irene phoned him and claimed a friend had tipped off newspapers, he blew a houseful of fuses. Gascoigne told her to deny everything and said: 'I have said I have never had sex with you, right? I just said I met you once at Chris Evans's house and we had a chat and you left.'

Gazza feared he had been set up by Irene. 'I effing hate women. Women, they can get f***ing out of my face. I effing hate women.' Publicly, however, he continued to deny the affair, saying: 'I've not had sex for five months. I'm celibate because I still love Sheryl.'

Sheryl said: 'Apparently he's going round denying it – which he would.'

Irene's cuckolded husband Melvyn Barnett was more pragmatic. 'I'm sure we will stay together,' he said. 'We are too old to break up. It does hurt but this is the '90s and, while it is not acceptable behaviour, we are not living in Victorian times. It could have been worse – it could have been Ian WRIGHT.'

Gazza had worked hard on his fitness for the 1998 World Cup, but when Hoddle left him out of the final squad – purely on form, he said – the fallen idol was devastated. Sheryl was his shoulder to cry on, as they were briefly reunited for a holiday in Florida while he sat out the tournament. He hoped for a permanent reconciliation but later that summer, exactly 785 days after their wedding, a divorce was granted on the grounds of his unreasonable behaviour. The abusive marriage had affected Sheryl's health, the court heard.

Gazza was not in the court in London for the two-minute hearing. He was back in Middlesbrough trying to regain his fitness and have one more crack at the big time.

The couple remained close at times. Gazza even paid for Sheryl to have breast implants and after the op he sent her flowers addressed to 'Dolly Parton'.

A year later, Gazza unwittingly shared a lover with Newcastle United boss Ruud Gullit. Both men fell for the charms of pizza waitress Lisa Jensen and had simultaneous affairs in 1999. 'Ruud had the biggest tackle, but as a lover Gazza was in a different league,' she reported.

Gazza is still fighting his alcoholism in American clinics and playing football in China, where he retains his legendary status. 'I don't want people saying Paul Gascoigne is a clown or a daft kid any more,' he says. 'I'm a different guy now. I've learnt and I just want to be respected for what I've achieved on the pitch. I know I haven't achieved much off it, but I do know I've given pleasure to people watching me play football over the years.'

But Sheryl, who works for battered wives' charities, insists: 'Paul doesn't like himself. If I thought he was capable of changing, I might still be with him because I loved . . . still love . . . the man. But he can't change.' By summer 2003 it appeared she had had another change of heart and they enjoyed a reported reconciliation.

● Gazza's name was used by soccer stalker Carolyn Pick when she left a phone number for her England international victim, Mr X, to call. 'I though it might be a wind-up,' said the player of the sexy phone call. 'Paul's prone to that sort of thing.'

GAY

Liverpool and England striker Robbie FOWLER was the first player ever to be charged by the FA for making gay insults on the field of play. Fowler stuck out his bottom towards Chelsea star and international teammate Graeme LE SAUX as he took a throw-in during an ill-tempered game in March 1999. Le Saux – married with a child – claimed the striker made lewd claims about his sexuality. The former Blackburn Rovers left-back got his revenge with an off-the-ball blow that flattened Fowler. No limp wrists there then . . .

Both incidents were missed by referee Paul Durkin but appeared on TV highlights. Fowler was banned for two matches for bringing the game into disrepute; Le Saux missed one game for violent conduct. Fowler later said he regretted the incident.

● Two Arsenal stars issued denials that they were gay after suffering years of taunts. Centre-half Sol CAMPBELL cleared the air after his free transfer from Spurs. Midfielder Freddie LJUNGBERG insisted his interest in fashion design was not a sign of his sexuality, adding: 'I'm not offended. Gay men can be very fashionable.'

See Ian BISHOP, Justin FASHANU, KISS, Trevor MORLEY, Tony POWELL.

GIGGS, Ryan

Born: Cardiff 29.11.1973
Career: Manchester United

With his chiselled cheeks, dark curls, mesmeric dribbling and spectacular goalscoring, it was inevitable Manchester United's new flying winger would be dubbed the latest 'New George BEST'. And with a torrid love life during more than a decade of success at Old Trafford, the brilliant Welshman has done more than most to live up to the billing . . . even if he's a modest Casanova.

'I'm not a flirtatious person,' young Ryan told an interviewer. 'I'd never go up to a girl and talk to her unless she was part of a crowd I knew. I'm a very shy person, people don't know that but I find meeting strangers difficult.'

Er, right, Ryan.

Behind the shy façade lay a soccer stud with world-class pulling power. His first long-term girlfriend was former school sweetheart Sue Rothwell. They met at Moorside High School, Swinton. Later she worked in a building society and the couple enjoyed holidays together, but soon the emerging soccer star had more glamorous goals . . .

By 21, the youngster had enjoyed flings with models Victoria Smith-Crallan and Daniella Lloyd. Victoria romanced Ryan for six months after meeting in a nightclub. When he broke the news that they were finished, she burst into tears. He believed she was using his fame to boost her own career. When sexy pin-up pictures appeared in the papers, he seemed vindicated. He apparently told friends: 'I've taken some incredible stick over all this and now I've had enough. I've blown her out in a big way.'

Vicky's ex, bar manager Mark Nordwind, was still licking his wounds after being dumped and went into print with his bitter accusations in the first place. He said: 'Giggs earns thousands a week and I suppose it would turn any young girl's head. I am only sorry the girl had to be my Vicky.'

Even when blond bombshell David BECKHAM replaced him as United's – and British football's – pin-up to launch a thousand schoolgirl fantasies, Giggs thrived in the shadows.

In 1994, he embarked on a relationship with TV host Dani BEHR after she interviewed him for a show. Dani dumped her own boyfriend and began a high-profile eight-month affair, but Giggsy's game suffered amid their romantic commuting between London and Lancashire. 'He's been playing crap since he met me,' Dani admitted. United boss Alex FERGUSON warned him to knuckle down to his career, the romance cooled, and Dani teamed up with NEWCASTLE UNITED striker Les FERDINAND.

When Giggs met schoolgirl Davinia TAYLOR, it was the start of a stormy 18-month ordeal. Davinia was just 17 and a sixth-form college student when she met Giggs in Manchester's famous Hacienda club in March 1995. An actress on Channel 4's *Hollyoaks* and an aspiring model, the wealthy daughter of a toilet-paper tycoon already drove a £20,000 BMW. Some schoolmates called her a stuck-up brat. Ryan's final verdict is not recorded.

The pair were instantly enamoured. When she cut her long blonde hair, she gave him a lock to keep. He was a regular visitor at her parents' mansion, and, after dating for less than a year, she moved into his own luxury home in Worsley. She said of Ryan: 'We are in love, we're happy. I want to marry him and have six little Giggsys. He is very good looking, a great lover and has a wonderful personality.'

Within weeks she was regretting her move. 'He watches football all the time,' she moaned. 'All I do is tidy up.' (Considering Davinia counted Liverpool's football-mad Jamie Redknapp as an ex, she should have known the score.) Soon she moved back to her parents' home. The relationship limped on with sporadic temper tantrums before ending in a very public altercation and a welter of bad publicity in June 1996, when, weeks after a kiss-and-make-up holiday in the Costa Del Sol, Davinia was linked in newspapers with 911 singer Jimmy Constable.

Jimmy denied any relationship. But when Giggs next saw Davinia at his favourite bar, Peruvia, in posh Wilmslow, he threw a glass of wine, which smashed on a wall at the nightclub and showered her in drink.

Four months later he spotted her in the bar again. This time bouncers raced to separate the warring couple. Friends then took her to be treated in casualty at Ormskirk Hospital.

Giggs maintained his silence when reporters called the following day. Davinia, 19, told them: 'I am OK now. I've nothing further to say about the incident. The whole chapter is closed. I will not be making a complaint to police. I just want to get on with my life.'

The FA refused to become involved, despite a clamour for action. 'It's something that happened in his private life, not on a football pitch or anywhere related to it,' said a spokesman. 'We're not sitting in judgment on people's private life.'

Another reason for Davinia's unhappiness emerged. While they were still together, Giggs had apparently pulled a stunning model on the dance floor of Manchester's Sticky Fingers launch party as Davinia watched. Model Beverley Parry said: 'He came up to me, put his finger on my breastbone and traced a line up my throat until he'd lifted my chin and stared into my eyes.' It was another breathtaking move by the United ace and the first recorded instance of The Giggsy Treatment – the United star's unorthodox but dramatic and effective pulling technique.

After spotting Giggs and his new friend, Davinia told him she was leaving, and that he should return to his 'slappers'. Redhead Beverley, 18, said: 'We were dancing next to each other and Davinia was shooting me filthy looks.' When furious Davinia departed, Beverley seized her chance.

'We kissed and began feeding each other ice cream,' she said, 'but he was very wary, looking around him constantly to see who was watching.' After giving him a lift home she gave him her phone number. He never rang.

Soon after splitting from Davinia, Giggs enjoyed an erotic night with tabledancer Christina James, 18. Christina danced for him at the Fantasy Bar in Manchester in July 1996 – then lost her job for breaking the house's no touching, no fraternising rule. Christina said Giggs couldn't keep his eyes off her as she danced at his table, where he sat with six friends. When she took off her bikini, she said Giggs was goggle-eyed. 'He suddenly grabbed my hair and started kissing me,' said Christina. 'He kept saying, "Come on, kiss me." I told him to stop because we're not allowed to do that with customers. But he kept telling me I was beautiful. He asked me what I was doing after work but I told him I wasn't into one-night stands and didn't care if he was a superstar. Then I started dancing at the other end of the club.

'Later that night, as I left the bar to go home, he was waiting for me – I couldn't believe it and I was flattered. He gently took my hand and just whispered, "Come on." I suddenly felt like melting. He was being so sweet and he had waited hours for me. He didn't even buy a dance off any of the other girls.'

After kissing in the cab on the way back to his home, they went to the bedroom and stripped each other. 'He said I didn't have to sleep with him if I didn't want to. But by this time I knew I wanted to spend the night with him,' said Christina. 'I felt completely relaxed. He was such a caring lover. He massaged me and played with my hair. He was so different from any other man I've ever slept with. I've never had a one-night stand before, but this was like a dream, he made me feel so sexy. And it was so intense because of the way he kept his eyes fixed on me. The next morning I took a shower and he made me a coffee. Ryan said he wanted to see me again and promised he'd be in touch. Then he called me a taxi and kissed me for the last time.'

Soon Christina found herself out of work. Bar manager Debbie Ryan said: 'She broke the bar's rules in going off with a customer. She said she'd spent the night with Ryan and that it had been fantastic. But we still had to apply the rules.'

By the age of 23, Giggs had now racked up a Best-like procession of former lovers, many of whom had earned small fortunes as a result of their time with him.

Teenager Donna Buxton told how Ryan had pulled her just two hours after stepping off his plane on the Greek holiday island of Kos in the summer of 1994. 'It was the best sex I'd ever had,' said Donna, from Derbyshire. 'He was a really considerate lover and we had a great time. I couldn't believe what a nice guy he was. But the second night was a washout. He was so drunk.' (Donna died tragically in a car crash near Buxton in 1997. She had kept a signed shirt Giggs gave her as a memento of their time together.)

Model Louise Callaghan told of her affair with the United star in April 1996. He was, she said, 'charming and witty'. She later dated his tearaway brother Rhodri, who was not. He smashed all the windows in her home with a hammer after one bust-up and was convicted of criminal damage.

Later that summer he dated stunning Spanish MTV worker Cai Ferrer. But Giggs courted disaster when police arrested air stewardess Lisa Susan Rys-Halska for drink driving in the early hours . . . and found him in the passenger seat. They had been heading back to his home from the Forte Crest Hotel near Manchester Airport where his friends carried on partying until 4.30 a.m. in rooms he had booked.

Giggs met blonde Manchester University student Roberta Simpson in a nightclub, but dumped her for telling of their romance. Then, in October 1996, he got a slap in the face from Michelle Pardy, 18, after telling her: 'I usually remember beautiful faces.' The Giggsy Technique, for once, failed.

In trendy Phil Black's boutique in 1998, Giggsy turned his attention to store assistant Gilena Hooton. 'Giggs put his hands on my cheeks and told me, "You'll be a porn star one day."' Who would be holding the camera wasn't hard to guess and Giggs did indeed go on to bed the Rochdale lass. 'He was good fun,' she recalled. 'He didn't play on his fame and status more than anyone else in the same situation would have done. He was just a young lad doing what young lads do. Girls were always throwing themselves at him. We went out for a few months and a couple of times we did end up sleeping together.'

Giggs even posed as a humble brass salesman to pull a Danish beauty he met in a Manchester nightclub in April 2000. Julie Jakobsen, 19, said: 'He was very convincing. He gave me a 100-year history of the brass business and went into great detail.' At the city's Midland Hotel, in Room 421, Julie said, they made love. 'It went on for ages,' she said. But half an hour after she drifted off to sleep, Giggs woke her as he dressed and left the room, leaving a mobile number for her to ring. The following day Julie learned the true identity of her brass salesman lover.

She also discovered that Giggs was living with his long-term girlfriend, student Emma Gardner, at his new mansion at Blackrod, near Bolton. Emma and Ryan were on a break in their rocky relationship. In 1998, Emma, sister of his former United youth team teammate Dave GARDNER, had suffered a miscarriage. The couple were said to be devastated by the loss of their child and seven months later they had apparently split up.

Ryan's continuing close relationship with Dani Behr could not have helped. She was said to have been the shoulder he had been crying on after the tragedy. But Emma and Ryan kissed and made up soon afterwards and Dani and Giggs parted once more (Dani returned for another fling with Newcastle United striker Les Ferdinand).

Emma and Ryan tried to make the relationship work, but during intermittent breaks he continued to play the field. During another separation, in 2001, Giggs, still only 28 yet a veteran of over 500 appearances for the Reds, was said to have had the hots for actress Patsy Kensit, ex-wife of Manchester City-supporting Oasis star Liam Gallagher.

Then he reportedly fell 'head over heels' for Rod Stewart's ex-girlfriend Rachel Hunter after meeting her on a yacht in Monaco during a World Sports Awards party. The New Zealand-born supermodel and actress had dates with Giggs back in England but Giggs continued to build his playboy reputation.

Wannabe singer Suzi Wiseberg found him in bed with her best friend. She was sure there were plenty of other women during their months together. 'He treats women badly,' she recalled, 'but at the end of the day he made me laugh.' She even wrote a song called 'God's Gift' about the player. 'People tell me every day you're with a different girl,' lamented the 20-year-old blonde.

Amazingly, Ryan *was* about to settle down . . . but his choice of partner was blamed for a damaging rift among the United first team.

As the Reds' form faltered and Arsenal roared ahead in the Premiership race in January 2003, Giggs dropped the shock news that his girlfriend was pregnant. But it wasn't Emma Gardner, who United friends believed he was still with. In fact, he had left Emma for a new love, Stacey Cooke, and she was expecting his baby. To make matters worse Stacey, 24, was the ex-girlfriend of his old pal Dave Gardner, Emma's brother. Dave was best mates with David Beckham and a high-powered agent who co-owned Elite Sports with Sir Alex Ferguson's son Jason.

Dave and Emma were said to be furious at Giggs' behaviour. Even Giggs' family apparently did not know he had subbed Emma for Stacey. And days later the plot thickened when Dave, 26, announced he was getting married to Ryan's old flame Davinia Taylor.

The couples – who had once visited the clubs and bars of Manchester as a foursome – had now effectively swapped partners.

Giggs' love life was now more tangled than an Arsenal defence with the United number 11 attacking it in full flight.

Dressing-room harmony – a key to United's flowing football and domestic domination – was reported to have reached rock bottom. 'Becks and Giggsy used to be near neighbours and socialised. That doesn't happen any more,' a source told reporters. 'They're not the friends they were – more like just work colleagues. This has caused problems in the dressing-room.'

After Giggs struck twice in a Champions League victory over Juventus in February, United's stars insisted they were still all good mates. Gary Neville said: 'We're all the best of friends and for people to suggest any of us have fallen out is a big insult. Ryan's a great lad and a great player and it's disappointing when there are rumours like that flying around.'

When Giggs' daughter, Liberty, was born prematurely in April 2003, Becks and Giggs – friends since childhood as they rose through the Old Trafford ranks – buried the hatchet. Beckham visited Stacey and Ryan at the Hope Hospital in Salford and fussed over the tiny 3 lb 3 oz baby. 'Becks was keen to be there as a gesture of friendship to Ryan,' one friend said. Harmony was restored and United roared back to steal the title from Arsenal with a sensational run of results, including a crucial 2–2 draw at Highbury, where Man of the Match Giggs headed the equaliser. In July, Beckham was best man at Dave and Davinia's wedding – it came as no surprise to anyone that Giggs was not invited.

The key to Ryan's sometimes rocky lovelife may lie in his father's character. Danny Wilson was a brilliant Rugby League professional who wrecked his hugely promising career through drinking and womanising. When manager Fergie found the teenage Giggs partying with teammate Lee SHARPE hours before a crucial game in 1992, he laid down the law to the pair of them. Sharpe continued living the high life and his career suffered. Giggs learned the lesson and became a Red legend. Proud Fergie now describes him as 'a fine young man who has never given me a problem since'.

United's most decorated player – with eight Premiership titles, four FA Cups, a League Cup, Cup-Winners' Cup and European Cup-winner's medals in the safe – settled down to fatherhood with a startling new blond hairdo. It may have been a fashion disaster (and was swiftly changed), but maybe it was also a sign that the ladies' man had deliberately changed his ways.

GILLESPIE, Keith

Born: Larne 18.2.1975

Career: Manchester United, Wigan Athletic (loan), Newcastle United, Blackburn Rovers, Wigan Athletic (loan), Leicester City

Faced a possible 14-year jail term after being arrested on rape charges after a boozy night out with LEICESTER CITY teammates in LA MANGA, Spain. Three woman later exposed as hookers said they were attacked by the star and teammates Paul DICKOV and Frank SINCLAIR at a hotel on the resort. All charges were later dropped.

GINOLA, David

Born: Gassin, France, 25.1.1967

Career: SC Toulon, Racing Club Paris, Brest, Paris St Germain, Newcastle United, Tottenham Hotspur, Aston Villa, Everton

The suave superstar admits beautiful women fall at his feet. 'Everyone wants to spend the night with me,' he complains. 'It makes me embarrassed that women want to go to bed with me.' But married Ginola, the sexy Frenchman famous for his haircare ads for L'Oréal, wasn't too embarrassed to team up with another ad beauty, Vicky Lee, for a night of illicit passion.

Blonde Vicky, a silicone-enhanced 37–24–36 who had appeared in ads for Guinness and Birds Eye peas, was introduced to him at London's Café de Paris in early 1998. Family man Ginola had left wife Coraline, a former model, at home with their two children while he partied.

Vicky said: 'I recognised him straight away from his modelling and adverts. He has the most piercing green eyes and beautiful hair I've ever seen on a man. I knew he felt the same about me because I could feel his eyes wandering across my body.'

No wonder. As Ginola once admitted: 'I like women with chests. I don't like girls such as Kate Moss. They are too skinny.'

Vicky continued: 'I was wearing a tight black dress with a plunging neckline and he couldn't suppress that naughty grin of his. Eventually we ended up in the VIP lounge downstairs. He seemed so gentle and attentive that I was completely captivated by him.' At 3 a.m., Ginola announced he was leaving with teammate Jose Dominguez, and heading for the Portuguese winger's flat in Loughton, Essex. And he invited Vicky along.

'We left in Jose's blue Porsche,' she said. 'David and I were sitting in the back together and it was clear both of us were getting turned on. When we arrived at Jose's flat, we sat down for a few drinks. Then David got up and disappeared into one of the bedrooms. I decided to powder my nose in the bathroom. When I came out, I walked past the open bedroom door and that's when I saw him lying bare chested on the bed. His body was so fit, lean and tanned I don't think any girl could have resisted him. He beckoned me over to the bed and spoke in that slow French drawl of his. He has a body to die for and oh, does he know how to use it. As I climbed on to the bed, I helped him take off his jeans. David was very aroused by this time so I knew what he wanted me to do.' She performed oral sex, 'which he seemed to enjoy very much. David seemed amazed by my chest and couldn't take his hands off me. His hands were lovely and smooth and I remember he had finely manicured nails. David loved me to draw my breasts up and down his body while I gently stroked his hair. After he was satisfied for a second time, we fell asleep for a short while. At first I thought it was strange he didn't want full sex. Now I realise that that was his married guilt coming out.' At 9 a.m., Ginola and Dominguez left for training and she returned to her home in Fulham, west London.

Vicky said: 'We met up a few times later but David seemed a lot cooler about things. When a friend later told me he was married, the penny finally dropped. He likes to portray himself as the ideal family man, but it's not true. He's just like all the others.'

Ginola, mindful of his wife and kids, later tried to deny the affair, but his publicist Lindy Woodhead confirmed: 'Of course David's been a naughty boy.' She added: 'David will flirt with anyone and sometimes it goes too far but that's between him and his conscience.'

Vicky had already enjoyed romances with singers Rod Stewart and Fun Lovin' Criminal Huey Morgan. She would later have an affair with boffin Sir Clive Sinclair.

Ginola had also enjoyed a racy past of his own. In his early 20s, he once confessed: 'I was crazy. I was just grabbing everything I could.' Including money and women. Newspapers once exposed the Parisian playboy's naked romps in the woods with nude Swedish *Mayfair* model Marianne Hallberg. 'He's top of the league for lovers,' the breathless model gushed.

But he claimed: 'Even when I was young and wild I was never a bastard, I was always a nice guy. In relationships, I'm always someone you can trust. I'll never be a hypocrite; I hate this. I am always honest with myself and others and this is something I'm proud of . . . '

Hmm. No mention of Vicky there.

Ginola, now retired and working as a campaigner against landmines, maintains that he is now a caring, sharing family man: 'You see I'm a very lucky guy. I've got no problems in my life. At the age of nine I dreamt of being a footballer and my dream came true. I married the girl I always wanted to marry. I got two beautiful kids.'

Let's hope he thinks about them next time he spies a busty blonde in a bar. Why?

Because they're not worth it, David!

GORAM, Andy

Born: Bury 13.4.1964

Career: West Bromwich Albion, Oldham Athletic, Hibernian, Rangers, Notts County, Sheffield United, Motherwell, Manchester United, Coventry City, Oldham Athletic, Queen of the South

The greatest soccer Glove Rat of them all! Scotland and Rangers' brilliant keeper was a tubby yet agile and fearless shot stopper. But it was off the pitch that his ability to twist and turn served him best – even if it cost him his chance of World Cup glory.

As his teammates prepared to face Brazil in the tournament opener at France '98, engaged Goram was on his way home, resigning after allegations that he had got another girlfriend, sales executive Janice Dunn, pregnant and paid for her to have an abortion. He claimed someone was trying to sabotage the nation's hopes of winning the competition and walked out.

Goram, born in England of a Scots goalkeeper father, had split from first wife Jacqui Taylor in 1989 after, she claimed, years of his affairs, booze benders and wild betting sprees. They had one son, Danny.

He wed former croupier Tracey Fitzpatrick two years later, after meeting her at a mutual friend's party while still married to Jacqui. But as he was swamped by mortgage arrears – despite his £1,000-a-week wage – the marriage hit the rocks. In 1997 they finally divorced, with Tracey looking after their son Lewis.

One reason for the breakdown of his second marriage was his night of passion with Susan Ingram – a car dealer's daughter – at her penthouse flat in Prestwick, Ayrshire. At the time he was out of action. With a groin strain! With the injury fully mended, Goram romped with 38D Louise Montgomery, 26 – dubbed 'Olga Orbs' for her impressive upper body.

Tracey later told how she took an overdose of valium, beta-blockers and wine when he dumped her and walked out on Christmas Day. Tracey said: 'I couldn't cope with the other women, the lies, the disappearing for days on end and the mounting debts. Eventually he turned up at the hospital to see me. He dissolved into tears, pleading with me to forgive him and begging for a new start. But I knew it was an act. A couple of days after my suicide attempt, he was cheating on me yet again.'

Tracey explained: 'When I took his clothes to the dry cleaners, I'd find dozens of telephone numbers hidden in the pockets. And from some of these notes it was obvious that he was seeing several women at the same time. Sometimes he'd try to hide the notes in his car or in the garage, but I'd usually find them. Some women had been seeing him for years. But the letters said the same thing – "I love you and I understand you." It was pathetic. There is no doubt in my mind that Andy has been with hundreds of women. He even cheated on me while I was pregnant with Lewis . . . I feel sorry for him because he's going to end up with nothing.'

Within weeks the keeper had begun a tempestuous on-off affair with kitchen saleswoman Angela Eadie, 21. She later revealed he begged her to wear silk knickers for their romps. And he used money from ex-wife Tracey to buy her perfume.

Soon he was seeing 17-year-old model Karen Johnston. They met for sex in an old caravan at a scrap yard in Penicuik, Midlothian, but it ended abruptly when Goram cancelled a planned trip to London with her and headed instead for a drinking session with other Rangers players, including his boozy pal Paul GASCOIGNE.

In July 1997, it emerged he had been ensconced with latest girlfriend Jacqueline Mathieson, a retired porn star, in his hotel room only hours before a game for Rangers – a breach of the club rules. But when the heartbreaker met blonde bar manageress and mother-of-one, Miriam Wylie, at the pub she ran in Ayr, he finally said he had found the love of his life.

Miriam, 35, and Goram were married at the romantic Brig O'Doon Hotel in Alloway, Ayrshire, in July 2001. He told their friends: 'I've found my rock', and vowed they would be together for ever.

Yeah, right! Weeks later Miriam announced that Goram – amazingly now playing for Manchester United – had gone out 'to buy a bit of FISH' and never returned. Miriam revealed trouble had flared within weeks of the wedding. 'We had a good month but then he didn't make the effort any more. I have been on my hands and knees and I have begged him to save our marriage but he's obviously not interested. The last time I spoke to him he told me he was off to buy a bit of fish. There wasn't an argument – his last words were that he loved me.

'I said to him not to do another disappearing act and he said no problem. Three days later I haven't heard from him and can't get him on the phone. If he wants to go out with some silly wee lassie who's going to accept the lies then he can go and get her and let me get on with my life. I never imagined life without him but I don't want life with him if that's the way it's going to be.'

● Goram had a brilliant tactic to stop himself giving the game away as he kept all his lovers on the go: he gave all of them the same nickname, 'Boobs', so he wouldn't get their names mixed up.

GRAVESEN, Thomas

Born: Vejle, Denmark, 11.3.1976
Career: Vejle, SV Hamburg, Everton

Flash is not the first word Everton fans would use to describe their shaven-headed £2.5 million midfielder. While his teammates roar up to training in Ferraris, Aston Martins and BMWs, the quietly spoken Dane parks his £5,000 Nissan Micra and gets stuck in.

But flash he did – as Denmark prepared for a crucial match with Romania in March 2003. A snapper at their training session spotted horseplay on the training pitch and was later stunned to see Gravesen pulling aside his shorts to dangle his tackle over a teammate's head.

The amazing photograph was shown in papers throughout Romania and Denmark. Boss Morten Olsen told Gravesen his behaviour was 'unworthy' of a national team member, so to speak, but refused to drop his midfield hard man. His decision was rewarded when Gravesen scored in a 5–2 victory as Denmark came from behind to seal victory.

Gravesen spotted Romanian keeper Bogdan Lobont off his line and lobbed him from the centre circle. And instead of public shame, Gravesen suddenly found himself very popular with women in his homeland.

GRAY, Andy

Born: Glasgow 30.11.1955
Career: Dundee United, Aston Villa, Wolves, Everton, Aston Villa, West Bromwich Albion, Rangers

Sky soccer expert Andy Gray would need all his TV gadgetry to explain the tactics behind his tangled love-rat past. The award-winning broadcaster – once a lion-hearted centre-forward, Scotland international and the most expensive player in Britain – is the dad of five children with four different women.

Over three turbulent decades, the once golden-maned lothario:

● FATHERED a son 16 months before marrying the mum – Vanessa Crossland-Taylor;

● WEPT as Vanessa gave the boy up for adoption;

● HAD a secret child by model Sara Matthews four months after marrying Vanessa;

● got DIVORCED after Vanessa found out he had fathered a daughter with mistress Janet Trigg;

● MARRIED Janet and had another daughter;

● LEFT her for model Jackie Cherry who had his fifth child;

● DUMPED her to move back in with his ex, Sara Matthews;

● WALKED OUT for former gymnast and fellow Sky TV star Suzanne Dando.

Gray, whose own dad walked out on his family when he was two, once said of himself: 'I'm a good father but relationships are a different thing. When women fall in love, they really fall. But it's difficult for me to give all. I get itchy feet.'

Too true, Andy. Let's just take a virtual reality replay through that love-rat career . . .

1975
Andy Gray is 22 – the hottest property in British football as he bangs in the goals for Aston Villa after moving from Dundee United in October. Gray has no problem pulling in Birmingham's clubs and discos – and, as usual, takes his chances well.

1976
In a city-centre nightspot he spots Vanessa Crossland-Taylor. 'I was dancing when Andrew tapped me on the shoulder,' she said. 'I'd no idea who he was. All I saw was this dazzlingly beautiful, fit young man with piercing blue eyes and golden hair. It was love at first sight.' Soon Vanessa had moved into the footballer's home in upmarket Sutton Coldfield. 'Making love with Andrew was electric, real fireworks,' she said. 'Often we'd rip our clothes off and do it in the car before we got home.' But there are rows over his flings with other women.

1977
Gray is voted PFA Player of the Year and Young Player of the Year in the same season – a unique achievement. The affairs, and the spectacular rows, go on. 'He was rich, famous, talented and good looking,' said Vanessa. 'Girls threw themselves at him and he couldn't resist.'

1978
His first child – Jamie – is born on 25 September 1978. But the couple split up over his constant infidelity. Vanessa said: 'One little slut came up to me in a nightclub and hissed, "I f***ed Andy last night." Then she stubbed her cigarette out on my cheek.'

1979
Fearing Gray would not be a reliable father to Jamie, Vanessa gives the baby up for adoption. 'It was my choice,' said Vanessa. 'Andrew

cried when I told him and begged me to bring him home. He came to see us every day but I was determined to stick with my decision. I knew Andrew couldn't provide the stability we'd all need. I couldn't put a child through that hell.' Amazingly, the story will remain secret for 21 years.

Meanwhile, Gray falls for model Sara Matthews and they become engaged. But he breaks it off to be reunited with Vanessa. In September, cash-strapped Villa sell him to Wolves for a British record £1.5 million.

1980
January: Gray weds Vanessa.

March: He hits the winner in Wolves' League Cup victory over Nottingham Forest at Wembley.

May: Sara gives birth to Gray's second child – incredibly it's another son named Jamie – but she refuses to name the boy's father (Gray will only discover he is the dad 15 years later).

1981
Gray falls for model Janet Trigg and begins an illicit romance. Vanessa discovers the affair – and that the secret lovers have had a daughter, Amy.

1982
Vanessa divorces Gray, saying: 'I must have been mad to marry him in the first place.'

1983–1985
Though 29 and cursed with dodgy knees, Gray is seen by Everton boss Howard Kendall as the cutting edge that will turn his side into champions. Gray moves to Merseyside in November and six months later scores as Everton beat WATFORD 2–0 to win the FA Cup. Another goal a year later brings home the European Cup-Winners' Cup against Rapid Vienna, days after Gray's Everton lift the League title.

1988
Switches to home-town club Glasgow Rangers after poor spells at

West Brom and Notts County. Gray splits from Janet Trigg, with whom he has had another daughter, Katy.

1989

Gray helps Rangers win the first of nine consecutive League titles, then weds stunning 6 ft fashion model Jackie Cherry in Malvern, Worcestershire.

1990

Gray signs up as a satellite TV soccer pundit. Friends believe he'll find plenty of new scoring chances. 'Andy has always been a bit of a lad and a womaniser,' says one. 'It was bad enough in football with women hanging round him but now he's involved with football and TV – it's bound to put a strain on the marriage.'

1991

He joins Rupert Murdoch's Sky TV for its launch. His telly career is about to rocket but he combines the role with the post of Ron ATKINSON's No. 2 at Aston Villa.

1992

Gray fathers baby No. 5 – Sophie – with Jackie.

1995

A tearful Gray confesses to Jackie that he has fallen for his old flame Sara Matthews and leaves their home, a converted mill by the River Severn in Worcester. He confirms: 'I am seeing Sara. My marriage is over. Jackie and I are divorcing.'

Sara tells him the amazing news that he is the father of her child Jamie, now a teenager. Andy says: 'Sara called me. She thought it was only right I should know. I must admit it came as a shock. She never told me she was pregnant and I don't blame her. After the way I had treated her, I had no right to know. Now I understand. She wanted Jamie to have as stable an upbringing as possible.

'I never expected to be part of his life, then I met Sara in a restaurant. Her marriage was over. So was mine. At first, I didn't recognise her. She said, "Hi, Andy" and I had to look twice. Then it hit me – she looked great, fantastic – better than she had done 16 years before. We got talking. We had both changed a lot, gone through similar problems. We talked on the phone a bit after that. Then we decided to get back together again. And it was the start of a whole new life for me.'

Wronged Jackie, 30, is philosophical. 'Andy Gray is Andy Gray and always will be,' she explains. 'I know who the other woman is but her identity is completely irrelevant to me. There have more than likely been others while we've been married.' She told friends how she had discovered his latest fling when she found matchboxes from hotels he denied staying in.

Andy admits: 'I've done some awful things and it's not something I am proud of. I haven't been able to make relationships work. I've been pathetic at them. But with Sara I have something I never had before. And I've reached the stage where I do want to work at it.'

Gray is reunited with son Jamie. He says: 'I can't tell you how difficult that first meeting was. It was stilted at first. He was aware of who I was. Sara had explained all that. I knew immediately that he was a great lad. Sara had done a great job bringing him up. We're mates, that's how I would describe us now.'

1996
Gray is embroiled in a custody battle with Jackie over their daughter Sophie. He wants the child to stay with him and his new family at weekends. Dumped Jackie calls in a solicitor to fight him.

1997
The former Goodison hero turns down the chance to manage Everton. He insists his desire to be a family man and not his reported £2 million Sky salary is the reason. 'I wanted to take the job, desperately,' he says. 'But I discussed it with Sara. And I knew I couldn't have done that to my family. Here, I see Sophie every other weekend. I couldn't if I was in Liverpool.'

1999
Birmingham chef Paul Davies discovers the identity of his real father. Although adoptive parents David and Jean Davies had told him he was adopted, Jean, dying of cancer, at last told Paul the full story.

He said: 'I was asking her questions like, "Do I know him?" and "Is he famous?" She said, "OK, if you want to know, he used to play for Aston Villa and he's Scottish." So I said, "Andy Gray?" And she said, "Yes." I was amazed.' Star-struck Paul, of Shirley, Birmingham, revealed: 'Once I was with some friends at a leisure centre and we spotted him and I said, "That's Andy Gray." I had no idea he was my real dad.'

2000

In February, Gray tells Sara he is leaving her for TV colleague Suzanne Dando. They set up home in a £750,000 converted barn in Warwickshire. Suzanne says: 'Andy is the one person I have been looking for.' Andy says: 'I think we both want to go softly, softly with this.'

Vanessa, who had been living in South Africa, finally reveals the amazing secret of her love child with Andy Gray. She adds: 'There hasn't been a day in the last 23 years when I haven't thought of Jamie and regretted that decision.' And she finally discovers the truth about his secret child with Sara Matthews back in 1980.

Paul contacts his father with the help of an adoption agency. 'We were on the phone for about half an hour. I was very nervous. I just kept talking and told him everything about myself. I can't really remember the conversation but he seemed interested. I'd like to meet him but I'd want my dad with me.' Gray insists it's a private matter.

2002

Son Paul Davies serves one month of a two-month prison sentence in Shrewsbury Jail for actual bodily harm after a pub brawl. 'It's going to look as if I'm a bad kid and I'm not,' said Paul, 23. 'I got into a fight in a pub but I'm not a wrong 'un and I hope Andy doesn't think ill of me.'

Fans will remember Gray as a fearless predator eager to dive in and score despite the consequences. So, sadly, will the women in his colourful life. Current love Suzanne Dando, a former Olympic gymnast, will have to bend over backwards to keep hold of her man.

GROBBELAAR, Bruce

Born: Durban, South Africa, 6.10.1957

Career: Vancouver Whitecaps, Crewe Alexandra, Liverpool, Stoke City (loan), Southampton, Plymouth Argyle, Oxford United, Sheffield Wednesday, Oldham Athletic, Chesham United, Bury, Lincoln City, Northwich Victoria

It wasn't just on the pitch that Liverpool's bungs-case keeper was accused of cheating – jurors in the libel action that finally ruined his golden reputation heard how his wife wanted to end their marriage because of his affairs.

Grobbelaar was secretly filmed calling air hostess girlfriend Wendy White to arrange a date in the presence of his business partner – and betrayer – Chris Vincent. The Zimbabwean action man told her: 'Next week for sure . . . we will try', and ended the conversation with the words 'Butala needs you.' He then told Vincent that wife Debbie wanted a separation because of his philandering and suggested they retire from the Southampton hotel room where the conversation had taken place to a nearby bar where they could look for 'fresh' – slang for women.

Grob's wife sat in the High Court as the tape was played during his libel case against *The Sun*, who, in November 1994, had accused him and fellow pros Hans SEGERS and John FASHANU of throwing matches to make money from a Far East betting syndicate. Vincent had been part of the scam that exposed him, playing the part of a middleman for another syndicate. When a jury found Grobbelaar not guilty, after his second trial at Winchester Crown Court in 1997, he sued the paper for huge damages.

The Anfield hero, winner of six League titles, three FA Cups, three League Cups and a European Cup, maintained he was stringing Vincent along in order to expose *him* as a crook. When the paper's QC George Carman asked why he had called Wendy if he didn't trust Vincent, Grobbelaar, famed for his agility and brilliant reactions, replied: 'Because that's what Vincent liked to hear. He liked all the macho image.' Asked why he revealed Debbie wanted to split up with him, he said: 'He said my wife was getting in his way. That's the reason I put this story to him.'

Grobbelaar – famous for the wobbly-legged penalty shoot-out antics that psyched-out the opposition to win the 1984 European

Cup – for once failed to get away with it. He initially won the libel case and was awarded £85,000. But in January 2001, an appeal court overturned the ruling.

Grob fought on. And scored a terrible own goal. In October 1992, Law lords reinstated the libel verdict but cut his award to just £1. They ruled the paper had proved he took bribes, but not that he had thrown matches. A month later he was landed with a £1 million legal bill for the case, his reputation in ruins. But his wife remains by his side.

GROUP SEX

Many a footballer's fantasy – well it is a team game! But it took on a sinister new twist with the ROASTING scandal in 2003.

See Celestine BABAYARO, Lee BOWYER, Titus BRAMBLE, Andrew COLE, Carlton COLE, Andy DIBBLE, Garry FLITCROFT, Robbie FOWLER, Craig HIGNETT, Alan HUDSON Anders LIMPAR, Nicholas MEIKLE, Sarah MOORE, Emma PADFIELD, PFA AWARDS, Nigel REO-COKER, WATFORD, Jonathan WOODGATE, Frank WORTHINGTON, Dwight YORKE.

GULLIT, Ruud

Born: Amsterdam, Holland, 1.9.1962
Career: Player – Haarlem, Feyenoord, PSV Eindhoven, AC Milan, Sampdoria, Chelsea. Player/Manager – Chelsea. Manager – Newcastle United

Ruud by name, rude by nature. The man who invented 'Sexy Football' played away with a PIZZA waitress and failed to found the greatest dynasty soccer could have ever known.

The dreadlocked Dutch master was already the biggest world star of his generation when he proposed marriage to Estelle Cruyff, a partnership that would have created a host of gifted young footballers. Sadly for the dreadlocked one, Estelle, niece of the great Johann and mother of Ruud's fifth child, discovered his fling with Lisa Jensen, a humble restaurant worker from Newcastle upon Tyne, and called off the ceremony.

Gullit, already married and divorced twice, had found Geordie Lisa, 21, an appetising prospect as he lunched at the popular Uno restaurant. She visited his hotel up to twice a week for eight months during 1999 as he passed the lonely hours in the North-east, where he was battling in vain to stop NEWCASTLE UNITED's post-Keegan slide under Kenny Dalglish.

What he didn't know was that Lisa, a divorced mother-of-one, was secretly seeing fellow Geordie and soccer legend Paul GASCOIGNE at the same time. She later told a Sunday newspaper Gullit had 'made the earth move for me', but added: 'Ruud had the biggest tackle, but as a lover Gazza was in a different league.'

England 1 Holland 0.

The turmoil was too much for Gullit. Citing the press's interest in his private life, he quit United, adding: 'For me, my family always come first.'

First wife Yvonne de Vries disagreed. Then 36 and mother of his daughters aged 13 and 17, she said of the debacle: 'That poor girl. Ruud cares only about himself.' Second wife Christina Pensa, with whom he had a boy of seven and girl aged four, added: 'Ruudi has let everybody down again. He has so much but always throws it away.' Christina did reveal that the sexy footballer was a master seducer in bed. 'Whenever I was very angry with Ruudi, he would put music on and dance the erotic dance with me and everything would be OK,' she said. When she complained her breasts weren't big enough, charmer Ruud told her: 'Don't worry, it's nice – it means you can run.' Hmm. He even chatted her up with the corniest line ever: 'Today we have sex, tomorrow we make love.' Ruud can speak 15 languages fluently – especially the language of *lurve*!

H

HALL, Douglas

NEWCASTLE UNITED's millionaire majority shareholder was disgraced when a trawl round Marbella's vice dens was recorded by an undercover reporter.

See Freddy SHEPHERD.

H'ANGUS

Fans loved the saucy antics of Hartlepool United's mischievous mascot H'Angus the Monkey. Once he grabbed a rival mascot's tackle before a game, another time he playfully simulated sex with a woman official. And he was even ejected from one ground on suspicion of being drunk and disorderly. But when he was elected Mayor of the town in May 2002 – promising free bananas for all schoolchildren – his monkeying around brought allegations of sleaze.

Stuart Drummond, 28, the man in the 7 ft furry chimp outfit, was caught watching naked blonde dancers perform a 45-minute lesbian sex show in a pub. Only five months earlier, Drummond had accepted the £53,000-a-year job and promised to clean up the town!

The new Mayor insisted he had only been at the The Office pub for a post-match pint with teammates from his Sunday football team. Bachelor Drummond, who still lived with his parents, said: 'I wasn't taking any great interest in what was happening on stage. Nevertheless it was an error of judgment to be there and I apologise if I have offended anyone.'

See MASCOT.

HARALDSTED, Eva

Born: Aarhus, Denmark

Sued George BEST for breach of promise when he promised to marry her then backed out. Best had tracked down the 21 year old by making a public appeal after signing an autograph for her at Copenhagen airport in 1969.

HARDING, Matthew

Born: Haywards Heath 26.12.1953; Died: 22.10.1996

Tragic Chelsea tycoon Matthew Harding's widow made a shocking discovery after his death in a helicopter crash in October 1996 – he'd fathered children with his mistress and another secret lover.

Playboy Harding – who rose from teaboy at an insurance firm to become the 89th richest man in Britain – had a wife, Ruth Harding; a mistress, Ecuadorian waitress, Vicky Jaramillo; and a lover, his married financial adviser, Maggie Nugent.

Only his love for Chelsea could match his passion for the three women in his life:

Ruth

They met aged 16 at school and were married for 20 years. The couple lived in a vast country estate in Sussex, with swimming pool, football pitch, tennis courts and panoramic views of the South Downs for their children Hannah, Luke and twins Patrick and Joel. She found out about his affair with Vicky when she saw them photographed in a newspaper. Ruth said later: 'He was a good dad for a long time then for a lot of years he wasn't.' In the summer of 1996 he began dividing his life between Ruth and the children at weekends and, during the week, living with . . .

Vicky

They met in 1992 when she was just 21 – 17 years younger than him – and working as a waitress to support her first child. 'I slowly got to know her and the more I got to know her, the more I liked her,' Matthew revealed. 'It was something that just developed.'

He tried to keep the affair quiet, but in June 1995, months after Ella was born, they were photographed at a West End premiere. She soon took Ruth's place by his side at Chelsea matches and they moved into a £1.5 million mock-Tudor mansion in Wimbledon, south London. After finally moving in for good in June 1996, he altered his will. But Vicky had no idea he had been sleeping with his adviser . . .

Maggie

Maggie gave birth to his daughter Megan in 1994, while Vicky was pregnant with Ella. He bought the 40 year old a £250,000 house in Hornchurch, Essex, which she shared with her husband Peter, a fireman. Peter was named as Ella's father on the birth certificate but after Harding's death rumours swept the City of London that he and Maggie – executor and beneficiary of his £150 million will – had been lovers. Lawyers insisted the child should have a DNA test to make sure any beneficiaries were catered for. The result was positive.

A close family friend, who did not want to be named, revealed: 'His family [Harding's] has been horrified to learn about the affairs he was carrying on while he was married. The latest one about Maggie Nugent is a total bombshell. No one knew he was treating the women in his life as if they were his own harem.'

Harding, a beer-drinking fan of the people, had risen from £17-a-week office boy to millionaire insurance company chairman and owner of Chelsea's Stamford Bridge ground.

When he tried to buy the club, he sparked a bitter boardroom feud with chairman Ken BATES. It ended abruptly on 22 October 1996. Harding was returning by helicopter from Chelsea's Coca-Cola Cup tie at Bolton Wanderers when it crashed in fog at Middlewich, Cheshire. Harding, three friends and the pilot died in the flames.

Shocked Vicky said: 'I loved him so much. We were looking forward to spending the rest of our lives together. Now I'm just trying to be as strong as I can for the children.'

Grieving Ruth allowed Vicky to be at Harding's funeral, but refused to talk to her. They sat three pews apart in thirteenth-century St Margaret's Church in Ditchling – each ignoring the other and instead gazing intently at the coffin draped in Chelsea blue.

The tycoon's lifelong friend, Tory MP Francis Maude, told the congregation Matthew was touched by genius but, 'Like many people born with a capacity to do great good, he could also cause hurt.'

Ruth was scrupulously fair in ensuring Vicky and her child were looked after when the will was settled. They were left £25 million in a trust fund. Ruth and her four children received £50m.

Soon each had new men – Vicky fell for financier Robert Macarthur; Ruth for NSPCC worker Richard Gist (he died just three years later after a long illness).

Ken Bates was asked years later why fans still chanted his rival's name. 'There's only one Matthew Harding?' spat Bates. 'Thank God there wasn't two of them!' The women in his life might agree.

HARVEY, Brian
Born: London 8.8.1974
The pint-sized pop singer's soap star fiancée Danniella WESTBROOK cheated on him with Spurs' hunky goalkeeper Ian WALKER. Poor Brian only discovered the truth when he read it in a newspaper and, in April 1995, called off the wedding.

HASHIMI, Sam
The Iraqi-born businessman failed in a £6.25 million bid to buy Sheffield United in 1990 then returned after a sex-change op as sexy Samantha KANE four years later with a new bid to buy the club.

HIGNETT, Craig
Born: Whiston 12.1.1970
Career: Liverpool, Crewe Alexandra, Middlesbrough, Aberdeen, Barnsley, Blackburn Rovers, Coventry City, Leicester City
Quizzed by police after an alleged three-in-a-bed sex session with teammate Garry FLITCROFT and a woman plied with drink in a Manchester bar. No charges were brought.

HILL, Jimmy
Born: Balham 22.7.1928
Career: Player – Brentford, Fulham. Manager – Coventry City
'We hate Jimmy Hill, he's a poof, he's a poof!' Scotland's mickey-taking Tartan Army couldn't have been more wrong when they sang

about the *Match of the Day* host they hated for his digs at Scottish keepers. If only they knew the sexy secret of the Big Chin!

A soccer revolutionary for six decades, Hill, 76, is a ladies man par excellence. At one point he had a wife, a mistress . . . and a girlfriend, as well as admitting other flings on the side.

But he wasn't always a skilled seducer. In 1950, as a shy, inexperienced 21-year-old, he married . . .

Gloria

'I went into the Army at 18, came out and, before I knew where I was, I'd got a wife,' Hill recalled later. 'The world was so different then in relation to sexual things. It was much more secretive and you buried worries and inhibitions inside you. It wasn't a bad marriage, apart from the sexual side. Gloria and I never talked about it. I'm good at communicating to lots of people but not in an intimate way to one person. It's part of male shyness. The trouble was lack of technique in love-making, because how did you learn? Before you married it was looked upon as something you shouldn't do. My Boys Brigade church upbringing frightened the life out of me about sex. You had to wait until that moment when you were married, otherwise it was a sin.'

Jimmy became a self-confessed 'compulsive' cheat during the ten-year marriage. He said: 'I don't think I was that different from a fair percentage of my contemporaries. Do I feel guilty? Of course. Everybody would rather have a normal life where you marry one person, have three or four kids who all go to university and you live happily ever after. It doesn't happen like that for lots of people and it didn't happen like that for me.' Despite being the father of three children under seven, he left Gloria after discovering the joy of sex with . . .

Heather

Heather and Jimmy married in 1961, a year after he became manager of Coventry City. They had two daughters, Joanna and Jamie, but it was a high-octane relationship. 'We didn't jump into bed straight away, but when we did actually make love it all became so much easier,' he said. 'I think God, or whoever devised the human race, needed to have the marauding male to keep the species going.'

But the fireworks weren't only in the bedroom. 'Heather was Welsh and very fiery,' said Hill, 'a bit volatile in temperament.' He quipped: 'I don't have a bad temper but I know what it's like to feel like throttling your wife.'

Hill at least understood the consequences of his new love. 'The tragic part of it is that it brings an awful lot of unhappiness,' he said. 'Leaving Gloria obviously made her a very unhappy lady. It must have been awful for her and her life became vastly different. We had three very young children. I never lost respect for Gloria or failed to appreciate what a sensational lady she is. Now she's happily remarried and, for her age, she's still very pretty.' He added: 'If I had not divorced Gloria, Jamie and Joanna would not be alive. There are rewards for misbehaviour. Weird, innit?'

On a club tour of the Caribbean after Coventry's promotion to Division One, however, Hill met young, glamorous . . .

Veronica

Now Hill broke up another young family for his sophisticated new lover. Heather stayed in the Midlands, bringing up their family as Hill left Coventry City for London Weekend Television, where he forged a new career and set up home with Veronica in Notting Hill. The couple didn't have children, but said Hill: 'Veronica was, still is, a very lovely lady and she grew to be a young mother to my children anyway.'

But Hill's quest for the perfect match was still only at half time. 'Maybe men were meant to have three wives,' he mused. 'Veronica was my secretary but also my lover and there came a point where it got too much. We advertised for another secretary and two girls came for the interview.' The lucky winner, and future lover, was . . .

Bryony

Beautiful, intelligent and in her early 20s, the former art school student had lived in France for five years. When Veronica and Hill decided to leave London for a 50-acre country estate in Gloucestershire, Bryony gave up the job. Hill, now divorced from Heather, was in his element in the country, taking up riding and hunting with the local bigwigs. 'I hunted and chased the horses and the girls,' recalled Hill. But years later, after a chance meeting in

London, Hill and Bryony went for dinner, retired to her Notting Hill flat and stayed till dawn.

'He was going to America the next day,' Bryony said. 'I thought: "What have I done?" I couldn't tell anyone. He rang me from America but I still couldn't see how it was all going to end up, except in tears.'

They began a passionate, secret and guilt-ridden five-year affair. Bryony said: 'I felt I was betraying Veronica. Once, Veronica came to London to take me out to lunch, before she knew Jimmy and I were having an affair. It was dreadful. I had to pretend nothing had happened. I used to have dreams where we would forgive each other and collapse in tears. I never thought he'd leave her, let alone marry me. It was all very fraught.'

Finally, in the early 1980s, he told Veronica the painful truth and they split. Hill and his lover moved to Sussex, where they still live happily together. Despite the anguish caused by Hill's broken relationships, his women remained friends. Bryony even nursed Hill's second wife Heather as she died of cancer.

Bryony, now 54, became Hill's third wife in January 1991. But six months later he was diagnosed with bowel cancer, an illness he fought bravely and successfully. 'He was absolutely amazing,' said Bryony. 'He wasn't going to let it disrupt his life. He wanted to deal with it clinically, professionally and efficiently – and he did.'

It was typical of the football legend's determination to succeed. A born winner, he played 297 games as a swashbuckling striker for Fulham, ended the minimum wage as chairman of the players' union and managed lowly Coventry City to Division One before turning to TV, where he launched LWT Sport, then made 600 appearances on *MotD*.

He was awarded the OBE in 1975, the year he famously ran the line in an emergency at a Liverpool v. Arsenal clash. He remains the only football man to have been player, coach, manager, director and chairman, after running Coventry City and Fulham in the 1980s. In 1998 he quit the BBC for Sky in a £400,000 deal.

Bryony is convinced that her husband's cheating days are over. 'If he were to stray I'd do a Bobbitt,' she joked. Hill also now proclaims himself a changed man. 'You can have a go at me for all the years before,' he says, 'but since Bryony I've been 110 per cent utterly faithful. We both rejoice in the fact that we're not tempted elsewhere. You could say, "Well, yeah, he's just worn out", but it's not that – no, no. I should be put on a pedestal for my behaviour.'

Hill says of his womanising past: 'It's like being a sort of compulsive murderer, isn't it? When I look back, I think, "Hold on a minute, that can't be me" – but it was. They were all lovely ladies. I've been very well blessed.'

HODDLE, Glenn
Born: Hayes 27.10.1957
Career: Player – Tottenham Hotspur, AS Monaco. Player/Manager – Swindon Town, Chelsea. Manager – England, Southampton, Tottenham Hotspur

From Spurs' midfield genius to millionaire businessman to England World Cup manager, Glenn 'Glenda' Hoddle's career had been one brilliant success after another. As well as triumphs on the pitch, including two FA Cup wins with the north London giants, the gifted playmaker had become a born-again Christian in the 1980s – to ad-men and future employers he was, quite literally, a Godsend. When England qualified for the 1998 World Cup finals with a heroic 0–0 draw against Italy in Rome, the boss's future looked rosy. But the beginning of the end was just one final whistle away.

Three days after that match in October 1997, Hoddle announced through the Football Association that he was leaving his wife Anne after 18 years of marriage. The football world was shocked. The couple and their three children Zoe, 15, Zara, 12, and Jamie, 6, had been the happy family face of Shredded Wheat breakfast cereal. The ads were taken off air instantly.

Soon the truth was out. Hoddle had fallen for Vanessa Shean, wife of a millionaire property tycoon, whom he had met at the Royal Berkshire Racquets and Health Club, near their Ascot homes.

It was Anne, then 39, who had tipped off Jeff Shean about his wife's affair with her own husband, though he had been suspicious for a while. They had been friends for some five years before consummating the illicit affair.

Jeff was furious. 'I thought she was just good friends with Glenn. She had £48,000-a-year pocket money, a top-of-the-range Mercedes, a petrol account, a Harrods account and the kids were at private schools. I gave her the world. Why should she leave?'

And he told the *Sunday Mirror*: 'He is supposed to be a Christian, so you would have thought he'd have heard of the commandment "Thou shalt not commit adultery."'

The wronged partners strengthened each other's resolve to survive the break-up of their marriages. They met occasionally, Jeff, 45, telling Anne: 'Don't forget, in all of this we're the good guys.'

Six months later, in January 1999, the Hoddles' marriage ended in a quickie divorce on the grounds of his adultery. A rumoured £1 million settlement was negotiated. It was deserved. Anne, a French language teacher, had helped her superstar husband settle quickly as a player with AS Monaco a decade earlier and earn his millions in foreign football.

The Sheans' own 20-year marriage had ended similarly weeks earlier with Hoddle named as the third party. And for the once-worshipped Hoddle, things would never be quite the same. A disastrous World Cup campaign in France had ended with England's exit on penalties to Argentina and a row then broke out over his dubious handling of stars like David BECKHAM and Paul GASCOIGNE and his subsequent decision to publish a tournament diary detailing his private conversations with them. When he told a *Sunday Times* sports reporter his belief that disabled people were being punished for their sins in an earlier incarnation, the uproar ended in his exit as England manager. After a spell out of the game, he returned as coach of struggling Southampton before his former club, Tottenham Hotspur, lured him back to White Hart lane as manager – only for them to sack him in 2003.

HOLDSWORTH, Dean

Born: Walthamstow 8.11.1968
Career: Watford, Carlisle (loan), Port Vale (loan), Swansea City (loan), Brentford (loan), Wimbledon, Bolton Wanderers, Coventry City, Rushden & Diamonds, MK Dons

Holdsworth begged his wife for forgiveness when she discovered his affair with heaving-chested, man-eating 18-year-old porn model Linsey Dawn McKenzie. The Wimbledon striker met her at a lapdancing club in London's West End where she worked in 1996. After Linsey stripped and dangled her enormous breasts inches from his face, they swapped phone numbers. Following an intimate, illicit lunch date, they met up as he 'rested' at a hotel before an away match.

Steamy is not the word. 'We ordered champagne and strawberries, then lay on the bed and slowly undressed each other,' said the 34GG model. 'He poured champagne down my breasts and licked it off. We put the strawberries all over each other's bodies and ate them off each other. We were both really excited and ended up rolling off the bed and making love on the floor. Dean was a very sensual lover. He has a lovely smooth body and a very athletic physique. We made love a second time in bed, but at midnight Dean had to put the light out to get some sleep for the game the next day.'

Less languorous love-making took place in a car park at a London golf club. Holdsworth even had the audacity to take McKenzie to a home game, where she sat with other players' wives and girlfriends. 'That was typical,' she said later. 'Because he was a top star he was so arrogant and thought he could get away with anything.'

When Holdsworth's wife Sam discovered the affair after a tabloid sting, she ordered him out of the family home and attempted to cash in by releasing a record – her own version of Viola Wills' 'Gonna Get Along Without You Now' – which she sang live on TV. The charts were not troubled and she relented, allowing Holdsworth to return to the marital home. Soon he had transferred to Bolton Wanderers and away from temptation.

The model was stunned too. She claimed Holdsworth had at first said he was not married. 'I was gutted. I'd really fallen for him. What girl wouldn't? He was fit, good looking and wore stylish designer clothes. Then he told me he wasn't sleeping with his wife any more and as I was only 18 at the time I naively believed him. Girls throw themselves at footballers and they know they can have their cake and eat it,' she whined. 'I'd never trust another again, let alone marry one.'

Sam Holdsworth, not surprisingly, was furious, describing Miss McKenzie as 'Uglier than our pet Rottweiler.' Ouch. Sam added: 'She said he caressed her all night. I know Dean and, believe me, Dean does not do caressing.' She warned other women: 'These days I see the young footballers' wives when their husbands get into the Premier League. They think they know it all. I think: "Watch out – he's coming home on time now, but a year down the line you'll be waiting for the phone to ring and you won't know where he is.'"

The Holdsworths' marriage never really recovered and in December 1999 the striker struck his wife at a charity bash in Liverpool because she was dancing with another man. Holdsworth admitted causing actual bodily harm and was given 18 months' probation, and a place on a domestic violence programme.

HOULT, Russell

Born: Ashby de la Zouch 22.11.1972
Career: Leicester City, Lincoln City (loan), Bolton Wanderers (loan), Lincoln City (loan), Derby County, Portsmouth, West Bromwich Albion

West Brom's kinky keeper hides two guilty secrets from fans: the married dad of one was convicted of kerb-crawling and accused – then cleared – of sending indecent letters to a 13-year-old girl.

Hoult, voted Baggies' Player of the Year as they returned to the Premiership in 2002, was nicked by undercover cops two years earlier. Police had staked out the red-light area of Normanton, in Derby, after complaints from residents who were fed up with the seedy goings on. Officers watched Hoult stop his car and pick up a hooker less than two miles from Derby County's Pride Park, the ground he had graced until a month before, when he had made a £300,000 move to ambitious PORTSMOUTH.

The 6 ft 3 in. keeper was arrested and taken to Derby police headquarters for questioning before being released on police bail. 'We acted after complaints from residents,' said a police spokesman. 'We are determined to clean up the area.' Maybe he meant the penalty area?

Hoult, then 27, appeared in court on 26 April 2000. He admitted soliciting a woman from his car and was fined £300. That same day, details emerged of a new sex case, involving letters sent to a 13-year-old girl who had innocently asked for his autograph after a game.

In December 2000, Hoult stood trial at Derby Magistrates' Court accused under the rarely used 1953 Post Office Act of sending four indecent letters through the mail. The court heard that the girl, who could not be named for legal reasons, had been bombarded with letters between January and March 1999 after she asked for his signature. Hoult was said to have asked the girl to send him pictures of herself in different poses and wearing various outfits. They came to light when the girl showed them to a teacher at her school.

The letters were not read out in court, to save the girl, now 15, from another embarrassing ordeal. Hoult's solicitor, Steven Mann, told the magistrates: 'Mr Hoult accepts that he was the sender of the four letters and that they were sent through the post. This is purely a legal argument as to whether or not the letters are classed as indecent. His view, his motives for sending them, and his connection with anyone is totally immaterial. I would ask you to compare them to the so-called saucy seaside postcards that used to be sent in Britain. Is what is put in these letters any worse and would anybody seriously say these postcards were indecent?

'It might be infantile and silly. It might not be particularly attractive or what you would want to read every day of the week. But is it indecent?' After 15 minutes' deliberation, chairman of the bench Susan Roberts told him: 'We find that, although the letters were to us distasteful, they were not indecent.'

He was cleared of all four counts. Mr Mann said outside court: 'He can now get on with his life.'

A month later, Hoult was on the move again, this time to West Bromwich Albion for £500,000. There, his brilliance between the sticks – he managed a club record of 27 clean sheets, including seven successive games – helped West Brom back to the top flight for the first time in 20 years. Hoult was, though, a very grubby hero.

HRISTOV, Georgi

Born: Bitola, Macedonia, 30.1.1976
Career: Pelister Bitola, Partizan Belgrade, Barnsley, NEC Nijmegen Zwolle

Barnsley's lovelorn record signing made himself public enemy No. 1 when he claimed t'local lasses were beer-swilling mooses too ugly to date.

After just one month in Yorkshire, the £1.5 million player said: 'I'm finding it difficult to find a girlfriend in Barnsley. The local girls are far uglier than the ones back in Belgrade or Skopje, where I come from.'

Ouch! Any other complaints, Georgi?

'Besides, they don't drink as much beer as the Barnsley girls, which is something I don't like at all.'

Barnsley lasses were, understandably, in an ugly mood. 'He wants to look in the mirror before he talks about us,' said one local, referring to the swarthy Macedonian's monobrow face.

Hristov was invited to judge local beauty contests and wet T-shirt contests but failed to find love.

Two years on, after moving to Nijmegen, in Holland, Hristov revealed he now had a girlfriend. 'She is from Macedonia. I always said the most beautiful girls were from there.'

Incredibly, Hristov later claimed victory. 'Last year, when I went back to Barnsley to see some friends, it was unbelievable how many more nice girls I see there. It made me think that after all that talk they started to take more care of themselves.'

HUDSON, Alan
Born: Chelsea 21.6.1951
Career: Chelsea, Stoke City, Arsenal, Seattle Sounders, Hercules Alicante, Chelsea, Stoke City

A midfield genius with supreme vision and impudent skills, Hudson scaled the heights of football – and hit rock bottom. Hailed by Chelsea fans as a god for his trophy-winning performances in their glittering side of the early '70s, he earned an England call-up at 22, then decided to stay at home and decorate instead. He finally made two brilliant performances for England in 1975, then was bombed out for good by boss Don Revie.

Hudson left Stoke City for Arsenal so he could pay a tax bill, then ended up unemployed after rowing with the boss. But it was in the days after his schizophrenic playing career that he really hit the rocks.

Out of work and desperate for cash, Hudson fronted a sleazy firm organising kinky orgies with prostitutes at £10,000 a time. He even boasted that he had tried out the £500-a-time hookers himself. One madame told how he wore a saddle and blinkers as a hooker rode him like a horse after a similar party.

Hudson and a business partner offered the sex shows to help new businesses launch with a bang. He boasted that other soccer stars would be there, but they would not take part in the orgies. In a conversation taped by a *News of the World* investigator, the fallen star said: 'We can arrange whatever you want for the opening night.

We've got the names and we can supply them. These girls are yours. They're 100 per cent, I can personally assure you. It's good fun. The girls go round serving drinks but the punters can't touch at first. Then the girls start making advances to your punters and it becomes an orgy.'

Then Hudson listed a number of soccer stars who could appear too, adding: 'Names are no problem – there'll be some shagging going on, but it won't be with them.'

Asked if he had slept with the hookers, Hudson said: 'Of course. I've done one show with them. They're 100 per cent.'

His partner Peter Garrett-Dare explained: 'Al has put on these ventures before with me and we've made a lot of money. We had the chairman of a football club and half a major league team at our last bash. It was great. What you're getting is a sex show of the highest quality, where anything goes. We want £10,000 but you'll be well happy.'

Vice madame Michaela Hamilton, who arranged girls for a party at an Indian restaurant in Stoke-on-Trent, told reporters of their business meeting in a local hotel. 'He had a few drinks and started getting frisky so we went up to a room and had some fun,' she said. 'He paid me £375 for sex but he wasn't up to the job.'

At the restaurant, she went on, 'We'd brought along a saddle and some horsey props and by the end, after most of the punters left, Alan got stuck in. He was wearing a saddle and blinkers. One of the girls was riding him round the stock room.'

The rider, Donna, 31, who claimed she was Michaela's sister – told the newspaper: 'I got on his back and he galloped round the room. He had sex with a couple of girls that night.'

Hudson, already divorced from first wife Maureen, had recently left his lover, Pam Rawlinson, a guest-house owner from Uttoxeter, Staffordshire. She claimed he had left her with a string of debts.

Exposed, Hudson blamed his business partner, Birmingham private detective Peter Garrett-Dare. Hudson said: 'I don't get involved with prostitutes. I have two big jobs in football management coming up. I've met these girls twice. The time before was for five minutes. I've never slept with one of them. I was with my son in the Sanam restaurant and we left early. I have a lot of witnesses who'll back me up. I'm not a pimp.'

But Hudson's transformation from soccer hero to zero was complete and his problems with women were part of his curse. Recalling his Chelsea heyday, he said: 'We used to go out after matches to the best bars, clubs and restaurants, where women used to make a beeline for us. At training in the morning, you could always tell the players who hadn't been home the night before because they'd turn up in the same clothes, reeking of alcohol. I had a glamorous wife, Maureen, who was a *Playboy* model, and we were together for 15 years. But it's very difficult being married to a footballer. Can you imagine your husband going out all the time and women being around? Players were put on a pedestal, which isn't the ideal situation for a marriage, although it wasn't the reason for the split. In 1978, I went to the States to play in Seattle. I came back to England after four years, but my wife wanted to stay there. We had two boys, now aged 27 and 22. I've also got another boy, aged 15, from a three-year relationship.'

Years later, personal tragedy would add to his woes. On 15 December 1997, he was hit by a car as he crossed a road in Mile End, east London, and hovered on the edge of death. The impact had shattered his pelvis and his sphincter. Surgeons had to remove blood clots from his brain and were minutes away from amputating his legs before his body fought back. The once great athlete was left with a remote-controlled device to empty his bowels, and a heavy limp.

Unconscious for a month and in hospital for 89 days, he finally left to find his second wife, Ann, 46, had fallen out of love with him just a year after their marriage on a yacht in Bermuda. Hudson said: 'How can she really fight to save my life one minute and then say she doesn't feel the same? She didn't even give me a hug or a kiss when I came out of hospital. I did ask her if she was seeing somebody else. She told me she wasn't.'

Ashen-faced Hudson told the *Daily Mirror*: 'I set myself goals to get better quicker. One was to go away with Ann for a couple of months in the sunshine after my operation. I still love the girl so much. But now everything has changed.'

Ann had seemed the perfect partner. They had first met 15 years earlier in Vagabonds, the stars' nightclub. Both were married and became friends first, he says. Only years later did it develop into something more.

In November 1999, Hudson, unable to work, was declared bankrupt. 'Frankly I don't give a stuff,' he declared before moving in with his mother in her flat close to Stamford Bridge.

In January 2001, he was arrested for shoplifting two bottles of wine and a bottle of vodka from a Sainsbury's store in Whitechapel, east London. Hudson, unkempt and wearing shorts despite the winter cold, claimed it was all a misunderstanding and two months later charges were dropped.

Nowadays Hudson earns his money writing about football for Stoke's *Evening Sentinel* newspaper, the Potteries town where he is still a hero. He says today: 'I don't feel bitter about the way my life has turned out.' Above all he has learned his lesson and steered clear of the vice trade. At least his readers can remember the maverick star in his pomp and not as a pimp.

HUTCHISON, Don

Born: Gateshead 9.5.1971
Career: Hartlepool United, Liverpool, West Ham United, Sheffield United, Everton, Sunderland, West Ham United

There are plenty of flash footballers, but Liverpool powerhouse midfielder Hutchison cornered the market in the early '90s. On holiday in AYIA NAPA in 1994 with teammates Michael Thomas and Jamie Redknapp, Hutch had a couple of beers too many at the resort's boozy Mini Golf Bar, dropped his keks and stuck the label of his Budweiser on his tackle.

Witness Chris Iaonnou said: 'In front of some holidaymakers Don Hutchison took his trousers down, pulled his dick out and put a Budweiser label on it. His attitude was "Have a picture of this!" He was out of it and thought it was funny, but everyone was shocked.'

When Liverpool bosses saw the unsavoury photo in the *News of the World*, his Anfield career was over. Boss Roy Evans said memorably: 'If Hutchison is flashing his cock again, that's out of order.' He was fined £5,000 and put on the transfer list. For it was his second flashing offence.

Just a year earlier, the fiery Geordie had flashed at a party of students in Labinsky's bar in Liverpool after their graduation ceremony. He was drinking at the club with teammates Ian Rush, Jamie Redknapp and Paul Stewart. Exposing his testimonials for the benefit of the camera held by 23-year-old graduate Catherine Brooks, he yelled: 'Zoom in on this!'

'To my astonishment,' said Catherine, 'he got his penis out and started waggling it about with his hand. I turned away in disgust, forgetting to turn the camcorder off. I was shaking and told him it wasn't worth it.'

Hutchison insisted: 'I told you to zoom in on this!' Minutes later one of the grinning stars handed the girl a glass of 'wine' that looked suspiciously like urine. She took a mouthful and spat it out.

Hutchison's dad was furious. 'It's a bloody disgrace,' he said. 'I don't know whether he had a few drinks too many but it's shocking behaviour. I'll be having words with him.' So would Liverpool. Although police took no action, he was fined £2,000 by the club and warned about his future behaviour.

Hutchison was eventually shipped out to West Ham United before low-profile moves to Sheffield United, Everton and Sunderland, and fewer Scotland caps than his talent deserved.

Hutch remained philosophical (some noted that, with his unimpressive tackle, he needed to be!). 'I've caused my own problems. I did silly things and I have to get on with it.'

HUTCHISON VALE

Hutchison Vale Boys Club soccer boss Ricky Graham did his best to prepare young starlets for the cynical world of professional football. But a Swedish sex and corruption scandal was the last thing the innocent lads' parents expected them to be involved in.

Graham, 48, used the annual Gothia World Youth Cup tournaments in Gothenburg as the perfect cover to bed Scandinavian University administrator Rose-Marie Anderson, whom he had met on a previous trip. With his wife back in Edinburgh, Graham spent hours between team talks cuddling up to the 40-year-old beauty. After three years of liaisons, Rose-Marie suggested she visit him in Scotland. And the truth emerged. Graham was married with three children. The wronged woman dumped him, insisting: 'I was very sad because he had made me think he was single and interested in me.'

At least there was success on the pitch. Hutchison Vale's youngsters followed in the footsteps of past players like John Collins by winning trophies in three age groups. But rivals suspicious of the Scots lads' towering frames and deep voices complained to organisers. It was discovered that Vale had included older players and were booted out in disgrace. As well as a £600 fine, Ricky received a ten-year ban from the Scottish Youth FA. Twelve other officials received lesser bans.

Graham protested his innocence, at least in the bedroom. 'I don't have any girlfriend over there,' he insisted. 'Last year I had a stroke and there's no way I could have had sex with anybody while I was in Sweden. People just want me out of this club.'

I

ICKE, David
Born: Leicester 29.4.1952
Career: Coventry City, Hereford United
The dotty former Coventry City keeper proclaimed himself the Son of God – then told his wife a blonde disciple was moving in with them to save the planet.

Icke, who gave up the game at 21 through arthritis, became a TV sports presenter and then a Green Party spokesman before announcing his bizarre conversion at a London news conference in 1991.

With wife Linda, 41, daughter Kerry and Canadian Deborah Schaw, 30 – his 'soul mate' – beside him, all clad in turquoise shellsuits, he predicted that by that Christmas New Zealand would disappear, Los Angeles would break off the American mainland, and that Teesside and the white cliffs of Dover would be under water.

He said: 'I channel an energy known as the Christ Spirit. Christ isn't a person, it's an energy known as pure love and wisdom and it resonates to the same frequency as the colour turquoise . . .'

Pure love was soon resonating in the Icke household when Deborah moved in. Bizarrely, Deborah and Linda announced they wanted to be known as Michaela and Mari. At first Icke denied a sexual relationship with Deborah. But eventually he confessed: 'It did get physical. But it was as if I were not really there in the room. I was floating somewhere else.'

Deborah later gave birth to a daughter, Rebecca – presumably the granddaughter of God. Linda, the mother of his three children, stood by Icke when Deborah eventually moved out. 'My husband is not insane,' she said. 'I have never doubted that, and I know several psychiatrists who agree.'

Icke began writing books on his bizarre conspiracy theories and began a series of global speaking tours. On one, in the West Indies in 1998, he fell for another woman, Pamela, and walked out on Linda. 'I have two families now,' he said, insisting he is still 'the best of friends' with his ex-wife.

Icke later described his conversion as a 'Headf**k'. He recalled: 'I had a Headf**k in 1991. I was no longer in a prison that everyone lives in – the fear of what everyone thinks. I didn't have a nervous breakdown . . . I had a breakthrough. Headf**k can set you free.'

Amen, David!

INTERCOURSE

Sex before a match can boost players' performance on the pitch – as long as it's good sex, scientists have proved. Sports physiologist Dr Tommy Boone put 11 athletes through a rigorous training programme after a night with sex and a night without. There was no difference in performance.

Contrary to the myth put about by trainers since the dawn of time, intercourse helps athletes by making the brain produce endorphins – opium-like chemicals which boost energy levels and kill pain naturally. And sports psychologist Jack Lamport-Mitchell discovered sportsmen's self-confidence increased if they had had sex that left their partner satisfied. But unsatisfactory sex left players anxious, and emotionally racked.

J

JAMES, David

Born: Welwyn Garden City 1.8.1970

Career: Watford, Liverpool, Aston Villa, West Ham United, Manchester City

England's calamity keeper David James dropped himself in it when he swapped e-mails with a childhood sweetheart on the FRIENDS REUNITED website. Blond-haired father-of-five James – married to Tanya for 12 years – even met Amanda Sutton, 31, for secret dates behind their partners' backs.

The pair had been close at their school, Sir John Newsome's in Welwyn Garden City, their Hertfordshire home town, 15 years earlier. But then their lives took very different paths. David became a millionaire Premiership soccer star, semi-pro Versace model and devoted family man. Amanda raised two children while working in an off-licence. But they still had plenty in common. They swapped banter about school days on the cult website for old school friends then exchanged phone numbers.

A friend of the footballer told *The People*: 'She had seen him on telly playing football so it was quite a shock when he e-mailed her out of the blue. But things just seemed to snowball from there. They got on like a house on fire and clicked again. It was as if they were still young and at school. Amanda was behaving like a giggling schoolgirl.'

The pair met up when Amanda took her two kids to see their grandparents in Welwyn and, the paper reported, they cuddled on a sofa. Amanda was said to be convinced 32-year-old James would leave his wife and family. But when her boyfriend Andrew Savva found out, he dumped her.

Tanya became suspicious and discovered the friendship too, but was determined to keep hold of her £25,000-a-week man. 'David held his hands up and admitted everything – he couldn't really deny it. Tanya hit the roof,' said a friend. Then she phoned Amanda directly and warned her off. Amanda was devastated.

'I think Amanda has got stars in her eyes,' said a friend. 'David James is a superstar who could have the pick of any Page 3 girl or any model he likes but Amanda really believed he would leave his wife for her. She has gambled everything on the dream of being with a rich footballer but has lost the man she loves and her children's father.'

Amanda told the paper: 'David and I have been friends for a long time. I e-mailed him a long time ago. There's nothing more to tell.' James narrowed the angle, saying: 'I've nothing to say.' Privately he was said to be trying to save his marriage. Andrew, a friend revealed, was 'fuming, and I would hate to be in James's shoes if they ever meet up'.

Two months later – only a month before his 12th wedding anniversary and amid West Ham United's dramatic battle against relegation – James was spotted visiting Amanda's parents' home in Welwyn. The marriage appeared to be over.

Shell-shocked Tanya, 35, said James had claimed he was visiting his own parents. She said: 'He claimed it was all nonsense. He said he's not living anywhere with her. But obviously I'm the one in the dark.' His agent Colin Gordon confirmed the split, saying: 'Dave has fierce family loyalties and I'm sure Tanya is going through a lot at the moment. But Dave is as well.'

On the weekend the Hammers were relegated, James was reported to have dumped Amanda. He faced a lonely future.

JENNINGS, Billy

Born: Hackney 20.2.1952
Career: Watford, West Ham United, Leyton Orient, Luton Town
The blond Hammer may not have been in his class as a footballer, but he achieved the unthinkable when he bedded George BEST's bird behind his back. Jennings met Angie MacDonald James in a London nightclub and carried on a secret two-month affair with her in 1976 while Best tried to rebuild his career with Fulham.

JOHNSTONE, Derek

Born: Glasgow 1.1.1951
Career: Rangers

Rangers' legendary '70s centre-forward was famed for using his head to devastating effect – but it was a vital organ a few feet lower down that cost him his marriage, children and £2,000-a-month alimony.

Fearless and lethal in the box, Johnstone became a TV and radio pundit after his retirement from a glittering career north of the border. It was as he prepared another big match bulletin for Radio Clyde that the star, then 47, met busty blonde producer Emma Dodds – at 19 she was one year younger than his own daughter.

They enjoyed a foreign holiday in Tenerife and intimate nights at his whitewashed country cottage in Bridge of Weir, Argyll. But his family were incandescent when the affair was revealed. Daughter Donna confronted him at Glasgow airport after one trip. 'All Donna could see was a girl who looked just like she did. He was her hero and she always stood by him – no matter what. But this latest blow has left her sickened,' said a friend.

Wife Marion booted him out of their home in Houston, Renfrewshire – and not for the first time. A year earlier she had given him his marching orders over a reported string of affairs, then forgave him. This time there was no reprieve. Four months later, in June 2000, Sheriff James Spy granted Marion a divorce and an alimony settlement of £2,000 a month to raise their four teenage children.

JONES, David

Born: Liverpool 17.8.1956
Career: Player – Everton, Coventry City, Seiko Hong Kong, Preston North End. Manager – Stockport County, Southampton, Wolverhampton Wanderers

It was in the dock and not the dug-out that popular soccer boss David Jones scored his greatest victory. The devoted dad of four had spent 18 nightmare months facing allegations of child sex abuse before being cleared. He had lost his £200,000-a-year job and faced public humiliation plus the prospect of a jail term spent as a 'nonce'.

Jones's personal hell began in June 1999 as Merseyside police pursued their controversial Operation Care inquiry into abuse at children's homes. When a knee injury had forced him out of the game he loved in 1986, Jones, 29, had worked as a care assistant at a home for children with behavioural difficulties, living-in part time. Four years later he returned to football with Stockport County. A move to Premiership Southampton in 1997 brought him huge wealth and a shot at the big time.

In August 1999, two months after being questioned voluntarily at a Liverpool police station in relation to the inquiry – where he denied all the allegations – he was arrested and charged. The following January, Saints chairman Rupert Lowe suspended him as manager. The club announced it had given the manager 'compassionate leave' to prove his innocence . . . then gave England coach Glenn HODDLE his job.

The wait for justice was agony. His wife Ann said: 'It was the worst thing somebody could possibly accuse you of. He said he'd rather be up for murder than something like this.'

Finally, on 31 November 2000, the trial began. David Aubrey QC, prosecuting, told the jury that soccer boss Jones 'carries with him a dark secret – a secret that will be revealed by those who assert they were physically or sexually abused while they were in his care'. He said the regime at the school gave Jones 'an opportunity to perpetrate acts on vulnerable young boys and to carry out his own sexual perversions upon them'.

Witness A, aged ten when he arrived at the home in 1986, said he was abused by the star when 'pretend fights' got out of hand. He claimed he was indecently assaulted five times and buggered by the ex-player, who let himself into a bath cubicle and made the naked boy perform a sex act on him. 'He said I must not tell anyone – it was a secret.' The witness added: 'He always had this look about him. He was looking at you in a certain way, as if to say, "Do it, don't mess." I saw him later, he said "Good lad" and gave me some sweets. I was terrified of him because he was so powerful and everyone knew he was a footballer.' In tears in court, Witness A turned to Jones and hissed: 'Fancy making me go through this again.'

The allegations made in court were vile, a bit like the four witnesses. Witness A was a crack-addicted prostitute serving three and a half years for arson and three-quarters of the way through a sex-change process. He appeared in court with auburn hair, wearing a black trouser suit and purple blouse showing off his cleavage. All four had led lives of crime – two were still serving prison sentences and not one of the four victims had complained at the time of the alleged assaults.

Day by day the prosecution case unravelled. The first 'victim' – who had 50 previous convictions – failed to turn up at the court. The second also stayed away and police were given 24 hours to find him but failed.

On day four, the fourth witness – whose allegations had kicked off the investigation – refused to give evidence too. With their case in disarray, the prosecution offered no evidence. Judge David Clarke ordered the jury of eight men and four women to return formal not guilty verdicts on two indecent assault charges and two of assault. Then he ruled Jones could not receive a fair trial now jurors knew of other allegations but would not hear the evidence, and threw out the eight further charges.

He turned to the defendant and told him: 'David Jones, Not Guilty verdicts have been entered in respect of all charges against you. I would just like to say this means you leave this court as you entered it – an innocent man. No doubt there will be people tempted to think that there is no smoke without fire. I can do nothing about that, except to say clearly in open court that such an attitude would be entirely wrong in my view. No wrongdoing has been established on your part. Indeed, many of the charges brought against you have not been pursued by those who brought them. I would like to congratulate you on the restraint and dignity with which you have faced these charges. I just express the hope that you will in time be able to rebuild your professional career in whatever field you choose to pursue.'

Jones's supporters clapped wildly. Moments later he kissed his wife at the back of the courtroom before leaving the scene of his greatest victory. Outside, he told reporters: 'It's been the worst time of our lives. I would not wish it upon my worst enemy.'

Jones's victory helped others. Media scrutiny discredited the practice of 'trawling' – contacting ex-residents and inviting allegations of abuse. 'Victims' believed they could earn up to £20,000 compensation if the people they accused were convicted.

In March 2003, two more men jailed during Operation Care, Basil

Williams-Rigby, 57, and Michael Lawson, 62, were freed by the Court of Appeal. One of the witnesses who had helped convict Lawson was Witness A in the David Jones case – and now the truth emerged. A fellow prisoner told the court that Witness A had lied to get money to complete his sex change.

The seven-year Operation Care saw 67 people charged with abuse offences: 36 were convicted (including 24 who had pleaded guilty), the rest cleared. Campaigners – and law chiefs – heaped derision on the operation.

Jones agreed: 'Allegations have to be investigated, but what followed is something that I'd like a little more time to think about.' But his hatred for the twisted 'victims' was clear: 'All I would say to them is not to step in front of my car on a dark night. They have crawled back to where they belong – back to their prison cells.'

In January 2001, a month after his vindication, David Jones emerged from his exile to become manager of Wolverhampton Wanderers. Two years later the quiet dignity that brought him victory in court helped put Dave Jones – and Wolves – back in the Premiership. But even his side's amazing 1–0 victory over champions Manchester United could not have been as sweet as his day in court.

JONES, Vinnie
Born: Watford 5.1.1965
Career: Wealdstone, Wimbledon, Leeds, Sheffield United, Chelsea, Wimbledon, Queens Park Rangers

The Crazy Gang hardnut turned toughguy actor confessed he was 'a disgrace' after being accused of a sex assault during a 7 a.m. jacuzzi party with three girls. Married Jones, 38 – a father-of-two – was said to have gone wild in the hot tub as he watched the sun rise over Cape Town, where he was filming a new £20 million movie, *Blast*.

Leanne Loots, 23, claimed the star of *Lock, Stock and Two Smoking Barrels* and *Snatch* twice tried to fondle her with his foot under the bubbles. Leanne said: 'He tried to put his foot on my private parts, but I pushed his leg away with my two hands. He did it a second time and I shoved his leg away again.' Her sister Stefane, 26, said Vinnie then grabbed her hair and held her under the water. Pal

Catherine Taylor, 24, said he screamed abuse at her when her watch went missing.

Vinnie explained: 'The director told me there was a party going on at a beautiful house overlooking the ocean. I'd been working really hard and hadn't had a drink for five weeks so I went for it. That night I downed three bottles of wine and was a bit drunk. When I got to the house, it was a proper gaff with a pool table and a lovely big bar.'

The former hod carrier and Welsh international footballer then had a scuffle with someone who tried to take his picture. As he headed for home after more drinks, he spotted the tub.

'There were two fellas well pissed in the jacuzzi – one of them had nothing on and the other just had a pair of pants. There was one girl in the jacuzzi with them and another sitting by the side. They both just had bikinis on,' he said.

Seconds later, Vinnie claimed, another man threw him in the jacuzzi.

'I was wearing jeans and a T-shirt and got totally drenched, but I didn't have the hump. I got out, went up to him and said, "Right then. Do you want a proper wrestle?" The two jacuzzi girls and the two blokes were laughing their heads off, so I got into the jacuzzi to dunk one of the fellas – but he got away. Then, as I got out, I pushed one girl's head under the water for a joke and said, "You can get your head wet if you think it's so funny." It lasted a split second and it was just a good laugh. I certainly didn't indecently assault any of the girls. The only way my foot could have come in contact with either of them would have been accidentally in all the splashing about. Then, seconds later, the big fella's girlfriend snapped at me, "Where's my watch?" I asked her, "Are you accusing me of stealing your watch? I've just been thrown in the swimming pool!" I was really upset that she was accusing me and told her, "Why would I do that? I've got 50 watches at home." Then she said, "Who do you think you are?" As the atmosphere got worse, her big boyfriend told me to cool down.'

Vinnie walked down the seafront and got a taxi back to his hotel at 7.30 a.m. That afternoon his agent told him the girls had complained to police. 'It hit me like a car crash,' said Vinnie. 'I was so upset I was shaking for two days. I've apologised to the ladies for my behaviour and I want to put the whole thing behind me.' He added: 'I go to a party, let myself down and everything that was great in my life all got undone in one night. When I told my wife what had happened, she screamed at me, "Why were you partying until 7 a.m.?" She was devastated. I'm disgusted with myself for putting my wife Tanya through hell. I'm a disgrace.'

Jones spent 45 minutes speaking to police at Sea Point police station probing the incident, which took place in January 2003. A week later the case was dropped. Police were concerned that the girls had apparently phoned newspapers with their story before calling them.

Jones said: 'I'd been warned many times to be careful in Cape Town because of what happened to Sir Alex FERGUSON. Of course, I thought, "That'll never happen to me."'

Tanya, back home in Hertfordshire, said: 'For Vinnie to do anything like this would be just completely out of character for him.'

JONSSON, Ulrika
Born: Sollentuna, Sweden, 16.8.1967

Ulrika won promotion into the Serie A of soccer groupies when she tried – and failed – to pinch England soccer boss Sven-Göran ERIKSSON from his Italian other half. The former weather girl who became a TV icon via *Gladiators*, *Shooting Stars* and *Dog Eat Dog* had a passionate four-month fling with her fellow Swede behind the back of his fiery partner, Nancy DELL'OLIO.

Highly sexed Ulrika-ka-ka already counted a doomed romance with violent ex-Liverpool and England star Stan COLLYMORE among her trail of failed affairs and broken marriages. She stood by the muscular striker even when he faced charges of assaulting the mother of his child – of which he was cleared – before he then battered her during a bust-up in Paris at the 1998 World Cup.

She later told of a cruel and abusive relationship with the fallen genius. Once, she said, he locked her out of his house in the early hours sobbing and wearing just a T-shirt and knickers.

After beating her up in Paris, he cut up her clothes. 'Stan was very abusive verbally and emotionally,' said Ulrika. 'He'd say, "You're crap, you're shit." I wanted affection, but he found it difficult to give. Then you'd get a little splurge which kept you going.'

Ulrika would later cause another storm when former *Blue Peter* host (and keen Sunday league goalkeeper) John Leslie was questioned when women contacted police following claims in her autobiography that she was raped by an ex-boyfirend. Leslie lost his job before all charges were dropped.

Amid the fall-out from her book, another footballer, Les FERDINAND, was identified as the third soccer star she had bedded. Ferdy, who had enjoyed affairs with TV host and soccer star collector Dani BEHR and *Vogue* model Eva Dijkstra while cheating on girlfriend Angelea Murray, was said to have dated her in the mid-1990s. A friend told newspapers: 'Both enjoyed it while it lasted but it just fizzled out. Ulrika was upset because the affair was very passionate.'

Within a year of her fling with Sven, Ulrika announced she was marrying posh Lance Gerrard-Wright, the unattached toff who was supposed to find love on *Mr Right*, the dating show she hosted. Can this really be the final whistle on Ulrika's footy romances? Watch this space.

KANE, Samantha

The sex-swap businesswoman vowed to buy Sheffield United and become the first woman chairman of a football club.

In the early '90s, with moustache and glasses, Sam HASHIMI had almost bought the Blades for £6.25 million on behalf of a Middle-East consortium. His wife Trudi had allowed him to wear her clothing in secret – now he had gone for the Full Monty. Ops totalling £60,000 had turned the lad who had learned to love football on the streets of his native Baghdad into a woman.

'Samantha' confessed the op had ended her playing career. 'I haven't played football since my transformation. My body is a woman's now. I have breasts, long nails, very long hair. It's all a bit restrictive. I don't have the testosterone necessary for such a muscular game.'

Her story – told in his autobiography *A Two-Tiered Existence* – was seared by tragedy, bad health and two bitter divorces. Now involved in the publishing industry, Sam Hashimi/Samantha Kane remains convinced that when it comes to making Sheffield United great again, he's the man – and woman – for the job . . . if he can ever decide which way he, or she, is kicking.

In February 2004, Samantha announced she was now becoming a man again, called Charles Kane, that the sex swap was a mistake and that he was suing the surgeon who, he claimed, had removed his tackle too soon!

'I missed talking about football and the stock market,' explained Charles.

KANU, Nwankwo
Born: Berri, Nigeria, 1.8.1976
Career: Federation Works (Nigeria), Iwanyanwu, Ajax, Inter Milan, Arsenal, West Bromwich Albion

The extravagantly skilled Nigerian star has lived the life of a king in his £3 million mansion after a £4.5 million move to Arsenal – complete with a coterie of courtiers. The star's fixer and right-hand man James Agu provided him with women for sex parties, the *News of the World* revealed in April 2001. One girl brought down for a bash from Yorkshire told investigators: 'It's wild over there. I couldn't believe it when I first went there. I got completely drunk and couldn't even remember how many I'd slept with. I can remember swimming naked in the pool and making love in the water, and I woke wearing my bra and Kanu's football shorts.' Another said: 'He tore my clothes off and said he loved my boobs. We made love for an hour and he kept asking me to call him "King Kanu". But he was a terrible lover, only concerned with satisfying himself.'

KEELER, Christine
Born: Hayes 22.2.1942

Keeler was the racy good-time girl at the centre of the PROFUMO SCANDAL of 1963. She was sleeping with the Secretary of State for War, John Profumo, while also seeing a Soviet diplomat, Yevgeny Ivanov, suspected of being a spy. Profumo lied to the House of Commons about his involvement and had to resign in disgrace.

Keeler's story was immortalised in the movie *Scandal*. But as well as her penchant for politicians and spies, Keeler later developed a taste for footballers – bedding soccer boss Malcolm ALLISON.

KERB-CRAWLERS
Stars caught in their cars with vice girls include John DREYER, Russell HOULT and David PLEAT.

KING, Howard
The Premiership ref bedded hookers all over Europe by telling clubs they wouldn't win unless they bribed him with local beauties. The Welshman, married twice, bragged he:
- CHOSE his dream woman when offered the pick of a Lisbon nightclub brimming with gorgeous dancers;
- ROMPED with a Czech vice girl who demanded he wear his referee's outfit after a match;
- DEMANDED the services of a blonde Russian bombshell who wasn't even on the game – and got her!

King maintained he never actually helped a team win, despite telling one official: 'This match is important to you. You need to win to qualify for the championships. I am the referee. Unless I go home with her you won't win, I assure you.'

King, by now retired and working as promotions manager at CARDIFF CITY, told the *News of the World* in 1995 how he was first offered sexual favours in Belgium 12 years earlier. 'The first time I was set up with a prostitute was when I was doing a UEFA Cup tie in Belgium. My chaperone was an ex-FIFA referee. He knew the score. He took me across the border into Holland to a brothel. He had no qualms at all about offering me some light entertainment. Obviously, he'd been the recipient in the past!' Home side Antwerp beat FC Zurich 4–2 in that match before being knocked out in the second round.

A year later in Portugal, King was really getting to know the ropes: 'The night before the game I was taken to this club in Lisbon. It was wall-to-wall with beautiful women. The guy looking after me said, "Take your pick. Whichever girl you want, you can have." I saw this blonde. She was the most beautiful girl I've ever seen in my life. She had an excellent body and had a short skirt on. Later I found out she was wearing white knickers and suspenders. Back at my hotel room, she had her arms around me and we were in a state of undress. She leaned forward, nuzzled my ear and whispered, "We must win the match tomorrow." She obviously knew I was going to referee the game. We had a great night together.' King continued: 'I always have three hours in bed to rest before the kick-off and I certainly needed it that day.' Lisbon won 2–0 although King was adamant he remained impartial during the game. 'Lisbon were simply too good,' he insisted.

The Welsh referee's weirdest night came in Czechoslovakia, after he officiated at Sparta Prague. 'I met a blonde at a party after the game. She said she knew I was the ref because she saw the match on TV, and she said, "When we have sex will you put on your referee's kit?" So I did. The kit stayed on all the time. She kept tugging at my shirt while we were doing it. It must have been a turn on for her.'

By 1986, King was becoming bolder still. Before refereeing Russia's European Championship qualifier with Norway, the vodka-swilling ref spotted another blonde at a pre-match banquet.

'By the end of the evening I was in love,' recalls King, 'so I threatened to make sure the team lost unless I got her. She wasn't a hooker. I asked a Russian official if she could come back to my hotel by any chance but he said: "No, no, no." I asked could I go to her flat? "No, no, no." Then I just ignored all diplomatic niceties and said, "This match is important to you. You need to win, I am the referee. Unless I go home with her you won't win, I assure you." My linesman was kicking me under the table.

'The official stormed, "You are crazy man!" Then he had a quick chat with his superior and I was told, "You can have an hour." Her name was Tanya, and she couldn't speak a word of English. The flat was just big enough for us to get along famously. Sure enough, after an hour there was a demand for me to leave. But it had been worth it. She was fantastic. The next day Russia won 4–0. They would have won anyway. They didn't need any help from me.'

Understandably he felt miffed when he arrived in Italy – the sex bribes capital of soccer at the time – and was met by a Juventus official who ordered him straight to his hotel bed. Alone! 'I was told the club had been threatened with expulsion from European competitions after being over-enthusiastic in supplying refs with goodies,' says King.

Cynically, he claims: 'Clubs could hardly report me if I did nothing for them on the pitch – it would incriminate them. But if they lost, there was no more hospitality – it was the cold-shoulder treatment.'

King retired from refereeing through injury in 1994 after over 500 first-class games and finally owned up to bonking escapades in Russia, Portugal, Germany, Holland, Spain and Denmark. 'I officiated in 44 matches in Europe between 1983 and 1993 with sides like Barcelona, Sporting Lisbon, Benfica, Ajax, PSV Eindhoven, Hamburg and Munich. I guess women were sent to my hotel bedroom about 12 to 15 times. They were usually in their 20s, often gorgeous creatures. They made it quite clear they knew who I was.'

Thankfully, King is adamant the curse of match fixing did not affect domestic football: 'I've never heard of it in connection with British sides. It was hard to get a cup of tea out of them!'

See REFEREES.

KISS

1970s soccer stars Alan Birchenall and Tony Currie became gay icons after being pictured kissing on the pitch. Leicester's Birchenall had collided with Sheffield United's long-haired midfield genius during a Division One clash in 1974. The Birch revealed: 'Just for a laugh, I said to TC as we got up, "Give us a kiss." There were no tongues or anything, but the picture went round the world. I even got asked to contribute to a gay magazine in Germany.'

KISS-AND-TELL

Classic tabloid tactic to expose footballers who play away. Some exponents have become household names, including Emma PADFIELD, Alicia DOUVALL and Emma Jones, and their notoriety has reduced their chances of bedding their prey. But nowadays every woman has her price – a nationwide survey in 2001 showed 51 per cent of women would tell all for £10,000 if they slept with a footballer. Married players, beware!

See Des LYNAM, Jane NOTTAGE.

KLEBERSON (Jose Kleberson Pereira)

Born: Urai, Brazil, 19.6.1979
Career: Atletico Paranaense, Manchester United

Manchester United's Brazilian World Cup winner put a Premiership move on hold – until his 15-year-old girlfriend could marry him.

Kleberson had dumped his previous fiancée for Dayane Wilians Da Silva when she was just 14. Kleberson, 23, and Dayane planned to marry on 14 February 2003, when she reached 16. Dayane confirmed: 'He told me he would not travel without me unless I agreed to marry him – I accepted within the hour.'

Leeds United target Kleberson, a revelation for Brazil the previous summer, said: 'Everything in my life happens very fast.' Except the transfer. By the time of the wedding, Leeds had run out of cash, boss Terry VENABLES had left, the team were facing relegation and the move was abandoned. Leeds' loss, was, as usual, Manchester United's gain. The midfielder joined the Reds for £5 million in July 2003.

KNEECAPPING

See Keith WELLER.

KNEE TREMBLER

See URETHRITIS.

L

LA MANGA

Nine LEICESTER CITY players were arrested over rape allegations by three hookers after a bonding session turned into a booze-up at the luxury Spanish sports resort in March 2004.

See Paul DICKOV, Keith GILLESPIE and Frank SINCLAIR.

LAMBIE, John

Born: Whitburn

Career: Manager – Hamilton Academicals, Partick Thistle, Hamilton, Partick, Falkirk, Partick

It seemed a good idea at the time. Hamilton Academicals' long-suffering boss swore he would stay celibate until his side won their first game of the 1986–87 season. Poor Lambie – and Mrs Lambie – had to wait *four months* for the lads to notch up their first victory, a 3–1 win away to Hibernian. Much to the boss's relief!

LAMPARD, Frank

Born: Romford 20.6.1978

Career: West Ham United, Swansea (loan), Chelsea

The son of West Ham's legendary midfielder inherited his football talent from his dad – but maybe an incautious streak too.

Frank LAMPARD snr played for over 20 years with hardly a booking, and established a exemplary reputation before it was revealed he had fathered a secret family at the height of his career. His son had already developed a dubious reputation of his own. In 2000, he was one of a group stars seen on a sex VIDEO of their romps with girls in AYIA NAPA. A year later, he was fined by the club for his part in drunken high-jinks, along with drunken Chelsea teammates Eidur Gudjohnsen, John Terry and Jody MORRIS, and ex- Stamford Bridge star Frank SINCLAIR, at a Heathrow Airport hotel the day after the 11 September atrocities in New York. One player was said to have dropped his trousers and exposed himself to horrified tourists. Contrite Lampard admitted: 'We made a massive mistake.'

Lampard seems to have put his waywardness behind him and during Euro 2004, with long-term Spanish girlfriend Elen Rives supporting him from the sidelines, his superb performances made him one of the tournament's stars.

See Kieron DYER, Rio FERDINAND.

LAMPARD, Frank
Born: East Ham 20.9.1948
Career: West Ham United

The Hammers' legendary left-back shocked his fans when a secret family he fathered at the height of his fame was finally revealed a quarter of a century later.

Married Lamps, who played 665 games for his only club in an exemplary 20-year playing career, had a daughter, Sophie, in 1979, and a son, John, five years later by long-term girlfriend Janet Butler.

Months before Sophie's birth, Lampard's loyal wife Pat had given birth to their third child, Frank jnr, later to follow in his dad's footsteps as an England international.

Lampard snr, an FA Cup winner in 1975 and 1980, kept his name off Sophie and John's birth certificates and had only occasional contact with them. In its unlikely exclusive, the *News of the World* said it believed he had never told his wife of his alternative family.

At least the East End icon – fresh from doting on his famous son in TV ads for Sainsbury's during Euro 2004 – now had the good grace to admit his folly. 'I accept what I did was wrong,' the 55 year old told the paper in July 2004. 'This was an episode in my life that was some time ago and it is important that I draw a line under it now. I have a happy marriage, a wonderful family and I love them all dearly. I made mistakes.'

LAURIE, Celina
Blonde Dane who said she slept with England skipper David

BECKHAM after a Manchester United friendly in 2002. She was the third woman to claim Beckham had played away.

LAWRENSON, Mark
Born: Preston 2.6.1957
Career: Player – Preston North End, Brighton & Hove Albion, Liverpool. Manager – Oxford United

The elegant Liverpool and Ireland defender turned TV expert landed five League titles, a European Cup, the FA Cup, four League Cups and 38 caps. But he had more troubles with women than any centre-forward he faced in a distinguished career.

- His first TEENAGE MARRIAGE to Ellie lasted just nine months;
- His second wife Vanessa ACCUSED him of being tighter than a Liverpool defence in Europe;
- He CHEATED on mistress Beth with another lover, Sue;
- Then DUMPED Sue when she became pregnant with his child before . . .
- DUMPING Beth to move back in with Sue!

Everton fans used to claim he was gay thanks to his Village People-style moustache, but his complicated love life was ample proof that he's 100 per cent bloke.

Second ex-wife Vanessa accused him of penny-pinching before their 1993 divorce. The blonde claimed he made her work in the pub they owned the night before their wedding, banned her from carrying a credit card and made her shop at the local Co-op while he lorded it on TV.

'After we married he changed,' said Vanessa. 'He didn't spend time at home. And as soon as I was off the scene my friends saw him with a new woman. He couldn't wait to get rid of me. It makes my blood boil when I see him on TV with everybody thinking how wonderful he is.'

Fashion store manager Beth Mitchell fell for the moustachioed macho man when he went in to her Newcastle shop in 1996 to buy a dress for another girlfriend. Smitten Beth dumped her own boyfriend for Lawrenson, who was coaching NEWCASTLE UNITED's defence for old pal Kevin Keegan. The lovers set up home together in a flat in Gosforth. For two and a half years they were an item, but lazy Lawro hadn't changed his ways.

Beth told how he lounged around watching TV as she cooked him his nightly roast dinner, watched football and *Coronation Street* and chomped his way through tin after tin of Quality Street chocolates.

She said: 'Mark is the most selfish man I've ever known. Football comes first, golf second and I was at the bottom. As soon as I moved in with him he made me feel like a lodger. I would always tell him what I thought. I was so up-front he nicknamed me "The Piranha".'

In 1998, Lawrenson met nurse Sue Culshaw at REUTERS in Southport, Merseyside. The soccer ace, then 41, whisked her to PARIS for a romantic weekend at the World Cup finals that summer (just like his *Match of the Day* colleague Des LYNAM). Despite their blossoming love, however, Lawrenson was still returning to Newcastle to carry on with Beth. After mysterious phone calls, he confessed his affair to Beth, promised to end it, but didn't. And in September 1999 Sue and Lawrenson moved into a flat in Southport.

That Christmas Sue, 32, discovered she was pregnant and on Christmas Eve, shocked Lawrenson cleared off back to Beth. According to friends, Sue considered an abortion. But then Lawro had second thoughts and returned, finally giving Beth the boot instead.

When his bizarre lovelife was exposed, Sue said: 'My relationship with Mark has never been a secret among our friends and family. He has never attempted to hide anything. He told me all about Beth, but I'm not saying whether he two-timed me or not.'

Scorned Beth could not disguise her fury: 'He told me the BBC were forcing him to relocate to Manchester. I didn't know any different. Then Sue rang me out of the blue and said, "Hi, Beth, it's Sue, Mark's girlfriend. I'm living with him now and we're getting married. I want to know if you are still with him." He still rang and told me he loved me and wanted to be with me. But he dumped me and went to live with his pregnant mistress.'

Sam – the baby boy he had wished for – was born in September 1999. Lawrenson, admitting he was indeed 'over the moon', at last seemed truly in love. Especially with his new son.

He said: 'I am New Man. When I'm home, I feed and change the baby and put him to bed. I get up with Sam. I enjoy having him. It would give me a reason to kill somebody if they ever harmed him. I'm so protective.'

Lawro, naturally, defended himself superbly against the allegations: 'When I was with Vanessa, we tried for a baby. There was nothing wrong with either of us but nothing happened. I suppose that was the beginning of the end for us. It was all very amicable when we parted but then it got nasty and I can't even tell you the last time we spoke.'

But what about his tangled love life? 'I was shocked when Sue told me she was pregnant,' he said. 'I didn't say anything for a while . . . it took a while to sink in. I mainly felt sorry for Sue because she got embroiled in all that nasty stuff and was pregnant by me at the time.'

Lawro's antics made him the butt of jokes from his quick-witted TV friends, he admits. 'Yes, they had their fun . . . plenty of it. But me, a womaniser? I don't think so.'

LEICESTER CITY

From the plush training pitches of LA MANGA to a hell-hole Spanish jail and relegation from the Premiership – how the Foxes came to regret a night of boozing that ended up with three women accusing them of rape.

City boss Micky Adams had taken his struggling side to the prestigious Spanish sports resort to recharge their batteries and bed new signings into a team on a miserable three-month run of fifteen League and cup games without a win.

After training on one of La Manga's eight full-size pitches, Adams allowed his players to unwind – gentle sunbathing in the Costa del Sol heat, perhaps, or a round of golf. Tennis, say, or even a dip in a pool or spa . . .

Or maybe a session in the resorts' bars to celebrate the 22nd birthday of reserve player Jordan Stewart. It developed into a boozy affair, even though Stewart retired early.

During the evening, those lads left on the lash met three women – Beatrice Wanjiro, 31, Ruth Lourenco, 36, and Martha Wilbert, 37 – who would later tell police a story of horrifying sexual violence.

According to the women, all Germany-based Africans, the players burst into their room – 305 – at the Hyatt Regency Hotel at 5 a.m. on Monday morning and attacked them, raping one and sexually assaulting the other two. They handed police a bracelet said to have been left by one player and a pair of bloodstained knickers ripped in the 'attack'. The women had been about to board a flight home to Germany when they decided to report the incident. Police convinced them to stay in the country. Doctors at the nearby Alicante hospital apparently found various injuries. After they identified the footballers from passport pictures, *nine* Leicester players were arrested: club skipper Matt Elliott; defenders Frank SINCLAIR and Nikos Dabizas; midfielders Keith GILLESPIE, Lilian Nalis and Stefan Freund; strikers James Scowcroft and Paul DICKOV; and reserve goalkeeper Danny Coyne.

Local police announced bluntly: 'For a sexual aggression to three women, the Spanish police detained nine English football players.'

The following morning, Spanish TV showed footage of many of the players being bundled into the back of a van on their way to court.

There was shock at home. Dickov's wife Jan said later: 'I saw them being handcuffed and put in a van on the lunchtime news. I broke into tears immediately and thought, "This is going to be something terrible." I knew in my own heart that Paul was not capable of doing this. But it was very difficult for the children. How can you tell them dad's been accused of rape?'

City fans were equally appalled at the pictures. 'Thanks for getting us relegated without even kicking a ball,' one pessimist wrote on an Internet bulletin board.

Their club went into overdrive to win the players' freedom . . . a Premiership place was at stake, remember. The rest of the squad was flown home (including Stefan Freund, who had been arrested but released without charge), manager Adams stayed in Spain as chief executive Tim Davies flew out.

Their efforts were rewarded. On Thursday evening, charges against Elliott, Coyne and Dabizas of breaking and entering and not aiding a crime victim were dropped. Lilian Nalis, questioned over sexual aggression and trespass, was also freed without charge. On Friday morning, James Scowcroft, accused of trespass and not helping a victim, was released on £13,443 bail.

For Sinclair, 31, Gillespie, 29, and 31-year-old Dickov, came only the grim realisation they might not be flying home for *fourteen* years. That night, investigating magistrate Pilar Perez Martin ordered all three to be sent to Sangonera La Verde prison. Banged up in a 12 ft by 6 ft cell designed for two, segregated from other prisoners in the intimidating overcrowded jail and said to be on suicide watch, each faced charges of sexual assault and breaking and entering.

'The prison cells were like a dungeon,' Paul Dickov later recalled. 'There were a few Spanish prisoners shouting and screaming. I was stunned and bewildered. I was sat on the step in the cell with my head in my hands crying. It was one of the worst moments I'll ever have in my life.'

Sinclair said: 'It was shocking. I've never been in prison before so it was hard for me to deal with. I was thinking a lot about my family and how they'd react.'

Now details of their night out began to emerge. Several players had been partying in the hotel's piano bar, where they first met the women. One guest had even taken a photograph of City striker — and father-of- three — Frank Sinclair at the bar at 12.45 a.m. with one of the women, her leg wrapped round his. The eyewitness said: 'As Frank walked in, one of the girls raced up to him. One of the women, the one dressed in a little black outfit with fluorescent stripes down it, suddenly wrapped her leg around Sinclair and ground her hips into him. He didn't exactly stop her, though. He held her leg with his hand and leaned slightly into her. He was grinning like a Cheshire cat. I thought it was so raunchy, something I'd never seen at La Manga before, that I took the picture of it. I never saw them kiss but there was a lot of touching and fondling. All the players there were loving the attention they got from the girls.'

Another witness, said to be a 35-year-old London businessman, said the players had been drinking heavily earlier that evening and were abusive. He said: 'About 13 of them started congregating in the bar about 9 p.m. They were loud and raucous and straight away started upsetting other guests.'

Soon they linked up with the three women. 'The women and the footballers were drinking Cristal champagne, shots and cocktails,' he claimed. 'The more the footballers drank, the worse they behaved. It was a disgrace. I felt ashamed a British team could behave in such a manner.'

Leicester City spokesman Paul Mace insisted other guests had said his players' behaviour had been 'impeccable'.

British diplomatic officials visited them in jail. George Outhwaite, vice-consul in Alicante, spent 40 minutes with them and said: 'You cannot describe them as being cheerful. They were the best they could be under the circumstances.'

The players' wives and girlfriends flew to Spain to support their men. A prison visit would not be a pleasant reunion – explaining their apparent partying with three dubious strangers would make it even worse.

'When I saw my girlfriend and my mum, it was pretty emotional,' said Sinclair. 'My mum was crying. We couldn't touch and it was just talking through a window.'

At home, the club sponsor, the Alliance & Leicester building society, was said to be reviewing its multi-million-pound deal. A spokesman said: 'We understand that our customers and the public are concerned by stories such as this.'

After a week in their intimidating Spanish prison, the players were hauled back to court for a further hearing in which accusers and accused presented their cases in a tiring and tedious day of courtroom argument. Finally they were allowed out on a combined £200,000 bail. They caught the first available plane, an Easyjet flight from Alicante to Luton Airport. Wafted in from paradise they most certainly were not. After sitting together at the back of the plane, the three millionaire footballers disembarked last at 2.45 p.m. and were bundled out of a side entrance away from reporters and photographers. Their partners had flown home the night before.

None of the stars was considered fit for the Foxes' Saturday afternoon clash with fifth-placed Birmingham City and the club faced the clash in disarray. 'The three players have had a very traumatic time and will not be considered for selection,' said Adams. 'We have been training all week without them and, given the ordeal they have been through, what is best for them now is that they have a quiet weekend with their families.'

(The boss also announced an alocohol ban in the players' lounge and on future training trips . . . well, at least they would be allowed out again.)

Incredibly a goal from veteran striker Les FERDINAND helped them bag three vital points after fifteen matches without a win. Maybe La Manga had bonded them in an unexpected way. But two draws and four defeats in their next six games left the Foxes relegation certainties.

How the saga affected the Leicester players can never be proved. But fans will always wonder whether Paul Dickov had really put his nightmare out of his mind when he took a penalty at 1–1 in a monumental relegation decider against Manchester City on 24 April . . . and missed.

The Foxes, inevitably, went down. But there was at last good news for the players.

In May, undercover *News of the World* reporters exposed the three women as hookers who charged £700 for group sex, blowing any credibility as witnesses.

Then Spanish prosecutors announced forensic tests on the women's clothes showed no trace of the footballers' DNA. All charges against the Leicester City players were dropped.

The players were mighty relieved. And very defiant.

Gillespie said: 'I am delighted that we have all been totally vindicated. Hopefully, all our lives can now get back to normal as quickly as possible and we can concentrate single-mindedly on football.'

If only they'd done that at the time!

Scowcroft added: 'My son Jody is six and he was getting asked at school about it. It was something that we couldn't hide from him, so my girlfriend Sara said there had been an incident in Spain and Daddy's helping the policemen. At times it was almost laughable, but I never panicked – I knew I was innocent.'

Dickov insisted trouble flared only because he was defending his wife's honour. 'The only thing I'm guilty of is having a late drink,' he told ITV's *Tonight* show. 'I don't feel I've let anybody down. With hindsight, I should have gone to bed earlier.'

The diminutive striker explained how a fight had broken out as they talked to the women in the bar. One of the women called him a 'a small, little white boy'. Dickov made a remark about her bottom: 'She lifted her skirt up and said, "I suppose your wife would love a backside like me?" I said, "No, my wife is tall and has a lovely backside." As I said that, one of the other girls grabbed me and scratched me above the lip.' Shocked by his arrest later, Dickov explained: 'We'd been down to the police station expecting to give a statement and then we were in the next room getting charged with rape. I told a policeman, "This isn't possible." It was one of the worst moments I'll ever have in my life.'

Sinclair seemed to miss the point totally, blaming the *club* for not imposing a curfew! 'I think clubs will change the way they do things now,' he said. 'If we did have a curfew, we would definitely have been home a bit earlier.'

Because footballers *always* stick to curfews, don't they?

And he had a bizarre explanation for the dirty dancing picture. 'A Bob Marley tune came on and she knew I played for Jamaica and got a bit excited,' he said. 'She came up to grab me and that's when the picture was taken.'

As Leicester cut costs ready for life back in Division One (they had only just come out of administration), all three were shown the door – Dickov was sold to Blackburn Rovers for £150,000, Sinclair was released and Gillespie offered on a free transfer.

The players had carved an infamous place in their club's long history. And in football's hall of shame. Sinclair summed it up: 'We'll always be remembered as the ones that were accused rather than the ones that didn't do it.'

LEILANI

Page 3 stunna split from NEWCASTLE UNITED and England star Kieron DYER after proclaiming she would remain a virgin until their wedding day. She soon swapped him for strapping Wimbledon centre-back Mark Williams.

LE SAUX, Graeme

Born: Jersey 17.10.1968
Career: Chelsea, Blackburn Rovers, Chelsea, Southampton
Taunted by Robbie FOWLER over unfounded allegations of his homosexuality.

See GAY.

LESBIAN

A women's soccer team boss was forced to quit because of lesbian love feuds. Gretna Ladies boss Barney Davidson walked out when he couldn't put out a team still on speaking terms to face Leeds City

Vixens in January 2003. Barney, 46, said: 'I have nothing against gays or lesbians, but when two players having a relationship fall out it causes all sorts of hassle. The final straw for me was all the lesbian fall-outs. It just got incredibly stressful. We're not talking about sordid stuff in the showers or anything sleazy like that to my knowledge, but there's a small section of the side in a butch sport like football who take their tiffs out on to the pitch. Premiership managers earning a lot of money have no idea what sort of problems I have had to face.'

The Northern Combination side's straight skipper Amy Davidson, 20, said: 'When lesbian girls fall out it can be pure hell – your whole preparation for a game is thrown away.'

LE TISSIER, Matt
Born: Guernsey 14.10.1968
Career: Southampton
He smacked in a few beauties in his time – but the big-hitting Saints striker won himself a steamy new reputation when he fell for an Aussie soap star who loved being spanked!

When sexy *Home and Away* star Emily SYMONS – dizzy beautician Marilyn Fisher in the show – starred in the panto *Goldilocks* at Southampton's Mayflower Theatre, the cast posed for publicity pictures at the Saints' training ground. Le Tissier and Symons hit it off, so to speak, immediately. Oh, yes, they did!

'I liked Matt right away,' said Emily, who once confessed she felt like 'a pair of breasts on legs' playing the busty character. But no sooner had the couple got together, in January 1999, than Emily's naughty secrets were revealed by a kinky ex-lover she nicknamed 'Nunkie'.

The soap star was said to have begged to be spanked after going on wild spending sprees. 'Too many spendies leads to bendies' would be the signal for her to bend over and accept her punishment. The spanking sessions would invariably be the prelude to fiery sex.

Chris Farries told how Emily, then 23, had begun a passionate affair with him in 1994, only three weeks after she had married her first husband, British musician Nick Lipscombe. Farries, a 51-year-old actor, had met her while playing in another panto, at Bristol. She was a princess. He, the villain. Within weeks, the familiar panto call of 'He's behind you!' had a new meaning.

Chris said their caning sessions began as a joke after she ran up fines on a rented video. He said: 'I told her she deserved a good hiding. She was sat on the sofa next to me laughing. I grabbed her, put her over my knee and smacked her four or five times – she didn't fight it off. I gave her some good firm smacks. We were laughing. After that first time we had several spanking sessions together.'

Their kinky antics culminated in a Christmas dressing-up session in a £12 schoolgirl outfit from Woolworths. Chris recorded the events. For posteriority, presumably.

Emily is heard calling him 'Sir', and asking to be punished for not returning the videos. The swoosh of his cane can be heard as he spanks her buttocks eight times. Emily tells him in a childish voice: 'I'm sorry.'

On another tape, transcribed in the *News of the World*, he punishes her for being late . . .

> Emily: I apologise dreadfully for being so late.
>
> Chris: I know. You know the routine.
>
> Emily: I know but . . .
>
> Chris: Three-quarters of an hour is totally unacceptable.
>
> Emily: I know, but I had to catch a taxi . . .
>
> Chris: I don't want your excuses. You know the position.
>
> [The cane can be heard.]
>
> Chris: Come on . . .
>
> Emily: No. It was because another lady was late, I wasn't . . .
>
> Chris: Two for three quarters of an hour. Put your bag down.
>
> Chris: How are you?
>
> Emily: OK.
>
> Chris: No. How are you positioned?
>
> Emily: Well, don't throw something new into the routine that I don't know.
>
> Chris: Bend over.
>
> Emily: Oh, God.
>
> [A swish of cane. Emily shrieks. The cane can be heard again. Emily shrieks again.]
>
> Chris: We won't be late again, will we?
>
> Emily: No-dles.

Chris: No-dles.
Emily: Hello, Nunkie.
Chris: Hello. All over now.
[They kiss.]

Farries said: 'I did smack Emily quite firmly – you can hear on the tapes that there's a good crack of the cane. But we both really enjoyed it. Our sessions were great fun. I asked her once why she liked to be spanked. She said she felt it did her good to be reined in, to be taught a lesson every now and again. She never had an objection. After the spanking we would be very intimate. We were lovers.'

But he insisted he was not the only man married Emily was seeing. 'But there's no fool like an old fool and I was in love with her and in a small way I still am. She was utterly adorable. Suddenly here's a gorgeous 23-year-old creature who lets me caress her boobs. I knew she was married but I'm a hot-blooded male. I was single. I thought it was fair enough.'

But it ended as quickly as it had begun. 'She told me she had a 25-year-old boyfriend who was a millionaire stockbroker and she was off to Paris with him.'

Le Tissier had skeletons in his own closet. In 1997, he left his wife Cathy and two children for a 19-year-old beauty he met in a nightclub. Le Tiss was said to be briefly besotted with Angie Nabulsi and heartbroken Cathy, 28, moved with the kids Mitchell, five, and Keeleigh, twenty months, to her native Guernsey. A family friend said: 'He misses his kids – they are so far away it's hard for him to see them.' But Cathy insisted: 'He hasn't tried to see his children for quite a while. It would be nice if he made the effort, but he hasn't. I did want him back but now I'm not too sure because his attitude stinks.'

The prospect of a painful divorce affected the unhappy footballer's game. But once Emily came onside, a fitter and rejuvenated Le Tiss responded on the pitch with match-winning performances and more epic goals.

Emily revealed: 'Matt gets hurt when people say he's got a fat bottom and a flabby tummy. He gets some stick about that on the terraces, but he's actually in great shape. And I like men with big noses, obviously. Matt's fabulous in bed,' she added. 'We have great fun together.'

You could say that again . . . 'When he sees my boobs,' she insisted, 'he likes to come out with the Austin Powers line, "Machine gun jubblies – how did I miss those?" And he goes, "I put the grrr in swingerrr. Yeah, baby!" I've lost count of the number of times he's watched *Austin Powers* and *The Spy Who Shagged Me*. Though if he ever went just too far and shouted, "Yeah, baby!" at the moment of passion, I'd kick him out of bed. He's got some funny tastes. He loves Shakin' Stevens and he's taken me to two of his concerts. He can also recite Frank Skinner's whole comedy routine about having sex.'

Emily quit *Home and Away* to move to Britain and Matt even proposed, pulling out a wedding ring at his seafront home on the south coast. But soon the cracks began to appear. That summer Emily revealed their wedding was 'on hold'. In October 2000, Le Tissier dumped her, announcing their relationship was finished, but that they would remain friends.

Injuries, fitness problems and age affected the star's final seasons at Southampton, but he finally bowed out of football with a classic Le Tissier moment – coming off the bench with minutes to go in Saints' last ever game at The Dell in May 2002 to score the winner against Arsenal with a stunning long-range goal.

Emily moved on too, landing a part in *Emmerdale*, the everyday tale of simple Yorkshire folk, where she plays (you guessed it) busty Aussie barmaid Louise Appleton. In July 2003, she married for the second time – to the Honourable Lorenzo Smith, 40-year-old youngest son of the Viscount Hambledon and heir to a £50 million fortune. The glutton for punishment will have plenty of chance for spendies now . . .

LIGHTBOURNE, Kyle
Born: Bermuda 29.9.1968
Career: Scarborough, Walsall, Coventry City, Fulham (loan), Stoke City, Swindon Town (loan), Cardiff City (loan), Macclesfield Town, Hull City (loan)
Honest Kyle paid £31,500 supporting his love child for 14 years before discovering the baby was not his! Veteran Kyle, now in the

twilight of his career, was told he had fathered a baby after a fling in Bermuda, his home country, when he was just 19. Even though he had his doubts, the striker handed over maintenance every month, until the child finally had a blood test. He had insisted on finding the truth during a holiday in the West Indian paradise with new wife RoseMarie in November 2002. When the result was revealed, the soccer hero demanded his name be taken off the teenager's birth certificate and began legal action to get his money back. 'This has really upset me,' said Kyle, with touching understatement. 'I feel I should be compensated, at least a little bit. I don't expect the full amount back, but it's the principle that counts.'

LIMPAR, Anders
Born: Solna, Sweden, 24.9.1965
Career: Young Boys (Switzerland), Cremonese, Arsenal, Everton, Birmingham City, AIK Solna, Colorado Rapids, BP

Limpar thrilled fans at Arsenal and Everton with exhilarating, attacking play that helped his unfancied teams land silverware. But the Swedish international winger must have wished he'd kept his Anders to himself as he partied after a tournament in the US.

Limpar, then playing Major League Soccer for the Colorado Rapids, had dazzled, as usual, at an All-Star Soccer Skills contest in Columbus, Ohio, but after a banquet that evening, 27 July 2000, things went a little hazy – such is life with footballers and drink.

Limpar ended up at the apartment of two caterers working at the banquet. During sex with one of the women, a 29 year old, Limpar asked whether her friend – asleep in her own room – would like to join them for a threesome. She said she laughed. Later he left the room and she fell asleep. Prosecutors alleged he was away for some 15 minutes, during which he entered the other, 30-year-old, caterer's room, pinned her down and fondled and kissed her before returning to her flatmate.

The following morning the 30 year old told her roommate she had been attacked, informed her boss and reported the assault to the police. One year later, after a protracted legal battle, Limpar was finally indicted by a grand jury in Franklin County, Ohio, on two counts of 'gross sexual imposition' – a charge carrying a possible three-year jail sentence.

In January 2002, Limpar appeared in court. He maintained his right to silence, and declined to give evidence. He even refused an offer to plead guilty to lesser charges in return for a lighter sentence. His attorney, Gerald Sunbury, said Limpar was innocent and had to be exonerated on all charges in order to keep his reputation.

The 30 year old told the court she woke up to find Limpar in her bed and repeatedly refused sex before he returned to her flatmate's room. There he had sex again. Limpar's defence maintained he had only left for around a minute to go to the bathroom.

Forensic tests apparently showed no evidence Limpar had been in the 30 year old's bed. Police believed force had not been used and Limpar was found not guilty. The former Swedish superstar said outside court: 'I just won the biggest game of my life.'

Limpar had been cleared, but, nonetheless, was exposed as a cheat. Luckily for him, Swedish newspapers could not reveal his name for legal reasons. He retired from soccer soon after the alleged assault and returned to Sweden with wife Madelaine and children Jesper, ten, and Josephine, six. He then played out his career with Stockholm second division side BP, while running a bar and restaurant in the Swedish capital.

Arsenal boss George Graham had paid Cremonese £1 million for Limpar in 1990, and, with 13 goals from midfield, he helped the Gunners win the title in his first season. Five years later, after a £1.6 million move to Everton, he won his second major honour – playing the game of his life as they beat favourites Manchester United 1–0 at Wembley.

Limpar loved the disciplined approach of the English game. As he prepared for a Masters five-a-side tournament in July 2001 – with the sex charge still hanging over his head – he said: 'George Graham was a hard man and a strict disciplinarian, but once you were away from the game you couldn't meet a nicer guy. Sir Alex FERGUSON is a similar sort of guy. They're from the same mould, aren't they? It's what made the game special when I was playing over there.' Pity some of that discipline didn't rub off on him.

LJUNGBERG, Freddie

Born: Vittsjo, Sweden, 16.4.1977

Career: BK Halmstad, Arsenal

Arsenal's fashion-victim Swede became the second Gunner to announce publicly: 'I'm Not Gay!'

Freddie – famous for his dyed red hair and bizarre outfits as much as his Cup-winning goals – has a legion of fans, male and female. And when the gossip got too much, Freddie, 25, announced: 'I know what I am. My family knows I'm not gay and my girlfriend knows. But I'm not offended – gay men can be very fashionable.'

Freddie would not reveal who his girlfriend was. 'There is always speculation about girls and stuff. I have a girlfriend and that's it.'

Freddie insisted he would steer clear of any soccer groupies. 'There are a lot of gold-diggers. It is difficult to know if they like you or they like your profession. You need to be careful. But as we say in Sweden, sometimes you walk on a mine and it will explode.'

The Swedish World Cup star also revealed in a 2003 documentary for Sky Sports how he planned to make a living in fashion when his playing days are over. 'It would be great to be able to do my own range.'

Freddie had already lifted the lid on one aspect of his sex life, when he revealed a year earlier how he prefers to perform for Arsenal than between the sheets. 'I usually don't have sex. Not on the same day as a match. I say no thanks. I guess that, mentally, I want to keep the feeling in my feet and that's why. I think the feeling sort of disappears out of your feet if you have sex before. I have tried before and my feet felt like concrete when you are supposed to kick the ball.'

See GAY, Sol CAMPBELL.

LOOS, Rebecca

David BECKHAM's personal assistant claimed in April 2004 she had a passionate affair with the lonely England skipper after his £23 million transfer to Real Madrid. Her revelations sparked the Beckhams' biggest marital crisis to date.

LYNAM, Des

Born: County Clare, Ireland, 17.9.1942

His silver tongue, twinkling eyes and debonair moustache have made Dishy Des TV's No. 1 charmer and a fantasy football figure for millions of women. When he switched from BBC for ITV his opening line was a raffish: 'Good evening. I thought we would be meeting again. We are both in exactly the right place . . . '

Irish-born Des's chat-up blarney has worked its magic on plenty of beauties – and landed him in trouble, including two disastrous flings he'd rather forget with a sex-swap Bond babe who had once been a butcher's boy from Norfolk; and a red-headed Irish beauty who revealed how he cheated on his long-term lover.

Des, born in Ireland but raised in Brighton, was married in 1965 to his childhood sweetheart, beautician Susan Skinner. Des was a young insurance salesman doing the odd bit of sports reporting. The couple had a son, Patrick, but the marriage ended in 1974 as his career took off and she fell for another man. Des – a rising star at the Beeb – enjoyed a string of flings. Conquests included TV newsreader Moira Stewart and actress Anita Dobson, later a star of *EastEnders*.

But the fling that would haunt him began in the summer of 1979 when he was captivated by a statuesque 6 ft beauty called TULA. The 37–25–37 stunner with dazzling emerald eyes would shoot to fame when she appeared in the James Bond movie *For Your Eyes Only*. But Tula, 25, had a bizarre secret past. She had been born Barry Cossey, in Brooke, Norfolk, and gone from humble beginnings as a butcher's boy to nude *Playboy* centrefold and trans-sexual icon via a sex change op paid for by topless dancing.

Des and Tula met at a party in a friend's house. They had a series of dates. 'His kisses were urgent, very sexy and seemed to last for ever,' said Tula.

Des learned about her past from showbiz friends. But when the *News of the World* splashed Tula's story on its front page in August 1981, she said Des dropped her. 'We would still talk and kiss but the relationship just fizzled out at the end of 1981.'

In her bestselling autobiography a decade later, she made no mention of a sexual affair. But four years later she told *The Sun* they had been lovers. 'He was a passionate and tender lover,' she claimed: 'Desmond told me he loved me. When we made love for the first time, he didn't know anything about my past life as a boy and the operation to turn me into a girl.'

But Des insisted: 'After I discovered her past, it was clear the relationship was not going very far. Unless I was absolutely psychotic, I don't ever remember making love to her.'

Romance followed with Scots actress and singer Barbara Dickson. They broke up because, she revealed, he did not want to be committed. 'Des is very uncommitted,' said Barbara, 'and I believe that people very, very rarely change.' She knew him so well . . .

Five years later, Des fell for the love of his life – beautiful blonde Rose Diamond. The model-turned-interior designer and the TV superstar enjoyed a quiet life out of the limelight, sharing a house in Sussex and a London home not far from the BBC Television Centre where he was by now a broadcasting legend and host of *Match of the Day*.

The renowned rogue's playing days appeared to be over. He insisted: 'I love the company of women, toying with the best looker at the party and having a giggle but that's as far as it goes.'

But in August 1996 – soon after being voted the person most Britons would like to live next door to – he risked everything on a secret affair with a neighbour.

Fiery redhead Laura Ewing, 48, was a wealthy widow said to have been married four times. The death of her 88-year-old stockbroker husband in 1988 had left her a woman of independent means. In December 1995, she moved into a £350,000 two-bedroom townhouse in a plush complex on the banks of the River Thames in Chiswick. Just a few weeks later she spotted Des, who owned a £750,000 house opposite.

'He was forever looking up at me, smiling and waving,' she explained. 'One morning I was sitting naked at my dressing table when I looked through the window and saw Desmond staring into my bedroom from his balcony terrace overlooking my house. I ducked down and tried to put something on.'

After two years of occasional meetings, the sexual tension was becoming unbearable.

In August 1997, she knocked to ask for advice about her council tax. Rose was out. Des was happy to help. The conversation turned to other subjects. Irish-born Laura said: 'He said he'd been thinking about me all the time and gave me a glass of wine. He told me what I needed was a good Irishman but I foolishly told him I didn't know any Irish people. Desmond saw his chance and raised his hand in the air to let me know what I needed was right in front of my eyes – he was Irish too, like me. I asked him about Rose. He said, "Rose and I are going through a tough time, it's finished. We're not in love with each other any more, we haven't had a sexual relationship for three years."'

She agreed to meet for a drink. 'Within two minutes,' Laura added, 'he was at my door, saying, "I'll have that glass of wine now."'

One Saturday, after presenting *Match of the Day* , Laura said, 'He just burst through the front door. We went upstairs and he started kissing me. He kept saying he couldn't believe it was finally happening, and he'd dreamed about this for two years.'

Des cut short a country break with Rose to meet Laura for lunch in London. After champagne, 'to mark the beginning of something great', wine and sea bass, they took a cab to her home where they made love before he dressed and returned to Sussex. Their affair was as red hot as her fiery hair: 'People joke sometimes about being a six-times-a-night man, but he really was. We were dead the next morning. I was offering something he wasn't getting at home – a very open sexual relationship where anything goes.'

Laura was so determined to win Des's heart that she had breast implants and liposuction, friends claimed. They talked of marriage and rented a £700-a-week mews house in London's Marylebone. Des even paced out the length of the garage to check whether his new Jag would fit in. On 23 February 1998, they moved in but spent only one night there together.

Des was terrified of tabloid exposure and worried he could lose his job. He promised once more to finish with Rose but didn't. And when Laura asked for help to cover the £34,000 a year rent, he said his money wasn't a 'bottomless pit' before agreeing to give her £20,000.

The World Cup in France in June 1998 proved the end of the affair. Des was in PARIS anchoring the BBC's coverage. What should have been a passionate liaison in the city of romance turned into a nightmare.

After one more night of loving, Des became convinced someone had spotted them. 'The next morning he called me to say he couldn't see me any more in Paris because he thought someone was on to us,' said Laura. 'It was more disappointing than you could ever believe.'

It was the last time she would see him, although he still phoned, she claimed, to say he was leaving Rose.

Bitter and alone, Laura now went public with her story in the *News of the World* on 27 September. 'This may be vengeance,' she explained, 'but I feel I've lost him anyway. I've got nothing to lose.'

Des remained supercool. He told the paper: 'While I will not go into any detail in my reaction, I will admit to an error of judgment which affects no one but myself and my long-term partner Rose. Rose has been aware of the situation for some months and has been both understanding and forgiving. Thankfully our 14-year relationship has grown even stronger, despite a hiccup which many couples unhappily experience.'

Loyal Rose, 50, kept her dignity too. 'Of course I still love Des,' she told the press outside their home. 'We are still together. I don't really want to talk about the affair. We've put it behind us. I have no intention of leaving him.'

On a TV chat show a year later, Des almost lost his cool, saying: 'I actually think anyone who kisses and tells for money is a hooker who defers payment.' Nowadays he insists: 'When I look in the mirror in the morning, all I see is this grey-haired old twerp with a grey moustache.'

Some of his women would have to agree.

McAVENNIE, Frank

Born: Glasgow 22.11.1959

Career: St Mirren, West Ham United, Celtic, West Ham United, Aston Villa, Swindon Town

'I must have had 500 burdz. Then again, I never was much good with numbers – it's probably twice that.' Meet soccer's bubbliest blond, Frank McAvennie – the sex-mad scorer who made Essex girls look bright.

Macca's golden goals transformed him from a gawky, ginger-permed road digger to blond-mulletted, champagne-swigging soccer playboy, dining in the finest restaurants and pulling blondes by the barful.

But a life of legendary excess would also leave him twice married, twice bankrupt, accused of drug smuggling *and* the most famous womaniser of his era. He was even immortalised in TV soccer comedy show *Only An Excuse*, with Macca's character constantly asking: 'Where's the burdz?'

Frank's 'burding' began as a young pro at St Mirren, where the town's nightclubs would echo to his usual chat-up line: 'Do you know who I am, darlin'?'

One woman who did was Anita Blue. Her boyfriend introduced them in 1982 in Paris . . . the Paisley nightclub, not the city of romance. Anita remembers: 'Frank had red hair in a tight perm and was wearing black leather trousers and white shoes. To be honest, he looked like something out of the Marx Brothers. He was very shy and it was only when he'd had a few drinks that he'd try giving it his terrible chat-up lines.'

Anita became his first serious girlfriend, and when he joined West Ham United, they bought a £500,000 three-bedroom detached house in Romford, Essex. Anita remembered, 'On Saturday nights after the matches, he'd go to the off-licence and buy champagne. We used to change into our tracksuits and sit in front of the fire, watching TV. We were happy and nothing came between us.' Frank even proposed marriage, handing over a ring encrusted with diamonds in the shape of a number 9.

But the bright lights proved more tempting than the home fires and he spent more and more late nights out.

'My eyes nearly popped out of my head when I first went down to London,' said Frank. There were girls walking about with very little on. When these girls were talking to me, I had to learn how to keep my mouth shut. My jaw used to just drop to the floor. All the time I'm thinking, "If you were in Glasgow, you'd be attacked wearing those clothes." When I was a kid, I never got a bird because I was so ugly. So I made up for it when I became a footballer. I even had guys introduce me to their wives and girlfriends and I didn't know what to say. If I kept talking to the girl, the guy might have whacked me.'

Anita explained: 'Frank was mobbed wherever he went, even in Marks & Spencer. We used to go on holidays to places like Ibiza and there would be one topless girl after another coming to talk to him as if I wasn't there.'

In 1986, Macca fired the Hammers to within a point of their first League title and reached the World Cup finals with Scotland. International trips gave him more opportunities to cheat on Anita. After a play-off win over Australia, Macca found himself with his teammates in a dimly lit Melbourne bar.

'Mo Johnstone was up against the pillar groping this girl's boobs and he shouted me over for a feel,' said Frank. 'All of a sudden her husband appeared and said, "That's my wife." I apologised and backed off because this guy was huge. But of course Mo wouldn't leave it at that and when we walked away he said, "By the way, big man, your wife's got a cracking pair." All hell broke loose and the guy leapt at Mo. The whole team waded in and got me and Mo out. We were just killing ourselves laughing.'

In 1987, Macca made his dream move to boyhood heroes CELTIC.

Anita stayed in Essex and they split up. 'Frank was getting out of control and I couldn't take it any more,' said Anita.

Soon after, he began seeing a lot of Page 3 beauty Jenny Blyth and they had a fitful relationship through the '80s. Macca claimed he blew £750,000 on drink, drugs and dodgy business deals during their five years together. He splashed out £500,000 on another Essex mansion at the very height of the '80s property boom only to see its value crash within weeks. Then a broken leg KO'd him for a year. Depressed, he turned to cocaine. 'I was on a downer,' he later confessed. 'I used the press to keep my face in the limelight. I spent all my time getting drunk then I'd take this stuff to wake me up.'

McAvennie's bed-hopping was now reaching epic proportions, even if he claimed he remained choosy. 'The girl had to be blonde because if it's good enough for Rod Stewart, it's good enough for me,' he said. And his job meant he didn't have to try too hard.

'I'm honest enough to admit that women didn't come after me because I'm an oil painting,' said Macca. 'It became easier to pull girls when I dyed my hair blond. I'm not the ugliest guy on the block either, but the fact I was a footballer helped. It wasn't as often as a different girl every night, but it could have been. I'm actually quite shy at home, until I get out, then I'm totally different. I used to party a lot with girls but that didn't mean I ended up having sex with them. I have loads of female pals I've never slept with – I respect them as friends. It's just many women never had any respect for me. A lot of girls would make it clear that they just wanted sex from me, and who am I to deny them that?

'I could never keep track of exactly how many, partly because I'm not very good at counting. It could have been a thousand for all I remember. The problem was half the time I was so pissed I couldn't do anything or my mates would never leave me alone long enough. I've easily crammed in about 500 females. I've certainly never been an angel.'

McAvennie was linked with dozens of beauties, including Page 3 girls Sam Fox and Maria Whittaker, though he denies bedding both women.

'But my best chat-up line used to be, "I know a lot of Page 3 birds, so I know a lot about boobs. Show me your boobs and I'll see how they compare." It might sound corny but you wouldn't believe how many would fall for it. One girl in Brown's nightclub in London was so gullible she just pulled her top up in the middle of the dance floor and said, "Well, how do these feel?" There I was standing there pretending I'm an expert feeling this poor, daft girl's boobs.'

Macca claims girls he never met said they'd slept with him to earn money from newspapers. But at least kiss-and-tells kept him in the spotlight. 'There was one girl and she was absolutely beautiful, a Page 3 girl, of course. She turned up to meet me at George BEST's bar, Blondes. She arrived late and by that time I was really drunk. Everyone's mouths dropped because she got out of the taxi in this sexy rubber dress. I remember thinking I'd better sober up here because I feel more rubbered than that dress. But I kept drinking all night. Eventually we went to bed and had sex at about seven in the morning. When she woke up, she asked me to take her home but I was so knackered I said, "Please get a taxi home. I'll pay for it." She must have taken the hump – I picked up a paper one day and she was on the front page saying I had been dating her for eight months. I had only been to bed with her once. But I didn't care. She was worth it at the time.'

In 1994, alone, unloved, back at St Mirren and desperate for cash, he sold the story of his affair with Jenny, including the confession that he snorted cocaine for four years. He revealed: 'Our home life was like Beirut – we did nothing but argue.' But if that was a battle, his next relationship would be a World War . . .

Laura McArthur was a model and hairdresser from Glasgow. After a year-long courtship, they were married in 1995, soon had a son, Jake, and moved back to London. 'I've never been with another woman since I met Laura,' he said at the time. 'She's the first girl to give me respect and the first one to trust me. I only wish I'd met Laura ten years ago.'

Laura insisted the feeling was mutual, and that she trusted him totally – even when she found him on a sofa with his Page 3 pal Tracy Kirby. 'They've been pals for years and I knew they wouldn't have done anything. People don't know Frank the way I do, he would never cheat on me.'

Laura was therefore less than chuffed when Macca was snapped kissing a nightclub singer, Nicole Turoff. Macca moved in with

Nicole and her two children in 1997. Predictably it did not last and once more he spun out of control.

Weeks after being made bankrupt with £200,000 debts, customs officers at Glasgow Airport caught him smuggling in a small amount of cocaine. He was fined £750. Investigators later froze £100,000 of his assets they feared would fund drug deals. In 1999, he was charged with drink-driving in Essex yet missed the hearing because, he claimed, he couldn't afford the journey from Newcastle.

There was an ill-advised dalliance with serial soccer groupie Emma PADFIELD, who kissed and sold a sorry tale. And in 2000 he hit rock bottom – on remand in Durham Jail accused of involvement in a £110,000 Ecstasy and amphetamine drugs deal.

His only comfort was new girlfriend Karen Lamberti, a 40-year-old divorcee, who visited him every day throughout his incarceration. In September 2000, he was dramatically cleared at Newcastle Crown Court. Their reunion had a surprise climax. Karen explained, 'We locked ourselves in an attic bedroom and made up for lost time. It sounds a bit dodgy but we were in bed when – in the middle of our love-making – he suddenly proposed. But I made him get out of bed and do it properly on one knee.'

Karen became the second Mrs Macca in a ceremony at romantic Lumley Castle, a few miles from their home in Newcastle in August 2001. Macca says of Karen: 'Other girls in the past have really got the best out of me and never given much back. Karen is different and we are very happy together. Of course I look at other women but I haven't tried to pull since I met her. Now that I'm getting older I've given up the womanising. I could probably still chat up women – Karen says I'm a real flirt – but I don't think I'd know if a woman was coming on to me, I just like talking.'

But he confessed: 'I was standing at the bar when I spotted this absolutely stunning female. She came up to me and asked, "Are you Frank McAvennie?" I nearly died with shock that she might be interested in me. Then she said, "You're a pal of my dad."' Time was catching up with the burding legend.

Loved-up Macca, now 43, free of bankruptcy and running a corporate golf business, says of his new wife: 'I searched a long time for her. Of course, you have to try a few before you find the right one. I just hope when I'm dead and buried people remember me for my football and not for the drugs and the women . . . although it was fun.'

McCOIST, Ally, MBE
Born: Bellshill 24.9.1962
Career: St Johnstone, Sunderland, Rangers, Kilmarnock

Super Ally ruined his cheeky-but-squeaky-clean image when it emerged he'd been cheating on his wife Allison *and* his rock chick mistress. The popular ex-Rangers striker-turned-TV star had a passionate affair with actress Patsy Kensit. And at the same time the dad of three was carrying on with air hostess Donna Gilbin. But McCoist, twice Europe's top scorer, found the Golden Boot was firmly on his wife's foot when she fell for a tattooed bouncer with convictions for violence and walked away with a huge slice of the star's fortune.

Super Ally's downfall began when, with the wife and bairns back in Scotland, he enjoyed intimate nights with Patsy at London's County Hall Marriot, after filming *The Premiership*. Three-times-divorced Patsy fell for old friend Ally, 39, after the collapse of her marriage to Oasis singer Liam Gallagher.

One insider revealed: 'Ally's marriage has been rocky for a long time. It's always been unconventional. He's always had an eye for the ladies. But this thing with Patsy is different. It's a love thing. He feels very strongly about her. And she feels the same.'

Not quite. When the shocking news of their affair broke in September 2001, she hoped he would leave his wife and children for her. Indeed, some believe troubled Patsy leaked the news herself in order to force his hand. If she did, it was a catastrophic own goal as McCoist dumped her instead and headed home to his £1 million mansion in Renfrewshire.

At first he denied the fling outright. But finally he was forced to confess. Outside the house, after a gloomy reunion with Allison, he announced: 'I just want to say I've been a complete fool. The only thing that matters now is my wife Allison and the three boys. If it's at all possible, we would appreciate a little privacy in the hope that we can sort things out.'

Allison, a former Miss Tyne and Wear he had met while playing for Sunderland 20 years earlier, kept her counsel, saying only: 'Everything is fine.'

Patsy's spokesman said bluntly: 'Patsy Kensit is entirely focused on her sons and her work, and her friendship with Ally McCoist is over.'

McCoist's public humiliation could not have come at a worse time. He had been due to help publicise his acting debut in *A Shot At Glory*, a movie starring Hollywood legend Robert Duvall. Reviewers praised his performance as Jackie McQuillan, a love-rat striker who leads his lowly side Portknockie to victory over Rangers in the Scottish Cup final. Ally certainly brought authenticity to the part but cancelled interviews.

At the premiere, Allison put on a brave face, walking hand-in-hand with her husband past photographers. And there were gasps of astonishment as fans spotted her startling new look. Allison had dyed her brunette hair blonde. Amazingly, she now bore more than a passing resemblance to Patsy.

Inside, an emotional Ally, announced: 'The only reason I'm here tonight is through the love, strength and courage of one woman who is sitting here tonight. I'd just like to thank you, Allison.'

Allison responded: 'Crisis? This is no crisis. A crisis is going through every emotion imaginable watching as our son has gone through life-threatening surgery. If we survived that, we'll survive anything.'

It was a reference to the turmoil they had faced after the birth of twins Argyll and Mitchell in 1998. Mitchell had a serious heart defect and spent a year in hospital. The McCoists' relationship was thought to have been strengthened by their ordeal. Ally said at the time: 'People ask how Allison and I cope, but you can't do anything else. There's no choice. We've been very lucky. When one has buckled, the other has been strong.'

And he added, with sad irony: 'Your priorities change when you have children. Before I only had Allison to think about, and, though I shouldn't say it, Allison came down a little bit in my priorities and I did in hers. But I know the most important relationship should be a husband and wife's.'

Only a few months earlier he had told how he would love to spend more time at home. Now he could. As he lay low, his place alongside Des LYNAM (no stranger to love-rat headlines) on that Saturday's *Premiership* panel was taken, ironically, by fellow football philanderer John BARNES.

If Ally thought the worst was over, he was horribly wrong. Sunday morning's papers would make grim reading. Air hostess Donna Gilbin revealed she was McCoist's second mistress. He had signed an autograph for her ten-year-old son on a British Airways flight from Glasgow to Manchester in February 1999. Next to it he wrote his phone number and politely asked if she would care to meet again, she said.

Donna described the player as 'gorgeous'. And yes, she would. A month later they did. And at a Manchester hotel they enjoyed, by all accounts, steamy sex. During their time together, he was said to have begged Donna, 28, to wear her sexy air hostess uniform.

Donna said: 'He was a wonderful lover and he made me melt.' But she never knew she was one-third of a secret love triangle – and, she believed, neither did Patsy.

She continued: 'I thought we had a future together, that he loved me, and that I was the only one for him. But now I know that he's just a liar and a hypocrite. My world fell apart when the bombshell dropped last week. Yet he called me and said he still wanted to see me regardless. But I want nothing more to do with him.'

McCoist could only squirm as he tried to put his TV career back on track. On *A Question of Sport*, his fellow panellists couldn't resist taking a pop – despite some having murky pasts of their own.

As host Sue Barker opened the 'Home or Away' round, fellow former Scotland striker Andy GRAY quipped: 'I'll do what Ally should have done . . . stay at home!' When Barker asked: 'What Happened Next?' Gray joked: 'Ally cancelled all his newspapers!'

There was no way back for the McCoists' marriage. And now Allison's new platinum look at the premiere took on a new significance.

What Ally didn't know was that his wife had been seeing a tattooed nightclub bouncer and landscape gardener with a criminal past and a taste for blondes. Scott Crawford, 39, had met Allison four years earlier at a pub in down-at-heel Saltcoats, Ayrshire, where he worked as a doorman. The McCoists later hired him to do work on the grounds of their home. Allison and Crawford had become inseparable, sharing dates at a £20,000 caravan she had secretly bought with cash at Seamill, Ayrshire, and having dinner in an Indian restaurant in the seaside town.

Crawford already had six children with four women and had just become a grandfather – he had allegedly got two teenage girls pregnant and met his last partner while bedding her friend behind his partner's back! A Rangers fanatic and keen Ulster loyalist supporter, his council house in Kilbirnie, Ayrshire, was festooned with a Red Hand flag.

Crawford had convictions for assault and breach of the peace. He had even been the target of a murder attempt for which the gunman was jailed. McCoist was said to be distraught that his young children would have any contact with such an unsuitable new father figure.

When exactly Allison's affair began remains a mystery. Some reports suggested it had been going for the four years since they met. Crawford was said to have told workmates: 'It's me Allison loves. She's only holding on in the marriage to make sure she gets money.'

The warring McCoists had a huge and violent late-night bust-up after a car chase through the quiet roads near their home in February 2002. Allison's BMW followed McCoist's 4x4 into a car park at Bridge of Weir, then she tried to drag him from the car. Both were screaming and Allison grabbed his keys from the car and ran. An unseemly wrestling match ensued.

A witness said: 'It was Ally McCoist and his wife. I was shocked, but I was more shocked when I saw what state his clothes were in. He had on a polo shirt which was ripped open. Allison was crying. I asked if she was all right and she pointed to Ally. She looked distraught. Ally just looked embarrassed, so I said to him, "Are you OK?" He replied: "Do I look OK? Look at what she's done – she's a maniac." Allison shouted back, "No, Alistair. You are the maniac."'

In August, a year after his affairs were exposed, Allison divorced him on the grounds of his 'unreasonable behaviour'. Crawford was reportedly now a regular guest at the McCoists' former marital home. The player, meanwhile, had bought a £450,000 farmhouse in nearby Kilmacolm. Lawyers moved in to divide the £5 million fortune amassed by their properties in Scotland and Portugal, other investments and the assets of Alistair McCoist Ltd. Allison's 19 per cent stake plus the value of their house meant she walked away from the marriage with about £1.2 million when they finally settled amicably out of court in January 2004. She had initially demanded a one-off payment of £2 million and £4,000 a month.

Ally, now 40 and alone, devoted as much time as possible to his children, but was soon playing the field again. He was said to be dating Vivien Ross, 27, who works for his beloved Rangers FC at Ibrox. And when he was reported to be in touch with London-based events manager Katie MacLeod, 25, Katie confirmed the friendship but added: 'I've got a boyfriend and any suggestion anything's going on between me and Ally is completely unfounded.'

Super Ally also tried to launch a pop career. But the man who once joked he was only married 'from the waist up' could have chosen a better debut single than 'Donald, Where's Your Troosers?'

McGRATH, Paul
Born: Ealing 4.12.1959
Career: Manchester United, Aston Villa, Derby County, Sheffield United

World Cup hero Paul McGrath drove his wife to a suicide bid after confessing he had secretly fathered a child with another woman. Booze-mad McGrath – a terrace hero for club and country despite the dodgiest knees in football – even moved a third woman into his house as wife Claire recovered in hospital.

McGrath had been married for ten years when he began a secret affair with divorcee Paula Hilton, of Chorlton, Manchester. It was the start of troubled booze-filled times that would change his life for ever.

Irish international McGrath, perhaps the most gifted defender in British football at the time, had been bombed out of Manchester United by new boss Alex FERGUSON for his uncontrollable drinking. Even as he signed his Aston Villa contract, McGrath had calmed his nerves with a bottle of vodka.

Claire, a nurse he met on holiday and married in 1984 as he established himself at United, explained: 'I only found out later that Paul used to have a bottle in his car and would drink as he headed for the training ground. In the afternoons back at home he would think nothing of downing a couple of bottles of wine.'

Within a year, McGrath made the first of the disappearing acts that would stud his career. After returning from the 1990 World Cup in Italy, he went missing for five days. When he got back, he told

Claire he had been 'drinking with the boys'. It was a lie. The English-born Irishman, dubbed 'The Black Pearl of Inchinore' after being snapped up from St Patrick's Athletic for just £35,000, was just five miles away from his Cheshire home, in Chorlton, Manchester, boozing and bedding his secret lover Paula.

With their marriage affected by his drinking, McGrath rented a house nearer Villa's training ground. 'For the first time he came clean to me that he was seeing another girl,' Claire said. 'At the time I thought that was fine. It was a clean break. We had been separated for a year and I had filed for divorce. Paul told me he saw a girl called Jane for three months, and then a girl called Debbie moved in with him for six months.'

In October 1992, however, the soccer star went missing again. Concerned Claire finally tracked him down to his Birmingham home where he had fled after a binge in Dublin. 'Whatever horrible things had happened between us, I couldn't help but feel sorry for him,' said Claire. Her husband was a mess – unshaven, shaking and smelling of booze. A woman emerged from upstairs. 'I had a screaming tantrum and told him to get her out. She went out of the front door.' The couple agreed to give their marriage one more try.

'I was with him all the time, so he couldn't get drunk or go missing. We had a great Christmas and I was delighted with the way things were going. We were like a family again. I really thought we had cracked it after all those bad years,' said Claire. But six months later, in April 1993, McGrath made two shocking confessions. He admitted his affair with Paula Hilton and that it had been going on for three years.

It got worse. Paula had given birth to his daughter, Danielle, by now 11 months old.

Claire said: 'I told him that as long as he would help me, back me up and support me, then I would forgive him. That night he went away with the team to play against Tottenham. But after the game he went missing for three days. I just presumed he had been with Paula.'

In fact, Paula had been left high and dry by her soccer star lover. She believed McGrath would leave his wife and children for her, but then she told him she was pregnant. 'He just blurted out, "Oh, my God",' said Paula, who already had a teenage daughter. 'He avoided me for seven months, then told me he was staying with his wife.'

If Paula was shocked, Claire was devastated. She took an overdose of sleeping pills in her bedroom and lay down to die. She spent four days in a semi-coma and eleven weeks recovering in a private hospital. 'I am ashamed at what I did,' she says. 'But I honestly didn't want to be around any more. Paul did come to visit me but it was plain he was back to his old ways. He turned up in my room one day so drunk that he fell asleep on my bed for six hours.' Claire still hoped to save her marriage, until bombshell number three arrived via the Sunday newspapers.

McGrath had gone on another mystery trip and this time been photographed with a woman – the same one Claire had spotted in his Birmingham home. The player had been having an affair with Liverpudlian Caroline Lamb, 27.

'I was in such a state that doctors sedated me and I was in for another nine weeks.' There, Claire admits, she found a new love, Matthew Shutt, 24. But to her amazement, that summer, with Claire in hospital, McGrath moved his new lover into the family home alongside his three children, Christopher, then nine, Mitchell, six, and Jordan, four.

McGrath's tactic at least meant the charade was over. 'I suppose it was a blessing in disguise,' said Claire. 'For the first time I realised he was not going to be an option for me.' She continued: 'Paul is a womaniser and, like most womanisers, no matter what they look like, the females seem to fall for them. Paul has ten tons of Irish blarney in him even when he's sober, and I suppose he can be described as a real charmer. But at the end of the day, I think it has been his football status which has attracted women.'

In 1999, McGrath, working as a newspaper columnist and TV pundit, claimed he'd beaten the booze thanks to wife Caroline, who managed his business affairs from their home in the Cheshire countryside.

'Alcohol really isn't an issue in my life any more,' he said. 'I haven't touched any in a long while and I'm not finding it hard.'

But after a long boozy flight to the Far East for the 2002 World Cup, McGrath, capped 92 times by Ireland, was booted off the BBC's TV panel. The following summer he was divorced from Caroline, mother of his children, Paul jnr, six, and Ellis, four.

'Drinking has been devastating for my family and everyone around me,' he once admitted, 'and I'm not proud of the hurt that I cause to the people who love me.'

Friends pray he will conquer his demons. Before he drinks himself to death.

McHARDY, Deirdre
Waitress reported to have had an affair with legendary Manchester United boss Sir Alex FERGUSON when he managed Aberdeen. He denied it.

McMINN, Ted
Born: Castle Douglas 28.9.1962
Career: Rangers, Seville, Derby County, Birmingham City, Burnley
Fans called him the 'Tin Man' – was it in honour of his thirst for lager, or his 'Wizard of Oz' performances on the wing? But Ted had a different reputation off the park. He left his first wife Jackie in 1988 after getting his girlfriend June Newman pregnant. Two more babies later, in 1990, they wed . . . only to split months later.

Next along was Heidi Cole, just 17 when they met and fell in love, but Ted carried on scoring. 'I know of at least seven women he'd been seeing in the seven and a half years I went out with him,' said Heidi.

In 1996, he moved abroad, combining football with a new job as an air-conditioning engineer in Connolly, near Perth in Western Australia. Heidi was ready to follow him until a tip-off that he was back to his old ways. 'Ted will end up as a very lonely old man,' she lamented.

McSTAY, Paul
Born: Hamilton 22.1.1964
Career: Celtic
Rapist David Stickings changed his name to Paul McStay, his CELTIC and Scotland hero, to disguise his string of sex crimes – allowing him to commit another disgusting offence. Scots-born Stickings had a record going back 20 years when, after being released from prison for rape, he took his idol's name by deed poll in 1998. The deception allowed him to evade security checks and

get a job at 1950s-style diner Frankie and Benny's in Bristol. After working his way up to supervisor, Stickings, 35, subjected an 18-year-old waitress to a terrifying five-hour rape ordeal after locking up the restaurant.

After he was jailed at Bristol Crown Court for rape, indecent assault and false imprisonment in August 2000, his victim said: 'That man is a monster. It was only at the end of the trial that I learned he had raped before. He's been given life, but he'll be out within ten years. He will attack again – and next time he may kill.'

MARBECK, Sarah
Australian former Gucci model turned £500-a-night hooker who claimed she bedded David BECKHAM during a Manchester United tour then had a two-year sex TXT affair.

MARTIN, Caroline
Call girl who found fame after her late-night cocaine-and-sex romps with Angus DEAYTON. The TV quiz show host and celebrity Manchester United fan had a long-term partner and child when their liaison was revealed in the *News of the World* in 2002. Martin later revealed her other flings with United's glitterati – including Dwight YORKE, Fabien BARTHEZ (none of the three knew she was a hooker and did not pay) and Martin EDWARDS.

MASCOT
See H'ANGUS, PANDA.

MASSAGE
See Wayne ROONEY, Peter STOREY.

MATTEO, Dominic
Born: Dumfries 28.4.1974
Career: Liverpool, Sunderland (loan), Leeds United
The Scotland international found himself at the centre of a love triangle when he was named as the other man in a divorce battle. Hannah Nicholls, 27, was said to have begun a secret relationship with the Leeds skipper when her husband Matthew asked for his autograph in a restaurant. Matthew told Matteo, 'You two are

colleagues', and explained that Hannah was a part-time physio with the club's youth team. Matthew, 27, now a broken-hearted Leeds fan, said: 'I am not denying my wife has been seeing Matteo. It is in the hands of my solicitors.' The four-year marriage ended in March 2004.

MAY, Eddie

Born: Edinburgh 30.8.1967
Career: Hibernian, Brentford, Motherwell, Dunfermline, Falkirk

The Scots soccer star's fling with a neighbour cost him more than just his marriage. The player walked out on wife Gail after falling for married mother-of-two Caroline Smith. But guilt-racked May soon realised his mistake and signed over his £100,000 Edinburgh home to Gail.

'This whole thing has been a total nightmare,' he told a newspaper. 'I will always regret what I have done. To try and make amends I've made sure Gail will never be without anything. The house is hers and everything in it is hers. I pay the mortgage, the bills, everything. Why should Gail have to start paying for something that was my mistake?'

Gail was touched but pragmatic. 'Eddie has come round every day to see how I am. But I think there has been too much water under the bridge to get back together, and I have told him that.'

MEIKLE, Nicholas

London nightclub PR who admitted setting up the GROUP SEX session with Premiership stars that sparked a football crisis and made the term ROASTING famous.

Meikle confessed to nine roastings already in the year up to September 2003, explaining the term meant: 'Roast, like a chicken – it [the woman] gets stuffed', and insisting it was normal behaviour for many young footballers. He told the *News of the World*: 'The last two years, three years, have been phenomenal. Girls are more up for it nowadays than ever before. Orgies are definitely happening. Before, I didn't get involved in sharing girls. But the more I've moved around with footballers, the more I've seen they just share their girls around.'

And the phenomenon is nationwide, he said. 'I've been to

Manchester, Leeds, Ipswich, Newcastle, even Bournemouth,' he added. 'It doesn't really make any difference.'

Describing one roasting, Meikle said: 'There were loads of girls in the hotel. They were going in the rooms and we were nipping in after them and having sex with them. Then we'd go in another guy's room and have sex with his girl. I shagged six girls in one night in the hotel. About ten of us had rooms on the same floor. We were there for four or five days, there was no game or something, and we were having a "Mad One" . . . a few girls, a few laughs, crazy stuff happened. Bournemouth is another place where the girls are well up for it. Five of us roasted a woman we pulled in a club. She came back to our hotel with her friends and we all had a few drinks and chatted for a while. Then her mates went home, but she stayed. She was a great roast.'

He claimed that it's not unusual for many of the new generation of young football players to get involved in such situations. He pointed out that footballers are like pop stars and said that girls are attracted to their wealth and celebrity. 'I've had about nine roasts this year. A lot of my friends get involved, that's the way it is.'

See Titus BRAMBLE, Carlton COLE, Kieron DYER, GANG RAPE, Nigel REO-COKER.

MELLOR, David
Born: 12.3.1949

The former Tory 'Minister for Fun' did for replica kits what Dracula did for blood transfusions when he reportedly made love to actress Antonia de Sancha in a Chelsea strip (despite his former allegiance to their west London rivals Fulham) during a scandalous affair in 1992. Despite parading his wife and children before the nation's press in a show of solidarity, his marriage also hit the rocks and he later lost his Cabinet role.

Mellor then fell for aristocrat Penelope, Viscountess Cobham, and became a newspaper columnist, football broadcaster and head of Prime Minister Tony Blair's Football Task Force.

MERSON, Paul

Born: Brent 20.3.1968

Career: Arsenal, Brentford (loan), Middlesbrough, Aston Villa, Portsmouth, Walsall

The drink, drugs and gambling addict's appetite for self-destruction led him to a new career low when he asked his lover: 'Do you believe in love at first sight?' – then dumped her for his ex-wife.

Merson, who has battled more demons than Buffy, dated blonde Gini Perris after moving out of the Hertfordshire home he shared with long-suffering wife Lorraine in November 1996. He admitted they had not shared a bed for three years as she tried to cope with his violent attacks, six-figure gambling losses, lager tops binges and cocaine sessions – and his one-night stands with groupies.

Blonde advertising executive Gini met the fallen idol at The Boat pub in Berkhampstead, Hertfordshire. She cheekily pinched his bottom as they stood in separate groups near the bar.

A week later, in the same bar, they met again. This time the brilliant Arsenal and England midfielder asked her out with him to the Kudos nightclub in Watford, near the house he was sharing with his brother Gary. After returning there for coffee, Merson made his move.

'He shut the kitchen door and kissed me,' said Gini. 'I never thought he might still be married. We talked about continuing to see each other and it was as though he was thinking of it being long term.'

A night later they went to bed. Gini recalled: 'We began kissing on the sofa and he asked me upstairs. We undressed each other. We didn't make love but did things to each other. He said I had a beautiful body as I sat on top of him. Afterwards he said he hadn't had so much fun for ages. It was then that he asked me, "Do you believe in love at first sight?" I answered, "Yes."'

Soon they were lovers, and, she claims, he discussed wedding rings with her. 'He noticed two rings on my finger,' she said. 'They're Cartier replicas and I said that's what I really want for my wedding and engagement.'

But when the soccer star did shop for rings, during a trip to New York, they were for his estranged wife as he tried to woo her back. Gini said: 'I couldn't believe it when I read he had flown to New

York to buy her a ring because he'd called me from his hotel and said, "I really miss you."'

Without Gini's knowledge he had been reunited with Lorraine. The couple even renewed their wedding vows during a romantic holiday in Barbados, before his shock £5 million transfer to Middlesbrough.

Devastated Gini said: 'I felt like a bimbo. I'd never have got involved had I known he was still married. Paul always referred to Lorraine as his ex, and even introduced me to his children.' Later she insisted she had shared intimate phone calls with Merson after his reconciliation, though his lawyers insisted: 'The relationship ended prior to his reconciliation with Lorraine. They have not met since.'

But what Merson really denied to Gini was the strength of his feelings for Lorraine, his childhood sweetheart of 14 years. During their split – in March 1997, as he battled his lethal addictions – he revealed: 'I'm probably the most jealous person in the entire world. It'll do my head in if Lorraine meets someone else. I'd crack. That will be my hardest time in recovery. I don't know if I can keep this up when my jealousy comes into play. Even now I sit indoors at my mum and dad's and wonder what Lorraine's doing at that moment. It's sad, really. I can't let go. Also, whoever I meet is unlikely to be a virgin and I won't be able to cope with that either. That's a real big thing with me. It made all the difference to me that Lorraine and I were both virgins when we met. I knew no one had had her before me and I need that. I haven't had sex since last year and I feel pretty frustrated on that score. But I'd have to meet someone nice before I jumped into bed and even then it would be tough. I'd feel very guilty even though I'm not with Lorraine any more.'

But not that guilty, as Gini learned.

MISS WORLD

1973 winner Marjorie WALLACE was fired over her romance with Manchester United legend George BEST. Later he bagged his second, 1977 winner Mary STAVIN, former girlfriend of QPR defender Don SHANKS and Middlesbrough hard man Graeme SOUNESS.

MOORE, Sarah

Soccer sex groupie who claimed to have bonked seven stars at the PFA Footballer of the Year Awards in 1993.

See Andy DIBBLE, GROUP SEX.

MORALEE, Jamie

Born: Wandsworth 2.12.1971

Career: Crystal Palace, Millwall, Watford, Crewe Alexandra, Colchester United, Barry Town, Forest Green

Moralee became WATFORD's best-known striker since Luther Blissett − not for his goals but for a real-life romance with a dangerous soap star.

Hunky Jamie had a fling with cocaine-addicted *EastEnders* actress Danniella WESTBROOK and found himself filling the front pages instead of the back. But the £425,000 signing wasn't the only man in the life of the wild-child actress. As Danni's life spun out of control, she admitted Jamie wasn't her only lover at that time. And when she announced she was pregnant in 1996, Jamie was one of *five* men she believed could be the father! The others were drug dealer Robert Fernandez; a jailed drugs baron, Keith Brooks; *EastEnders* actor Paul Nicholls; and financier Jake Stevens.

Luckily for Jamie he took a blood test which proved he was not the father and eventually − after Danni tried to sell the name of the father to papers for £100,000 − Robert Fernandez was revealed as the lucky dad of baby Kai.

But Danni, an Arsenal fan in real life, admitted she would always have warm memories of her centre-forward. In a frank interview in *Loaded* magazine, she explained: 'Jamie was really good in bed. Everything he done was good. Brian [HARVEY] weren't bad but Jamie was the guv'nor. He was a giver, not a receiver.' Oh, and how could she forget: 'He also had a big dick.'

Later she would play a more appropriate tribute: 'Jamie's special and means a lot to me. It's thanks to him I've kept away from the circle of people I've been mixing with. Jamie is a good influence on me and he's a caring person.'

Jamie, then 22, accepted her praise as only a footballer could. He said: 'It's very flattering. She has slept with a whole load of people and for me to come out top is a real boost.'

Jamie later moved on to Crewe and later Barry Town. Danniella moved on to Spurs.

See Ian WALKER.

MORLEY, Trevor

Born: Long Eaton 20.3.1961
Career: Corby Town, Nuneaton Borough, Northampton Town, Manchester City, West Ham United, Brann Bergen, Reading

'Come on you Irons,' sing the West Ham faithful. But when their tempestuous striker joined the select band of footballers to be stabbed (see George BEST, Mickey THOMAS), that chant acquired a spectacular irony.

Morley received knife wounds in a domestic incident at his house in Waltham Abbey, Essex, in February 1991 – injuries bad enough to keep him out for eight matches. Newspapers, naturally, were keen to know the soccer star slasher's identity but strongwilled Morley refused to answer their questions.

Bizarre rumours grew and, even a decade on, unfounded tales persist that it happened when his wife Monica walked in on a GAY bedroom tryst with Hammers teammate Ian BISHOP. The pair had an almost telepathic understanding on the pitch during their days together at Manchester City and West Ham, from where they had moved in a joint deal in December 1989.

'The wound was caused by a drunken accident but the biggest mistake I made was not commenting on it,' Morely explained in a 2001 interview. 'The papers said my wife caught me in bed with another woman, then they came up with the line that one of my kids had done it after catching me in bed with another woman. Eventually, it came round to, "Your wife caught you in bed with another man." Then it came around to me and Bish being together. I even got a phone call from my sister in Nottingham saying there were rumours about me and Bish up there.'

More confusingly, Morley continues: 'I should have come out with some sort of story because the papers were offering me money. There was no story because it was an accident but I should have made one up. They never actually printed the story but I wish they had because I'd have been a rich man after suing them.

'I've nothing against gay people but when you're not gay and people accuse you of it, it's very hard. I'd go into a pub and people would shout "Queer" and I'd want to fight them. Then, of course, you know what football fans are like and matches away from home were very hard. Bish handled it a lot better but it wasn't easy for him either.'

Morley left the Hammers in 1995 for Reading, after twice helping them to promotion from Division Two, before settling in Bergen, Norway, where he manages a local side. What the 'drunken incident' was, or who, exactly, had been wielding the weapon, Morley has never chosen to explain.

See STABBING.

MORRIS, Jody

Born: Hammersmith 22.12.1978
Career: Chelsea, Leeds United, Rotherham, Millwall

From England to Rotherham via a rape charge . . . has any football starlet sunk faster than the hard-drinking, hell-raising former Premiership player?

Morris flushed one career down the toilet thanks to his boozing with the bad boys in AYIA NAPA and stripping drunkenly with Chelsea teammates days after the 11 September tragedy. And he wasted no time doing the same at Leeds United.

The fallen Yorkshire giants – around £100 million in the red – invested £20,000-a-week wages in the combative 25-year-old midfielder who, they prayed, would stave off relegation, save them from liquidation and ensure the club's very existence.

Instead, Morris headed for the bright lights, taking new teammates Jermaine Pennant and Seth Johnson, and old friend Kristofer Dickie, on a Monday night out with a difference – cut-price drinks all round on student night in the buzzing city centre.

At Leeds' famous Townhouse pub they met a 20-year-old woman – one of 15,000 students out on the town that night. And at the end she accepted a lift with them. In the early hours, the girl would later tell police, in a lay-by at Collingham, 12 miles from Leeds on the A58 to Wetherby, the car stopped and she was attacked.

Detectives arrested Morris at the club's Thorp Arch training ground the following morning, Tuesday, 7 October, drove him to Leeds, cautioned him, held him overnight in a cell and questioned him on and off for 36 hours. Morris's friend Dickie, 26 – the son of a senior Scotland Yard detective – was also arrested. Both men were later bailed. Johnson and Pennant were questioned as witnesses by police. Neither was ever accused of any wrongdoing.

Morris was in deep trouble. But worse was to come. A 20-year-old woman who read the allegations in newspapers contacted West Yorkshire police to say she had been attacked by Morris years earlier.

He was arrested again at his home in Weybridge, Surrey, and driven the 200 miles to Leeds to be interviewed over the new allegations. Another man, aged 26, was also arrested and questioned. In November, Leeds announced the star Morris had been fined two weeks' wages and suspended for two weeks after an internal inquiry into his boozing on the night of the incident. The club announced that they had 'considered carefully the employment position and has taken legal advice. In English law there is a presumption that a person is innocent until proven guilty.'

On 18 November 2003, Morris and Dickie, of Fulham, west London, were charged with rape and told to appear again in March for a trial – date to be fixed. The trial would never take place. On 30 January 2003, prosecutors announced there was no 'realistic prospect' of a conviction after the discovery of 'fresh forensic evidence'. West Yorkshire's Chief Crown Prosecutor Neil Franklin announced: 'Having looked at this evidence we have decided the case should not proceed.' With the second rape allegations also now dropped, Morris was totally in the clear and said to be relieved: 'He's always maintained his innocence but is pleased he did not have to go through a high-profile court case to prove it,' said a Leeds United colleague.

No wonder. Another high-profile court case had already caused him acute embarrassment. When lapdancer Simone Hayes read reports of his trial in 2002 for assaulting a nightclub bouncer as he celebrated the birth of his daughter, she worked out they had been cheating behind his pregnant partner's back. They had begun an affair fuelled, she said, by 'sheer lust' after he paid £50 for private dances at For Your Eyes Only, a club in west London. 'When he came round, it was always just for sex. We were head over heels in lust. His favourite thing seemed to be threesomes. He asked me time and again to fix one up with my modelling friends. But I was shocked when I read in the paper that Jody had a daughter and that his girlfriend was pregnant all the time I was seeing him. Jody is a lying rat who needs to start thinking with his head and not with what's in his football shorts.'

Morris was cleared of assault, but soon split with Louise and moved in with model Jamelah Asmar, 25. Two years later she booted him out for sleeping with her best friend! Jamelah now announced she was having a tattoo of his name removed from her foot because of the publicity over the rape case. 'I had to erase him from my memory,' she explained. 'The fact that I see his name on my foot every morning didn't help me, so it has to go.'

Yet another lover emerged – lapdancer Destaney Beckford, who told how she spent the night with him at Chelsea Village Hotel, next to the west London club's ground. 'I asked the hotel to get me a cab back to my home in Battersea,' she told *The People*. 'I laughed when they called to say, "Mrs Morris, your cab has arrived." They must have thought I was his wife.'

Of their five-times-a-night session together after meeting in a London club, she recalled: 'Jody told me to stop dancing so close because staring at my bum was turning him on. We began flirting and when I left the dance floor to leave the club, I asked him for his number. He said, "You don't need my number, you're coming back to my hotel."

'He was fascinated when I told him I was a quarter Brazilian, Chinese, Jamaican and English [sounding like a modern Premiership back four!]. I've known a few men in my life but Jody is one of the best ever, if you know what I mean.'

The publicity must have been galling for Louise Winstanley, now reunited with her fun-loving partner and trying to bring up their daughter Romy as a family. She, at least, maintained a dignified silence.

Morris was now free to rejoin Leeds' desperate struggle for survival. But, predictably, Morris could not keep out of trouble for long and when the end of his Premiership career came, it was, inevitably, due to drink. The fallen star reportedly failed a breath test at training and was fired.

The club confirmed: 'Leeds and Jody Morris have reached an agreement today, as a result of which Jody will be leaving the club. Jody's career has not progressed as he would have wished and he has not featured regularly in the Leeds team.'

Eleven starts in one desperate season for a struggling side was indeed poor. But then he'd had other things on his mind . . .

Now Morris swallowed his pride and accepted a chance at Division One strugglers Rotherham. Boss Ronnie Moore insisted: 'I think Jody knows this could be his last chance, really. He's a hell of a player who has lost his way and sometimes you have to take a gamble. He's hungry because he realises if he's not careful he is going to make a cock-up of his career.' The following summer, Jody's old teammate Dennis WISE gave him one more chance at redemption with a move to Cup finalists Millwall.

See VIDEO.

MORRISON, Clinton

Born: Wandsworth 14.5.1979
Career: Crystal Palace, Birmingham City
The Premiership prodigy fell for serial soccer groupie Emma PARRIS at a nightclub.

N

NEWCASTLE UNITED

The Geordie giants were plunged into crisis when the club chairman and his deputy got down to business in a brothel instead of the boardrom.

Drinking pints of lager in the seedy Milady Palace in Marbella, Freddy SHEPHERD and Douglas HALL:

- GROPED half-naked hookers;
- ORDERED £325 sex shows with vibrators and handcuffs;
- WATCHED lesbian performances and were . . .
- FONDLED by vice girls.

As if that wasn't bad enough, the dirty directors began bragging

about their sexploits and slagging off their club and their fans.
They:

- BOASTED of how they travelled the world hiring hookers;
- DUBBED £15 million striker Alan Shearer 'Boring . . . we call him Mary Poppins';
- BRANDED Geordie women 'ugly dogs';
- BRAGGED that £50 replica United shirts cost £5 to make.

What they did not know was that the whole conversation was being recorded by undercover *News of the World* reporter Mazher Mahmood.

The pair had flown to Marbella by private jet after watching Newcastle United in an FA Cup tie at St James's Park. After midnight, they met the famous fake sheik in a hotel where champagne and brandy loosened their tongues. Married Shepherd, 56, said: 'Newcastle girls are all dogs. England is full of them.'

Hall, 39, and married with two sons, said: 'I've got 600, 700 mistresses.' And added: 'I've got one wife – but she's more trouble than 40.' Shepherd said: 'We've had Penthouse Pets, the lot. The best in the world.'

After moving on to the brothel, each described their preferences. Hall said: 'I prefer a beautiful face first, long legs, and I like a nice tight bum.' Shepherd explained: 'I like blondes, big bust, good legs. I don't like coloured girls. I want a lesbian show with handcuffs.'

As he eyed up a prostitute, Shepherd said: 'Shearer is boring – we call him Mary Poppins. He never gets into trouble. We're not like him.'

Groping a hooker, he asked her: 'Have you got any sex toys or handcuffs? How much do the girls charge? What's the price?'

After paying for a sex act from a blonde Spanish girl, the pair dropped more clangers. Andy COLE, they explained, had been sold for £7 million to Manchester United even though they alone knew he needed a career-threatening leg operation. Shepherd, a millionaire scrap-metal merchant, told how they once failed to convince former boss Kevin Keegan to go into an Amsterdam brothel with them. They also laughed at the huge profits they make selling 600,000 shirts a year for £50 with players' names and numbers on them. 'We get £30 million turnover from sales – but the shirts only cost £5 to make in Asia,' said Hall. They listed their favourite stops on their sex-filled world tour while on official business – relating tales of their brushes with prostitutes in Geneva, Amsterdam, New York, Las Vegas, Atlantic City, Denmark, the south of France, Lisbon, Thailand and London, and also revealed they have one woman, Maria, flown around the world from Athens to entertain them wherever they are. 'She is the best. The dirtiest. She's a Greek,' said Hall, offering the reporter a night with her.

At another strip club, Crescendo in Puerto Banus, both men chatted up two English strippers and disappeared into the back of the club with them. The bawdy binge carried on until 4.30 a.m.

When the paper splashed their scoop, the repurcussions were enormous.

Sunday, 15 March
Fans are furious. 'They've brought shame and disgrace on the name of Newcastle United and we don't want people like that in our football club,' says Kevin Myles of the Independent Newcastle Supporters' Association.

Alan Shearer was the only Geordie not offended. He insisted: 'I've had worse things said about me than that. I am boring, aren't I?'

Monday, 17 March
A share plunge wipes £9 million off Newcastle United's stock-market value. Other club directors, women's groups and Roman Catholic leader Cardinal Basil Hume join the protests. Even Prime Minister Tony Blair expresses his concern.

Thursday, 19 March
Relegation-threatened United lose 2–1 to bottom-of-the-table Crystal Palace. Afterwards 1,000 fans gather outside the directors' box demanding their resignation. Toon legend Malcolm MacDonald says: 'This is the result of the past few days, not of the last 90 minutes, and sadly the women supporters are going to push and push because the apology is not good enough.'

Friday, 20 March
Shepherd goes to the High Court to win an injunction banning the

paper printing more allegations. But after a three-hour hearing, Mr Justice Lindsay says a 'series of lewd and boastful claims about whoring his way around the world' could not be made confidential. He added: 'If someone wanted to keep something confidential, talking about it in Spanish brothels is not the way to do it.'

Hall and Shepherd insist they have been 'set up' and will not step down.

Tuesday, 24 March
Shepherd and Hall step down. But the pair retain their 60 per cent shareholding in the club and appoint their own representatives to the board. At 12.20 a.m., after a marathon board meeting, a statement faxed to the media says it is 'in order to ensure that the allegations made against them do not further affect Newcastle United and to enable them to concentrate their energies on restoring their reputations'.

Wednesday, 25 March
Hall's father, Sir John, 65, returns as stand-in chairman 114 days after retiring. Hall says: 'The vilification of Freddy and Douglas is terrible to watch. Yes, it's self-inflicted, but why were they targeted? Why were they set up? Why were they the subject of such an elaborate and expensive scam?'

Shepherd is on holiday in Barbados with his wife Lorelle when the news is announced. Shares rise by 5p to 100p – ironically Hall earns £5 million as his 57 per cent is valued at £81.7 million.

Thursday, 2 July
Hall's wife Tonia, 35 – a former glamour model – has filed for divorce. She is said by friends to be 'utterly sickened' by the revelations and demands a £15 million settlement for herself and their two sons, aged 12 and 9.

Tonia's mum, Sandra Pallister, says: 'Tonia filed for divorce this week and served the papers on Douglas. But pressure was put on her to keep the family unit together for the good of the boys.'

A friend says: 'There are very few women who could remain married to the kind of man Douglas has been exposed as. It was not just a case of him committing adultery discreetly or having the odd one-night stand. It was uncontrolled and perverted lust and Tonia has been totally humiliated by his behaviour. The last thing he wants is a divorce, it would tear his family apart and cost him a fortune. But Tonia wanted to make sure she and the two boys could live in the manner they are accustomed to.'

Wednesday, 15 July
Tonia changes her mind and decides to stay with her seedy husband for the sake of their boys. 'Mr and Mrs Douglas Hall wish to confirm that any difficulties they may have had have been resolved,' says an official statement.

Friday, 24 July
The disgraced directors are reinstated to the club board. Freddy Shepherd announces: 'We were very, very stupid and we apologise unreservedly for our behaviour.'

Shares fall from 98p to 92p. Shepherd announces his wife Lorelle, 53, has stuck with him. Telling her about the allegations was 'the worst thing I have ever had to do,' he says. 'I have been extremely lucky. She was not happy but she understands all the circumstances surrounding the conversations and she has been extremely supportive. Anyone who says that sort of publicity doesn't hurt is lying, believe me.

'But I am not making excuses,' he insisted, before making excuses . . . 'What I did was stupid but was never as bad as was made out. Most of the conversation was drunken bragging. There is no way we could have got up to half those things, it's humanly impossible. I have learned my lesson. I want to go forward and hope that people will see how genuinely sorry I am.'

Tuesday, 8 December
Shepherd and Hall vote themselves back on to the board of Newcastle United Plc. Three directors resign in protest. Shares fall 3p to 95p at the news. A city analyst says: 'It was always obvious they would be back. On or off the board, they have such a huge shareholding they basically run the company as their own private fiefdom.'

Considering their crimes against their own fans, the price the sleazy Toon twosome paid – a seven-month exile from board meetings – was small change. The private toll was heavier.

For three years after the scandal, Douglas Hall lay low in his Gibraltar tax haven. When he did return it was without his familiar moustache and with his bouffant hair cropped short. If he seemed a man in hiding, it was because he was. 'It's been a difficult three years,' he said. 'I've hidden in the background because I got more than I could stand from the newspapers. The newspaper thing was unfair, but it's history now and my intention is to pass my shares on to my children.'

By 2003 those shares were trading at around 25p – a quarter of their value at the time of the scandal. Rumours are rife that Hall and Shepherd intend to take the club off the stock market. Maybe then their indiscretions will cost them dearly . . .

NOEL-WILLIAMS, Gifton
Born: Islington 21.1.1980
Career: Watford, Stoke City

The powerhouse striker and part-time preacher extolled family values from the pulpit – then prayed away with his secret girlfriend.

The gifted goalscorer, still only 22 but married with three kids, walked out on his family after a summer of horrendous rows. Wife Dee demanded a divorce after discovering he:

● CHEATED on her while she was in bed with pneumonia;

● MET lover Rachel Odonzo while out blessing new houses for members of his congregation;

● GAVE her the family's pet dog, a Staffordshire bull terrier called Zion;

● GOT her pregnant then

● INVITED her to join worshippers at his church secretly, while Dee and their kids stood just a few pews away at the Mount Zion Spiritualist Baptist Church.

Dee, 26, discovered her husband's secret after he moved out of their £500,000 *Footballers' Wives*-style house in Bushey, Hertfordshire. She said: 'My son Dejon came home from visiting Gifton and said: "Daddy is going out with Rachel and she's having his baby." I couldn't believe it.'

The ace then told Dee to leave the house and banned her from using their Mercedes and Land-Rover. When he stopped giving her money for their kids, Daje, six, Dejon, four, and eleven-month-old Gene, she reported him to the Child Support Agency. Dee said: 'I couldn't believe someone who loved God could act that way, particularly with his own children.'

She moved with their children into a smaller three-bed semi and got a job on the checkouts in Asda to make ends meet. And when newspapers confronted her about her cheating husband, Dee compared him to *Footballers' Wives* bad boy Jason Turner.

She told the *Daily Star*: 'Jason can't hold a candle to Gifton in real life. Neither of them can keep it in their pants, but what makes Gifton worse is he portrays himself as a man of God. When I watch the show it reminds me of the life I used to lead – the big house, flash cars, and luxury holidays. But it also hammers home the downside to being a footballer's wife – the footballer!'

The couple had once seemed a match made in heaven. Noel-Williams became a hero to Hornets fans when he made his debut aged just 16 – the youngest player in the club's history. Dee supported her teenage toyboy financially as they had their first baby. In 1999, he was the club's top scorer as they reached the Premiership – even though a serious knee injury at Sunderland in January stopped his season in its tracks. For 18 months the prodigy's career lay in the balance as he battled back to fitness. It was a testing time. But Gifton was a clean-living kid with an old head on his shoulders.

When he returned in 2000, with WATFORD relegated in his absence, he said: 'I was in a bad way and there were times when I didn't think I would play again. But my faith in God and my family helped pull me through. I have a deep faith in God and go to church every Sunday. That helped me through the darkest hours – and believe me, times were tough.

'Apart from my faith, my family kept my feet on the ground when I had success and they lifted me when I had tough times. There's mum, Dee and our kids – with them around, you can never get too big-headed and you can never get too down about things. There was a time when the doctors had to refer me to a specialist in the States, so the whole family flew out to Boston and the treatment seemed to do me good.'

He added: 'So much has happened so soon in my life that sometimes I wonder how I coped. My dad died when I was 13 so I had to become the man of the house. Then my fiancée Dee and I had our first child when I was 16, around the time I was making my Watford debut. Everything was going great until the injury.'

And until he became the horniest Hornet of them all.

Sheepish Noel-Williams, who moved to Stoke City in June 2003, said of his fall from grace: 'This has nothing to do with the church. It is my personal affair. It is true that Rachel had my baby last week. I still go to the church. It is still part of my life.'

NORTHERN IRELAND

'Win or Lose, on the Boobs!' After a 3–1 drubbing away to Czechoslovakia which left them bottom of their group and out of the European Championships, the men in green donned their glad rags for a night on the town – and all hell broke loose.

The boys headed for the sleazy Nancy Show Cabaret Club just off Wenceslas Square in the heart of cosmopolitan Prague. The resident strippers performed their acclaimed tabledances for the downhearted Ulstermen and thoroughly earned their £200-a-night takings. But the players all showed their composure by rising to leave the club at 7 a.m. – anxious to get their heads down for a couple of hours before flying home to Belfast. Then disaster struck.

Club owner Pavel Schick said: 'There was no problems until it came to paying the bill. They were escorted to the cash desk by some of our lovely hostesses but refused to pay. They claimed it was too much money. They were horribly aggressive and a flowerpot was thrown at the bouncer who was trying to calm the situation down. We did nothing to provoke them. When the flowerpot was thrown we just called the police and left them alone.'

The 16 st. doorman was left with a black eye, a swollen nose and stitches. Meanwhile the players made their getaway in a fleet of taxis and returned to their luxury hotel.

At 9.30 a.m. Czech police arrived and ordered the squad to hand over their passports. Next they had to line up – and it wasn't for a team photo! The injured bouncer picked out five from the impromptu ID parade, and Michael Hughes, Glenn Ferguson, David Healy, Peter Kennedy and goalkeeping coach Tommy Wright were thrown unceremoniously into police cells.

Boss Sammy McIlroy insisted his men were innocent. 'There is great doubt over who caused this injury to the nightclub security man and over who started the fight. They're a good set of lads and they've done nothing wrong.' The former Manchester United and Northern Ireland hero was proved right when twelve hours later all five were released without charge.

'This is great news,' said a relieved McIlroy. 'It's been a very difficult day but it's had a happy ending.' The squad returned home to fight another day.

NOTTAGE, Jane

Scotland boss Andy ROXBURGH OBE would have impressed his own athletic players when his mistress described sex with him as 'supersonic'. The 50-year-old married manager was so sexy, she reckoned, even her mother fancied him!

Roxburgh met Jane Nottage, 37 – a businesswoman, football writer and Paul GASCOIGNE's former minder in Italy – at an expo in Atlanta, Georgia, in 1991. She was there to interview England boss Graham Taylor for soccer magazine *Shoot*. But it was the Scotland boss, married for 30 years and a father-of-one, who was something to write home about. They 'fell into each other's arms' and retired to his hotel room where they 'talked' into the early hours. Soon they were romping their way across the globe as a frantic three-month affair began.

'It was like two stars colliding,' she panted. 'He took me to new peaks of ecstasy. Andy was by far the greatest lover I have ever had – I was totally bowled over. It was the best sex ever. He was tall and slim without an ounce of fat.' Roxburgh even recorded a tape of romantic songs for her, inscribed 'Roxy Music'.

Three months later the rampant affair ended, reportedly because of the soccer boss's guilt at cheating on wife Catherine.

It was two years before their affair became public. Jane blamed a leak from one of her old pal Gazza's camp to the tabloids in September 1993, in the same week Roxburgh quit his £70,000-a-year job after failing to reach the World Cup finals.

Jane decided to sell her story, posing for sexy photos and including lurid descriptions of their love-making. It was a kiss-and-sell she was to regret. 'Now everyone thinks I'm the bimbo,' she said.

And it was the last time she would ever talk to raging Roxburgh.

Later she confessed: 'If there were only 100 women left in this world, I'm sure I'd be number 99 and a half on his list after what's happened. I would like to get in touch with him again, but I'm not hungering after him. We had a great relationship, the sex was supersonic, fantastic, but there are other fish in the sea, I hope! I'd like to think he still remembers our friendship and has good memories about me. But that may be difficult to expect after all that's gone on.'

She talked of her 'guilt', told how she hoped he could patch up his marriage and added: 'It couldn't have been particularly nice for Andy's family, but he came out of it very well because he's the good guy who just happens to have been caught up with a bimbo. Everyone thought he was boring and strait-laced until it all appeared.'

OAKLEY, Matthew
Born: Peterborough, 17.8.1977
Career: Southampton

The saintly Saints playmaker dumped his girlfriend on her 21st birthday – and not even for another woman! Oakley told Helen Moody he had to concentrate on his football – despite her sexy late-night dances for him in her shortest skirt. Helen said: 'It wasn't a normal relationship. We'd go to clubs sometimes, but he seemed to prefer being out with the lads than me. Then he dumped me after two months together. He said he was worried the manager thought he was spending too much time with me.'

Helen lamented: 'He had a groin strain most of the time that I knew him so we only did it once a week if I was lucky.'

O'BOYLE, George

Born: Belfast 14.12.67

Career: Manchester City, Distillery, Linfield, Bordeaux, Dunfermline, St Johnstone, Raith Rovers, Brechin City, Queen of the South, Glenavon, Ards

The Ulster-born star is notorious north of the border for booting out his wife and child for a blonde shop boss, allegedly snorting cocaine in a nightclub toilet and being named in a sex-and-bribes scandal in France.

O'Boyle fell for married mum Karen Scobie while visiting her fashion shop to buy clothes for his two-year-old daughter Georgia in 1997. He sent wife Joanne, 28, and little Georgia packing from their luxury home near Perth, then defaulted on £5,000 maintenance payments. In a final insult, when the CSA forced him to pay he reportedly sent a cheque signed by his new woman.

Two years later, Northern Ireland international O'Boyle, a £20,000 signing from Dunfermline in 1994, was named in a report into corruption at French side Bordeaux, where he had transferred from Linfield, in Northern Ireland, nine years earlier. Around £580,000 was apparently siphoned off from his fee without the player's knowledge.

In 2001, bad boy O'Boyle – battling back after abdominal surgery – suffered further disgrace when he was discovered by Saints physio Nick Summersgill apparently snorting cocaine in the toilet of Perth's trendy That Bar during a Christmas party for the club's injured players. O'Boyle, after 82 goals in 164 games, and teammate Kevin THOMAS were fired days later.

OYSTON, Owen

It was the most extraordinary board meeting in football history – held inside the prison where Blackpool FC's multi-millionaire chairman was beginning a six-year sentence for rape.

Bearded jailbird Owen Oyston, 62, sat with his wife Vicki and an associate to discuss the future of the club, his radio and media empire and the five farms he owned. Guards sat in at all times on the meeting and, after any other business, the chairman returned to his bleak cell at Wymott Prison, near Chorley, Lancashire.

The socialist tycoon's downfall had been spectacular and costly, involving three trials and an estimated £1.5 million defence fund to try to secure his freedom.

At first his heavy spending on the finest legal brains appeared to be helping him stay out of jail. Magistrates threw out one rape charge and two of indecent assault, and on 22 May 1996, after an 18-day trial at Liverpool Crown Court, a jury of eight women and four men found him not guilty of raping an 18-year-old former model (Miss A).

His reprieve was short lived.

The same jury – after another eight hours and twenty-one minutes of deliberation – found him guilty of raping a 16-year-old model (Miss B) at his home – a castle-like sixteenth-century manor house with 50 rooms in Lancashire, and guilty of indecently assaulting the same woman on the back seat of a sports car.

Oyston had said during an earlier trial: 'Anyone who commits rape deserves the worst kind of sentence. Any woman who suffers rape has an awful ordeal.' Now justice would be done.

Mr Justice McCullough announced his sentence after a withering attack on the tycoon, worth an estimated £40 million. He was to serve six years for rape and three years, to run concurrently, for indecent assault.

Oyston, flamboyant as ever in a double-breasted navy-blue suit with silk marigold hanky in his breast pocket, bit his lip and fought back tears as the judge told him he had committed 'horrendous offences' and shown no hint of remorse.

He had lured the girl to his home after meeting her through a friend's modelling agency, the court heard. 'You were 58 and Miss B was 16,' said the judge. 'You were rich and powerful with a strong personality. She was young, dependent and vulnerable. This aggravates the offence. I do not believe she led you on in any way. I am, however, prepared to assume you hoped that your advantages – age, wealth and position – would influence her to agree to what you wanted. When it came to it, she didn't and it must have been obvious she did not. As she so accurately put it, "He treated me like an object and I am not." It is impossible to know to what extent she has been traumatised by the experience of that night.'

From inside the jail, Oyston still, it appeared, pulled the strings at the Oyston Group, owners of Blackpool FC, although his wife Vicki, with power of attorney, was now chairman. 'The same people are running the Oyston Group,' she explained. 'The only difference is Owen is no longer chairman. I am, and I am having to work 16 hours a day and learn at the same time.'

Of the jail meeting, she said: 'Everyone sent to jail is allowed one meeting to sort out his affairs. Mostly we discussed farming – we have just taken over a big farm locally and now have five covering 3,000 acres. We also touched on property, football, radio, publishing and one or two legal matters. I would like to nail this lie about Owen conducting his business from jail. He simply cannot have much influence from where he is, although, obviously, I might ask his advice on some things.'

Blackpool manager Sam Allardyce, now boss of Premiership Bolton Wanderers, certainly felt Oyston was behind his sacking from Blackpool soon after. 'It was lunacy,' said Allardyce. 'We had missed automatic promotion by one point and then lost in the play-off semi-final. Two months later I was out. I had taken the club to their best position in 16 years and that was the reward I got.' Vicki later handed control of the club to their son Karl.

Oyston was released on parole from Wealston Prison, in Yorkshire, in January 1999 after serving three and a half years of his sentence. He refused to confess to his crime, but admitted to an MP he had had sex with young women. He said: 'There will be no celebration until my name is cleared.' The former Blackpool chief remains convinced he was set up.

P

PADFIELD, Emma

Notorious seducer of soccer stars who hung up her knee-length boots in 2002 to become – she claimed – a quiet country housewife. A dedicated professional who carried spy equipment and had her own press office, the Yorkshire lass boasted of:

- BEDDING former Manchester United winger Lee SHARPE;
- BAGGING Leeds United midfielder Lee BOWYER;
- BLAGGING cash for tales of her romps with fallen idol Frank McAVENNIE.

The platinum blonde – a former Miss Great Britain finalist – was just 19 when she met Lee Sharpe, 29, in Leeds bar Evolution. Sharpe's career was in freefall, but he was celebrating a move from Leeds United to Italian aces Sampdoria. She said: 'He had a really cheeky smile and I thought he was cute.' By the end of the night she had his phone number.

After two dates she visited his home in swish Roundhay, Leeds, where, after watching MTV and downing Hooch, they retired to his bedroom. 'It was very spacious,' she said, 'because he had his wardrobes in another room. The wall opposite the bedhead was completely mirrored and there were those candles everywhere – dozens of them – big fat ones, cream ones, multi-coloured ones. And he insisted on lighting them all – almost as if it were a sort of ritual before we started to make love. Inside the bedroom he disappeared for a few moments. I knew what he had in mind and I definitely wanted it as much as he did. Luckily I always carry a condom in my purse.'

Emma stripped and climbed into the bed to wait for him.

Moments later Lee returned naked. 'He looked irresistible,' she recalled. 'He was every inch the athlete – and it didn't take me long to realise that he could act like one in bed, too. I felt a wave of pleasure rippling through my body. It was electric. Then Lee carefully rolled on top of me and we made love twice as he whispered my name over and over in my ear. Afterwards I laid my head on his chest as he wrapped me up in his arms. It did occur to me at the time that I probably wasn't the first person to get this treatment because he's so gorgeous, but he still made me feel like a princess.'

Bed was good, but breakfast was boring. 'I knew his fridge was empty from the night before, but not even I bargained for what he produced – a few pieces of chicken PIZZA left over from a takeaway.' It was their last supper. Or breakfast. Lee moved abroad and Emma continued her manhunt for famous footballers and tabloid fortunes. She sold her first kiss-and-tell, about Sharpe, to the *News of the World* in February 1999.

After a publicity-seeking appearance on TV's *Blind Date* (she wore no knickers and, of course, told the world), Emma spotted, and bedded, her next prey. She met midfield powerhouse Lee Bowyer in Leeds' Majestyk nightclub – the scene of a future notorious attack on Sarfraz Najeib. 'I thought Lee was ugly, but he grew on me,' she said. 'Once I got chatting to him, I thought he had a great personality and we had a laugh. I don't normally sleep with guys straight away, but things just felt right and we went back to my hotel room. He started kissing me and touching me all over. He had a nice smooth body. We had sex for about an hour, then fell asleep exhausted.'

Two months later, in his mansion after a party to celebrate his Player of the Season award, Bowyer suggested a tactical switch with his teammate Jonathan WOODGATE. 'Lee suggested we went to bed, but then added, "Oh, there's an odd number – there are three of us." I'd had a fair bit to drink so I agreed. Jon followed us upstairs and I could tell from the grin on Lee's face what he had in mind. But I went along with it because I trusted him. When we got into the room, I undressed and climbed into bed while Lee took all his clothes off. Jon watched as Lee got into bed and started kissing me. Lee and I began to have sex and Jon could not take his eyes off us. Soon he undressed and sat down on a chair, watching me and Lee. I didn't mind because I'd had a few drinks and lost my inhibitions. You could tell Lee was really turned on by knowing we were being watched. Lee asked if Jon could join in and Jon got into bed and started kissing me. Lee wanted me to have sex with Jon but I didn't want to go all the way. I only kissed and cuddled Jon but Lee kept trying to get me to go further. He kept saying, "Go on, it's a team game", but I insisted I did not want to have sex with Jon.' Woodgate, she informed *The People* in June 1999, then left the bedroom and went to join Emma's pal Kerry and fellow Leeds star Alan Smith who were partying in the next room.

A month later her relationship with Bowyer was over. When he showed friends a video of them making love, Emma claims she blew the whistle for full time. 'Bowyer's a prat,' she hissed. 'Fame goes to footballers' heads and they think they can get away with anything.'

Emma – the undoubted queen of soccer kiss-and-sells – gave away her trade secrets in a high-profile TV documentary in April 2000. She explained how she carried a Dictaphone to record incriminating conversations and a small camera to collect evidence when her target fell asleep after sex. In her home she had an office complete with photocopier to do her deals with the papers. On average, she revealed, she could earn £10,000 each time she bagged a player, but, she revealed, 'If you have two or three Premiership footballers at the same time, it's £20,000.'

When fallen CELTIC, West Ham United and Scotland ace Frank McAvennie was on remand over cocaine peddling charges, for which he was subsequently acquitted, Emma decided to cash in again. She offered Scotland's *Sunday Mail* an exclusive story about their romps inside prison. It proved a lurid tale too far. A far-right terror group – the Justice Organisation – sent a chilling death threat to her home warning her to change her lifestyle or die. With stars wising up to her tactics – and the tabloids screwing down the price for soccer sex stories – Emma announced the end of her career. She was giving up the kiss-and-sell to settle down with a new boyfriend and a life mucking out horses and, she hopes, having children. Premiership players – and their wives – can sleep easier from now on.

See GROUP SEX.

PALIOS, Mark

Born: Liverpool 9.11.1952

Career: Tranmere Rovers, Crewe Alexandra

Former lower-league defender-turned-financial-firefighter who became chief executive of the FA – then crashed and burned after a fling with a secretary. Palios, 51, a twice-divorced father-of-five, had a brief fling with Faria ALAM, who also bedded England boss Sven-Göran ERIKSSON. When an FA spokesman's offer to discredit Eriksson in newspapers and leave Palios untainted was revealed, the chief executive resigned. It was a blow for the national game. In his 18-month reign, respected Palios had cut the game's spiralling debt, taken a tough stance on discipline and put the new Wembley Stadium project back on track.

Alam claimed she had twice made love to Palios after falling for his 'sexy voice and charismatic presence' in July 2003, but added that it was uninspiring. She said: 'He wanted the FA to be like the Vatican and stand for the highest principles.' But when the scandal broke, she said, Palios told her to deny their relationship.

PALMER, Carlton

Born: West Bromwich 5.12.1965

Career: Player – West Bromwich Albion, Sheffield Wednesday, Leeds United, Southampton, Nottingham Forest, Coventry City, Watford (loan), Sheffield Wednesday (loan). Player/Manager – Stockport County

The gangly England midfielder was all arms and legs and never knew when he was beaten – just like the boozy night the married dad of two groped an 18-year-old girl and offered to show her his tackle.

It was near closing time in Leeds' Square On The Lane pub – the biggest bar in Europe – on a freezing night in January 1997 when the £2.6 million Leeds United captain struck during a night out with teammates Ian Rush, Lee SHARPE, Brian Deane and Rod Wallace.

The girl, an office worker, told magistrates: 'I was talking to Rod Wallace and Carlton Palmer turned round and asked me what my problem was. I replied, "Nothing." He pulled his mobile phone from his pocket and put it in front of my face and said, "Ring my wife and tell her I'll be home next week." I was quite shocked.'

The court heard that Wallace made a remark about the size of a black man's penis. The girl added: 'I said I wasn't interested and as far as I was concerned it was a myth. Carlton Palmer said, "Come here and I'll show you." He put his hand in between the top of my legs over my trousers. I did nothing to provoke this behaviour. I was very upset and shocked and crying. I felt shocked, humiliated.'

She continued: 'I pushed him away and told him to get his hands off me. As I said that, he grabbed me by the shoulders and pushed me into a one-armed bandit. I slapped him with my right hand and told him he was bang out of order.' Striker Brian Deane pulled Palmer away and the stars left the bar. The girl told the doorman what had happened, then left for a nightclub.

In the early hours of the morning, the second half kicked off. The girl spotted Palmer and his teammates in a club and left to report the attack to police in a van outside. In court, Palmer claimed the girl was drunk and 'out for a good time', denied indecent assault and said the case had threatened his career and marriage.

She insisted she'd drunk just four halves of lager all evening and denied pestering him for his autograph. Witness Ashley Farmer, a student, told the court Palmer had tried to touch the girl's breasts before she 'ran off crying'.

Palmer looked stunned as he was convicted of indecent assault. Stipendiary magistrate David Loy Palmer told him: 'I am conscious of the effect this conviction will have on you. Bearing this in mind and also because the assault wasn't for a very long period and the gravest offence, I am going to fine you.'

Palmer had been lucky. Earning a reported £7,000 a week, he would have to work just four hours to cover the £600 fine plus costs of £338. To be paid within 14 days, if at all possible.

The leniency shocked many. Legal advice group Rights of Women said: 'The magistrate seems more concerned about the effect of the case on the perpetrator than the young woman.'

Palmer announced he would appeal. But first there was the small matter of his trial for assaulting a policeman on the same night.

As Palmer and his teammates crossed from the pub to a nightclub, he had screamed obscenities at police officers. 'I earn more than all you wankers put together,' he told the boys in blue. 'Get some f***ing work done, you wankers.' After allegedly pushing an officer, Palmer was arrested. In court he said the policemen had poked fun at him for clubbing instead of training. A week after being found guilty of indecent assault he was fined another £450, with £190 costs, for disorderly conduct. He was acquitted of assaulting a police constable.

Four months later Judge Brian Walsh threw out his appeal, branded him a liar and increased his fine to £1,000 and hit him with an extra £1,500 costs. The judge said teammates Lee Sharpe and Rod Wallace had been 'ill at ease' in the witness box because 'they were not giving a fair and honest account to the court'. And he told Palmer – now transferred to Southampton: 'You are plainly guilty on the evidence of a grubby little offence.'

PANDA

Soccer MASCOT Paisley Panda was told to cool down his act when he taunted rival fans by simulating sex with an inflatable sheep before a clash with rivals Queen of the South. Furious visiting fans – upset by his insinuations about their sexual leanings – complained to police at St Mirren's Love Street ground and officers warned the man in the furry suit, Chris Kelly, 24, to tone down his act. He escaped without a formal charge.

Chris said: 'When the cops spoke to me, I was a bit worried I'd lose the slot as Paisley Panda. They said they knew I had a job to do but I had to drop the sheep gimmick. I was pretty gutted.'

Lifelong St Mirren fan Chris, of Uddingston, Lanarkshire, volunteered for the job after the last mascot quit. And, though unpaid, took pride in his efforts at winding up the club's opponents. He explained: 'I'm at the cutting edge of football mascotry and I have a duty to entertain my fans. If adopting risqué routines means I'm labelled the black sheep of the mascot world then so be it. My girlfriend thinks I'm crazy but turns a blind eye.'

A police spokesman said: 'The Panda was told to ensure his behaviour was appropriate for a football match.'

PARIS

City of romance, and, for love-rat football personalities in 1998, a perfect place to mix business with pleasure. Stars entertaining their mistresses at the 1998 tournament in France include Viv ANDERSON, Mark LAWRENSON, Des LYNAM and Bryan ROBSON.

During the same tournament, Stan COLLYMORE attacked his then girlfriend Ulrika JONSSON.

PARRIS, Emma

Notorious soccer groupie who kisses and sells her tales to tabloids.

In 2002 the sales and (self) promotions girl, from Selhurst, south London, boasted of flings with three players.

First up was Millwall midfielder Bobby BOWRY in 1994. 'His body was rock hard,' she reported. 'He's quite skinny but his legs are big and firm. We did it standing up in a nightclub but it only lasted about five minutes. We had to be quick because of the bouncers.' Two years later, she claimed, she met him again. 'He told me he had a girlfriend and baby. I was upset, but let him come back to my flat. As soon as we got in the door he pinned me up against the cupboard. We ripped each other's clothes off and made love four times, then he went home.'

Emma next pulled Orient ace Jason BRISSET. She was by now earning the nickname 'Chopper Parris' – and not after the 1970s Chelsea stopper.

Birmingham City star Clinton MORRISON – 18, single and a rising star at Crystal Palace – was easy meat. 'We had it the first time he came round to my flat on the living room floor. He may be well endowed, but he's very quick,' she said. 'I used to say to him, "I'm not sleeping with you again because you're rubbish." He used to tell me to shut up and say he'd been practising and that he had some new moves for me. But the sex was always the same. When I first started seeing him, we used to have sex twice a week. But he never stayed over. He was a real mummy's boy and went home to his mother. It was very selfish.'

PEEPING TOM

See Martin EDWARDS.

PFA AWARDS

The players' annual awards bash turned into a wild sex orgy when seven stars did the honours with a fan. Sarah MOORE claimed she bagged the players at London's Embassy Hotel in March 1993 and that Manchester City's goalkeeping lothario Andy DIBBLE was the No. 1 performer. She claimed Dibble bonked her seven times in just three hours as she went from room to room. He apparently knocked at the door and walked in with a friend to take over as she recovered from bedding another player. Other players, she said, took photos of the action for a scrapbook she was keeping of her big night out. She even claimed that at one point she shared a single bed with five men covered in cream!

Moore later explained her motive – 'It was my wildest fantasy come true' – but complained that most of the players had ignored her at breakfast the following morning – except Dibble. 'They were fine when they were getting it off me,' she complained. 'For three solid hours I was on my back. But they just turned their backs on me the next morning.'

See GROUP SEX.

PICK, Carolyn

Sex-craved stalker who blackmailed a former England star for five years.

See EROTOMANIA, Mr X.

PIZZA

See David BECKHAM, Paul GASCOIGNE, Ruud GULLIT, Emma PADFIELD, Lee SHARPE.

PLEAT, David

Born: Nottingham 15.1.1945
Career: Nottingham Forest, Luton Town, Shrewsbury Town, Exeter City, Peterborough United. Manager – Luton Town, Tottenham Hotspur, Luton Town, Sheffield Wednesday

The Tottenham Hotspur boss was forced to resign after being cautioned three times for kerb-crawling. Pleat, famous for galloping wildly across the pitch when his Luton Town team beat relegation at Manchester City in 1982, was exposed to a shocked football world by *The Sun* in June 1987. Prostitute Wendy Branagan told how he had picked her up from Luton's red-light area of Bury Park in his car and drove her to a deserted car park behind his team's Kenilworth Road ground. After sex in the car – in view of his office just yards away – he drove her back to Bury Park, where vice cops pounced. Pleat was cautioned – and incredibly picked up another caution three days later. Wendy later claimed he once paid her £80 for a lesbian act with another hooker in the back of his car. Another prostitute Heather

Barrett told how he tried to haggle the £15 fee for sex down to a fiver! 'I told him to f*** off!' she revealed.

Pleat, who had just taken up a £90,000-a-year job as Spurs boss, was backed by his new board. But four months later new scandal emerged. Pleat had been cautioned again, this time by undercover officers as he cruised George Street in London's West End in his Merc. Pleat resigned, though his wife Maureen stood by him. He later bounced back with spells at Luton Town, Sheffield Wednesday and as director of football (and caretaker boss) back at Tottenham.

● In 1996, Arsenal star Ian WRIGHT was charged with misconduct after calling Pleat a 'pervert'. Pleat, then Sheffield Wednesday boss, had criticised Wright for pulling the dreadlocked hair of Regi Blinker and stamping on Dejan Stefanovic. 'It was just a joke,' Wright protested.

PORTSMOUTH FC

The words 'Portsmouth' and 'top of the table' were rarely mentioned in the same sentence for 50 years until their League title win in 2002–03 – apart from the time commercial manager Julie Baker was axed over allegations of rumpy-Pompey on the boardroom table. Miss Baker, 50, was forced out after claims that, as directors sipped their drinks after a friendly game against Birmingham City, she bragged about making love perched on the expansive table. She told an employment tribunal in Southampton she was 'devastated' when then chairman Martin Gregory made the allegations of 'bawdy behaviour' and said she was told she must resign or face a scandal.

Tribunal chairman Neil Jenkinson called the club's behaviour 'outrageous' and, in March 1999, awarded the £25,000-a-year worker £55,000 compensation for unfair dismissal and sexual discrimination. Sadly, with the club in the hands of administrators, she discovered she would have to join a long list of creditors before getting her hands on the cash.

POWELL, Tony
Born: Bristol 11.6.1947
Career: Bath City, Bournemouth, Norwich City, San Jose Earthquakes,
Seattle Sounders

> Knocker Powell
> Superstar
> Walks like a woman
> And he wears a bra
> And a frock
> *– Anon*

Norwich City's hard man defender sparked a 'womanhunt' when the
club tried to find former players for a centenary reunion. The ex-
Canary was said to have disappeared in San Francisco after a sex-
swap op, and become a bird – wearing women's clothes, high heels
and lipstick.

The blond-maned man-mountain they called 'Knocker' had left
the club in 1981 . . . then simply vanished. When club officials
couldn't find their 1978 Player of the Year, newspapers stepped in.
And found their *man*.

Powell, now a greying 55 year old, was discovered working as the
manager of a rundown Hollywood motel. And he was gobsmacked
by the rumours. 'It's ridiculous,' he told an intrepid reporter from
the *Mail on Sunday*. 'I don't know where this started. I am all bloke,
I can assure you. I've never worn a frock in my life and my tackle is
still intact. I'm the least likely man to have a sex swap. I had a
reputation as a hard, but fair, player.'

He explained how he had dropped out of sight after leaving
Norwich for the San Jose Earthquakes then the Seattle Sounders.
When the club went bust, he hung up his boots. Then his marriage
failed. 'I dropped off the radar because I hated all the celebrity
stuff,' said Powell. 'When I came to the States, I left all that behind.
My wife came with me from England but we divorced in the States.
I have a brother and sister in the UK but I haven't been in England
for years and I never kept in touch with my mates. My parents are
both dead. I still see my kids but the divorce was nasty.'

Powell explained: 'I lead a quiet life and I can promise you it doesn't involve stilettos and lipstick. Not even in the privacy of my own room.' A room in a modest flat, he explained, that he shared with another man. 'But I promise I'm straight,' he added quickly.

A 'nasty' divorce was an understatement. As readers of the *Mail on Sunday* would soon discover.

Powell's ex-wife Marilyn read the story aghast, then called the paper to give her side of the story and make amazing revelations of her own. Marilyn was pregnant by another man when she met the 23-year-old Powell on a girls' night out in 1970 in Bournemouth, where he was a rising star with the Cherries.

Marilyn, then 20, said: 'He had an amazing body. I was pregnant and amazed that he even showed an interest. When Kelly was born he was great with her. Our relationship started very slowly. I was living at home and he was in digs so there was little opportunity for hanky-panky. We made love a few times in the car.'

On 19 August 1972, Bournemouth boss John Bond was guest of honour as the couple married. 'We got married in the morning and Tony played that afternoon,' said Marilyn. 'We didn't make love on our wedding night because he told me he was too exhausted from the game. It sounds crazy but I didn't know any better. Tony was always telling me he couldn't have sex because he needed all his energy for the game. He was always macho in public, but in private was sensitive and quiet. We'd have sex maybe once a month. I thought that was normal.'

In 1974, Bond, now boss of ambitious Norwich City, bought Knocker to bolster his defence. Fans loved his 100 per cent, all-action style. 'Girls were after him but he would always come home,' said Marilyn. 'He was drinking quite heavily in those days but only between Sunday and Wednesday. Then he'd stop and prepare for Saturday's match.'

The couple had a child of their own, Danielle, in 1975. 'He was a perfect father. He loved the baby. He liked to dress and feed her. We had a fairly normal relationship except that he found it hard to be affectionate.'

Marilyn also revealed that Tony became great friends with Norwich City's new striking sensation Justin FASHANU – who would later hang himself after being accused of GAY sex assault crimes.

The couple's life began to unravel in 1981 when Powell, nearing the end of his career, was signed by San Jose. His friend George BEST was already there and put the family up. Marilyn recalled, 'Tony got £30,000 for signing for San Jose. I was looking after two little girls. I didn't even notice our sex life had become non-existent.'

Two years later, Powell moved on to Seattle, but the soccer league in America, already failing, went bust. To earn money, Marilyn went out to work while Tony stayed at home. 'One day I left and he said he was going to play golf. I was sick and so I came home mid-morning; his car was still outside. I went into the house and went into the bedroom. Tony was in bed doing something disgusting with a young black man. He turned his face and he saw me. I just stared at him. Then I walked out. I was shaking. I felt sick. I went to the supermarket and shopped. By the time I got home, Tony and the man had gone.'

The following day she filed for divorce. Then she discovered thousands of pounds in their bank account had vanished. 'I found hotel receipts and evidence Tony had been keeping this boy for a year. He came back about a week later and I screamed at him and told him I hated him.'

Soon after, Knocker vanished, evading even the private detectives Marilyn hired to find him so he could pay his way. 'We honestly thought he was dead,' said Marilyn, who claimed their daughter Danielle grew up to be a heroin addict because her dad left.

In his missing years, Powell too, the *Mail on Sunday* reported, hit rock bottom, and was arrested for shoplifting and drug offences while working as a youth soccer coach and barman.

Marilyn is still furious at the former football hero. 'Tony Powell has lived a lie his entire life,' she says. 'He lied to his fans, he lied to me. It infuriates me that his legacy in football was that he was a hard man. People compare him to Vinnie JONES but the Tony Powell I knew is a fraud. He says he never wore a dress. Yes, he did,' she adds, brandishing a photo of the centre-half in pink ballgown, curly wig and Dame Edna Everage glasses at a fancy-dress party. 'He was happy that night. He insisted on going down the pub in drag, it was the happiest I'd ever seen him.

'Tony wasn't a transvestite but he is gay,' she said. 'He hid his sexuality from everyone, including me, for years. I want people to know the truth. He is no hero. He is a liar, a coward and a cheat.'

PROFUMO AFFAIR
Both beauties involved in the sex-and-spies scandal that almost
brought down the government in 1963 later had soccer star lovers.
    See Malcolm ALLISON, Christine KEELER, Mandy RICE-DAVIES,
Frank WORTHINGTON.

Q

QUINN, Micky
Born: Liverpool 2.5.1962
Career: Derby County, Wigan Athletic, Stockport County, Oldham
Athletic, Portsmouth, Newcastle United, Coventry City, Plymouth
Argyle (loan), Watford (loan), PAOK Salonika
'It's not easy being a footballer's partner,' says tubby goalscoring
talisman Mick Quinn with remarkable understanding, 'especially
when the footballer in question is out shagging all the time.'
    Believe it or not, the much-travelled barrel-chested bruiser
(nicknamed 'Sumo' for his Billy Bunteresque appearance) was a
soccer sex symbol who had more women than clubs – often all at
once.
    Quinn, born and bred on the mean streets of Liverpool, confessed
to cheating on his partner with *four* barmaids at the same time as he
banged in the goals for PORTSMOUTH in the early '80s.
    He explained: 'Women would throw themselves at me. If I was
in a club, gorgeous women would come straight up to me and
whisper in my ear, "I want to f*** you." Others would slip me bits
of paper with phone numbers on. I felt like Rod Stewart. When I
was at Portsmouth, I actually had four birds on the go at one time.
They were all barmaids, which says a lot about the life I was
leading. I had moved down with my girlfriend Sheila and it was
tough for her.'

Sheila discovered his womanising ways when she listened in to a phone call from a 19-year-old barmaid called Cindy. During the call, he told her their relationship was over.

'She started to wail and say she still loved me,' Quinn recalled in his book, *Who Ate All The Pies*, 'then I heard a click. F★★★. Sheila had been listening on the upstairs extension. After a couple of hours of bare-faced lies, I thought I had talked her round and we went to bed. But Sheila wasn't stupid. After training the next day, I decided to have a booze-and-horses afternoon with a few of the lads. We went to the bookies and then round to mine to watch the racing. As I strode through the front door with the lads behind me, my jaw hit the carpet. The house had been stripped bare. All the furniture had gone, every last stick of it. It turned out Sheila had got her brother to come down from Liverpool with a removal van and gut the place. But we didn't let it stop us. She had left the fridge and it was still stocked with cans of beer. I found a radio and we all sat on the carpet listening to the racing results.'

Quinn's taste for bets, boozing and bedding girls became legendary during a career that brought 231 League goals in 512 appearances. He even landed in jail for three weeks in 1987 when he was twice caught driving while banned.

QUOTES

'He's pulling him off! The Spanish manager is pulling his captain off!' – George Hamilton, RTE commentator, as Emile Butrageno was subbed by Luis Suarez in a World Cup qualifier with Ireland in Seville, 1992

'I used to go missing a lot: Miss Canada, Miss United Kingdom, Miss Germany . . . ' – George Best

'I certainly never found it ever had any effect on my performance. Maybe best not the hour before, but the night before makes no odds.' – George Best

'I dated three Miss Worlds – it should have been seven but I didn't turn up for all of them.' – George Best

'People always say I shouldn't be burning the candle at both ends. Maybe because they don't have a big enough candle.' – George Best

'In her youth the Queen was quite a stunner. Who knows what might have happened if I'd met her at Tramp in my heyday.' – George Best

'Hump it, bump it, whack it might be one possible recipe for a good sex life, but it won't win us the World Cup.' – Ken Bates discussing Graham Taylor's tactics as England manager 1998

'I've always believed in treating the ball like a woman. Give it a cuddle, caress it a wee bit, take your time, and you'll get the required response.' – Former Rangers star Jim Baxter

'Burnley have reached the semi-final of the FA Cup for the first time in 20 years. The Cottagers have been outed.' – Gary Lineker, on *Match of the Day* 2003

'When you've curled the ball into the back of the net once, you know you can do it again.' – Gay striker Justin Fashanu claims to be heterosexual again in 1990

'I get loads of grief, especially if Harry misses a goal. I get "Oh, you're keeping him up too long – stop shagging him."' – *Emmerdale* actress Sheree Murphy, wife of ex-Leeds United and now Liverpool striker Harry Kewell

'The worst thing about sex is that you have to stop and go to work.' – Adriana Karembeu, wife of former Middlesbrough maestro Christian

'They can wear jeans and earrings for all I care but I draw the line at stockings and suspenders . . . until after the match.' – New Wimbledon boss Joe Kinnear orders a revised dress code

'My idea of relaxation: going somewhere away from the wife.' – England and QPR defender Terry Fenwick, 1986

'Who's my most dangerous opponent? My ex-wife.' – Serial soccer seducer Frank Worthington, 1982

'It's certainly an exceptional feeling, but it's not as good as having sex with him.' – Posh on Becks scoring, 2000

'When you're in bed with David Beckham, you don't look at the clock.' – Sarah Marbeck on Becks, 2004

'Germany benefited from a last-gasp hand job on the line.' – Freudian World Cup slip by soccer chief and ITV analyst David Pleat

'I don't know whether to kick him or kiss him.' – Argentina's Diego Simeone on his World Cup tactics against Adonis-like David Beckham, 2002

'Women should be in the kitchen, the disco and the boutique but not in football.' – Villa boss Ron Atkinson in 1989

'Sven can move in with Miss Piggy as long as England deliver on the pitch, which they haven't.' – Henry Winter, *Daily Telegraph* sportswriter

R

RAITH ROVERS

Scandal struck the Scottish club when three young players were accused of raping a teenager. John Cusick, Shaun Rouse and Colin Telford were charged by police after the girl complained she had been attacked at a flat in Kirkcaldy, Fife. Cusick told how he was in bed when his teammates returned with the 19 year old in the early hours. 'The police arrived at 8.30 that morning when I was still in bed. I didn't know what was happening. The next few hours were a nightmare.' Later that day the three – and another man accused of indecent assault, James O'Connell – who was unconnected with the club – were charged and released on bail. Hours after their arrest, Rovers sacked all three players. Six months later, in February 1994, charges against all four were dropped.

Cusick said: 'I feel bitter and angry about what the girl did to us. Football is my life. This has ruined my career.'

REDMOND, Steve

Born: Liverpool 2.11.1967

Career: Manchester City, Oldham Athletic, Bury, Leigh RMI

Married Steve Redmond's name was wrongly dragged through the mud by a randy imposter who trawled Lonely Hearts columns looking for sex. Salesman Mike Gregory advertised himself as 'Professional footballer seeking adult fun'. He promised 'Discreet afternoons of fun' for married or single women, and said he was available 'after training'. He told one would-be partner: 'I'm after adult fun, whatever you want and takes your fancy – that's what it's all about.' To impress his dates he told tales of his friendship with soccer stars like Bryan ROBSON and John BARNES.

Finally, in 1993, Gregory, who lived at home with his mother in Bramhall, Cheshire, was exposed as a fraud by *The People*. He confessed: 'I've got into trouble before for this. I've got a girlfriend and I don't want her to find out what I'm doing.' The real Redmond – whose wife was expecting their third child – was relieved, explaining: 'People always believe the worst of footballers and if this guy had done something stupid the finger would have been pointed at me.'

REFEREES

Greedy Howard KING didn't just blow the whistle on top players when he refereed crucial matches around the world, he also confessed to bedding scores of hookers laid on by top soccer clubs bent on using him to fix their results. King, now retired after years as a top UEFA official, admitted he told one club official: 'This match is important to you. I am the referee. Unless I go home with her you won't win, I assure you.'

Premiership ref Rob Styles found his love life in the headlines twice in a month when he was spotted KISSING a fellow man in black before a match, then SWAPPING his wife for a widow next door. Styles, 39, was seen on TV appearing to kiss fourth official Phil Dowd before Fulham's clash with Manchester City in September 2003. He laughed off the incident, insisting: 'I was saying, "Have a good game, sweetie!"'

A month later, newspapers told how the dad-of-three had set up home with next-door neighbour Caroline Cleeve, 45, after leaving the home he shared with wife Trudy in Meon Valley, Hampshire, after 17 years of marriage. Amazingly, civil servant Trudy then got together with Caroline's motor mechanic son Nick, 21, and he moved in to the ref's £675,000 home! This time, Styles – the strictest ref in the Premiership – was less obliging to quote-hungry reporters. 'This is a small personal matter associated with a public profile,' he said. 'I've got no other comment to make.'

An under-16s match was abandoned when a man stormed on to the

pitch and accused the referee of flirting with his wife! Referee
Richard Smith had to call off the match to sort out the disturbance,
much to the chagrin of Forest Oak Rangers, who were beating
Burgess blues 5–3 in Keymer, Sussex. The ref said later, 'There was
a misunderstanding which has been sorted out.'

REID, Peter
Born: Huyton 20.6.1956
Career: Player – Bolton Wanderers, Everton, Queens Park Rangers.
Player/Manager – Manchester City. Manager – Sunderland, Leeds
United

The soccer boss was a bustling, hustling midfield dynamo in his '80s
heyday, but he didn't expend all his energies on the pitch. As a young
pro with Bolton, the Scouser's home apparently looked more like a
porn movie set! Wanderers teammate Frank WORTHINGTON said:
'The place often resembled one of those orgy rooms in ancient
Rome. It became known as the "den of iniquity" due to all the
comings and goings.' Married Frank even had his own set of keys to
the cottage in Edgworth, Lancashire, so he could meet a married
lover there.

REO-COKER, Nigel
Born: Southwark 14.5.1984
Career: Wimbledon, West Ham United

The 19-year-old prodigy helped heap shame on football by revealing
how soccer stars planned their orgies – and admitted his own part in
them.

As police investigated the infamous ROASTING gang rape at the
Grosvenor House Hotel in London in October 2003, Reo-Coker, an
England Under-21 star, boasted: 'If a girl comes up to you and starts
saying I want to do this to you . . . if you turn it down then there'd
be something wrong with you. Women will come to you and start
leaving the signs, start talking dirty and everything. So obviously a
young footballer would really just go with it, just go with the flow.
I've met loads of girls who've said, yeah, they'll do a threesome.'

The teenager told ITV's Martin Bashir how sessions usually took
place on Saturday or Sunday nights after matches, because players
weren't allowed to drink 48 hours before games. But he added: 'If it

happens right after you've been on a night out then you could find yourself in big trouble if she decides to call out rape.' The giggling youngster, transferred from crisis-hit Wimbledon to West Ham weeks later, added: 'My mum's gonna kill me when she hears this.'

See GROUP SEX.

REUTERS

Not the global news agency but the Southport wine bar where soccer stars regularly pull.

See David BECKHAM, Mark LAWRENSON.

REVENGE

Student Claire Lloyd-Evans made her football-mad boyfriend pay the ultimate price for playing away: she ripped up his prized collection of NEWCASTLE UNITED programmes. Claire, 21, explained how she stormed to his flat and let herself in after a friend tipped her off. 'I didn't find any evidence, but I did find his programme collection. He'd been collecting them since he was a boy. I started to rip them up. There were hundreds of them. I know it was a stupid thing to do, but it seemed like a good way of getting back at him.' Mark later confessed. Claire, from Devon, added: 'He didn't discover the programmes until later. He seemed more upset about them than at losing me.'

RICE-DAVIES, Mandy

PROFUMO AFFAIR good-time girl. Enjoyed an affair with '70s soccer stud Frank WORTHINGTON.

RIX, Graeme

Born: Doncaster 2.10.1957

Career: Player – Arsenal, Caen, Le Havre, Dundee. Assistant Manager – Chelsea. Manager – Portsmouth, Oxford United

Chelsea's tactical mastermind found his life and reputation in tatters when he was jailed for a year for indecent assault and unlawful sex with a 15-year-old schoolgirl.

Assistant manager Rix had made his name as a bubble-permed playmaker at Arsenal – his golden left foot cross had set up the winner in the dramatic 1979 FA Cup final against Manchester

United, then put them in the Cup-Winners' Cup final the following year. Sadly, after a glittering career and 17 England caps, he will now be remembered not only for the penalty shoot-out miss that handed the Cup to Valencia.

Rix, married with four children, was said to have met the girl – a Chelsea fan, who cannot be named for legal reasons – in a street near her home. On a summer's day in 1997, Rix saw the girl playing football with her brother. For months he allegedly contrived to bump into her until, on 8 January 1998, he invited her to his flat, plied her with wine and put on a CD. Rix asked if she was still a virgin and she replied that she was. Slowly, Rix seduced her, rubbing her back, kissing her and groping her before she insisted on leaving. He gave her his mobile phone number and asked her to call. She said later: 'I was walking in the street when he started chatting and invited me to his home for a coffee. I thought he was really nice and friendly. When I went to his flat, we watched *The Simpsons* on TV and then he told me about his life at Chelsea. He was really flattering and said I was a very pretty, intelligent girl. Then he started kissing me and used his tongue. It all came as a shock. I had never even had a boyfriend before. I told him to stop and he did.'

Later, at his new flat, she performed oral sex on him after he smoked a joint with her. She explained: 'He had some pot and gave it to me to smoke. It was the first time I had ever taken drugs and it made me feel a bit giddy. Then he started kissing me and indecently assaulted me. He wanted to have sex, but I wouldn't let him.'

On 27 February 1998, Rix invited the girl to the Novotel hotel where Chelsea were preparing for their Premiership clash with Manchester United. He told her to meet him in room 615. There, Rix told her 'Don't tell anyone or we'll both get into trouble. It's our little secret', then indecently assaulted her as they shared a naked jacuzzi. They slept together and the following morning he gave her £20 cash to pay for a taxi home.

The girl said: 'He was staying in a room on a different floor from the players. He gave me the room number and told me to knock on his door. That night he gave me a glass of red wine. I drank one and then I had another half a glass of wine. It made me feel a bit dizzy. Then he seduced me. He had sex with me and it hurt. I didn't like it at all and afterwards felt ashamed and dirty. That was not how I wanted to lose my virginity. I was far too young. But I stayed with him until the early hours of the morning because I had told my parents I was staying overnight at a friend's house.' Afterwards, he stressed – like he had done before – "You must keep this a secret. Otherwise we're both going to be in trouble." When I got home, I shut my bedroom door and cried my heart out. But I didn't dare tell my parents because I felt so ashamed.'

Hours later, the girl's writer father took her to the match. 'I knew there was something wrong,' he said. 'But when I asked her she insisted, "Nothing. Nothing's wrong."' Weeks later she finally told her father about her liaison with Rix. She told him: 'I was in love with him. He said he loved me.' She told the *News of the World*: 'I hate Graeme Rix. He used and abused me and then, after getting his way, just cast me aside. I felt guilty and dirty. He very nearly destroyed me and my family. I hope he gets kicked out of Chelsea Football Club and goes straight to prison.' The father revealed: 'I was horrified when she told me what had happened. If Rix had been walking down the road I would have mowed him down. It affected her so badly that she became a chain-smoker.'

With no evidence, the father decided to write to Rix's lawyers and demand the coach's resignation. 'I couldn't put her through a court ordeal, so I decided I just wanted him out of Chelsea.' Rix refused then arrived at the family home to deny the allegations. The father said: 'Rix admitted my daughter had been inside his flat and even admitted talking to her about contraception. But he continued to deny anything had actually happened. I told Rix I was going to leave the room for five minutes and leave him alone to think about what really happened. I told him, "When I get back I want the whole truth. Do you understand?" Rix replied, "Yes, I understand." I then went upstairs to my office and got my mini-cassette. Then I walked back into the sitting room. I said to him, "So it happened as she told me." He confessed, "Yeah, it happened. I'm being straight with you."'

Rix admitted lying and apologised for his actions. The father said later: 'Rix spent weeks seducing her. I wanted to kill him. But I just let him dig his own grave and carry on blabbing while he had a drink in his hand in my living room. Because what he didn't realise at all was that I had hidden a tape recorder in my pocket and got every word he said. Rix is a drug-taking paedophile who should never be allowed anywhere near a family football club. He even befriended my son and offered to help him become a professional footballer as part of his plan to have his wicked way with my daughter.'

The girl's father wrote to Chelsea demanding again that Rix be dismissed. The club challenged the father to go to the police if he had evidence. The girl's father alerted police on 23 September 1998. Rix was arrested on 12 November.

In a ten-minute hearing at Knightsbridge Crown Court on 19 February 1999, Rix pleaded guilty to indecent assault and unlawful sex. He denied two further charges of indecency and they were allowed to remain on file. His counsel, Desmond de Silva QC, told the judge Rix was of 'hitherto impeccable character' and that this was an 'exceptional case'. On 26 March 1999, Judge Timothy Pontius handed down his sentence – 12 months' imprisonment.

It was a second shattering blow for Rix. His wife Gill, 40, had already moved out of their £800,000 home in Harpenden, Hertfordshire, after forgiving him only two years earlier for a reported affair. That time Rix had been bedding ex-model Sharon Balzanelli at his flat near Chelsea's ground at Stamford Bridge.

But otherwise there was widespread support for the jailed coach. Chelsea manager Gianluca Vialli said: 'I love Graeme Rix. He has been punished for something which he has done and when that finishes, there is no reason why he should be punished again. When he comes back, he will be made welcome – especially by me.'

And the club's pugnacious chairman Ken BATES came out fighting for his man. He revealed he had received thousands of letters – and that fans had backed him by more than six to one. In the club programme, he blasted the victim's father. 'I believe there is more in this than meets the eye,' wrote Bates. 'I ask three questions. Firstly, did the father get paid for selling his story? Secondly, if the crime was committed in February 1998, why did the father not go to the police until September? And thirdly, is it true the father and daughter came to the Manchester United match the day after the crime?'

Bates added: 'He tried to get Chelsea involved but we told him we were a football club not a judge or magistrate and he should go to the police if his allegations were correct.' He also rejected the suggestion that the club should have sacked their coach when he admitted the crime. 'Until the matter was resolved by the courts, we had to await the outcome.'

Rix was released in September 1999 after serving six months of his sentence. 'The first thing I did was take a cold can of Guinness, even at that time in the morning. And then I had bacon and eggs.' He added: 'I have no problem with the sentence, none at all. I admitted the offence. I have now served the punishment and I came out a different man.'

Rix lost his job a year later when Vialli was replaced by Claudio Ranieri. He spent a disappointing season at PORTSMOUTH before being fired again.

His name will live on for ever for fans of Arsenal and Chelsea. And, sadly, will stay on a sex offenders' register until 2009.

ROASTING

It was the shock headline that made traditional boozing, brawls, bungs and bed-hopping look like a rejected plot from *Footballers' Wives*: EIGHT PREMIERSHIP STARS PROBED ON GANG RAPE.

Readers of *The Sun* reeled at allegations of a GROUP SEX attack by players on a 17-year-old girl in a London hotel room. Football braced itself for the backlash . . . and hoped for the best. Fleet Street would now inevitably shine a light on the national game's murky recesses – and the sexual excesses of wealthy young stars worshipped by fans. Though the number of soccer stars involved in the orgy would eventually fall to two – and both would be cleared of any crime – the revelations that followed were sickening; the reverberations seismic. And a new word, 'roasting', would enter football's vocabulary.

Friday, 26 September 2003
Struggling NEWCASTLE UNITED stay second from the bottom of the Premiership after losing 3–2 at Arsenal on a drizzly night in north London. After showering, midfield dynamo Kieron DYER and a bunch of defeated teammates head for the swanky Grosvenor House Hotel in London's West End, the perfect base for a cruise of the capital's up-market clubs and restaurants. Several rooms are reserved – including Room 316, where, in the early hours, the

depressing drama would unfold. After checking in, Dyer heads straight into town for a dinner date he has previously arranged with a girlfriend while his friends visit the subterranean Funky Buddha Club, just off Oxford Street.

Saturday, 27 September
Centre-back Titus BRAMBLE has teamed up with old pal Carlton COLE, a young Chelsea starlet on loan at CHARLTON ATHLETIC, nightclub PR and party organiser Nicholas MEIKLE and his friend Jason Edwards, an engineer.

One of their party spots a young woman in high-heeled shoes and a black halter-neck dress slashed across the chest, and asks if she'd like to join his friends at their table for a drink. The girl, a former convent school pupil and wannabe model celebrating after doing her first charity catwalk show, agrees.

'I was flattered, so I went along with it,' she would later tell *The People* newspaper. 'He then introduced me to the other men, including Meikle, Cole, Bramble and Edwards. At the time I didn't know their names – but I do now. We just chatted generally. They had two bottles of Laurent-Perrier champagne on the table and I'd never drunk that before. I usually have fruit juice when I'm out.

'One of the men introduced himself and said he was a player for Newcastle. That was Bramble, but I didn't recognise him. The only footballers I'd know are David BECKHAM and Ian WRIGHT. But we were having a laugh and they all seemed like nice men. I didn't feel worried and sat with them. I felt like I could trust them.

'Then the Newcastle guy asked if I wanted to go to Browns club with them. I couldn't find my friend to tell him, but it seemed like a fun idea at the time. Now I wished I'd just gone home.'

The players pay for her to enter Browns nightclub with them, then buy more champagne.

'I was drunk and enjoying myself,' she said, 'and I fancied Nicholas Meikle – he was really nice looking. We were flirting with each other and when he asked me if I wanted to go back to his hotel, I said yes. I'd never done that before but I didn't think about the consequences. It wasn't because I was starstruck about meeting footballers and their mates. That meant nothing to me. But I'd been treated with respect, given champagne and charmed. And I really liked the guy. In the cab to the Grosvenor House, it was obvious Nicholas was chatting me up and seducing me. And I did fancy him.'

The couple take the lift to Meikle's room, 316. 'Nicholas kissed me and then we started touching each other,' said the girl. 'We ended up going all the way and I was fine with that. He behaved like an utter gentleman. It wasn't rough or anything like that, we both wanted to do it. I've never gone to bed that quickly with anyone, but I knew I really liked him and it all seemed right. But I thought it was just going to be me and him.'

At 4 a.m. they were interrupted, she said, by someone entering the room then leaving.

'We both stopped and looked around. But then we were kind of cuddled up together in bed when the door opened again. That's when I realised things had changed and there wasn't just one man in the room.'

The girl told how she discovered another man was now having sex with her.

'I could see his face, he was directly above me and he was smirking, kind of laughing. And Nicholas was just laughing, too. I remember just thinking that I really wanted to be at home. There were four of them in the room and they all had sex with me – oral sex, too. None of them spoke. And I remember looking at Nicholas and wondering how he could let it end up like this. I thought he was a nice guy.

'It went on for a couple of hours, but I felt ashamed of what was happening. Eventually I just passed out. Maybe it was the drink, I don't know, but I woke up at about 10 or 11 in the morning and there was Edwards laid on one side of me and Meikle on the other. I remember waking up and thinking, "Oh, my God!" I wanted to get out and went straight to the bathroom. From there I heard someone else come into the bedroom and they all started talking about me and calling me a slag.

'One of them had my knickers and I heard the other asking why he was throwing my pants around the room. They were proud of what had happened and I thought it was disgusting. I was in pain and I just wanted to go home. I was in there naked for about an hour.

'They were asking me to come out but I ignored them. When I heard two of them go, leaving Meikle and Edwards, I came out, got my clothes and asked to use the phone. I rang my friend and left a message saying I needed to speak to him. The two men were ordering breakfast and asked if I wanted any. But I said no. I couldn't believe they were asking me that. I was in a state of shock. They asked if I was OK, but they meant if I was OK about what I'd heard, not about what had happened earlier. When I got down to reception, I phoned my friend again and he came to get me straight away.'

The girl visits Marylebone police station and tells police her story. In her confusion, she told officers eight men had been in the room. 'I was just in a state of shock,' she said later.

The investigation, codenamed Operation Tougo and led by Commander John Yates, begins instantly. Police seal off the rooms, take CCTV tapes and swab for DNA evidence. In addition, they cleverly let the players check out to discover exactly who was staying where that night.

Monday, 29 September

The *Sun*'s crime reporter Mike Sullivan breaks the story in the morning's paper. The paper does not name the players said to be involved. But police announce they will question up to eight stars who had stayed at the hotel that night and even their embarrassed manager, who could all be vital witnesses. (Sir Bobby Robson was said by some sources to have offered to resign as Newcastle boss over the incident, though he later called a press conference to deny it.)

Scotland Yard detectives also interview Manchester United defender Rio FERDINAND and Joanne Beckham, sister of England skipper David Beckam. There was no suggestion that they had been involved in the incident, but they had partied with the players the following day and could have seen the girl.

Tuesday, 30 September

There's just one question on Britain's lips: who are the gang rape footballers? Several clubs deny their players were involved. One glance at the Premiership fixtures for the previous Friday is a massive clue. Internet chat rooms and fan sites are filled with suggestions. One site is closed down amid legal threats.

Sunday, 5 October

As rumours sweep Britain about the identity of the players involved, Meikle breaks cover and tells his story to the *News of the World*. He insists only two players were among the three friends who joined him in bed with the girl, and that she consented to sex with all of them.

He also names Newcastle United midfielder Kieron Dyer as the mystery England star being linked with the investigation – but insists Dyer is totally innocent.

Meikle tells the paper how his group had met up in the bar of the Grosvenor at 11.30 p.m. Dyer met them briefly before heading to Sketch – London's most expensive restaurant – for dinner. (He was pictured leaving there by photographers in the early hours.)

'Not only did Kieron do nothing wrong,' insists Meikle, 'he wasn't there at any stage with the girl. I feel so sorry for him. The rest of us ended up in Funky Buddha at about 1 a.m. We had a few bottles of champagne.'

There, he said, the girl was at their table 'getting cosy with one of our mates, then cosy with the Chelsea player. I can't remember her name. Eventually I tried chatting her up. She had this short black dress on and you could see her underwear. I asked what kind it was and she pulled up her dress to show me. It was black with silver lettering that read something like "Xmas present". She had a few glasses of champagne and then came with us to Browns.'

When he asked her back to his hotel, she agreed. Back in his room, they undressed. He insisted they had protected sex, at his own suggestion. Minutes later, he admitted, his friend Jason Edwards walked in. 'Usually when we go out, people always try and get in each other's rooms,' Meikle confessed. 'The girl carried on having sex. She didn't tell him to get out,' said Meikle, 'so I thought, "Oh, she doesn't mind, I don't really care." So I finished and found he was in the corridor by my bathroom. He asks me, "What's she saying?" And I go, "Why? Do you reckon you can get involved?" And he told me that in the club he asked her if she liked any one of us and she said, "I like all of you." So I said, "Try your luck."'

As Edwards had sex with the girl, Meikle explained, first Cole, then Bramble walked in to watch. 'Carlton says to my pal, "Go on, boy." She didn't stop. She knew there was other guys in the room now. So then Titus says, "I wanna get involved." He moved closer and received oral sex.

'No one got heavy with her,' insisted Meikle. 'This is normal. She didn't say no, she didn't push anyone off.'

When Bramble stopped, Cole joined in. Edwards moved round so the girl could perform a sex act on him while the Chelsea player had full sex with her. Next, said Meikle, the girl had sex with Cole and Edwards.

Meikle explained: 'It's not unnatural for everyone in our crowd to have sex with a girl for 15 or 20 minutes and then get up and wonder what the other boys are doing.'

Soon afterwards, he recalled, the sex stopped and she cuddled up with them in bed. Amazingly, Meikle insisted the girl even gave them a back rub and walked on their spines. (What the players' physios would think is not recorded!)

At 6.30 a.m., Cole returned to his own room. Edwards, Meikle and the girl slept till around 1 p.m., when they ordered breakfast.

As the girl showered, Meikle's friends reconvened to discuss the night's events, and, he admitted, swapped crude jokes and even threw their conquest's underwear around the room for about 15 or 20 minutes as the girl stayed in the bathroom.

'There was a lot of talking about what the other guys had been doing, like, "Yeah, I shagged this bird." So if you was only hearing bits of it, maybe you'd think it was all about you. Looking back, I suspect she could hear bits of conversation and thought it was about her and we were laughing at her. Even so, when breakfast arrived, she stayed to eat. By now it's about 2.20 p.m. and she asks, "Can I use your phone to ring for my mate to pick me up?"'

The girl, he said, then went to reception while he packed. Downstairs, she was alone. 'I said to her, "I've got to catch my mates, bye and that." I never saw her again. After we said goodbye to the girl that afternoon, I joined the boys to go shopping. We had a top afternoon.'

That evening, Meikle and his friends party again – this time at The Wellington Club, another favourite West End haunt of footballers.

'The the next thing I know on Monday was: "Eight Premiership players raping a girl." We never held her down. No one forced her.

She gave us oral sex. And there weren't eight of us in total, never mind eight Premiership footballers! And none of us were claiming to be footballers.

'And we never knew she was 17. She looked 21, 22. After all, she was in a top club dressed up to the nines. I can't understand how she can cry rape and stay overnight until the afternoon. The night was nothing special until the rape allegation – by far was it not unusual, by far.'

Perhaps Meikle's – and presumably his friends' – casual attitude to such a high-risk pastime will dawn on him one day. Then again, perhaps not.

Meikle called the sex session a 'roasting'. 'Roast, like a chicken. It gets stuffed.' A new depraved and disgusting term entered the lexicon of soccer sleaze. 'It's not unusual for a girl to s**g all of us, no,' he continued. 'But it's the first time I've been caught up in this sort of scandal.'

Wednesday, 8 October
Meikle is arrrested, questioned and later released on bail.

Thursday, 9 October
His friend Edwards, 26, is also arrested, quizzed and bailed.

Friday, 10 October
Amid fevered speculation about the identities of the footballers involved, Cole, 19, and Bramble are arrested after volunteering to attend a London police station. DNA swabs are taken from each player's mouth as a matter of course, but their identities, at least, are protected, as newspapers are warned about prejudicing the case. Cole is questioned for six hours by detectives at Belgravia, Bramble for two hours at West End Central. Police announce the men have been 'arrested in connection with an allegation of rape and sexual assault made by a 17-year-old female'.

Hours later, with his name now inextricably linked to the case, Kieron Dyer makes an official statement. 'I checked in together with several other people and totally unbeknownst to me, the hotel entered the other people's rooms under my name. I checked in at approximately 11 p.m. One of my representatives and a friend met he hotel shortly thereafter and we left together at ~~lately~~ 11.30 p.m. We went to Sketch on Conduit Street in w 1 and the three of us remained there until it closed, leaving at about 2.20 a.m. My friend and I were dropped back at the hotel and went directly to our room, alone, where we stayed until late the next morning. The following day, we left the hotel for lunch, completely unaware of anything having happened. Unfortunately, the fact that my name was mistakenly attached to someone else's room has provoked wild speculation. I was appalled by a supposedly "blurred" photograph of me that appeared during a storm of publicity, which had suggested that I was at the centre of the criminal investigation. Until now I have felt trapped and it has been very frustrating that I have been unable to clarify publicly the facts, which clearly exonerate me. I have not been fined by Newcastle United Football Club nor reprimanded by its management, directors or chairman. My teammates are fully aware that I had nothing to do with this and reports of them launching personal attacks on me are categorically untrue. I had no involvement in this matter, let alone being "at the centre of it", as suggested in e-mails, websites and elsewhere. I am aware that this has been clarified for the authorities by witnesses. I have, from the very beginning, had a number of witnesses who can and have corroborated my whereabouts, which proves I had no involvement in the alleged events. I recognise the claims being made by the woman are of the most serious nature and warrant a thorough investigation, that is without doubt. I do not wish to trivialise these allegations. It is for this reason that I have not stated my position until now.'

Saturday, 12 October
Dyer plays for England against Turkey. A penalty ballooned over the bar by David Beckham and a punch-up in the tunnel spare Dyer from media attention.

Monday, 13 October
Poor Meikle can't help feeling sorry for himself. He tells a reporter: 'My life has been hell since all this started. I have been keeping a very low profile. I haven't been able to eat, so I have lost loads of weight. I can't sleep and I feel depressed all the time. Sometimes I

just want a hole to open in the ground and swallow me up. Anything to escape all this.'

Tuesday, 25 November
The two players – Carlton Cole and Titus Bramble – are at last named in news bulletins after the Attorney General says 'identification procedures' have been completed and lifts his gagging order.

Friday, 9 January 2004
The teenaged object of the players' lust is 'devastated and distraught' as Crown Prosecution Service lawyers announce that no charges are to be brought against any of the men. A CPS statement reads: 'We have concluded that there is insufficient evidence for a realistic prospect of conviction against any of the four suspects for any offence.'

The footballers' lawyer Graham Shear says: 'My clients have always categorically denied these allegations. This significant announcement marks the closure to an exhaustive four-month police investigation and demonstrates that my clients have not committed any crime whatsoever.'

Relieved Carlton Cole tells reporters: 'I was definitely victimised and if I wasn't a footballer, none of this would have happened. The media made out that we were guilty already. We were guilty of going out and having a few drinks, but girls can say anything they want and you become guilty straight away. It's not fair.'

He added, 'I was in the room with her and another player. I won't lie about that, but there was nothing unlawful. My experience changed me a lot and I'm determined to conentrate on football. It was a horrible time but also a learning experience.'

Bramble refuses to talk, but Newcastle United boss Sir Bobby Robson says: 'Titus is fine. He has played through all of that turbulence without any real ill-effect. He must have had difficulties with it from time to time, but it's over now.'

As the players picked up the threads of careers so nearly ruined, the girl promises to launch a case in the civil courts. 'I want to get those men into a courtroom so everyone can see who is telling the truth,' she says. 'I have been branded a liar and a tart, and my reputation has been dragged through the dirt. Every time I hear that word roasting I feel physically sick. What I went through was so dreadful that I thought things couldn't get any worse.'

ROBINSON, Paul

Born: Beverley 15.10.1979
Career: Leeds United, Tottenham Hotspur

England's new goalkeeping hope confessed to a fling with a childhood pen-pal just *thirteen days* after his wedding!

Robinson, 24, married fiancée Rebecca in May 2004, nine months after their first daughter Lucy-May was born. But what proud bride Rebecca didn't know was that the keeper had been carrying on with dance teacher Joanna Kilminster since the previous Christmas, when she got back in touch to congratulate him on his football success.

And less than two weeks after the big day, as he prepared for England's Euro 2004 tournament, Robinson was forced to confess all to reporters from the *News of the World* . . . and to his new bride.

'It was purely sex,' said the keeper. 'I hold my hands up. I blotted my copybook. Yes, I feel guilty, horrendous. Still do now.'

Robinson, snapped up by Spurs for a bargain £1.5 million as Leeds slashed their wage bill, claimed he had seen Rebecca six or seven times when Leeds were playing away in London but ended it the moment Lucy-May was born.

'I came to my senses when my little girl was coming home,' he told the paper. 'I just thought: I don't want this – I want my family. I love my wife. I love my family. It was a mistake and I'm big enough to stand up and say, "Yep, I'm sorry and I apologise for doing it." We're strong. We'll come through this together, all three of us.'

Joanna, who first met Robinson when they were both teenagers on a caravanning holiday, told a different story. She claimed the affair went on until March 2004. 'He already had the baby when we were having our affair. The baby was no wake-up call for him. He told me his relationship with Rebecca had ended and never even had the guts to tell me he was getting married.'

When she discovered the truth, she recalled, 'It was such a shock. I thought we had an unbreakable bond. But he built me up and let me down.'

ROBSON, Sir Bobby

Born: Sacriston 18.2.1933

Career: Player – Fulham, West Bromwich Albion, Fulham. Manager – Fulham, Ipswich Town, England, PSV Eindhoven, Porto Sporting Lisbon, Barcelona, Newcastle United

NEWCASTLE UNITED's legendary local hero shook off his whiter-than-white reputation by two-timing his wife of forty years with two scarlet women.

As Sir Bobby guided England towards the 1990 World Cup, and an epic semi-final with Germany, the master manager and father-of-three was battered by revelations that he had had a five-year affair with divorcee Janet Rush. He then got his marching orders when Rush found out he had bedded Pauline Ridal, who sold her sensational story to the papers.

Robson's devoted wife Elsie was said to be devastated by the shock revelations in 1988. And 15 years on, Robson knows the damage he did: 'What I did was daft, I was pretty stupid. I haven't seen her or spoken to her [Ridal] since the story was in the paper. She wrote twice, but I recognised the handwriting and I tore up the letters. I didn't even read them. I hurt my wife; I hurt my family. It was a difficult time, it hurts me so much to hear talk of it.'

Robson admits he must be one of the worst husbands in football. When asked what his wife was planning for his 70th birthday party, the soccerholic boss said: 'I don't think she knows I'm in Germany actually, because we play Bayer Leverkusen that night. She might have arranged a dinner party. I will have to tell her. She doesn't know, honestly. I do feel guilty. I'm aware I've been a chauvinist – that's the word.'

Capped 20 times as a midfielder with Fulham and West Bromwich Albion, Robson then enjoyed a brilliant coaching career, propelling unfancied Ipswich Town to glory, England to the World Cup semi-finals and Romario and Ronaldo to greatness at PSV and Barcelona. Until August 2004 he managed Geordie giants Newcastle United. (He supported the club as a boy and says his parents' joy at the Magpies' FA Cup final victory over Arsenal in May 1932 even led to his birth nine months later!)

'A good football manager now has to be psychiatrist, psychologist, father, confessor, priest, and dictator sometimes,' he once said. At Newcastle he had more than his fair share of confessions to take, thanks to the antics of stars like Kieron DYER, Carl CORT and Craig Bellamy.

After defeating life-threatening cancer, he now lives in Langley Park, just yards from the dance hall where he met Elsie more than 50 years ago. He is the ultimate local hero. But, best of all, he has won back the love of his wife. 'Elsie hasn't forgotten but she has forgiven me,' he says proudly.

ROBSON, Bryan
Born: Chester-le-Street 11.1.1957
Career: Player – West Bromwich Albion, Manchester United, Middlesbrough. Manager – Middlesbrough, Bradford City

Soccer superhero Bryan Robson's wife was hopping mad when she caught him in a hotel room with his crocked young girlfriend and battered him with the girl's crutch.

Suspicious Denise had tracked down Captain Marvel and TV reporter Claire TOMLINSON to Leeds' Crowne Plaza Hotel one morning in January 1999 at 2 a.m. When she burst through the door, she found Claire and Robson clad in their bathrobes. Claire, recovering from a broken left ankle, tried to hide under the bed but left the tell-tale stick, well, sticking out.

Denise, 43, grabbed the crutch and rained blows on Claire and her love-rat husband – for once not the one in plaster. Finally the 43-year-old millionaire Middlesbrough manager dragged her away.

Robson, dubbed 'Pure Gold' by boss Ron ATKINSON after his record £1.7 million move to Manchester United in 1981, had at last been rumbled. The hard-running, fearless-tackling, epic-goalscoring, hard-drinking, hell-raising inspirational former skipper of Manchester United and England returned to the family home with his tail between his legs to try to repair the marriage.

It was the end of a passionate and complicated 18-month affair with the Sky TV girl. They had first met around 1993, when she was working for the FA, became close at the Euro '96 tournament, when he was England's assistant manager, and later became lovers.

'There were always rumours about her because she was so pretty, but I knew about her affair with Robson,' said one friend. 'They were very discreet – she always used to join him before matches and they'd stay in a hotel. As a press officer, she was quite authoritarian and very efficient. But she was fun-loving. She used to drink pints in the pubs and bars with the lads until two or three in the morning. She was very outgoing and flirtatious, but quite classy as well.'

Another said: 'She quite often went away with the team and thought nothing of sitting around the hotel pool just wearing her bikini. She is a very attractive girl with a great figure and many of the lads couldn't take their eyes off her. She was always very popular and was quite flirtatious, but they knew they didn't really have a chance with her.'

The university history graduate had worked for Spurs and Arsenal before joining the FA, and had even done a six-month stint as a personal assistant to self-styled PR guru Max Clifford.

Confronted by TV crews, Robson said only: 'It is my private life and I have no comment to make.'

Claire told friends she was still in love with Robson but accepted the affair was over. 'She is devastated,' said one friend, 'but didn't want to break up his family. Now she is getting on with her life.'

Robson, a father-of-three (and still fit enough to play Premiership football until a fortnight before his 40th birthday), had the perfect ally for his philanderings – his Boro assistant Viv ANDERSON was playing away behind his own wife's back, with restaurant boss Nicole Burton. The boss and his backroom boy could plan their tactics in detail, and, with their wives and families hundreds of miles away in Cheshire, even play the old one–two.

Robson and Anderson regularly wined and dined their secret partners as a foursome at Teesside hotels, bedded them in rooms just yards apart and even took them to PARIS and Marseilles to watch the 1998 World Cup. The two other halves became friends. But when Robson's wife discovered his secret affair in autumn 1998, Anderson's playing-away days were also numbered. His wife Debra had been comforting Denise during her own troubles – unaware of her own man's infidelities.

When Anderson finally dumped her to try to fix his own marriage, Nicole confirmed: 'Viv and Bryan have gone running back to their wives with their tails between their legs.'

Denise remained suspicious of her husband, and four months later launched her hotel raid. But the affair apparently rumbled on.

Weeks later, as she tried to repair the damage, she saw newspaper pictures of Claire getting out of a sleek Mazda MX5 convertible and hit the roof. It confirmed her suspicions that Robbo had bought his lover a car. 'She went nuclear,' said a friend. 'Denise is convinced he has blown family cash on a sports car for the other woman. He has assured her that he hasn't paid a penny and that he was only pulling a few strings to help her get a better deal. But she won't believe him.'

In December 1999, nearly a year after her grim discovery, Denise was still fuming. In sedate Yarm, Cleveland, she spotted Nicole Burton, who, as lover of Viv Anderson, had shared secret dates with her husband and his own mistress. Denise's revenge was served piping hot as she burst into intimate Chadwick's restaurant in Yarm, and began hurling insults at the former mistress, branding her a 'marriage wrecker' and she and her friend Claire Tomlinson 'sluts' before storming out. Outside, Denise's humbled soccer boss husband sat in his car with their son and his parents.

Hours later, Denise, still 'steaming' according to family sources, crashed her black BMW in a ditch, fracturing three ribs, though friends insisted a muddy road had caused the crash.

The car was a write-off. Amazingly, the Robsons' 17-year marriage was not.

A year later the couple were still together. Denise's one proviso to her husband was that he must never see the TV presenter again. So, when she discovered that Tomlinson was to cover Middlesbrough's clash with NEWCASTLE UNITED in October 2000, she was said to have hit the roof and insisted Boro make alternative arrangements. After calls to Sky TV, Tomlinson was apparently assigned to other duties for the day. But it was Robson's own career that would really suffer. His affair, and the shadow it would cast, was said to be one of his reasons why he ruled himself out of the England job in 1998. Then, as Boro's form dipped disastrously, the club brought in Terry VENABLES to help him. Boro survived. Robson didn't. In August 2001, he was fired. It was three years before the supreme midfielder returned to football as boss of struggling Bradford City, only to suffer relegation to League One.

  ● A Casanova conman seduced dozens of female football fans by claiming to be Bryan Robson's cousin. The 35-year-old trickster targeted women at football matches across Britain. One woman told detectives: 'He charmed me into bed then four days later he came back and burgled my house.' Despite a nationwide alert in 1993 the conman was never found.

ROONEY, Wayne

Born: Liverpool 28.10.1985
Career: Everton, Manchester United

England's teenage genius discovered the flipside of fame weeks after his golden goals at Euro 2004 made him a megastar – when a hooker claimed he paid her £140 for sex behind his childhood sweetheart Coleen McLaughlin's back. Rooney was even said to have given the vice girl a note saying: 'To Charlotte, I shagged u on 28 Dec, loads of love, Wayne Rooney.'

Hooker Charlotte Glover, 21, had told reporters how she went with two other girls – including her twin sister Katie – to a shabby flat in Croxteth, Liverpool, after a late-night call to their escort agency in December 2002. There were four men inside, including a ginger-haired lad they recognised instantly – despite the Santa hat he wore and his claim that he was actually a boxer! He appeared to have had a few drinks to celebrate his winning goal against Birmingham City earlier that day. Charlotte claimed she had sex in the tiny bathroom with Rooney because the apartment was so crowded. 'We started to have sex on the floor but there wasn't enough room,' she said, 'so Rooney suggested we stand up and we had sex with me bending over the bath. It lasted about 10 to 15 minutes. I was laughing all the time because I couldn't believe I was having sex with Wayne Rooney. He was laughing as well. He seemed to be enjoying it.'

Before the girls left, Charlotte even persuaded him to give her a memento. 'I said I needed something to prove it all to my mates, like his autograph. I told him what to write, just for a laugh. I couldn't believe he was so stupid.'

The following October, Rooney and Coleen – his girlfriend since they were both 12 – were engaged. Soon they moved into his new £1 million mansion in upmarket Formby. After his brilliant performances in Portugal, the couple sold the exclusive story of their life and love for around £250,000. There was a possible move from Everton in the offing once his broken foot healed . . . and a wedding to plan.

Coleen was 'heartbroken' by the *Sunday Mirror*'s revelations in July 2004. His tryst was a sordid and humiliating betrayal.

The couple answered rumours of a split (and claims that Coleen had thrown her engagement ring away in a squirrel sanctury!) with a kiss for photographers. But there was more pain to come. In August, the same paper's front page showed a picture of Rooney leaving a BROTHEL, and detailed his visits to prostitutes there. He admitted the visits: 'When I was young and immature'. She forgave him once again and days later he signed for Manchester United for a massive £27 million.

ROXBURGH, Andy MBE
Born: 1.8.1943

The former Scotland boss now heads UEFA's technical section. And sports writer Jane NOTTAGE told of his technical excellence under the duvet during an illicit affair in 1998.

RUDDOCK, Neil
Born: Battersea 9.5.1968
Career: Millwall, Tottenham Hotspur, Millwall, Southampton, Tottenham Hotspur, Liverpool, Queens Park Rangers (loan), West Ham United, Crystal Palace, Swindon Town (player/coach)

Hell-raising 'Razor' Ruddock was a man on a mission to destroy opposing sides – but it was his own family he almost wrecked with his drinking, womanising and wild nights out.

In one nightmare year, Liverpool's raging bull centre-half almost threw away his career and his marriage for a leggy blonde lingerie model.

April 1995

Razor, 27, meets posh BA Honours graduate, model, dancer and part-time barmaid Fiona Robinson, 23, in his local pub, The Grapes. Fiona explained: 'When I asked what he did, Neil said he was an athlete. He was a bit sturdy and I thought he was just spinning me a line. Much later people started asking for his autograph and I asked about his job again. He said he played football for Liverpool FC. I said stupidly "You mean *the* Liverpool, who play in the Premier

League?" Afterwards we kept bumping into each other. We'd have a chat and a drink. We had the same sense of humour and shared the same outlook on life.'

June 1995
The friendship becomes an affair. They are spotted in pubs, clubs and even the Anfield players' lounge, as well as sneaking off for a romantic water-skiing break in the Lake District. 'I knew Neil was married right from the start but we just couldn't help ourselves,' said Fiona. 'After our first kiss he said he loved me. I told him I loved him too. From that moment we would go to hotels whenever an opportunity arose.'

July 1995
Ruddock meets Fiona's parents at their detached home in upmarket Formby. Fiona said: 'They told him they could never approve of their daughter going out with a married man and Neil said he understood their feelings.' Divorce is on the agenda.

August 1995
Fiona heads for a holiday in Ibiza without her married boyfriend. 'She carries around photos of him,' a friend confided. 'She's even got one of him wearing a pair of Liverpool shorts with his willy sticking out the side. She kept showing it to me and saying "I'm missing it."'

September 1995
Ruddock's wife Sarah, 25, bursts in as they canoodle on the dance floor of a club in Southport. Ruddock's pals Alan Shearer and Mike Newell and their wives are with them.

Fiona said: 'Sarah asked Neil who I was. He told her I was his girlfriend and he loved me. Neil told her he was desperately sorry to have let her down – but he was in love with me and couldn't give me up.'

Sarah – 'hurt and humiliated' – moves out with her kids to her parents' home in Essex after a furious row at their £400,000 mansion. Ruddock says: 'Fiona's not a scarlet woman. I am to blame and I will have to take it on the chin. I'm really sorry for Sarah and the kids, and I still love them – but I'm not the first married man to fall in love with another woman.'

Sarah calls Fiona. 'She wanted to know all the details,' said Fiona. 'She seemed calm and was very polite. I felt awful. I tried to explain that a genuine friendship had grown into love. Sarah was really civilised about everything in the circumstances.'

Sarah is shown pictures of the model topless on holiday being groped by another man and says: 'The girl is making a fool of herself. But I don't want to get into a slanging match.'

Wound-up Ruddock breaks teammate Robbie FOWLER's nose after a brawl boarding a plane for a European tie. He's fined a week's wages.

October 1995

Sarah watches Ruddock against Manchester United at Old Trafford, raising hopes of a reunion. But Fiona, who has rented a two-bedroom flat with her new man, hits back, telling a newspaper of their 'electrifying' sex. 'Neil is a wonderful lover with a great physique. He's very attentive and has great stamina.'

Ruddock hammers the final nail in the coffin of his marriage: 'I think we were both a bit too young when Sarah and I got married in 1989. Things were great at first and when the kids came along I was the happiest man alive. But we seem to have grown apart.'

November 1995

Razor dumps lover for wife . . . 'He told me he couldn't live without me and the kids. I am delighted,' said Sarah. 'I know he wouldn't have come back unless he knew it was right.'

December 1995

Razor dumps wife for lover. After just four days, the star decides he still wants Fiona after all and moves back to their rented home. Out injured, Ruddock piles on the pounds comfort-eating and boozing. 'Most players can drink ten pints and eat five hamburgers a night and not put on an ounce,' he moans. 'But I can't.'

New Year's Eve 1995

Razor dumps lover for wife . . . again. He is said to be furious that Fiona has been seeing too much of skinny pub footballer Mark Price, 22, who explained: 'I was at the flat she shared with him. We were kissing in the kitchen in the early hours. She told me the relationship was rocky.' He added: 'I heard a message Razor left and he was really cut up about her seeing me. He was effing and blinding, and obviously very angry.'

January 1996
Dumped Fiona plots to get Razor back. She allegedly tries to lure him to a meeting staked out by newspaper photographers, explaining: 'When he leaves, I'll follow him out and kiss him goodbye. Then you'll have your picture, his wife Sarah will throw him out and we can be together.' She claims Ruddock confessed to a string of other affairs during his marriage. But the plot backfires when the *News of the World* exposes her.

February 1996
Remorseful Razor reveals: 'When I moved out, my wife filed for divorce and I found my entire life consisted of 15 bin bags, 10 CDs, a bag full of sweaty unwashed training kit and my fishing tackle. I missed my kids and my personal life was in turmoil.' He added: 'Thankfully I came to my senses. I'm back with the missus.'

May 1996
Ruddock is dropped by Liverpool for the FA Cup final with Manchester United. 'I was gutted,' he confesses. United win.

June 1996
Hell hath no fury like a woman scorned – except two women! Sarah confronts Fiona in the ladies' loos at The Grapes pub. Fiona later complained that a bruised arm, scratches on her breasts and a black eye had cost her modelling jobs. No charges were brought.

July 1996
Ruddock pays £6,000 for Sarah to have a boob job. Sarah says: 'They look brilliant and I feel like a new woman.'
. . . So did Razor. Five years on, Ruddock was over his guilt. And apparently all over a new woman.

Coaching Swindon Town and living in a flat 100 miles away from his wife and family in their Essex mansion, Ruddock was spotted embracing busty blonde former model Ashleigh Fogg, 40, as she arrived on a train from London.

After a trip to the theatre, the pair collected a takeaway curry and returned to his penthouse, only emerging the following afternoon. Ruddock had already collected eight cans of Red Bull, the energy drink! A friend told *The People* newspaper: 'Neil might be married but he's absolutely smitten with Ashleigh. Normally he's a rough and ready type – but now he's acting like a lovesick kid.'

Ruddock left Swindon after a bust-up with the club bosses and returned to the family spread in Essex. In 2003, he took part in ITV's reality show *I'm A Celebrity . . . Get Me Out of Here!* Now he plans an acting career . . . How about the Lust Action Hero, Razor?

S

SAUSAGE

'All kinds of sausages remind me of you' was the dirty ditty sung to a married former England ace by sex stalker and blackmailer Carolyn Pick.

See Mr X.

SEAMAN, David MBE

Born: Rotherham 19.9.1963
Career: Leeds United, Peterborough, Birmingham City, Queens Park Rangers, Arsenal, Manchester City

England's pony-tailed number 1 blundered when he dumped his wife and kids for a promotions girl and started a messy divorce. The keeper – now a veteran of over 1,000 first-class games – was accused of cutting two young sons who idolised him out of his life.

Married Seaman had known of Arsenal worker Debbie Rodgers for four years before finally talking to her at a club Christmas party in 1993. Debbie, who escorted wealthy fans to their executive boxes on match days, said: 'When David started chatting to me, I felt relieved. He was one guy in the room who wasn't trying to pull the girls and I thought, "David's safe – he's married." He's not like some footballers – not in the least bit laddish. I enjoyed his company, but at the end of the evening I left, thinking, "That's it."'

Days later he asked for her phone number – then lost the piece of paper he scribbled it on. She was in two minds when he asked again. 'I didn't want to get involved with a married man,' she said. 'But I have to admit now, I was secretly flattered. I felt guilty about it. But he was a kind, sensitive guy. He didn't strike me as the womanising type. There had to be a genuine reason for him wanting to talk to me.'

Their relationship grew during constant phone calls, then became more serious.

'We both felt a lot of guilt,' she said. 'I'd say, "If we start a relationship, we may fall in love." I asked him if he could rescue his marriage and he said, "I'm not happy, and that's it. I haven't been happy for a while." His main worry was how a split would affect his children. For a moment it crossed my mind that he was being a typical footballer. Footballers do have a bad image because they're always surrounded by girls, but I knew David was different.'

She added: 'I'm very much in love with him. He's got it all – he's tall, dark and handsome, and his Yorkshire accent is just the icing on the cake. I enjoy having someone who's a heart-throb.' (Well, they say beauty is in the eye of the beholder!)

In May 1994, Seaman turned up at her flat near Wormwood Scrubs in west London, with just his overnight bag. 'David told me that he had left his wife,' said Debbie. 'I felt a mixture of emotions – elation, sadness, fear – and the first thing I said was, "What are you doing?" I had told him, "If you can patch your marriage up, do – at least for the sake of the children." I wanted to be sure that I wasn't wrecking a marriage – that he would have left his wife even if I hadn't been around.'

The couple kept their relationship quiet. But a tabloid storm broke. 'I was labelled as a mistress and I had done nothing wrong. But David was very reassuring. He just said, "To hell with it all, we're together and that's it."'

Within months the lovers had moved to a £500,000 mansion in Chorleywood, Hertfordshire. And a year later Seaman and Sandra were divorced. They had married in 1984 in Peterborough, where Sandra worked as a veterinary nurse, and settled in Waltham Abbey, Essex. Even Seaman admitted she had played a big part in his success. After England's disastrous failure to reach the 1994 World Cup, Seaman had thought of quitting international football. 'I was on a real low but my wife Sandra talked me round and restored my self-confidence,' he said at the time. 'I cannot thank her enough.'

The split was horrific. At Christmas 1996 – six months after his heroic efforts as England reached the Euro '96 semi-finals, and days after he was honoured with an MBE – his boys Daniel, then 11, and Thomas, 10, were said to have received only a card from their millionaire dad, with the message: 'Hope you get lots of presents, love, Daddy.'

Sandra's sister Kath told papers: 'People think David's a wonderful bloke and a hero, but they don't know him. He hasn't seen the boys for at least 18 months. We feel he doesn't want to because they're part of his past. He phones frequently and speaks to Thomas, but Daniel won't talk to him. When his name is mentioned on TV, Daniel walks out of the room. It's really sad.' Sandra and their boys had moved back to their native Yorkshire.

When Seaman and Debbie married, pictures of their extravagant wedding were sold to *Hello!* Despite a series of high-profile blunders (Nayim's lob, Koeman's free kick, Ronaldinho's cross), Seaman's dedication kept him at the top of his profession with Arsenal and England for a decade. With Debbie now working as his agent, and a best-selling autobiography on the bookshelves, the couple enjoy a lavish lifestyle. Seaman boasts of his cellar of wine and collection of expensive Davidoff and Monte Cristo cigars. Now the couple have two young children of their own – Georgina, four and Robbie, nine. But the pain of a broken first marriage remains.

SEGERS, Hans

Born: Holland 30.10.1961

Career: PSV Eindhoven, Nottingham Forest, Stoke City, Sheffield United, Wimbledon, Wolves, Hamilton Academicals

It was the last line of defence he wanted to use, but Wimbledon legend Hans Segers had to own up to cheating on his wife to fight match-fixing charges.

Accused with Bruce GROBBELAAR and John FASHANU of helping fix games for cash, Segers claimed phone calls between him and teammate Fash were not to arrange fixes, but to cover their cheating tracks.

Segers was asked by his QC, Desmond de Silva: 'In your domestic life, to coin a phrase, did you always play at home?'

Embarrassed Segers replied: 'I played a few away matches.'

He explained how in the early '90s he had been exposed after an affair. His furious wife had been 'really upset', he told the jury at Winchester Crown Court, but they had 'scraped through'. He added: 'If anything happened again, I was to pack my suitcase.'

Mr de Silva said: 'She showed you the yellow card?'

Segers told him: 'Yes, I was booked.'

But, the crafty keeper confessed, he had been 'naughty' again and agreed with teammate Fashanu that they would cover for each other.

'I asked John quite a few times to cover for me,' he admitted, as his wife looked on from the public gallery. In return he had done 'quite a few favours' for Fashanu while the England striker carried on with a 'quite well-known pop singer'.

When questioned, Segers at first claimed he only talked to Fashanu about once a month during 1993 and 1994. This, he later admitted, was another whopper.

'I was a naughty boy in that period as well, and I would have to explain that to the police, and the consequences of it, and there's no way I would do that. When the arrest was made, my marriage was back together again and I thought, if anything will pop out, I'll lose my wife, lose my kids, everything.'

All three, together with Malaysian businessman Heng Suan Lim, denied match fixing and were finally cleared, after two trials, in 1997.

While Grobbelaar pressed his case and sued *The Sun* newspaper, which had made the accusations, Segers kept his head down. There were enough questions being asked back at home . . .

SHANKS, Don

Born: Hammersmith 2.10.1952
Career: Luton Town, Queens Park Pangers, Brighton & Hove Albion, Wimbledon

QPR's bearded midfielder stole MISS WORLD Mary STAVIN off Graeme SOUNESS then lost her to George BEST.

SHARPE, Lee

Born: Halesowen 27.5.1971
Career: Torquay United, Manchester United, Leeds United, Sampdoria, Bradford City, Portsmouth, Exeter City, UMF Grindavik

The handsome former Fergie fledgling treated one conquest to left-over chicken PIZZA after a night in his candle-lit love temple bedroom. The ex-Manchester United title winner and England ace had fallen for kiss-and-sell merchant Emma PADFIELD. And soon the nation knew of his culinary shortcomings.

Moussaka was on the menu, however, when Lee pulled a sexy actress on holiday in Greece. The star was said to have pursued Ivana Horvat, 24, for two weeks before finally bedding her. Ivana, who had starred in a One-2-One mobile phone commercial, was lapping up the sun when she noticed how one man kept bumping into her.

The raven-haired beauty said: 'He told me his name was Lee, but didn't give me his surname because I think he expected me to recognise him. I just remember him following me everywhere for the whole holiday. I would be in a bar or a restaurant or on the beach with my friends and suddenly he would be there too. At first I thought it was a coincidence, but then I realised this guy had to be following me.'

Finally, one sultry evening, Sharpey's girl-hanging paid off. 'He swept me off my feet – I just couldn't resist his huge, sexy thighs,' said Ivana. 'When he kissed me, I could have melted. I was totally in love with him. And he was perfect in bed. He knew exactly what to do to turn me on. He was wonderful. It was very romantic and I couldn't help falling for him. He took me for barefoot walks on the beach and the whole thing seemed like a fairytale.'

The lovers remained in touch back in England, until, she claims, fame went to his head. 'We used to see each other every weekend,' said Ivana, 'and I would go up to Manchester most of the time. Lee was probably my first true love. But then he started to behave in a slightly arrogant way. He was doing very well in his career and started to believe all the hype about himself. He was also earning a lot of money and splashing out on expensive cars and clothes. We grew apart and didn't really have anything left in common.'

SHEPHERD, Freddy

Chairman of NEWCASTLE UNITED caught 'whoring his way round the world' by an undercover reporter.

See Douglas HALL.

SHILTON, Peter

Born: Leicester 18.9.1949
Career: Leicester City, Stoke City, Nottingham Forest, Southampton, Derby County, Plymouth Argyle (Player/Manager), Wimbledon, Bolton Wanderers, Coventry City, West Ham United, Leyton Orient

England's brilliant last line of defence for 20 years never shirked an oncoming striker in his career – until eyeballing an angry husband at 5 a.m. as he canoodled in his Jaguar with a woman who was not his wife.

Suspicious Colin Street tracked his wife Tina and the Nottingham Forest goalie down to a deserted country lane on the outskirts of the city. He said: 'Both of them were partly clothed. They were definitely making love. I knocked on the window and said, "I know you, Shilton, I've got you." I heard Tina say, "It's my husband." Shilton slid back in the driver's seat and roared off' . . . into a lamppost. Police were called, he failed a breathalyser and later needed stitches in a cut jaw.

For getting his angles wrong just this once, Shilts was fined £350 by Nottingham magistrates and banned for drink driving for 15 months. But he maintained the rendezvous in September 1980 was innocent. 'Nothing untoward took place,' he insisted. He had merely met the woman in a nightclub, taken her for an Indian meal and was giving her a lift home. 'I don't even know her name – I'm terrible with names, you know.'

Tina added: 'There was no hanky-panky between me and Peter Shilton.' But Colin told of his 'burning hatred' for the star and began divorce proceedings.

Thankfully he survived the crash to make an incredible British record 1,005 League appearances during a magnificent 30-year career and win 125 England caps.

SILKMAN, Barry

Born: Stepney 29.6.1952
Career: Hereford United, Crystal Palace, Plymouth Argyle, Luton Town, Manchester City, Brentford, Queens Park Rangers, Leyton Orient, Southend United, Crew Alexandra

1970s soccer-star-turned-agent Barry Silkman faced a five-day trial in November 2002 for allegedly French kissing a 14-year-old girl. Silkman, 50, whose clients included Arsenal's Brazilian star Gilberto Silva and Middlesbrough star George Boateng, was said to have taken the girl and her 16-year-old sister to a trendy West End bar after an audition for a *Pop Idol*-style show he was organising. Afterwards, he drove them to a friend's house where they were staying.

Snaresbrook Crown Court heard the talented playmaker had taken the girls to a West End nightclub where they drank peach schnapps and lemonade, while he sipped water.

Prosecutor Iain Morley asked the 14 year old what they talked about during a car journey from central London to West Hampstead. 'About Barry's friends having sex for the first time,' she replied.

Asked what happened next, she said: 'He kissed her then said to her, "Excuse me while I kiss your sister. She's such a lovely kisser." He used both hands to turn my face. He kissed me just like a peck at first. I felt his tongue touch my lips and I jumped away. He had his tongue in my mouth. If I hadn't, he would have gone further.'

Silkman, of Northaw, Hertfordshire, denied indecent assault and after a five-day trial in November 2002 a jury took just two hours to find him not guilty.

SINCLAIR, Frank
Born: Lambeth 3.12.1971
Career: Chelsea, West Bromwich Albion (loan), Leicester City, Burnley
Spent a week in a Spanish jail facing rape charges after three women claimed they were attacked at the LA MANGA sports resort. The £2 million LEICESTER CITY defender and teammates Paul DICKOV and Keith GILLESPIE were eventually cleared of all charges.

SINSTADT, Gerald
Born: Folkestone 1930
As the days to the 1994 World Cup ticked by, the BBC's legendary voice of football could have been forgiven for watching videos of the Swedes warming up or the Italians in action, but it was a steamier kind of movie that turned his life upside down.

Sinstadt, then 64, whose distinctive voice had graced BBC's *Match of the Day* and ITV's *Star Soccer* for more than 20 years, was arrested by police as they raided the Fantasty II porn cinema club in Islington, north London. Vice cops who burst in allegedly found the former *On The Ball* reporter fondling himself as a blue movie played.

The twice-married father-of-three was charged with gross indecency. But on 9 May, as he was due to appear in court, the case was dropped. The Crown Prosecution Service had decided there was insufficient evidence. 'The allegation has put a great strain on him,' his lawyers said. 'He now intends to resume his work and looks forward to taking part in the BBC's coverage of the World Cup in America.'

Sinstadt did indeed return to his job. Now in his 70s and still working on BBC TV and radio, in 2002 he covered his 12th World Cup tournament as Brazil again lifted the glittering trophy. In 1999, the BBC marked his 50th year in broadcasting with a special award. Though his second marriage broke down, he now lives quietly in Staffordshire with third wife Margaret, commercial manager at Port Vale FC, whom he met doing a feature on the club in 1997. 'I am privileged to have enjoyed such a great career,' says the telly legend, 'and I hope there is more to come.'

SLADE, Steve

Born: Hackney 6.10.1975

Career: Tottenham Hotspur, Queens Park Rangers, Brentford, Cambridge United, Chesham United

Spurs starlet Steve Slade got to grips with a millionaire's girlfriend – and with the new, improved 32C breasts her sugar daddy had paid for!

Blonde Debbie Jager, 24, was already dating businessman Philip Woods, 36, when she netted the soccer ace at the Global bar in Romford, Essex, in February 1996.

Even though generous Woods had given her:

● a classic MERCEDES sports car – £13,000;

● CLOTHES – £3,000;

● an engagement RING – £2,000;

● a BOOB JOB – £3,000;

● a MOBILE PHONE, CASH and HOLIDAYS;

● and let her use his GOLD CREDIT CARD . . .

the brazen gold-digger offered the 20-year-old footballer massages after his gruelling training sessions. 'I gave him the works – a full body massage plus extras. He loved it.'

Soon the massages turned into sizzling sex sessions – even though Slade had his long-term girlfriend Donna waiting at home. And after Debbie's boob op at a north London clinic – and with Philip abroad on business – the player was eager to test them out.

Debbie explained: 'The first thing he said was, "Show us your tits." He couldn't wait to get his hands on them. When it came to sex, Steve was fantastic. The myths about black men being well endowed are rubbish, but he certainly had rhythm. Being a footballer, he had a very athletic body and lots of stamina. The sex was great. It was that good I overlooked certain strange things about him. He refused to kiss me and was sometimes happy to just have a massage and "relief" without full sex.'

Slade regularly visited Debbie's flat in Westcliff-on-Sea, Essex, and baby-sat her son Chay, five. He even gatecrashed an Ann Summers sex aid party and modelled posing pouches for her friends.

When Philip returned, he discovered her fling and ended their ten-month affair. Slade was worried Spurs would find out and dumped her too.

A friend of Debbie tried to sell the tale to the tabloids for £5,000, explaining: 'You've got a perfect story here you know – mad girl with footballer and manic sex all over the place.'

Slade denied having sex with Debbie. 'I have met her twice and was accompanied by a friend.' He admitted taking her phone calls but added: 'I most certainly have not had any sexual contact with her. I am engaged to my girlfriend and we are perfectly happy.' Soon, Slade was on the move, to QPR then Brentford.

But Debbie was unrepentant. Thrusting out her costly chest, she said: 'Between those two and my new boobs, I know which pair I'd rather keep.'

SOUNESS, Graeme

Born: Edinburgh 6.5.1953

Career: Player – Tottenham Hotspur, Middlesbrough, Liverpool, Sampdoria, Rangers (Player/Manager). Manager – Liverpool, Galatasaray, Torino, Benfica, Southampton, Blackburn Rovers

He was called 'Rembrandt with a Razor Blade'. When he wrote his autobiography *No Half Measures*, he said: 'Being successful has always been more important to me than being popular.' So it should have been no surprise that when Graeme Souness's marriage exploded, the fall-out was nuclear . . . with allegations of affairs and sexual jealousy.

The moustachioed macho man had married Danielle, daughter of a millionaire Merseyside businessman, during his days as on-pitch leader of the Liverpool machine. Danielle was the latest in a string of beauties he had romanced, including former MISS WORLD Mary STAVIN.

In six years at Anfield, the Scottish international landed three European Cups, six League titles and four League Cups. A cameo role in *Boys From the Blackstuff* confirmed his cult status.

After a spell in Italian football he became player/manager of Rangers, where he turned Scottish football on its head by buying in Englishmen and Catholics, and destroying CELTIC's dominance with four titles on the trot. But in December 1988, Danielle walked out of their £500,000 Edinburgh mansion. She claimed he devoted all his time to Rangers and neglected his family. The divorce settlement was generous. Danielle received £560,000 cash plus land in Majorca worth £500,000, £30,000-a-year school fees for their two sons, Frazer, 14, and Jordan, 10, up to the end of university, as well as maintenance. She even lived in £800,000 Norton Farm, in Worplesdon, Surrey, which he had bought.

In 1991 Souness did his own walk-out, leaving Rangers to fulfil his dream of managing Liverpool. This time, he insisted, he would handle the pressure better. 'When I was new to being a manager, I took it home with me,' he said. 'It ruined one relationship. I'm not going to allow it to happen again.'

But this time he became the victim. Souness fell seriously ill and needed a triple heart bypass. His new girlfriend, former model, Miss UK runner-up, Bond girl and *Sale of the Century* host Karen Levy, visited him every day. But Souness sold the exclusive story of the operation and his new girlfriend to *The Sun* – still reviled on Merseyside for its coverage of the 1989 Hillsborough tragedy in which 96 fans died. The story ran on the third anniversary of the carnage. Souness would never be forgiven. He returned weeks later to see his beloved Reds land the FA Cup with victory over Sunderland, but, amid poor results and deepening unpopularity, resigned the following January.

Whether the messy divorce from Danielle had played a part in his illness could never be proved. But the pressure must have been immense. It took six painful years for the divorce to become absolute. Souness was also at Karen's side as she faced a three-day court hearing in September 1992 into her own bitter divorce that June from fashion millionaire John Levy at the High Court in Manchester. In June 1994, a month after his own divorce became absolute, Souness married Karen, 35, in a chapel in Las Vegas. 'I am the happiest woman alive,' said Karen.

But he could still not escape Danielle.

Months earlier she had sold the story of her split with Souness to *The People* for £15,000. In a story headlined YOU'RE A DIRTY RAT, SOUNESS, she claimed he gave her and their children 28 days' notice to move out of the farm just before Christmas 1992, refused to pay maintenance and school fees and forced her to sign a man ban, so lovers could not stay overnight.

Furious Souness sued the paper for libel, and kicked off 'Sourness v. Sourness' – the bitterest courtroom battle in football history.

(The warring couple warmed up with a pre-match legal tussle in which Souness asked for Danielle to be given a suspended jail sentence. She had taken him to court claiming he had not revealed full details of his wealth when their original settlement was decided in 1989. He counter-claimed that she was refusing to give details of her own bank accounts. The judge, Mr Justice Slot, hit the roof when he discovered Danielle was on legal aid. Result . . . match abandoned.)

On 7 June 1995, the libel case began with an unlikely sight – Souness, the midfield enforcer, wiping away tears as he denied the claims in London's High Court. Karen and Danielle sat just yards away from each other, watching him intently.

When legendary QC George Carman accused him of trying to control Danielle, he rasped: 'A BENGAL TIGER couldn't do that to my ex-wife.'

When Mr Carman accused him of treating Danielle 'indifferently', he hit back, saying: 'That's not true. I was a good husband and a good father. I wanted the very best for my wife and children. She didn't like being in Edinburgh where we were living because it was too cold and wet. She wanted me to pack in the Rangers job – a job I was enjoying and at the time doing very well – and she wanted me to go back to Spain with her.'

Souness added: 'I've worked hard for everything I have. I'm very fortunate to have been given a reasonable amount of talent. I was given something and I made the most of it. I have worked for it.'

When Mr Carman suggested everyone in the court worked hard for what they had in life, Souness came in with a crunching tackle. 'Well, I can see one person in this room who hasn't,' he sniped. 'She has never been hard-up since the day she was born. In all the time I've known her she has never done anything, she's never had a full-time job.' He said of his marriage to Danielle: 'It was me giving, giving, giving. Being abused by her. Her taking advantage of me.'

When Mr Carman referred to Karen as the soccer star's 'mistress', his famous hackles rose. Souness hit back: 'Who is now my wife, and I don't like you using that word.'

Mr Carman replied: 'Lover – would you prefer that?' Souness said: 'Yes, I would.'

Mr Carman continued: 'She became your lover and cohabited with you before marriage – there's nothing wrong with it.'

Souness agreed: 'We were in love, yes.'

Mr Carman said: 'And your children, after you began to cohabit, visited you, didn't they, in 1992? So would you explain why your wife was not entitled to have a lover come and stay in her home where she lived?'

Souness told him: 'I had paid for Norton Farm and I wasn't willing for someone else to stay in the house I'd supplied.'

Danielle put the boot in too. The steely Souness must have had a sneaking admiration for her skill. On day five of the trial she told the court: 'I thought Graeme had been having an affair and when I questioned him about it he just disappeared out of the house for two days. It was my birthday as well.' She added: 'I asked him what he wanted from us and he said he was going to give 100 per cent to his job. I took that to mean me and the kids weren't in his plans.' She added: 'He vented his feelings on me and I lost all confidence in myself. He made derogatory remarks about everything I did in the house and with the children.' And she claimed when she told Souness she planned to open a boutique with a friend, he replied: 'Who's going to cook my dinner?' Danielle denied telling the newspaper Souness was a 'dirty rat' but said she agreed with the sentiment.

The court even heard of an amazing race to Majorca to grab £500,000 held in a joint bank account there. Danielle's dad, Austin Wilson, flew to the holiday island and reached the bank first, moving the cash into a new secret account. Souness flew out and arrived at the bank just as her father was leaving. 'Graeme looked furious,' Danielle told the court.

The half a million seemed like small change when it was revealed how much money Souness had made from football. Since leaving Liverpool as a player in 1984 he had earned at least £2.2 million in wages, signing-on fees and bonuses, as well as a £245,000 loan he had never had to repay Rangers and a £135,000 gift from a businessman after the Gers won a championship. He had made another £2.2 million when he realised share options in the Ibrox club.

Danielle claimed Souness had boasted he had £8 million in his bank account. She added: 'As far as I am concerned, he has had a personality change. Up to his operation he seemed OK but since then he has gone downright ridiculous.'

Crucially, the court heard, Souness's solicitors had sent legal notices for her to quit the couple's property without his knowledge, and they had never been carried out. And pay-outs for their children had only stopped when Danielle moved them to Majorca with her.

Judge Mr Justice Morland told jurors: 'Graeme Souness loved his children dearly. He was very generous, providing luxurious homes for Danielle and their children. The genuineness of his love and his generosity have been confirmed by Danielle Souness herself in her evidence, although she was the instigator of the defamatory articles.'

Whatever their decision, Mr Morland told the jury, any damages must be 'sufficient to vindicate his reputation', but 'fair and reasonable to the injury done by the complainant'.

On 15 June, after the corpse of Souness's marriage had been dissected in public for eight painful days, the jury of ten men and two women retired to consider their findings. Just two hours later they returned and awarded Souness an incredible £750,000 damages – the fourth-highest payout ever in a British court.

Souness hugged Karen, then walked hand in hand with her from Court 13. Five hundred thousand pounds of the award was frozen pending an appeal by the newspaper, which said it was 'disappointed and disgusted' by the verdict.

Danielle too was shocked. Looking pale and drawn (or was it overdrawn?), she vowed to press ahead with a new court fight to increase the divorce settlement, saying: 'I've been put through hell and I'm emotionally drained. I'm in a corner with nowhere to go' – except for the four-bed detached home in Cheshire with the boys and Chantelle, 20, her daughter from a previous marriage.

In June 1999, Souness and Danielle were reunited, briefly, at Chantelle's wedding in Majorca. Although they were described by pals as 'not exactly lovey-dovey', they put aside their differences for the bash. Souness's new wife, Karen, also attended, six months pregnant.

Mellowed and more relaxed, Souness became a dad again in August 1999, to James. With time on his hands after leaving Benfica, Souness enjoyed his role as doting father, but was soon back in football with Southampton then Blackburn Rovers and was favourite to be new boss of his first club, Spurs, after Glenn HODDLE's exit in September 2003. But one tongue-in-cheek reference brought back memories of his nightmare first marriage. After a training pitch bust-up with star striker Andy COLE, Souness was asked if the former Manchester United ace had a future with Rovers. 'I argue with my wife every day,' said Souness, tongue firmly in his cheek, 'and she's got a future.'

SPANKING

Former favourite pastime of *Emmerdale* star Emily SYMONS, ex-lover of Southampton legend Matt LE TISSIER.

See Mark BOSNICH, Frank LAMPARD, VIDEO, Dwight YORKE.

SPEED, Gary

Born: Mancot 8.9.1969
Career: Leeds United, Everton, Newcastle United, Bolton Wanderers

'We wuz robbed,' goes the classic soccer cliché. And for Gary Speed it came horribly true. Speed, then 26, engaged to be married and starring for Wales and Leeds United, picked up two blondes in a bar in Hale, Cheshire, as he amused himself after an abandoned match in February 1996. The handsome midfielder couldn't believe his luck as he chatted up the mysterious beauties at Mulligan's wine bar and disco, and persuaded both to return to his room at the swish Copthorne Hotel, not far away in Salford's upmarket Quays quarter, for a nightcap.

Speed was said by staff to be the worse for drink as he arrived back at the hotel. Hours later he woke to find Bonnie and Bonnie had done a runner with his clothes, his £2,000 watch, £150 cash, his credit cards and his mobile phone!

The only description he could give was that the girls were aged around 23, slim, about 5 ft 5 in. tall, with long blonde hair and they were wearing jeans. Or was that not wearing jeans?

Luckily, the girls had some scruples. A taxi turned up at the hotel and the cabbie handed over his clothes. A hotel worker told the *News of the World*: 'Gary was very relieved. It's one thing to tell your girlfriend you've been robbed. But it's another trying to explain where your clothes went!'

STABBING
See George BEST, Trevor MORLEY, Mickey THOMAS.

STAVIN, Mary
The flawless Swede who won MISS WORLD in 1977 had a bizarre penchant for hirsute footballers. Stavin was already dating Middlesbrough's moustachioed hard man Graeme SOUNESS when she met QPR's shaggy-haired defender Don SHANKS at, of all places, a greyhound track in Gosforth Park, Newcastle.

Stavin was handing out prizes at the Friday night meeting when she spotted Shanks and his Rangers pal Stan Bowles and began chatting. Bowles wagered Shanks £100 he couldn't get a date with her. Shanks, still living with his mum in a council flat, was happy to take his money.

Weeks later, Middlesbrough played QPR at Loftus Road. 'Ten minutes into the match I sidle up to Souness, who's prowling round the centre circle,' said Bowles. '"Graeme, I've heard Don's shagging your bird." Two minutes later – and a minute after the ball had gone – Souness cuts me in half with a scything, waist-high tackle. I give my on-pitch minder Dave Webb the green light to dish out Souey a taste of his own medicine.' Souness declined a drink in the bar.

After two years with Shanks, Mary walked out for another beardy player – the legendary George BEST. It was a rumbustious affair. Best claimed her squeaky-clean image hid a more sinister side. She enjoyed kinky sex, and, said Best, 'liked to go to sleep at night with something in her mouth that wasn't her thumb!'

Mary later left Best to pursue a semi-successful Hollywood acting career and is now happily married with a daughter.

STOREY, Peter
Born: Farnham 7.9.1945
Career: Arsenal, Fulham
There are plenty of midfielders who couldn't score in a brothel, but not Arsenal and England star Peter Storey. The uncompromising ball-winner moved into the sex industry when his Double-winning days at Highbury ended in 1977.

Storey turned player/manager as he ran three call girls from the incongruously named Calypso MASSAGE Parlour on downmarket

Leyton High Street, east London. The self-confessed womaniser and boozer was fined £700 with a six-month suspended sentence in 1979 for running a BROTHEL.

After a brief dabble in the world of counterfeit currency (three-year jail sentence in 1980) and stolen cars (he did the double again – two six-month sentences in 1982), he returned to sleaze, attempting to smuggle hardcore porn videos into Britain from the Continent in his spare tyre. Another 28-day sentence followed.

Storey famously said: 'When I became a pro, I learned what the game was all about – drunken parties that go on for days, orgies, birds and fabulous money. Football's just a distraction.' Porn movie legend Mary Millington was a regular at raunchy parties at his north London pub.

In 1983, Storey was made bankrupt and confessed: 'I blew it all on birds and booze.' In 1991, he got another month in jail for abusing a traffic warden. So he's not *all* bad!

STRANRAER

Sleepy Stranraer were forced to fire their social club chairman over a case of sour gropes! Three women – all waitresses or barmaids – complained that Leo Sprott, a retired businessman and father-of-three – had groped them at club functions. Club chairman James Hannah announced: 'With regret, Stranraer FC unanimously have agreed to withdraw Mr Leo Sprott's membership from the club with immediate effect.' Now that's what you call a Sprott of bother!

STRIPAGRAM

Sunday league keeper Luke Milne let in 12 second-half goals after a stripagram performed on the pitch at half time to mark his 40th birthday. Luke, of Margate, Kent – whose Westwood Saints side had been leading 4–0 – said: 'I couldn't concentrate on the game once the girl had stripped before me. I was expecting something to happen to mark my 40th, but not a girl stripping on the pitch.'

SUBBUTEO

The table-top football game has been an innocent pastime for kids for decades. But Staffordshire sports shop owner Tom Taylor threw the finger-flicking game into disrepute when he introduced a

Subbuteo streaker! Tom sells the tiny nude figure – made entirely to scale – to players anxious to put off opponents at vital moments. Sensibly, Tom also sells a tiny Subbuteo policeman to chase him off the pitch!

SUMMERBEE, Mike

Born: Preston 15.12.1942
Career: Player – Swindon Town, Manchester City, Burnley, Blackpool. Manager – Stockport County

The swaggering and combative winger was George BEST's right-hand man as they bedded the soccer-mad city's women in the swinging '60s. Summerbee and his United rival even rented a flat together in unfashionable Crumpsall, where they could bed their conquests away from public gaze, but Best was forced to go it alone in 1968 when Buzzer married and settled down.

SUTTON, Chris

Born: Nottingham 10.3.1973
Career: Norwich City, Blackburn Rovers, Chelsea, Celtic

Once half of Blackburn Rovers' title-winning S.A.S partnership with Alan Shearer, the £21-million man's motto is more likely to be 'Who Dares Sins'.

The striker was just 19 when he fathered a child with an air stewardess old enough to be his mum. Sutton met Lynne Briggs, 38, in Florida, where his Norwich City team were playing in a pre-season tournament.

Back home, Sutton introduced her to his club colleagues and even talked of marriage. But when Lynn, of Warrington, Cheshire, discovered she was pregnant, the relationship hit the rocks. When she was 11 weeks pregnant, he was said to have asked her to have an abortion – Lynn refused. After the birth, in March 1993, Sutton insisted on a DNA test to prove little Jordan really was his son. 'She didn't need to bring it into the world,' was his cutting verdict on fatherhood.

There was no first Christmas card for the boy. 'What kind of man is it who ignores his own son?' said Lynn. 'He's behaved like a real rat.'

Sutton called Lynn 'cunning and conniving' and claimed he had been 'used'. He finally agreed to pay £90 a week towards Jordan's upkeep. It would hardly dent his £250,000-a-year wage.

Soon after, Sutton met Page 3 model Samantha Jane Williamson – to the dismay of his mum. When it became clear the romance was for real, however, she accepted it.

In July 1994, just two years after playing at centre-half in a Norwich side hammered 7–0 by Blackburn Rovers, the Lancashire side's boss Kenny Dalglish made him Britain's first £5 million player. Sutton celebrated his new £12,000-a-week job with a riotous night on the town with his Norwich City teammates. After a bust-up with a barman in the Chicago Rock Café, he became involved in a fracas with a motorist outside Hy's nightclub then fled in a black cab. Police arrested him half a mile away after a bizarre chase. He spent a night sobbing in a police cell, then accepted an official caution. His family – and in particular his teacher father and mentor Mike – were deeply ashamed. Sutton admitted sheepishly: 'I embarrassed myself and let my club down, I have absolutely no excuse.'

Sutton and Samantha planned a summer wedding, but brought the date forward to January 1995 when Samantha found she was pregnant. 'Understandably they want to be man and wife before the child is born,' said a guest.

Lynn Briggs – still receiving just £90 a week – demanded more support, adding: 'I hope he makes a better dad to his new child than he did to his last one. Chris has never even seen Jordan. I want him to face up to his responsibilities.'

Rovers' Premiership title in 1995 was followed by embarrassment for Sutton. In December it emerged that his paltry payments for Jordan had actually been paid by his old club, Norwich City! Sutton claimed former Canaries chairman Robert Chase had agreed to help him pay maintenance – and that it had even been written in to his contract. Eighteen months after Chase's own exit, the club stopped paying. The player threatened to sue.

Sutton, now having £1,000-a-month maintenance docked from his Rovers pay packet, settled in a luxury converted country farmhouse. He thrived on family life and had another child with Samantha before Dalglish's exit, a fall-out with England, niggling injuries, relegation and a disastrous £10 million move to Chelsea.

Glasgow became his salvation. After a £6 million move to CELTIC, the goals returned and he landed League and cup medals. Happily settled in the Scottish countryside, Sutton and Sam have, at the last count, four boys and six dogs. 'I love spending time at home relaxing with the dogs and the kids.'

But not all the kids, Chris.

SYMONS, Emily
Born: Sydney, Australia, 10.8.1969
Soap star lover of Southampton striker Matt LE TISSIER was exposed as a love cheat who loved being spanked.

See SPANKING.

T

TAYLOR, Davinia
Born: Wigan 11.11.1977
Former lover of Manchester United wing wizard Ryan GIGGS. Their 1998 split was bitter, to say the least. Davinia later married Giggs' best pal Dave GARDNER, while Giggs dumped Gardner's sister Emma for his ex, Stacey Cooke.

TAYLOR, Peter
Born: Rochford 3.1.1953
Career: Player – Southend United, Crystal Palace, Tottenham Hotspur, Leyton Orient, Oldham Athletic (loan), Maidstone United, Exeter City. Manager – Southend United, Gillingham, Leicester City, England (caretaker), Hull City
As a player, England winger Peter Taylor once boasted he had scored twice after a night of passion – but it was a night without sex that rocked his brilliant managerial career.

The highly respected LEICESTER CITY boss – and caretaker manager of England – was caught in a hotel room in the early hours with a busty former Page 3 model. And, just like City's in the months that followed, his defence was embarrassing.

Taylor had booked a room in the Kensington Hilton hotel after the annual BBC Sports Personality of the Year awards in November 2000. But instead of enjoying a quiet nightcap in the bar before bed, Taylor headed for a more exciting liaison in a room that was not his own and with a stunning 36FF–25–38 blonde in just bra, knickers and stockings.

Unknown to his wife Jenny back in Southend, dad-of-two Taylor had arranged a secret reunion with a friend he had not seen for 20 years – ex-Page 3 model Gemini Reynolds.

Gemini said: 'Peter looked just as gorgeous as when he was playing for Crystal Palace when I first met him. He still had that sexy rugged look that can melt a woman. I can't deny I was very physically attracted to him. In his dark shirt and tight-fitting trousers, he looked years younger than he is and I fancied him like mad.'

The old pals sprawled on the double bed and chatted about the olden days over drinks. They had met in the '70s when Taylor's dazzling wing play for Palace made him one of only a handful of Third Division players in history to play for England.

He was already married at the time and on the verge of a move to Spurs. She was a soft-porn model dating a millionaire publisher she would later marry and divorce before moving abroad.

Gemini revealed: 'We chatted about all the players and managers we met in the '70s. Peter looked into my eyes and made me feel very special. I wanted to make love to him – and he must have known. I was sat on my bed at midnight in my undies with my dressing gown open.'

Suddenly Taylor announced he had to leave. Gemini told a friend: 'Maybe he just felt guilt. Maybe he thought his wife would be ringing his hotel room. A bit of me hoped he would stay the night, but when he looked at me sheepishly and said he had to go I didn't complain.'

Taylor's problems were about to start. *The People* newspaper heard about his midnight assignation and pieced together his movements.

Gemini would confirm only: 'We sat on the bed and had a drink but I'm not saying what happened next, it's private.'

When they put the story to him, Taylor insisted: 'I did not tell my wife I'd met Gemini, either before or after . . . [why, exactly, he would not admit] . . . but I can categorically say we did not have sex.'

Despite the embarrassment, City backed their man. Chairman John Elsom said: 'Peter has done a fantastic job since he joined us. This in no way affects his position at the club.'

An FA spokesman said: 'This is a personal and private matter for Peter Taylor.'

But his ill-judged tryst was the start of a nightmare period for Taylor. Poor results, the failed record signing of £5 million Ade Akinbiyi and a relegation battle cost him his job. He was left to rebuild his once high-flying career at Hull City and manage England's Under-21s.

THOMAS, Kevin
Born: Edinburgh 25.4.1975
Career: Heart of Midlothian, Stirling (loan), Morton, St Johnstone, Berwick Rangers, Montrose

It wasn't the passion of a Hearts v. Hibs Edinburgh derby that brought Kevin Thomas and Willie Miller to blows – instead, they were battling for possession of the same woman.

Blonde former model Leeann Mackay had been cheating on each player with the other for four months. Hearts defender Thomas – engaged to be married at the time – would slip away from his fiancée every Sunday night for sex with the beauty. During the week, father-of-two Miller would visit after training sessions with Hibernian to keep her satisfied. And after a fierce 90 minutes on the pitch during the match in 1997, the men's fury erupted. Inside the tunnel, Thomas hurled abuse at Miller and the pair traded punches.

Thomas would hit the headlines again after being allegedly caught snorting cocaine in a nightclub toilet with St Johnstone teammate George O'BOYLE during a Christmas party for the club's injured players. Sidelined by a cruciate ligament operation, Thomas, a £150,000 signing from Morton, decided to make the most of the party at Perth's trendy That Bar in December 2000. But physio Nick Summersgill saw them snorting cocaine and blew the whistle. Days

later, in January 2001, Thomas, 25, and O'Boyle, 33, were fired by
the club.

THOMAS, Mickey
Born: Mochdre 7.7.1954
Career: Wrexham, Manchester United, Everton, Brighton & Hove
Albion, Stoke City, Chelsea, West Bromwich Albion, Derby County
(loan), Wichita, Shrewsbury Town, Leeds United, Stoke City, Wrexham,
Notts Country

The little Welshman was one more Red Devil dubbed the 'New
George BEST' when he joined Manchester United in 1978. For once
the new boy lived up to the billing, but not just because of his long
hair, the number 11 on his back or even his intermittent brilliance.

Thomas's tangled love life put even the Irish icon in the shade
when, in August 1991, he was stabbed in the bum (just like Bestie)
while having sex in a car with his ex-brother-in-law's wife. With an
accomplice, Erica Dean's furious husband Geoffrey ambushed the
Welsh international – now a Sky TV pundit – as he romped with her
in a secluded country lane near Prestatyn, North Wales, wounding
him in the buttocks, body and arm. It emerged in court later that
Erica had actually lured the footballer into a trap sprung by her
husband, who wanted to avenge Thomas's acrimonious divorce from
his sister. The judge told Erica: 'You lured Mr Thomas into what can
only be described as a most vulnerable position.'

It wasn't long, however, before Thomas followed them into
prison. In July 1993, he was found guilty of peddling counterfeit
money and jailed for 18 months. The star had handed out fake £10
and £20 notes to youngsters on Wrexham's YTS scheme in order to
launder the dodgy wonga. It was a sad and sorry end to a unique
playing career.

A season earlier, 37-year-old Thomas's magnificent FA Cup third-
round free-kick had helped knock out champions Arsenal in one of
the great giant-killing acts of all time. If only *that* had been his final
football act . . .

THONG
Found in an executive box after Aston Villa's floodlights failed,
plunging the ground into darkness for 80 minutes. Cleaners found

the saucy undies the morning after the Worthington Cup clash with Liverpool in January 2003. At least two supporters enjoyed a thrilla at Villa!

TOMLINSON, Claire
Sky TV soccer reporter allegedly hit with a crutch by the wife of her lover Bryan ROBSON.

TULA (Barry Kenneth Cossey)
Born: Brooke 31.8.1954
Sex-swap model, Bond girl and, she claimed, former lover of TV football legend Des LYNAM.

TXT
England skipper and Vodafone figurehead David BECKHAM was said to have let his fingers do the w★★★★★g with hundreds of X-rated txts to a string of women.

URETHRITIS
Sexually transmitted disease that can wreck a philandering footballer's knees. Scientist Paul Oyudo found eight out of ten sportsmen with arthritic knees – including five Premiership stars – also had non-specific urethritis, a painful inflammation of the urethra. An identical bacteria – sexually acquired reactive arthritis – can attack the knee joint. Five of the stars admitted they'd had more than eleven lovers – twice the national average for 18 to 24 year olds. Mr Oyudo reckoned that on average each of the players battled the injury for eight months before being diagnosed. He reckoned the STD cost clubs £500,000 per player in wasted salary.

V

VAN DEN HAUWE, Pat

Born: Dendermonde, Belgium 16.12.1960

Career: Birmingham City, Everton, Tottenham Hotspur, Millwall

The chiselled-cheeked Welsh international was one half of the 1990s equivalent of Posh and Becks – until his career and marriage went down the pan in a haze of birds, booze, cocaine and cross-dressing sex.

'Psycho' Van Den Hauwe was living the high life on Merseyside as the 1980s came to a close, with two League titles under his belt and plenty to celebrate. 'I was doing a lot of nightlife,' he recalled. 'My wife was suffering. We had a baby girl and the great team we had was breaking up. My wife thought moving back to London would be good for our marriage – a new start.'

How right she was – and how wrong. Her soccer star hubby did make a new start. But with a new woman – former wildchild Mandy Smith.

Mandy had achieved notoriety as the child bride of Rolling Stone Bill Wyman. They met when she was 13 and he was 47. A year later they first had sex (police began an under-age sex inquiry but no charges were ever brought) and, in June 1989, when she was 18, they wed. But within three weeks, after a honeymoon with Mandy's mum Patsy, Wyman's son Stephen, and her sister Nicola, she had walked out, and they divorced three years later.

Handsome Van Den Hauwe met model Mandy after a big-money move to ambitious Spurs. The attraction was mutual, and, in 1991, he walked out on wife Susan and daughter Gemma, six, for her.

In January 1993, Van Den Hauwe re-mortgaged his house to buy a £40,000 engagement ring for Mandy – a grand gesture not entirely welcomed by Susan and Gemma, who were still living there. 'I couldn't believe Pat would be so stupid or so cruel as to risk our home for the sake of a ring,' said Susan.

Mandy spent another £50,000 on a lavish ceremony and reception for stars of soccer and showbiz. Fashionably, she arrived at the Marylebone Register Office half an hour late, and without her knickers! She had forgotten them in the rush. Pat slipped the wedding ring, a matching band of solitaire diamonds, on her finger.

The omens were clearly good. But as his own career waned, Mandy plummeted to just six stone in weight due to her well-publicised wasting illness. The passion fizzled out.

Van Den Hauwe once boasted: 'There's a theory that sex on the eve of a match weakens you, but I think that's rubbish too. Don't get me wrong. I don't have sex every Friday night before a game, but if it happens, it happens.'

In fact, it didn't happen very often for the tough-tackling defender – at least not at home, the three-bed Muswell Hill home dubbed the 'House of Dolls' that the couple shared with Mandy's mum and sister and Nicola's Spurs striker boyfriend Teddy Sheringham.

'Mandy's consent to sex seemed to come in waves,' said Van Den Hauwe. 'Once or twice she made me wear a nurse's uniform and painted my privates with different lipsticks.' The couple were reported to enjoy wearing each other's clothes in bed and pictures of Van Den Hauwe cross-dressing appeared in a national newspaper, to the mirth of fans across the country.

As the marriage collapsed, Van Den Hauwe confessed: 'I hit the town big time. For three months I was Mr Party. My life and my money were dedicated to booze, birds and charlie. Two months into the season I woke up one morning in some bird's house and I just knew I couldn't make training . . . again . . . ever. I quit.'

Van Den Hauwe had also been packing away curries and takeaways. His fitness had gone, his career was finished and Millwall put him out to grass. He then began blowing his £25,000 pay-off.

'I went majorly on the booze. Full time, day and night and, of course, as many women as I could find. On a few occasions I saw

Mandy but it wasn't the same. Eventually I just said "f*** it" and walked away. I'll always wonder if Mandy would have stayed with me if I had remained at the top in the game.'

The break-up was a huge blow for Van Den Hauwe. 'Not long afterwards I sat down one night and watched the video of our wedding, in tears. It was all there, captured on the screen, the beautiful thing we had once and had somehow lost. She was a good wife and a good influence on me.'

Van Den Hauwe headed for South Africa, where he hit rock bottom. 'I'd blown everything I earned from football. So I took my pension dough of £55,000, which was a fortune in South Africa. I spent it all in two years on trips back to England, lending money to so-called mates and on my usual old friends – booze, birds and coke – of which there were plenty in sunny Cape Town.' The former Welsh international ended up sleeping rough on a beach.

Thankfully, however, salvation, at long last, was close. Van Den Hauwe began playing again and married third wife Caroline in 1995. She helped him kick the drugs and drink into touch and he now works as a gardener in South Africa, where he has also written his X-rated memoirs.

VARADI, Imre
Born: Paddington 8.7.1959
Career: Sheffield United, Everton, Newcastle United, Sheffield Wednesday, West Bromwich Albion, Manchester City, Sheffield Wednesday, Leeds United, Luton Town (loan), Rotherham United, Oxford United (loan), Mansfield Town, Boston United, Scunthorpe United

The swarthy Leeds United striker's wife put up with his affairs, boozing and gambling for nine long years – but when Jane Varadi snapped, she *really* snapped!

After their divorce, she went public in a TV documentary about the terrible lot of footballers' wives, betrayed not just by their husbands, but by the managers and coaches who let them get away with it. Blonde ex-model Jane told TV viewers: 'My biggest dread was the summer holiday and the week before Christmas. The wives are virtually never invited on those club trips for one very good reason – it's playtime for the boys, married or not. Christmas week was just one long binge. I blame football for a large part of what happened to Imre and myself.

'I was naive. When we first went to Sheffield Wednesday, the manager, Howard Wilkinson, told us that he didn't care what a player did off the park as long as he did it on the pitch. He said he would sign Jack the Ripper if he could play, so what chance did I have with my problem?'

Ten years on, with Wilkinson now his boss at Leeds and Varadi's womanising out of control, Jane asked for a meeting.

She says: 'Howard was very nice and he said he'd speak to Imre. I thought he'd do it discreetly without disclosing my visit. Instead, Imre came home raging that the boss had told him I was making trouble and that it could cost him his career. I was shattered.'

Jane says that the marriage collapsed when Varadi began to be violent towards her. While he was away on a club tour, she changed the locks on their luxury home in Dore, Sheffield. On his return, he broke in and trashed the house he had shared with Jane and their children Georgina, then eight, and six-year-old Danielle, leaving £10,000 worth of damage. 'When he broke in through a window, he smashed up the TV and everything else,' said Jane. 'All that was left was a settee and two chairs,' she told a court.

In 1992, Varadi enjoyed his finest season, helping sleeping giants Leeds United to their first championship in 17 years. He earned £1,000 a week that season, but failed to pay maintenance for the children. At one point, his union, the PFA, stepped in with a one-off interim payment. At a hearing that October, Varadi, who said he was 'extremely ashamed' by his actions, was ordered to pay £2,200 in maintenance arrears and £7,500 compensation or face jail. Jane said: 'Football worries about players using the elbow but doesn't care about the suffering of some wives and families.'

VENABLES, Terry

Born: Bethnal Green 6.1.1943
Career: Player – Chelsea, Tottenham Hotspur, Queens Park Rangers,
Crystal Palace. Manager – Crystal Palace, Queens Park Rangers,
Barcelona, Tottenham Hotspur, England, Australia, Crystal Palace,
Portsmouth, Middlesbrough, Leeds United

El Tel sparked the infamous Blackpool Eight scandal when he and
seven Chelsea teammates did a bunk from the team hotel for a night
on the town – and a liaison with a secret girlfriend.

The Blues were spending a week in the seaside resort to prepare
for a vital title decider at Burnley in April 1965. On the Wednesday,
the lads were allowed out – but with an 11 p.m. curfew. Half an hour
later, skipper Venables, 22, and seven pals sneaked back out through
a fire escape. When they crept back in at 3 a.m., manager Tommy
DOCHERTY was waiting for them.

The Doc immediately ordered all eight back to London after the
escapade. There they called a press conference, claiming they had
merely left to have a meal because they were hungry and that they
had been harshly treated. 'There were no girls in our company,' their
statement said.

But soon it emerged that the players *had* met women – 19-year-
old Pauline Monk and her friend Shirley Clarkson, 18. Pauline added
to the mystery when she explained: 'I've known Terry since October
when I met him at a dance.'

The escapade was the beginning of the end for Venables at
Chelsea – 12 months later he was sold to Spurs.

Docherty, no stranger to controversy, would recall the Blackpool
incident – one of the first mini sex scandals to hit the game in an age
of relative innocence – years later. 'Basically, they'd been out on the
piss,' said the Doc. 'One or two may have seen a bird. By today's
standards, that's nothing.'

● The ex-England boss's wife Yvette banned his nude centrefold
shoot for *Cosmopolitan* magazine in May 2001. Venables was to have
appeared in the flesh with, among others, Eminem. She must have
realised Terry may be shady, but he's not so slim . . .

VERON, Juan Sebastian

Born: La Plata, Argentina, 9.3.1975

Career: Estudiantes, Boca Juniors, Sampdoria, Parma, Lazio, Manchester United, Chelsea, Inter Milan (loan)

The £15 million misfit is known as '*La Brujita*', the Little Witch, for his magical midfield skills, but he has another nickname in his native Argentina. '*Managuillo y Putanero*', altar boy and whoremonger. For shaven-headed, goatee-bearded dad-of-two Seba, who once cost Manchester United a record £28 million, has a controversial past. As well as stealing cash from his mother and nicking cars from his dad, young Seba lost his virginity at 15, he says, 'like everybody, with a prostitute'.

He is reported to have collected the knickers of his later conquests and even had an affair with a model, Laura Franco, dubbed 'Pan Am' for her giant silicon breasts that stuck out like jet engines.

As a star at Lazio, there were car crashes, brawls with photographers and unsubstantiated rumours of cocaine abuse. He was even innocently caught up in the passport scandal that rocked Italian football, though cleared of any personal wrongdoing.

Seba's father, Juan Ramon Veron – another Argentinian soccer legend – says he will one day return to La Plata with model girlfriend Maria Florencia and their children Lara, six, and Deian, three.

'Football and fame will go, but your character stays with you for ever,' says Ramon.

VIBRATOR

Bad boy Dennis WISE got the LEICESTER CITY party buzzing with his Christmas present to teammate Robbie Savage at the club's 2001 bash. The battling midfielder handed over a teddy bear in a City kit with a vibrator placed where the sun doesn't shine, and told him: 'This is for you, Robbie, 'cos you're the only prick in a Leicester shirt at the moment.' Savage, enjoying a poor run of form in a struggling side, had to be prised from Wise after trading insults.

VIDEO

End-of-season videos were never like this! When England stars Kieron DYER, Frank LAMPARD and Rio FERDINAND went to AYIA NAPA for their summer hols after a gruelling season, the sexual highlights were captured on film.

The trio – all tipped for future stardom – had flown to the trendy Cyprus beach resort with pals Jonathan WOODGATE and Michael DUBERRY, of Leeds United, Chelsea's Jody MORRIS and other friends at the end of the 1999–2000 season.

As England's senior players prepared for the ill-fated Euro 2000 tournament in Holland, the young lions unwound with the sun on their backs and a few cooling beers. Girls flocked around them, and inside their bedrooms at the Grecian Bay hotel, a video camera recorded their not-so-private moments.

Ferdinand, now the world's most expensive defender after his £30 million move from Leeds United to Manchester United, was a 20-year-old superstar in the making at West Ham United. In one scene from a video Ferdinand says was made with the young woman's consent, he and a beautiful blonde writhe naked on the bed. Afterwards, he faces a camera and waves, before pretending to kick a ball and celebrate a goal, then 'cackles with laughter'. When speaking about the incident, Rio maintains that he had consensual sex, that it was with just one woman, and that Dyer and Lampard were never in the same room with him when the video was made. And he insists: 'The camera wasn't hidden. The girl consented. If I'd been caught degrading a woman, I'll put my hands up, but I've never degraded a woman in my life.'

In another scene on the video, Lampard, son of West Ham United legend Frank Lampard snr, appears naked receiving oral sex from a blonde. Behind them is another man having sex with a girl. Lampard's partner spots the camera and hides her face. Lampard laughs and the film cuts away. Soon he has persuaded her to continue but is not satisfied and asks her to perform lesbian sex with the other girl. As they roll together on the bed, Lampard sups lager from a bottle and laughs: 'Go on, darling. Go for it!' He is said to spank her bottom and joke: 'He's not filming. He's just practising for when he comes to film.'

Dyer, then 21 and just transferred for £6.5 million from Ipswich

Town to NEWCASTLE UNITED, was unwittingly filmed having sex
with a girl he met dancing in a bar. She claimed she was tipped off
two days later by one of his friends. 'I went numb,' she said. 'I was
absolutely horrified. This was a private thing, an intimate thing.'

In one scene, the cameraman creeps up on Dyer and a different
unidentified blonde. Both wake up and the girl insists: 'Go away.
Please go away.' The cameraman laughs: 'Mr Dyer, King of
Newcastle and Ipswich! You're the Don.'

Later, Dyer, about to be a father for the first time, is filmed from
the balcony making love to another unsuspecting girl. Then, clad
only in purple boxer shorts, he kisses her neck as a friend implores:
'Go on, Kieron, my son!' Dyer whispers to her: 'Will you remember
this night for the rest of your life?' Seconds later he simulates sex
astride her and taunts: 'Don't you want it?' The gleeful midfielder
finally laughs: 'You've got to laugh. This is amazing!'

And it's still not the final whistle. In another scene, he is said
to creep into a room where another couple are sleeping. He
exposes himself close to the girl's face and laughs. Kieron Dyer
denies any involvement in group sex, insists none of the girls were
filmed by him and maintains that he did not know the video was
being made.

A brief extract from the Ayia Napa video, allegedly involving
Dyer and Lampard, was seen for the first time on ITV's docudrama
Sex, Footballers and Videotape in August 2004.

See also Mark BOSNICH, SPANKING, WATFORD, Dwight YORKE.

WALKER, Clive

Born: Oxford 26.5.1957

Career: Chelsea, Sunderland, Queens Park Rangers, Fulham, Brighton and Hove Albion, Woking

The flying blond winger admitted flashing at two schoolgirls as they rode past his house on their bikes. Walker had only just got married when he performed his act of madness in 1978. 'As one girl rode past he stood on the doorstep, undid his trousers and exposed himself and smiled at another girl,' said the prosecution. The Chelsea ace's solicitor could say only: 'The offences have devastated my client. He can't explain why he did it, except that he was in something of a daydream.' Months before he had scored a stunning 20-yard winner to knock mighty Liverpool out of the FA Cup. Now Walker admitted indecent exposure and was fined £50. If only he'd had been a pro 20 years later when even average footballers own a country mansion at least a mile from a public road!

WALKER, Ian

Born: Watford 31.10.1971

Career: Tottenham Hotspur, Leicester City

Spurs' slick shot stopper avoided a boot in the goalies when he bedded *EastEnders* wildchild Danniella WESTBROOK behind the back of her furious fiancé.

Walker – on a trial separation from topless model Suzi Howard, 24 – slunk off to a hotel with the cocaine-addicted actress, and only escaped because staff sent East 17 singer Brian HARVEY the wrong way!

Pint-sized Harvey, a household name thanks to a string of No. 1 hits, said: 'I was told she was staying with him at the Swallow Hotel in Epping Forest so I went down there to find her. I said, "You've got my bird in 'ere – I've got to see her." The guy on reception denied she had booked in and even let me check the register. He told me, "There's no Miss Westbrook with us tonight."' Harvey then went to search a local nightclub. Danni and Walker carried on cavorting till the soccer star left at 7 a.m., interrupted only by room-service waiters. Walker opened the door to the £112-a-night room sporting only boxer shorts. Inside, Danniella lay on the bed.

Hotel staff were amazed the next night when Danniella, 23, who had stayed on, took Harvey to dinner in the hotel's restaurant. 'She walked in there all lovey-dovey,' said a worker. 'The staff couldn't believe how much front she had.' Danniella reportedly sent the hunky keeper a TXT message saying: 'Thank you for last night . . . and I mean everything.'

Furious Harvey later called off their engagement. But, ironically, Ian's fling with Danniella brought him back together with Suzi. She said: 'We split up for a while but he kept calling me. We went on holiday to Barbados and he proposed. I said no. He asked me again in the morning. He said "I want to be with *you*", and he'd met some quite gorgeous girls while we were apart. I forgave him.'

But changes had to be made to the wobbly relationship. The jealous keeper insisted Suzi keep her kit on. And Suzi insisted he follow suit. Walker – described by Suzi as 'the sexiest man on the planet' – incurred her fury when he posed nude in *For Women* magazine. In one photo, only the keeper's hands covered up his embarrassment. He earned a whopping £10,000 for the shoot. 'It was just for a laugh,' said Walker. 'It's nothing special.' Such modesty!

The couple, who had met on a blind date three years earlier, were married at Weybridge Register Office in July 1995. Suzi landed a chat show, *Hiya! with Suzi Walker*, on cable TV. 'Ian asked me to give up modelling when we got married because he didn't like me being pictured with other men,' said Suzi. 'We are both jealous people. I do trust him but there is always that thought at the back of my mind that he might be tempted. I know it's not Ian's fault. He can't help being sexy.'

Ian's football addiction has also brought pressure on the marriage – particularly as he insists on separate beds on a Friday to save his energy. Frustrated Suzi said: 'He's even harder to resist than a bar of chocolate for me. But I could walk around starkers on a Friday – and sometimes I have – and he would still tell me to go away. There are times when it can be frustrating.'

WALLACE, Ian

Born: Glasgow 13.6.1956
Career: Dumbarton, Coventry City, Nottingham Forest, Brest, Sunderland

The former £1 million man was accused of helping wreck a marriage after his football career finished and he turned to booze. The livewire Scotland star – Britain's third £1.25 million player when he moved from Coventry City to Nottingham Forest in 1980 – spent three years managing home town club Dumbarton before being fired in 1999 amid accusations of heavy drinking. A year later wife Carol walked out, he sold their home and moved to a dreary tenement block.

Working as a catalogue salesman, he became close to colleague Ann McNeill, 46, and her husband Colin, sometimes sleeping on their sofa. But when the McNeills' own marriage hit the rocks, Wallace got the blame and a battering. The fallen star appeared bruised and bloodied as he went to an off-licence to buy more booze.

Colin said: 'We were good friends – past tense.'

Ann revealed: 'I don't want to wash my dirty laundry in public. I love Colin but I'm not in love with him.'

Wallace muttered: 'Colin might think Ann and me are having an affair but we're not. We never have. We are just really good friends. I've got a sore face because I got pissed and fell into a bush. You could say the three of us get pissed and fall into bushes together.'

It was a pitiful downfall. Literally.

WALLACE, Marjorie

America's first MISS WORLD was stripped of her crown in 1973 after just four scandalous months of flings with, among others, George BEST. She is now a US TV star.

WATFORD

Elton John's favourite side were never known for rock 'n' roll excess
– until two stars were filmed romping at an orgy next to their
Vicarage Road stadium. Guests swapped partners, had GROUP SEX
and watched blue movies till dawn at a property developer's
specially appointed house in March 1991. But the stars, one an ex-
England international, were secretly filmed as they bedded a 22-
year-old waitress clad in stockings, suspenders and French maid's
outfit. A man then tried to sell the footage to *The People* for £200,000
but the paper turned the tables and reported him to police. Luckily
for the stars, police destroyed the VIDEOS and their identities never
emerged.

WELLER, Keith

Born: Islington 11.6.1946
Career: Chelsea, Leicester City

The England striker was said to have been threatened with
KNEECAPPING for allegedly playing away with the wife of an East
Midlands gangster in 1974. LEICESTER CITY teammate Frank
WORTHINGTON said: 'Keith, a bit of a ladies man, had incurred the
wrath of a local heavy for dallying with his wife. He was left in no
doubt that the husband was deadly serious.'

WENGER, Arsène

Born: Strasbourg, France, 22.9.1949
Career: Player – Mulhouse, Strasbourg. Manager – Nancy, Monaco,
Grampus Eight, Arsenal

Took the unprecedented step of calling a press conference just
months after arriving at Arsenal to deny false and malicious rumours
sweeping Britain that he was a paedophile. It emerged later that the
rumours were part of a city betting scam that he would quit before
the end of his first season. The plot failed and Wenger, a French
title-winner in 1991, coached the north London side to the Cup and
Premiership Double in 1998 and 2002, and a third title in 2004.
Some fans still remind him of the scandal with mindless chants.

WEST, Taribo

Born: Lagos, Nigeria, 26.3.1973
Career: Julius Berger, Auxerre, Inter Milan, AC Milan, Derby County, Kaiserslautern, Partizan Belgrade

The Rams could have done with divine intervention as they crashed out of the Premiership in 2002 – shame their flamboyant centre-back Taribo West was busy saving other fallen souls instead. Little did many of the despairing Derby County fans know, but their centre-back was actually a pastor, who specialises in clearing the streets of prostitutes and delivering them to God.

Green-haired Taribo, world renowned for his brilliance at the heart of Nigeria's World Cup back line and an Olympic Gold medal winner in 1996, turned to God when his club Inter transferred him to rivals AC Milan. He was ordained as a pastor in Milan in 1998 and, soon after, began his own church in the city with a shelter aimed at removing the scourge of young Nigerian women selling their bodies on the streets.

Fr West says: 'My shelter is working hard at getting prostitutes to quit what they are doing in Italy. God will give us divine direction so that we can restore those people who are part of his kingdom to the eternity of God's salvation.'

Tragically, Taribo's own marriage has suffered. Wife Atinuke West sued him for divorce in Lagos in February 2002, claiming he refused to sleep with her. Taribo at first denied he was even married but then insisted: 'These are lies from the pit of hell. Nowhere in the world would a man marry a wife and refuse to sleep with her, even a pastor! This is a ploy to tarnish my image and dampen the spirit of God in me. I am a man of God.'

WESTBROOK, Danniella

Born: London, 5.11.1973
Wildchild actress counts two footballers on her list of conquests. After bedding Spurs keeper Ian WALKER behind both their partners' backs, she then seduced hunky WATFORD striker Jamie MORALEE. Ex-*EastEnders* star Danni once admitted she likes a bit of rough, including 'builders, roofers and footballers'. Charming!

See Brian HARVEY.

WILLIAMS, Robbie

Born: Stoke-on-Trent 13.2.1974

Singing superstar and celebrity Port Vale fan seduced one fan while wearing his Port Vale shirt. Sandy Palermo, a 23-year-old 32DD lapdancer he met at London fleshpot Stringfellows, explained: 'When I got to his flat, Robbie answered the door in a Port Vale football shirt. He was swigging a can of lager. I walked in and sat on his sofa. We started chatting then he began whispering and nibbling my ear. Moments later he was leading me to the bedroom.' Another woman fell for his charms after he claimed as a joke he was manager of Partick Thistle . . . there's no accounting for taste.

WISE, Dennis

Born: Kensington 16.12.1966

Career: Player – Wimbledon, Chelsea, Leicester City. Player/Manager – Millwall

See VIBRATOR.

WOODGATE, Jonathan

Born: Middlesbrough 22.1.1980

Career: Leeds United, Newcastle United, Real Madrid

The talented centre-half and unlikely *Galactico* took teamwork too far when he allegedly asked for a three-in-a-bed romp with teammate Lee BOWYER and kiss-and-tell girl Emma PADFIELD. When she refused, he left. He is now dating *Big Brother* 2002 winner, Kate Lawler.

See GROUP SEX, VIDEO.

WORTHINGTON, Frank

Born: Halifax 23.11.1948

Career: Huddersfield Town, Leicester City, Bolton Wanderers, Birmingham City, Leeds United, Preston North End, Brighton and Hove Albion

With his Cuban heels, tasselled jackets, macho moustache and non-stop bonking, big Frank was football's original 'Cowboy Casanova'. The gunslinging '70s striker devastated defences with his brilliance on the ball – and when he unbuckled his jeans he devastated women's defences too. The boy wonder was such a bird-bandit he even blew a dream £150,000 move to Liverpool!

Discovered by Huddersfield Town, big Frank only needed to pass a routine medical to join Bill Shankly's all-conquering Anfield machine in 1972. 'I was living a little fast at the time,' he admits. 'I was out every night of the week, bar Friday, till the early hours.' He was gutted when the Liverpool doctor told him his blood pressure was abnormally high and the move was off.

'Go away on holiday and relax,' said Shanks, 'then come back and take it again.'

Worthington, then dating Miss Great Britain Carolyn Moore, did take a break – for a birds-and-boozing holiday in Spain. On the plane on the way over, he pulled the girl sitting in the next seat and spent the night with her in a hotel near the airport.

'Majorca was like a conveyor belt of good-looking available young women,' said Worthington, who then enjoyed a three-in-a-bed romp with two Swedish stunners waiting in his friend's villa. 'I put on some music and got them a drink,' he recalled. 'One thing led to another and I took one of the girls into a bedroom. We made passionate love and then she disappeared only to come back with the other girl. The three of us had a romp. So much for taking it easy.' He also managed to accommodate a Belgian beauty whose breasts 'defied gravity'.

Back in Liverpool, Worthington had another medical. And failed again. The transfer was off. His penchant for sex had raised his blood pressure to an abnormal level. Rumour mongers claimed a dose of VD had cost him the move (he had had an infection months earlier but claimed it was cleared up by the club doc). But Worthington confesses: 'It was high blood pressure caused by burning the candle at both ends. If I had my time again, I'd have got my feet up in Majorca with a good book and some early nights.'

His blood pressure restored by five days' rest in a hospital, Worthington joined LEICESTER CITY instead. The sex-fest he had begun in his native Yorkshire (he had so much sex he couldn't even remember losing his virginity, and fathered a love child aged 20) continued.

Frank was dating a Swedish beauty, Birgitta, he had met in Majorca a year earlier, and Denise Gibbs, an E-type-driving Leeds lass. In 1973, he married Birgitta, though he said he didn't want to settle down.

'I never messed around with other women when Birgitta and I were together,' he confessed in his brilliant autobiography *One Hump Or Two*. 'But if we were apart . . . I did whatever I liked.'

To prove it, England international Worthington:

● BEDDED beauties non-stop in the hotel he called home;

● BROUGHT UP a daughter as a one-parent family when Birgitta did a runner with their son;

● ROMPED in a Mini with tinted windows outside Euston Station;

● PLEASURED a cabaret singer with a *toothbrush* attached to her *vibrator*;

● BEDDED comic Dick Emery's make-up artist, whose technique 'could have put Linda Lovelace to shame';

● PULLED three women in three days on a club tour of Barbados – including one who made his eyes water in the back of a taxi;

● LET a teammate watch from a wardrobe as he bedded a woman on tour. 'He must have spilt his Bacardi in there,' said Frank, 'because when he climbed out there was a big wet patch down the front of his trousers';

● JOINED the mile-high club on a 747 with a French woman as her boyfriend slept;

● PULLED Miss Barbados Lindy Field as she watched him play (she later kissed and told of her affair with cricketer Ian Botham);

● BECAME front-page news in the *Daily Mirror* thanks to boasts of sex 'five times a week . . . but never on a Friday'.

A £90,000 move to Bolton Wanderers in 1977 brought new opportunities. At a house owned by teammate Peter REID, he regularly bedded a married lover and met long-standing girlfriend Joanne Russell.

At Birmingham City he two-timed the catwalk model with Page 3 girl Joanne Latham. On a trip to London he chatted up a fellow passenger, Mandy RICE-DAVIES – the call girl infamous for her part in the PROFUMO AFFAIR of 1963. 'To say Mandy was experienced would be an understatement,' he said. 'As I discovered, when I got her into bed.' But he also found time for an illicit sex session with the randy wife of a Blues teammate, who turned up wearing just stockings and suspenders under her coat.

Perpetually strapped for cash, Worthington spent summers

playing abroad. In America he agreed to meet a mystery woman fan who wrote asking for a date. After smoking pot and having mind-blowing sex in a mirrored room, he drove home and nearly killed himself in a car crash. He also dated Lindy McDonald James – sister of George BEST's wife Angela – then dropped her for an exotic dancer he chatted up in a club. In Sweden he seemingly slept with every Scandinavian teenage girl he could find – and their mothers.

Worthy's next Page Three girl was buxom Carol Dwyer – they met at a Birmingham club, Rumrunner, made famous as the home of pop's New Romantics. In 1986, Frank, the old romantic, married Carol, and his playing-away days ended. But not his playing days. The Yorkshireman with the Brazilian skills oozed class until he was 40 – so much for that dodgy blood pressure. He also turned to after-dinner speaking to help bounce back from bankruptcy.

Frank once told a reporter: 'George Best wants every girl to love him – I just wanted them to go to bed with me.'

A Worthy epitaph.

WRIGHT, Ian
Born: Woolwich 3.11.1963
Career: Crystal Palace, Arsenal, West Ham United, Burnley

Arsenal's cocky yet charismatic centre-forward carefully cultivated his image as a clean-living family man who would never stray from wife Debbie and their baby boy . . . then two-timed her first with a burger waitress, then a BBC researcher! And while his wife publicly forgave him for the first fling – but warned him it was his final chance – he was said to be still secretly bedding the second beauty.

'Deborah knows the sort of guy I am,' he once proclaimed. 'I never had any girlfriends all over the place. I've only had about five in my whole life. She knew I wasn't the type to mess around.'

Until Wright met TGI Friday waitress Tina Hodgson, 27, during a lunch with his Arsenal teammates in Mill Hill, north London, in October 1995. They swapped phone numbers, and, after she broke up with her boyfriend, met for sex in the afternoons on her days off.

She said of their first tryst: 'He was the best lover I've ever had. He was really gentle, just beautiful in bed. He really satisfied me like no one before. I told him that I loved him but it wasn't real romance. But from there our relationship became really close.'

The lovers tried to halt their illicit affair. 'We decided just to be friends. But the next time he came into the restaurant we just couldn't resist each other and ended up back home in my bed again. Believe me, he makes the earth move for me every time.'

The fling finally ended in January 1997 when the *News of the World* exposed him. Wright confessed: 'It happened, I hold my hands up. I admit I did sleep with her but it was just a few times. But I was the one who wanted to finish it.'

Wright, who had three sons from previous relationships (including Manchester City's teenage sensation Shaun Wright-Phillips, whom he adopted when Shaun was 18 months old), moved out of the £2 million family mansion in Croydon, south London, while Debbie, 29 – mother of his fourth boy Stacey – agonised over whether to call time on her errant husband.

She revealed they had already been trying to rekindle the three-year marriage with romantic breaks, but said: 'When you get as much attention as he does, I suppose at some stage he's going to give way. But I'm not sure I can forgive him.'

Wright, stung by criticism in the nation's papers, hit back with a typical piece of showmanship – a tattoo of a verse from the book of St John inscribed on his right arm: 'Let he without sin cast a stone'.

A week later, Debbie announced she would give their three-year-old marriage another chance. 'Ian's disrespected me and he is very sorry. I'll forgive him – in time. He won't make the same mistake again.'

Yeah, Wright!

Blonde BBC radio researcher Venetia Williamson-Noble had already become another conquest after meeting him at the Brit Awards ceremony a year earlier. The romance was an open secret among her colleagues.

One said: 'Venetia is always talking about Ian and what a fantastic player he is. She often goes to Highbury to watch him, even though she is a Spurs fan.' Wright even took her to the players' lounge after matches. But tired of being stuck in a love triangle, she decided to end it. Wright, too, came clean, confessing to Debbie for a second time within weeks before more tabloid revelations exploded onto the front pages. The affair ended messily.

A year later, as Wright began his new TV chat show *Saturday*

Night's All Wright, he finally talked about his duplicity. He admitted in a TV documentary that there had been other affairs, revealed he was still trying to win back his wife's trust and showed off a new tattoo – a line of hearts under Debbie's name. 'Other women will see that name on my arm,' he explained, 'and ask me who it is, and I will tell them it's my wife. How much of a hypocrite would I be?' He also told of how a session with Glenn HODDLE's faith healer Eileen Drewery saved their marriage.

And he confessed he had 'lost the plot', adding: 'I realised with a shock how bad it was, that I had to tell lies and get people to cover for me. But by then it was too late. I was like a runaway train. I didn't intentionally set out to inflict hurt on my wife. I was trying to get something I thought I needed. It was all tied up with being macho and having an ego. I have seen the pain and hurt it brought me and, more importantly, it brought my wife. I will never do that to her again.

'I'm sure women will try it on with me again, but once they realise this man is not for turning I think they'll respect the fact that I'm going to stay faithful to my wife. I must be the luckiest guy in the world. Despite all that has happened, I still have the woman I love.'

In 1998, Wright left his beloved Arsenal as its greatest ever scorer and, a year later, had a daughter with Debbie. 'I've learnt from the whole experience,' he said later. 'I've got my daughter Bobbi and hopefully everything has now turned out for the best. Unless Jennifer Lopez gives me a call!'

Ian, that was just a joke, Wright?

WRIGHT, Mark

Born: Dorchester 1.8.1963
Career: Player – Oxford United, Southampton, Derby County, Liverpool. Manager – Southport, Oxford United, Chester City
England's former Lionheart defender was banned from seeing his wife for a year after bombarding her with menacing phone calls when their 14-year marriage broke up. Wright, 38, ignored police warnings to stop pestering Sarah, who stayed on in the family home with their four children when they split. Chester magistrates heard he had begged her to dump her new boyfriend

and get back with him. Peter Hussey, prosecuting, said: 'Mrs Wright was fearful of what would happen if she did not call police to take things further.'

The 1992 FA Cup winner, then managing Vauxhall Conference Chester City, admitted making the calls. His solicitor Michael Hogan said Wright was 'a very loving and doting father' who made the calls 'to ask her to resume their relationship for himself and their children. He has lost his good name and character and he is truly remorseful.' In April 2002, he was ordered not to call Sarah for a year and to pay £75 costs.

Mr X
Born: Censored
Career: Censored

It was the most humiliating appearance he would ever make: after a career in which he graced the finest stadiums in the world, the former England star stepped slowly into the witness box at Newcastle Crown Court. In the dock, just feet away, former Miss England contestant Carolyn PICK gazed adoringly at him, smiled, tossed back her brunette hair, licked her lips and winked suggestively. At last they were face to face – the married international footballer and the pathological sex stalker who had plagued him and his family for *five* years.

Deranged Pick stood accused of blackmailing him over tapes she claimed to have made of telephone sex sessions with him. The court heard she had:

- BOMBARDED him with sick sexual messages;
- MAILED his friends pornographic pictures of men with his head on;

- SENT him topless photos of herself and saucy pictures from her modelling days;
- SUNG lewd songs about him on five hours of sinister tapes;
- LEFT threatening messages on his phone and
- DEMANDED an apology and treats for 'treating me like a prostitute'.

The retired international star's nightmare had begun in 1995 when Pick sent him a photograph of herself in a yellow bikini. As he had done thousands of times, middle-aged Mr X, who can never be named for legal reasons, sent back an innocent autographed picture. He thought no more of the woman in the photo.

But when Pick left a message at his office asking him to call Paul GASCOIGNE and leaving a North-east phone number, his life would change for ever. Hers would end in tragedy . . .

The star told the court: 'I know Paul quite well, so when I got the message I phoned the number from my car after leaving work. A female answered and at first I thought it might be a wind-up, as Paul is prone to that sort of thing. But it was quickly apparent that it was not. The conversation soon turned to sexual innuendo, quite provocative. It was completely one-sided. I was mildly amused by it but I brought the call to an end.'

Under cross-examination, the soccer star denied committing a sex act during the call. But he confessed he might have 'joined in' the conversation, adding: 'She was mentioning suspenders and things like that. I think it would be fair to say that I did not discourage it.'

He revealed how, months later, the woman called his office again, claiming to be his wife's sister. He took her call, but, he said: 'From the accent I could tell it was the same person. She started saying, "We had an intimate conversation some time before, why aren't you calling me?" She said she would go to the press with it. It shook me.'

Mr X told of his shock at the BLACKMAIL threats: 'She said if I didn't get in touch she had a tape of our conversation and she would go the papers. It was very worrying even though I feel that there was nothing on that tape to be particularly embarrassed about.'

When defence counsel Richard Bloomfield put it to the player that he had visited Pick's home and her mother's house, and had twice had phone sex with his client, Mr X replied: 'It gets more absurd. Absolutely not. I can categorically deny that.'

Mr Bloomfield continued: 'You are not telling the jury the truth when you say that.'

The footballer insisted: 'Yes, I am telling the truth.'

Mr X said he put the phone down when she became aggressive, but within weeks he began to receive lewd photos of the caller. He said: 'I was horrified and disgusted by them. They were not the sort of thing you wanted lying around the house with kids around. I disposed of them. Then a circle of my friends started receiving pictures of naked men with my head superimposed on top.'

Letters arrived every third week, he explained. 'I was more and more disturbed by it. You don't really know what you are dealing with. I am a family man and I was very worried when these letters were getting sent to people I know. It was degrading stuff, and was very distressing. Some were very suggestive, and pleading with me to contact her. Others were very abusive and threatening. They called me names and different things, fairly vitriolic things – pervert and much worse than that. My wife was mentioned – not in a negative way, just that this person wanted to make her aware of what I was supposed to be.'

In 1997, Mr X called the police, who tracked down Pick and cautioned her for harassment. Mr X said: 'For six months to a year I received no further mail. I was hopeful that was it.' But stung by his reaction, and excited to be involved even in such a sordid way with a star, Pick stepped up her campaign. She began making the tapes that would eventually seal her fate.

The footballer told the court how he received the first in 1999. He said: 'The parcel was again marked "Private and Confidential". I recognised the writing and the Tyne Tees postmark. There were two audio cassettes and a newspaper cutting referring to me. I listened to one, and it was weird. It started with strange laughing and then something along the lines of "I've been near where you live." There was an eerie tone to it. It was certainly a bit more frightening this time.'

A transcript of the tape was read out in court. It began:

> Hello. This is the girl you had telephone sex with twice. It seems you have been seen and you are worried that I might tell everybody that you rang me up, and you wanted me to

feel myself. Now could it be that you are famous and you
don't want anyone to know that you rang me up and wanted
me to feel my nipples for you? I don't think that you want
anyone to know, do you? I know you've got yourself into
trouble by pretending you don't know me. You said you
liked my photograph in my bikini, and I am not going
quietly.

In another tape later played to the court she told him:

What was it that you said to me when your wife was out,
'What are your fantasies, Carolyn?' And, of course, I told
you I would like to tie you up in handcuffs in your football
gear and rip it all off. I was kidding, but you got very
excited. It's quite pathetic really, it seems like you are not
getting enough at home, doesn't it? It seems you were
obsessed with me or madly in love with me, telling me I had
a sexy voice.

Pick then compared herself to a *Dynasty* TV character played by Joan
Collins, star of *The Bitch* and *The Stud*.

I'm like Alexis Colby. She always gets the better of men who
try to protect their marriage or career. I can blow your little
world apart. I have a tape recording of you and I could ruin
your career. I want revenge. I will carry on doing it for the
rest of my life unless you are nice to me. If you don't want
the whole world to know about this, you should say sorry
to me very soon . . . I'm not shutting up about this unless
you want to be nice to me.

When he refused to meet her, she threatened to release tapes of their
alleged telephone sex session. She told the player:

You know I have your career in the palm of my hand. I've
got you around my little finger. I've got complete power
over you. You are going to have to say sorry. I think you are
going to have to apologise to me for what you did to me. I

do like fine wine, champagne, smoked salmon, caviar,
Jaguars and BMWs. I like going to nice restaurants. If you
don't want anyone to know that we had sex on the
telephone, then you should apologise to me very soon. It's
up to you to keep me quiet, if you know what I mean.

But as well as blackmailing the star, Pick was hell-bent on
humiliating him too. In one tape she said:

Hello . . . yes, you are dying to see me. You are trying to see
me and have been to my house but you have the wrong
address. This is the girl you had telephone sex with twice,
in 1995 and January 1996. You wanted me to feel myself
while you were playing with your tiddlywink and you
wanted me to say sexy things to you while you played with
your pork sausage.

She could be heard singing:

All kinds of sausages remind me of you,
Big ones, small ones, shiny ones too,
Lancashire, Cumberland, green and blue ones,
You drop a big one, tender ones too,
Succulent, juicy ones, baked in a stew,
All kinds of sausages remind me of you.

Then Pick laughed hysterically . . .

Jurors heard how Pick had even travelled to the town where Mr X
lived and shopped in his local supermarket. In yet another tape
played to the jury, she told him: 'It was such a nice place. There were
a lot of nice shops. There was one called Bottoms Up, which you
should know a lot about, being a sex addict.'

(Bizarrely it emerged that Mr X was not the only innocent victim
of the unhinged stalker. Pick combed through phone directories and
found a man in London with the same name but who was not related
and called him over 100 times. The man said: 'The calls were coming
thick and fast, at all hours of the night. She told me she knew where

I lived. I was scared to leave my flat.' The man later had a heart attack and suffered depression because of the ordeal.)

Though the evidence against her grew and grew, Carolyn Pick remained locked in her deluded world. As she preened in front of the footballer during his evidence, Judge David Hodson had to warn her to stop her 'improper gestures'. When it was her turn to be questioned, she continued with her twisted lies. In court, she claimed the star had called her first after she sent the revealing beach photo, taken years earlier; visited her flat in Washington, Tyne and Wear, six times – but that she had never let him in; winked at her during a TV appearance; and blanked her when she made a third phone call, prompting her drastic blackmail plan to win him back.

Pick told the court they had phone sex within minutes of their first phone call. 'He wanted me to say sexy things to him,' she insisted. 'I pretended I had on black stockings and suspenders and he got very excited.'

She claimed he phoned her a number of times then suddenly stopped. 'He treated me like a prostitute and broke my heart,' she said.

Most bizarrely of all, she even proclaimed her love for him in court: 'If he could only speak to me for five minutes he would know that I didn't mean what I said to him in the tapes. I love him.'

Pick denied blackmail but admitted harassment. But on 18 October 2000, after just 30 minutes' deliberation, the jury returned its verdict: guilty.

Pick, wearing high heels, garish red lipstick, a black blouse and checked suit, initially looked blank. But she fought back tears as Judge Hodson told her: 'The usual punishment for an offence of blackmail is a substantial term, numbered in years, of imprisonment.'

The England star was not in court to see victory.

Pick was remanded under the Mental Health Act to St Luke's Hospital in Middlesbrough after reports indicated she might stalk the star again if released.

After the trial, her sister Doreen told how she had developed a fixation on TV star Michael Barrymore before turning on the footballer. She explained: 'She wrote off for an audition to go on *My*

Kind of People but she didn't get on. She was very disappointed.' Soon she had the footballer in her sights. 'I knew she liked the footballer,' said Doreen. 'She used to talk about him all the time. We used to go out for a meal and she used to say "He's on TV tomorrow and I'm going to watch him." I used to warn her "You can't have him, he's married", but she wouldn't listen. She was selfish, self-centred.

'She received a caution from the police a couple of years ago and she ignored it, which was stupid. I told her to forget him. I think she has become obsessive because she's lonely. It's not good for you to be on your own all the time. Your mind starts to play tricks.'

The loyal sister added: 'What she's done isn't that wrong – there are rapists, murderers and burglars out there. The only harm it could have caused is to his marriage. She's not a bad girl, she's just selfish. She thinks all men are after her.'

The clues to her twisted crime litter Pick's early life. Brought up by strict Catholic parents, she longed to leave behind her mundane life in Washington. In 1986, aged 22, she reached the local heat finals of the Miss England contest. Her ambition, she told a local paper, was to 'travel the world and meet Nick Kamen of Levis 501 fame'. Instead, she left school and became a secretary. Though tartily dressed, with make-up, low-cut blouses and miniskirts, she was said to have had few boyfriends. One neighbour said: 'Carolyn was always weird. At school she would fantasise about where she'd been or who she'd been with, when everyone knew none of it was true.'

After her father, Thomas, died of cancer in 1992, her mother developed Alzheimer's disease. Pick visited her every day but had a lonely existence. Her love life was sleazy, at best. Keith Martin, who met her in a nightclub, said: 'She was always wearing stilettos and revealing clothes, and a few of my mates said she had a reputation for being easy. We started talking and she was very flirty. After just a couple of hours, she said, "Can we go back to your place?" It was obvious what she wanted. I was a young lad and she was fairly attractive, so I wasn't about to say no.'

Their sex session ended at 3.30 a.m. Hours later she called demanding more sex and the following day she turned up at his local pub. 'We had only slept with each other once, but she assumed she owned me. I can understand how this ex-footballer has run into trouble. Sometimes she would call four or five times a day. She just wouldn't take no for an answer. It was a nightmare.'

Psychiatrists spent six months preparing reports ready for Pick's sentencing on 3 May 2001 and concluded: 'It is almost certain that she was suffering from EROTOMANIA – a paranoid delusional disorder in which sufferers convince themselves wrongly that a stranger from a higher social or work level is in love with them.'

Sometimes called de Clerambault's syndrome, the psychosis can persist despite obvious evidence to the contrary and the fact that nobody else believes it. About 1 in 3,333 people is believed to be affected by similar delusions, and the condition is more common in women. But Pick was never diagnosed.

On 21 April 2001 – two weeks before she was due to learn her fate – she ended her own life. Staff at St Luke's found her body hanging in her secure room. She had apparently used a window blind cord as a noose. A hospital spokesman announced: 'There were no suspicious circumstances and it does not appear to be the result of an accident.' An internal inquiry was launched. Her family, still reeling from the court case, were shocked. Her sister Doreen said: 'We are devastated because we are her family and the only people who really care about her. She's dead and that is all that anyone needs to know.'

A former neighbour of deranged Pick said: 'What she put the footballer through was terrible, but she wasn't in her right mind. It's tragic. She was a sad person with no interests and no friends.'

Even police on the case were sorry at her demise: 'This is a tragic end to a young life,' said one officer. 'Carolyn Pick was a woman driven by her obsession with the rich and famous, but she was more deserving of pity than punishment.'

YORKE, Dwight

Born: Canaan, Tobago, 3.11.1971

Career: Signal Hill, St Clairs, Aston Villa, Manchester United, Blackburn Rovers

As laid back as his giant waterbed, Treble-winning Dwight Yorke played football with a dazzling smile on his face – no doubt thinking about his latest conquest off the field. A permanent fixture on the gossip pages as well as the sports sections, the extrovert striker filmed his orgies with a teammate, bedded two women in six hours, abandoned his pregnant model girlfriend and even potted another beauty on his pool table!

Extravagantly skilled Yorke, brought to England by Aston Villa for a bargain £120,000, announced his arrival in British football with a delicate chip under the crossbar from the penalty spot in a fierce FA Cup tie against Sheffield United. Such audacity convinced Alex FERGUSON to pay £12.6 million to take him to Manchester United and helped make him soccer's biggest playboy since fellow Red George BEST. Sometimes Yorke's antics outshone even the dirtiest Devil of all.

Before joining United, Yorke had already been accused of paying £400 a time for romps with a busty vice girl called Jade between February 1997 and April 1998. Another of his conquests, TV presenter Louise Brady, described the striker as a 'love machine'.

When Dwight invited his former Villa teammate Mark BOSNICH round for the evening in August 1998, it was purely to discuss tactics. Six-a-side tactics. In Yorke's luxury detached home with them were four women and a secret VIDEO camera. Footage from the ensuing soiree showed the two footballers, and an unidentified male friend dressed in women's clothing, giving a thumbs-up to the camera and enjoying a drinks and sex session, including spanking by a belt-wielding blonde. While Yorke romped on a double bed, Bosnich was captured being spanked and having his toes sucked.

Anxious to keep the embarrassing memento out of the wrong hands (namely Fergie, who had signed him just weeks earlier), Yorke dumped the videotapes in his wheelie-bin. Surprise, surprise: the video ended up in the offices of *The Sun*, and all over its front page.

If Yorke was embarrassed, it didn't show. That same month Yorke was said to have enjoyed non-stop sex with married brunette Denise Jeffrey, 30, in a hotel suite before bedding sexy stripper and underwear model Gaynor Royle, 24.

Gaynor said: 'We met at a champagne bash to launch Ryan GIGGS' latest video. Somehow Dwight and I got chatting . . . for two hours! As soon as we met there was a spark between us.' After dinner dates, it was back to Dwight's.

'That was when we made love. And he was wonderful in bed – so gentle, loving and affectionate. He showed me a lot of respect. There was nothing whatsoever coarse about him. It was wonderful for both of us. He's a perfect gentleman and really knows how to treat a lady properly. But I cooled our romance because I wanted the same commitment from Dwight that he gave to football. But that's something he just couldn't give to me.'

There was no stopping Fergie's new signing off the park or, to be fair, on it. Yorke was scoring non-stop for his new employers.

Manchester's Midland Hotel, where the superstar was staying while selecting a pleasure palace of his own, should have installed a revolving door on his suite. A week after his transfer from Villa, Yorke put two notches on his new bedpost in one day. And reporters from his favourite paper, *The Sun*, were on hand again to record his exploits.

Around 2 p.m., leggy Australian blonde Patricia Wade, wearing a short skirt and leather boots, arrived at the Midland after a £100 taxi ride from Birmingham. She checked in to her £150-a-night room, 515, then met the player in the lobby. After lunch at an Italian restaurant in town, the couple returned separately to the Midland.

Five hours later, at 10.10 p.m. Yorke emerged . . . and not from his own suite. Yorke then asked for a valet to bring his £94,000 Aston Martin DB7 to the front of the hotel. After studying a road map of his new city, he roared off.

At 11.20 p.m. he pulled up at posh Mottram Hall, a luxury country house hotel and haunt of northern celebrities. After collecting his key, he met up with a mystery brunette waiting for him at a side entrance and went to his room.

At 9.45 a.m. the following morning they walked to the car park together, smiling and laughing. After passionate kisses, Yorke left for training and his friend drove off in her own car. That night he was reunited with Patricia at the Midland. 'I'm a single man,' insisted Yorke.

Now a millionaire megastar at the world's most famous club, Yorke could be seen with beauties including *Baywatch* babe Tania Zaetta and model Debbie Anderson. But it wasn't just flashing the cash in Manchester's bars and clubs that impressed the ladies. When Yorke met glamorous blonde Lin Eastwood in the city's Kells nightclub on New Year's Eve 1998, she was bemused that so many people recognised him. The United ace had told her he was a postman called Brian!

'People were coming past and saying hello to him and he said it was because he delivered their letters. I believed him. He seemed a lovely sweet bloke. I kissed him that night and he was really passionate and gorgeous.'

Five days later, when he arrived in his £30,000 Mercedes, he carried on the ruse, and claimed he was looking after the car for a friend. Lin, a market researcher from Crewe, Cheshire, said: 'Next day he rang and said he was a footballer. I said, "So what?" Then he said, "For Manchester United. I'm really called Dwight Yorke." He said he'd lied because he didn't like people just being with him because he was a star.'

At his mansion, Yorke proved his real identity by watching football on his giant TV. Lin was having none of it. 'After a few minutes I grabbed his hand and whisked him upstairs.'

Lin dumped her boyfriend and regularly spent nights of passion on the dirty Devil's waterbed during a three-month affair until she read a tabloid exposé of a group-sex session. 'The first conversation we ever had was about trust,' said Lin. 'Now I know I shouldn't have trusted him.'

By teaming unpredictable Yorke with the quicksilver Andy COLE, United boss Alex Ferguson had created a lethal cutting edge which would propel United to a history-making European Cup, Premiership title and FA Cup Treble. But it wasn't just in the penalty area that the pair clicked: hours after helping destroy Inter Milan in the European Cup to take United to the semi-finals, United's potent strike force ended up in bed with Yorke's own teenage girlfriend, Nikki Conroy.

He had pulled her at Manchester's Royals disco. 'I was wearing a sexy black catsuit,' said the 18 year old. 'He called me over and within minutes we were snogging. He invited me back to his house. Then he unzipped my catsuit and stripped me naked. When he took off his trousers, I just went, "Wow!"'

As United's plane landed at 3 a.m. in April 1999, Nikki was waiting. She explained: 'Dwight asked me if I'd give Andy a lift home. I dropped Andy off and he was getting his bag out of the car when Dwight told him, "You can't stay there alone. Why don't you come back to my place?"'

Nikki found herself alone with them and playing spin the bottle. 'He explained the rules – each time the bottle pointed towards you, you had to take off an item of clothing,' said Nikki. 'He kept on losing and ended up naked. I said, "Right, that's the end of the game." But Dwight changed the rules and said, "No. The game only ends when we've all lost all our clothes." After half an hour I was left with only my bra on. I wasn't wearing any panties that night because I didn't want to spoil the outline of my catsuit. Then I lost again and felt very nervous. Andy was bare-chested but still had his trousers on. He asked me, "Would it make you feel any better if I took my trousers off first?" I replied, "No. Not really." But Andy took his trousers off anyway. They both kept pressing me to take my bra off so I gave in. I felt very uncomfortable. Dwight told me, "Come upstairs and I'll get you a towel." Then Andy said, "Do you want to come up with me and get it?" I said no. Then they both came over to me and Dwight said, "Right, then. We're going to have to carry you up." Andy got hold of my legs and Dwight grabbed my arms. Then they hauled me upstairs to one of the spare rooms in Dwight's house and flung me on to the bed.'

After sex, Cole vanished, but Yorke and Nikki carried on until dawn. 'He was a real exhibitionist. He sat naked on the windowsill in broad daylight and beckoned me over. Then he got me to do things to him. He was a very big boy – Dwight made Andy look small in comparison. When I eventually got home, I couldn't believe what I'd done. I'm a big Manchester United fan and I'd just had sex with the team's top two strikers. I'd only ever had two lovers before them, and both of those were long, caring relationships. But I'd been drinking wine and got totally carried away.'

Nikki revealed Dwight described himself as a 'sex machine' and had boasted about losing his virginity at 12 to a 17 year old.

One man less than chuffed was Nikki's boyfriend Mark Glynn . . . and not just by her betrayal. Mark, 27, was a Manchester City fanatic and being cuckolded by a Red rubbed salt deep in his wounded pride. Mark said: 'It was bad enough her sleeping with someone else, but going off with two men, and United players at that, is the lowest of the low. I can't believe she has done this to me.'

Yorke now subbed Cole for Chelsea defender Celestine BABAYARO for a rumble under the sheets together with two women in June 1999. Blonde Adele Hartshorn, 23, and a friend were at the Coliseum nightclub in London when Yorke spotted them at the bar. 'My friend Lisa fancied Dwight too,' said Adele, 'but he was mine that night from the moment he saw me in my little white cowboy hat.' Class!

At the Met Bar, Adele, a sometime porn TV presenter, gave him oral sex in one of the bar's quiet corners, before the party transferred to Yorke's room. The two girls offered to demonstrate the art of the combined twin-striker themselves. 'We all had a bit more drink and me and Lisa started dancing, having a laugh. We said, "We'll do a two-girl dance for you", and stripped each other off.' By the time they were naked, only Babayaro and Yorke were left in the room and the action was about to hot up. Adele said: 'They took their clothes off and we had a gang bang.' The following August, as United prepared to kick off the new campaign, Adele's sex session was revealed in the *News of the World*, and she passed her verdict on Dwight . . . 'He's a bit of a boy.'

No doubt, a similar verdict to that reached by newly ennobled Sir Alex Ferguson. Yorke's goals had helped land the Treble that sealed Fergie's knighthood. Now his wayward behaviour was becoming a knight-mare! Especially when he chose to play for Trinidad and Tobago instead of United. The fall-out coincided with Yorke's high-profile affair with Jordan, the surgically enhanced soft porn model, voracious party animal and insatiable sexual athlete.

The romance even caused friction at the club, where David BECKHAM's wife Victoria – Posh Spice to her fans – laughed heartily as Teddy Sheringham's girlfriend Nicola Smith sang 'Who Let The Dogs Out' to Jordan in the players' wives box. Teddy had once romanced the model.

The boss put Yorke in the reserves. Fergie hoped he would settle down when Jordan became pregnant. But by the time Jordan gave birth to his child, in May 2002, the couple had already split up. At first, Dwight even denied the boy, Harvey, was his, before facing his responsibilities and attending the birth. Yorke became a doting dad to the little boy, who was born blind. But incredibly, it would not be the first disagreement over paternity that summer.

Social worker Julie Francis, 34, insisted she had had a secret affair with Yorke between August and November 2001, while he was dating Jordan. He had chatted up the mum of two at Manchester's hip Sugar Lounge. 'I suppose I was taken by the glamour of dating a footballer,' Julie reportedly told a friend. 'Looking back I should have known better.' Four weeks after Jordan gave birth to Harvey, Julie produced Soloman at Manchester's St Mary's hospital seven weeks' premature. Dwight would deny even knowing her and refused to take a DNA test. It was more scandal the United boss found impossible to ignore.

Soon after, Yorke, still a super-fit 31, was shipped out to Blackburn Rovers in July 2002 for just £2 million. Back in harness with Andy Cole, the goals flowed again. And he hit back at Fergie. 'He's 60 years of age and I'm sure when he was a player, they used to [settle down] much earlier, but I've never felt it was the right thing for me to do. When he bought me, I was a single man who likes to enjoy life. He knew exactly what he was buying into. When it's going well for you, these things are overlooked, but as soon as it goes bad, they analyse every little aspect of your life. I tried changing but it made me very unhappy. I just wanted to be me – a free spirit. When I try to become somebody else, it doesn't work.'

So Dwight stayed the same. Busty TV presenter Emma Jones revealed more of the Blackburn striker's amazing sex secrets after he dumped her for his latest beauty. Emma gave Yorke her phone number after a heady night at London's Funky Buddha club. Emma – 32DD – said: 'He is definitely a boobs man and he loved mine so much he couldn't take his eyes, or his hands, off them. But I decided I had to draw the line at full sex. I didn't want it to be a one-night stand.'

Playing hard to get didn't last long. Emma soon ended up at his Alderley Edge love palace on what Yorke called his 'Altar of Love' – the waterbed with black silk sheets on a raised dais in the middle of the bedroom. Beside it, bizarrely, was a chrome pole, apparently to support the telly, but useful if he pulled a poledancer!

Emma told *The People* how, after sex on his waterbed, he led her to his 'playroom'. I knew I was about to have some fun when he cleared all the balls off the pool table. He lifted me up and laid me on the green baize. Dwight was grinning and loving every minute of it. All I can say is we had a great deal of fun.'

Emma went equally potty when Yorke failed to show up as arranged at another showbiz bash and was later pictured in the papers with another girl, blonde Scots model Leanne McGill, 23.

Leanne and Yorke met in a Glasgow bar and soon he was regularly flying up for nights with her, including a two-hour rendezvous at the city's Hilton Hotel. Dumped Emma was philosophical: 'Dwight didn't have the guts to tell me it was over, but good luck to Leanne. He's world-class in bed.'

See Alicia DOUVALL, GROUP SEX.

Z

ZORRO

Fulham striker Facunda Sava donned a Zorro mask pulled from his sock after scoring against Charlton in October 2002. The Argentinian star had secreted the prop in his sock and, after a fumble, whipped it out after lashing home a rebound from close range. What Sava was actually trying to explain by his celebration may never be known. But let's hope every soccer swordsman doesn't follow suit!